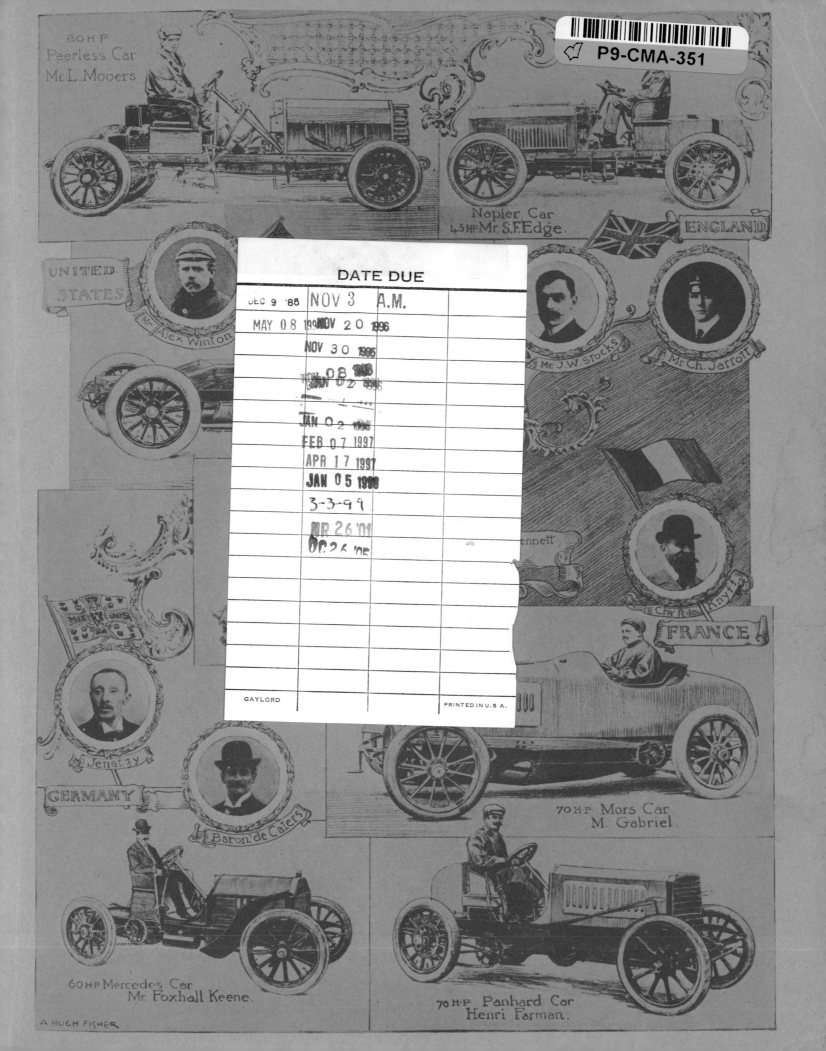

80 H.P.
Peerless Car
Mr. L. Mooers

Napier Car
4.5 H.P. Mr. S.F. Edge.

ENGLAND

UNITED
STATES

Mr. Alex Winton

Mr. J.W. Stocks

Mr. Ch. Jarrott

Jenatzy

GERMANY

Baron de Caters

FRANCE

Chr. R. de Knyff

70 H.P. Mors Car
M. Gabriel.

60 H.P. Mercedes Car
Mr. Foxhall Keene.

70 H.P. Panhard Car
Henri Farman.

A HUGH FISHER

American Automobile Racing

An Illustrated History

American Automobile Racing

An Illustrated History

Albert R. Bochroch

A Studio Book

The Viking Press   New York

Design: Christopher Holme
Copyright © 1974 by The Viking Press, Inc.
All rights reserved
First published in 1974 by The Viking Press, Inc.
625 Madison Avenue, New York, N.Y. 10022
Published simultaneously in Canada by
The Macmillan Company of Canada Limited
SBN 670–11686–6
Library of Congress catalog card number: 73–20660
Printed in U.S.A.

Contents

Introduction

The sport of auto racing has played a unique and rarely understood role in the history of the United States. Varied in its forms, it includes a bewildering variety of interests, purposes, and motivations.

On any particular summer weekend there are literally hundreds of thousands of spectators and tens of thousands of participants at the hundreds of tracks and drag strips throughout the country.

Initially, the automobile was the rich man's toy, and the most adventurous and daring would race one another in what was as much a social occasión as a sporting event. By 1905 professionalism had entered the sport and with it the opportunity for all Americans to take part. Down through the years we see a constantly expanding participation, not only at the premier level but at the grass roots—the county fairgrounds, the drag strips, the desert trails, the vacant shopping-center parking lot, and, underground, on deserted night-time streets and highways.

Diverse economic interests have found a place within this unique sport: large corporations acting as sponsors for advertising purposes; automotive companies promoting and developing products; wealthy sportsmen owning race cars; professionally competent team managers; superbly innovative mechanics ranging from engineers to "file and fit" corner garage geniuses; promoters who stage the events; race track investors; entertainment media; race car builders; and finally the race drivers, who today come from all walks of life.

It is indicative of the many and diverse aspects of American auto racing that it has taken seventy years for a "comprehensive" history to emerge. The literature of auto racing is varied and it is extensive, but it has been specialized, directed to a particular individual, a track, a constructor, an era, or a particular type of racing. Now, in this volume, Al Bochroch has surveyed the entire field of American auto racing.

He has searched and found the roots of the sport and then has traced them to the trunk and limbs we know today. Starting with the Americans in Europe, where the first organized races were held, he has chronicled both the independence and the interdependence of road racing, oval racing, drag racing, sports cars, stock cars, speedway cars, and specialized speed-record machines.

With his inquiring mind and patient research Al Bochroch has uncovered new facts and corrected established errors, but, more importantly, he has not let the facts run away with the story. The general reader will not just learn what happened in past years; he will find the spirit of racing within this history as well—and the spirit of racing is what gives it its legitimacy.

One may list the many and unique contributions of the sport to automotive development, to safety on the highway, and to the development of mechanical talent. No other sport can boast of such contributions to our society. Yet, there is still something more important, more fundamental. Automobile racing symbolizes the spirit of man challenging himself to pierce new barriers, overcome unassailable obstacles, establish new frontiers, come closer to "perfection" than ever before. It requires sacrifice, dedication, a willingness to squeeze out all our talents. In the case of the driver it requires physical bravery as well, for injury or death is a very real alternative to success.

Officials, with the help of participants, constructors, and specialized engineers, are constantly striving to diminish the risk to the driver. Much success has been achieved in recent years. While completely accurate statistics are difficult to come by, it is probable that today fewer race drivers than football players are killed annually and only a fraction as many as are drowned in water sports. The goal, of course, will not be reached until death and serious injury are completely eliminated.

Meanwhile, one must bear in mind that the race driver is not forced to compete. He does so willingly and with full knowledge of the possible consequences. For him, the reward is worth the risk; the challenge is his life.

Al Bochroch's history of American auto racing is the history of the American response to the challenge of speed and, as such, reveals a significant and intriguing aspect of the spirit of man as developed in twentieth-century America.

Thomas W. Binford

For Fran, who loved races,
and
for Ginger, who has just seen her first

Preface

What a mixture of pleasure and frustration writing this book has been—satisfaction and enjoyment galore on digging into racing's past, dejection on being unable to unravel racing's mysteries, recount its gossip or take you, lap by lap, to more races. What a letdown when I could not locate correspondence between young Vanderbilt and Gordon Bennett. And the riddles: What would be the shape of American racing today if the Indianapolis Speedway had been built to include a road course, as originally planned? How did that unlikely pair of Broadway musical-comedy stars Elsie Janis and Barney Oldfield get along? Was Joel Thorne the pleasant, well-to-do whiz kid that thoughtful John Oliveau told us of, or was he the mean, hell-raising, spoiled playboy as described by journalist Brock Yates?

I have tried to write a lean book, one that "puts it all together," that stays close to what I, arbitrarily, consider the mainstream of American racing. However, I have slipped down a few side roads when I thought that history had overlooked an interesting personality or incident, one that would add to the reader's understanding of the times.

Because American automobile racing is so enormously varied, many of its fans and much of its literature are devoted to a particular branch of the sport. There are good reasons for this specialization. Hundreds of different kinds of race cars competing in a myriad number of events are bewildering. Stock cars, dragsters, and road racers, each with a multitude of classes —championship cars, sprint cars, and midgets—formula machines from 1 to Vee, and the almost separate world of modified and supermodified back-yard specials that probably run on close to a thousand of America's 1100 or 1200 tracks.

The sport, at seventy-nine, is young enough for me to have met many of those who have helped make its history. And it is fortunate that auto racing is blessed with such a large population of wonderfully cooperative scholars. Although a bibliography of books and magazine articles that I found useful appears in the back of this book, I would like to single out four outstanding volumes: *The Checkered Flag* by Peter Helck, Griff Borgeson's *The Golden Age of the American Racing Car*, Al Bloemker's *500 Miles to Go*, and *Ford: The Dust and the Glory* by Leo Levine.

Of the many drivers and car owners who gave generously of their time I especially want to thank young Billy Vukovich and Dan Gurney. Chris Economaki, Bill France, and NASCAR's Jim Foster were most informative, and Bill Dredge and Bob Thomas helped me with information and photographs. The Ormond Beach Birthplace of Speed Association and Mal Currie at Watkins Glen were helpful, and George Rand supplied me with valued information and photographs on the revival of American road racing. I am grateful to John Peckham for his help on steam, to Phil Drackett for arranging a visit to the Royal Automobile Club's hallowed archives, and to Cyril Posthumus, my former editor at *Motoring News*, for loads of help overseas. FIAT, Daimler-Benz, and Renault supplied me with information and photographs, as did Firestone and Goodyear, the Chevrolet Division of General Motors, and the Ford Motor Company. Photographer Bob Tronolone, Dean Batchelor, and Bob Russo came through with hard-to-find pictures; Jack Fox was quick with information on West Coast racing; Bob Kovacik made available his fine series on Corona; and Melitta Hartung of the AAA supplied information on the club's early years. The Speedway's Al Bloemker and John Fugate were a gold mine of information and a delight to work with, as were John Oliveau of ACCUS and Walter Fasbender and Verna Martinsen at the Vanderbilt Museum.

Henry Austin Clark was an important source of photographs and information, as was the distinguished artist-historian Peter Helck, one of whose paintings honor these pages. Mary Cattie of the Philadelphia Library Automobile Reference Collection and Jim Bradley of Detroit's Public Library Automotive History Collection make it a pleasure to conduct automobile research. Motoring writers are lucky to have such cooperative, well-informed people in charge of these magnificent collections.

I was privileged to have the manuscript read and corrected by two outstanding auto racing historians, Charles Lytle and Charles Betts, both of whom allowed me to use photographs from their collections. In addition to guiding me over many rough spots, Charles Betts has contributed an updated version of his valuable reference work, *Auto Racing Winners,* as an appendix to this volume.

My thanks also to Olga Zaferatos of The Viking Press for steering me through the maze of publishing an illustrated book. To Tom Binford a final word of thanks for contributing the thoughtful Introduction and for playing midwife to the idea for this book.

Albert R. Bochroch

Bridge House
August 1973

Getting Started

Reporting on the Paris–Rouen reliability run of July 22, 1894, Gerald Rose, in his classic *A Record of Motor Racing 1894–1908,* notes that "many now well-known people were present at the start, amongst them Mr. James Gordon-Bennett, the proprietor of the New York *Herald,* who sent a special reporter on a bicycle to follow the race through to Rouen." We quibble with the otherwise impeccable Mr. Rose on two counts—his use of "race" (no doubt he tired of writing "trials," the term used most often in describing this first of all automobile contests) and the superfluous hyphen in Gordon Bennett.

Le Petit Journal, the newspaper that sponsored the Paris–Rouen trials, considered them a success. A large crowd saw the start on the Boulevard Maillot. Reports indicate that the lunch stop at Mantes was enjoyed by both the townspeople and participants and a remarkable seventeen of the twenty-one starters completed the 78.75-mile run.

Encouraged by the reception given the trials, a group of French enthusiasts, led by the Baron de Zuylen of Belgium and Count de Dion, asked the *Petit Journal* to lend its support to a more testing event in 1895, perhaps an all-out race of seven or eight hundred miles! After showing initial interest, the paper regretfully withdrew its support, fearing that its competitors would call the *Journal* irresponsible for encouraging a speed contest. Not easily discouraged, on November 2, 1894, the enterprising Count de Dion called a meeting at his home. The committee, which one year later was to form the Automobile Club of France, eventually decided to hold a race in 1895, from Paris to Bordeaux and back, a distance of 732 miles. The winner was to be the first car to finish which had seats for more than two passengers. Thus did our racing forefathers help placate their critics by demonstrating that if speed were motor racing's only objective, the regulations would have been written to permit the faster two-seaters to be eligible for awards. The 1895 Paris–Bordeaux race actually started from the Place d'Armes in Versailles on

June 11. The rules were simple: drivers could be changed en route, repairs were to be done under the supervision of race officials and then only with materials carried onboard the car. The winner was to receive 50 per cent of the purse, second place 20 per cent, third 10 per cent, and fourth, fifth, sixth, and seventh each 5 per cent of the remaining prize money. An exhibition of Paris–Bordeaux entries created considerable interest, and 69,951 francs in prize money was raised by subscription.

Two prominent Americans—William K. Vanderbilt, Jr., and James Gordon Bennett—were Paris–Bordeaux contributors. William Kissam, the great-grandson of Commodore Vanderbilt, then an eighteen-year-old Harvard student, gave 3000 francs. James Gordon Bennett's donation was 10,000 francs. Young Vanderbilt was a true motoring enthusiast, and he was to become a first-class race driver. William K. Vanderbilt twice held the land speed record. He finished well up in several of the early European races, his books on touring were among the very first on motor travel, and he was the founder of the history-making Vanderbilt Cup series.

By the time Gordon Bennett became interested in automobile racing he was known as a successful, albeit flamboyant, newspaper publisher and an outstanding sportsman. He attended the Ecole Polytechnique in Paris and was as much at home in France as in his native New York. Gordon Bennett came back to the United States to serve as a Navy lieutenant in the Civil War but returned to Paris following a scandal in New York that involved a duel. In 1887 he founded the Paris edition of his father's newspaper, the New York *Herald.*

In 1869, as managing editor of the *Herald,* Bennett had been responsible for sending Henry Morton Stanley to Africa to find David Livingstone. He helped to finance the 1875 search for the Northwest Passage and in 1877 sponsored the tragic De Long expedition to the Arctic. An erratic but generous man, he gave $100,000 to the *Herald* relief fund for Irish sufferers of the agrarian outrages, yet was known to fire a man if he did not like his looks. As a sportsman he helped introduce polo to the United States, and he personally skippered his yacht, *Dauntless,* in the transatlantic race of 1870.

Bennett became an early member of the Automobile Club of France and regularly gave financial support to European racing. But he remained an American patriot. The idea of the Gordon Bennett races was the result of his conviction that an American machine could beat the best of Europeans and his showman's instinct that told him the sponsorship of a series of international automobile races would be a good thing for his newspapers. Gordon Bennett began to realize his idea in 1899 when the pioneer American car maker, Alexander Winton, challenged Fernand Charron to a match race of 1000 miles. Winner of the 1898 Marseilles–Nice and Paris–Amsterdam races in his Panhard, Charron quickly accepted Winton's challenge, posting 20,000 francs with the *Herald*'s Paris office. Nothing came of Winton's dare, but one month later Bennett announced the Gordon Bennett Cup series and commissioned famed Paris silversmith Auroc to prepare the trophy.

Automobile racing in the United States got underway on November 2, 1895, when H. H. Kohlsaat, who bought the Chicago *Times-Herald* in April 1895, had visited Europe in 1894. In July 1895 he persuaded his editor to sponsor a contest. As with the 1894 Paris–Rouen Concours, as its sponsors called it, many more entries, close to a hundred, were received than were ready to race. So few were fully prepared when race day neared that the event was postponed to November 28, Thanksgiving Day. However, so as not to disappoint the public, an "Exhibition Run" was scheduled for the original race date, November 2. For running from Chicago to Waukegan and back, a prize of $500 was to be divided between all finishers within a thirteen-hour maximum time limit. A Duryea Motor Wagon, driven by Frank Duryea, accompanied by his brother Charles, and a Mueller-Benz, driven by the builder's son, Oscar, were the sole starters. However, two Kane-Pennington Electric Victorias and a Morris and Salom Electric were exhibited at the start. The Duryea and Benz left the Midway Plaisance in Jackson Park at 8:15 a.m., the "race" proper starting at Halsted and 55th Street. The Duryea lost forty-eight minutes repairing a snapped drive chain and, after almost catching the Benz, was ditched by an errant farm wagon. Mueller's Benz completed the ninety-two miles in eight hours and forty-four minutes actual running time after being on the road for nine hours and thirty minutes. As the only finisher it won the $500 prize.

Driving on Thanksgiving Day, 1895, would have been difficult for today's motorist. The U.S. Weather Bureau's Chicago report for November 25 through November 28 read, "A severe snowstorm which visited Chicago on November 25th and 26th left 12 inches of snow . . .

The Gordon Bennett Trophy.

As a newspaper publisher, Gordon Bennett may have had more interest in racing as a promotion than for love of the sport. However, it was the Gordon Bennett series that stimulated international automobile competition.

William K. Vanderbilt, Jr., in his 70-hp Mors prior to the 1903 Paris–Madrid. Willie K. was one of six Americans in this last of the great city-to-city, open-road races.

temperatures ranged from 8 to 33 degrees . . . winds attained a high of 60 miles an hour." Race-day temperatures did rise to the low 30s, but eight to ten inches of snow, slush, and ice remained. Of the eleven competitors that had claimed to be ready the day before, only six made it to the start: Duryea Motor Wagon, De la Vergne Refrigerating Machine Co. Benz, Morris and Salom Electric, R. H. Macy-Benz, Sturges Electric Motocycle, and the Mueller-Benz, which was over an hour late for the start.

At 8:55 a.m. J. Frank Duryea and his umpire, Arthur White, were the first off. The De la Vergne Benz followed but soon withdrew because of trouble getting through the slush between Jackson Park and the official 55th Street starting point. Jerry O'Connor, driving the Macy-Benz, with Lieutenant Samuel Rodman as umpire, started at 8:59 a.m. Within minutes, nearing the Art Institute, the Macy-Benz slid into the rear of a horse-drawn streetcar, crossed the Pennsylvania railroad tracks, and collided with an overturned sleigh that had just dumped its occupants, including the *Times-Herald* reporter, in the snow. Later O'Connor made contact with a hack, further bending the Benz's already damaged steering. This last misfortune forced the Macy-Benz to retire. The Sturges Electric left at 9:01 a.m., followed one minute later by the Morris and Salom Electric. Sixth and last to leave was the tardy Mueller-Benz, with

Oscar Mueller and umpire Charles B. King. They started at 10:06 a.m.

Large, good-natured crowds lined the route. Those attending the Michigan–University of Chicago football game in Lincoln Park paused to cheer the "motocycles"; willing hands helped lift stuck machines out of snowbanks, and the Chicago police hustled from point to point clearing a path for the approaching machines. At Evanston the Macy-Benz had less than a two-minute lead over the Duryea, with the Mueller-Benz forty-five minutes behind. Minor delays were caused by the Cottage Grove Horse Cars. Time was lost, and meticulously recorded, for mechanical adjustments: "2 minutes to oil engine; 8.5 minutes to tighten belt; one-half minute right chain off; 6 minutes to bend clutch." Two relay stations supplied gasoline and pails of broken ice for cooling. Charles Reid, a third rider in Mueller's car, was removed after thirty-five miles, exhausted and cold. Nearing the finish, Frank Duryea lost ten minutes when he took a wrong turn, but by then his only competition was the Mueller-Benz, far behind.

As the crowd chilled, its mood changed. At Douglas Park, a group of two hundred youngsters first snowballed the police and then drove them into the street. An attempt to call patrol wagons found that all phone lines had been down since the beginning of the storm. The streets became all but deserted as darkness fell,

J. Frank Duryea behind tiller with umpire Arthur White. The Duryea, No. 5, won the first organized race in America—the Chicago *Times-Herald* contest of November 28, 1895. George H. Hewitt, president of Duryea, stands on the right, behind the car's rear wheel.

The start at Jackson Park: No. 7 is the De La Verne Benz, No. 5 the Duryea, and No. 25 the Sturgis Electric.

The winning Duryea making time in Evanston.

The accident-prone R. H. Macy Benz.

The Sturgis Electric receiving help. Some versions of this historic photograph were retouched to show deep snow in the foreground.

Although the Duryea Motor Wagon won $2000 "for the best performance in the road race, for range of speed and pull, with compactness of design," the gold medal went to the Morris & Salom Electrobat "for the best showing made in the official tests, ease of control, absence of noise or vibration, cleanliness and general excellence of design."

Some of the 400 guests at the Ardsley Country Club who welcomed the *Cosmopolitan*-New York to Irvington-on-Hudson racers.

and fewer than fifty people were in Jackson Park at 7:18 p.m. to see the Duryea win America's first automobile race. At 8:53 the Mueller-Benz crossed the finish line, only twenty-four minutes running time behind the Duryea, because it had started over an hour later. The Duryea completed the 54.36-mile run in ten hours and twenty-three minutes total time, seven hours and fifty-three minutes actual running time, for an average speed of 6.66 mph. For the final hour, umpire Charles King drove the Benz with one hand on the tiller, the other supporting Oscar Mueller, who had collapsed from exposure.

This is the same Charles Brady King who, on March 6, 1896, drove the first automobile on the streets of Detroit and, beginning in 1909, manufactured his own car. King also was one of those responsible for the formation of the world's first automobile club, the American Motor League, established in Chicago on November 1, 1895. Twelve days later, the Automobile Club of France was organized by the Count de Dion at his Quai d'Orsay home in Paris, and December 12 saw Great Britain's Self-Propelled Traffic Association formed.

On December 5 prizes were awarded to the two Chicago–Evanston finishers and seven other entrants: $2000 to the Duryea for best performance, range of speed, pull and compactness of design; $1500 to H. Mueller for performance and economy of operation; and $500 to the Macy-Benz for its showing in the race. The farsighted judges also made awards based on tests, as well as race performance, for "ease of control, absence of noise or vibration, cleanliness and general excellence of design." However, giving the *Times-Herald* gold medal to the Electrobat, a non-finisher, did cause some dismay.

In addition to local newspaper accounts, contemporary reports, calling the event a motocycle race, appeared in America's first automobile publications, *Horseless Age* and *The Motocycle*. The *Times-Herald,* looking for a term to replace "horseless carriage," had sponsored a $500 contest to find a new name. "Motocycle" was the winner, but not for long.

The second automobile race held in America was run on May 30, 1896, and was sponsored by *Cosmopolitan* magazine. Its editor, John Brisbane Walker, arranged for the course to run from New York's City Hall to Irvington-on-Hudson. *Cosmopolitan* was published in Irvington, which also happened to be where Walker had his home. Following a "parade" of the race cars from City Hall to Kingsbridge, where the race actually began, the field ran up the Hudson to the Ardsley Country Club in Irvington, where the race judges (who included John Jacob Astor, Chauncey Depew, president of the New York Central Railroad, and Frank Thompson, president of the Pennsylvania) awaited them. The officials were transported from New York City by the New York Central and Hudson River Railroad. They were joined by four hundred guests celebrating the country-club opening. Although the *Cosmopolitan* had thirty entries, only six started. Frank Duryea won the thirty-mile run in seven hours and thirteen minutes, pocketing the complete purse of $3000 in prize money as the only finisher.

In 1899 Walker, with A. L. Barker, a New York paving contractor, paid $250,000 for the design rights to the

Stanley Steamer. Walker founded the Mobile Steam Car Company in Tarrytown, New York, and Barber began making the Locomobile Steam Car. Two years later the steam patents were resold to the Stanley Brothers. The Mobile continued to be made until 1903, however. Locomobile discontinued its steam car and began production of a gasoline-driven machine designed by A. L. Riker.

The forerunner of state-fair auto racing that still thrives was held at the Rhode Island State Fair, Narragansett Park, from September 7 to 11, 1896. Five Duryeas were entered, but the event, a series of one-mile sprints, was won by the Riker Electric, driven by A. L. Riker and C. H. Whiting. The final heat, run early on Friday evening, September 11, was reported to have been seen by a crowd of over 50,000. Accounts of the Narragansett meet indicate considerable dissension, with several of the complaints sounding surprisingly current. Because of heavy rains, only three heats were run, although five were advertised. The drivers were unhappy over the $100 entry fee; the promoters were criticized by the press for garaging the race cars a good distance from the track and the main fair buildings, which made it difficult for the public to visit the "work sheds"; the sheds were not suitable for the cars; there were no signs telling the public where the racing carriages could actually be seen; the race-horse owners complained of the noise made by the automobiles, and the automobile racers complained about the vagueness of the rules. "What is needed," said one contemporary report, "is a strong racing association such as the newly formed American Motor League." However, first place did earn Riker $900.

The first American to race in Europe was George Heath, a resident of Paris. His Panhard was thirteenth of twenty-two in the 1898 Paris–Amsterdam, and in 1899 he finished sixth in the Tour de France and fourth in Paris–St. Malo. Heath's finest year was 1904, with two victories over the Circuit des Ardennes in Belgium and a historic triumph in the first Vanderbilt Cup, held on his native Long Island. Heath, who never raced any make but Panhard, continued to participate until 1909, his last notable finish being a second in the 1905 Vanderbilt Cup.

Not counting his fastest-time-of-day in a hill climb at Newport, Rhode Island, in September 1900, William K. Vanderbilt, Jr., began to take motoring seriously in 1902. April of that year saw his Mercedes travel 65.79

During the *Cosmopolitan* magazine race of 1896: the winning Duryea being pushed up a hill near Ardsley.

mph on the Acheres road near Paris (the fastest mile up to that time), the first time the record was held by a gasoline-powered car. Before the year was out he had pushed his Mors to 67.78 mph at Albis and then drove the giant 80-hp, 12-liter Mors to a new official mark of 76.08 mph. But young Vanderbilt soon lost his laurels to Fournier's Mors, which clocked 76.60 mph. He entered the 615-mile Paris–Vienna race in June 1902, his Mors completing only the 233-mile first leg from Paris to Belfort. However, Vanderbilt must have enjoyed his racing debut, as the following month found him in Belgium running the difficult Circuit des Ardennes. Following the catastrophic Paris–Madrid race of May 1903, which the French government ordered stopped at Bordeaux and in which "Willie K." fell out with a cracked cylinder on the first day, motor racing shifted from town-to-town events to closed circuits over public roads. Another American, J. B. Warden, finished fifth in Paris–Madrid in his Mercedes.

The Ardennes race of July 1902 became the forerunner of modern road racing. In the same event a year later, Vanderbilt finished third to Jarrott's Panhard and

Gabriel's Mors, his 60-hp Mors covering the hilly 318 miles with a 50-mph average.

In January 1904 Vanderbilt set a new world speed mark at Ormond Beach, his 90-hp Mercedes running the mile in 92.30 mph to edge out the 91.37-mph record made by Henry Ford over the ice of Lake St. Clair a few weeks before. Before the 1904 Ormond Beach season was over Vanderbilt had run the mile in 102.85 mph, the first to travel faster than 100 mph. Unfortunately, that effort did not go into the record books, since it was not timed officially. That same year, in January, Vanderbilt opened a bright new chapter in American racing when he presented the American Automobile Association with the Vanderbilt Cup, becoming the patron of America's first international series.

Actually, the Vanderbilt Cup of 1904 was the second he gave. In September 1900 J. H. McDuffee won a cup inscribed "donated by William K. Vanderbilt Jr." when McDuffee's Mobile won a five-mile race for steam carriages over a half-mile track at Newport.

Vanderbilt's interest in automobiles went beyond racing. He fought for better roads in America, and his

Start of America's third race, its first on a closed track, at the Rhode Island State Fair, Friday evening, September 7, 1896.

The Riker Electric, winner at Narragansett Park, Rhode Island State Fairgrounds. A. L. Riker, with moustache, faces camera.

three books—*Log of My Motor, 1899–1908, Log of My Motor, 1908–1911,* and *Through Tunisia and Algeria by Motor*—were among the first automobile tour guides.

Although young Vanderbilt was the most active, he was not the only American racing in Europe during the pioneering pre-Grand Prix days.

Foxhall Keene became a European regular in 1901. He drove a Mercedes in the 1901 Paris–Bordeaux and a month later a Mors in Paris–Berlin, in which he lay sixth before retiring at Hanover. A contemporary account of Paris–Berlin noted, "Mr. Foxhall Keene, the only American competitor, blundered into a potato-field where his car capsized, although he miraculously missed injury. . . ." He was in the Paris–Vienna the following month and in 1903, with four other Americans—Warden, Heath, Terry, and Keene—started the Paris–Madrid, which was the last of the great city-to-city marathons. His best race was to be the 1903 Gordon Bennett at Athy, Ireland, in which he drove one of three Mercedes representing Germany, and set the fastest lap. He led during the early stages but ran into axle trouble and retired at the halfway point.

Fabulous Foxhall Keene could only have happened when and where he did. Program notes for the 1903 Gordon Bennett read, "An American sportsman, much given to steeplechasing in England. A son of James R. Keene, a millionaire stock-operator in New York, who was born in England but migrated to the United States in 1852 soon after the bonanza boom. Mr. Foxhall Keene is a well-known Wall Street millionaire, and one of the smartest motorists on either side of the Atlantic. Drives a powerful Mors car, but does not confine himself to one type. Is a familiar figure on the Coney Island Boulevard. Is a thorough sportsman, and either in hunting field, where he has been frequently dislocated or fractured, or on the polo ground, can give many men points. . . ."

Should Foxhall Keene be remembered it will be as a horseman. In one year he won 79 of 101 races, and at seventeen he was the nation's champion jockey. His father, who lost several fortunes tangling with Jay Gould, offered to bet $100,000 to $10,000 on his son in any of ten sports. There were no takers. A trim 140-pounder, young Keene boxed, shot championship golf, played college football, excelled at both court and lawn tennis, and enjoyed a ten-goal polo rating. He bought his first car, a three-wheeler, in Paris in 1895, but his racing record never matched his other honors. He continued to race, usually in a Mercedes, until 1909, but rode to the hounds up to 1917, when he was forty-seven. Foxhall Keene died lonely and broke in 1941, in a cottage provided by his sister.

One of the better early "gentlemen drivers" was John B. Warden. Out of more than two hundred entries, his Austrian Mercedes finished sixth overall in the curtailed Paris–Madrid of 1903. Warden's 90-hp Mercedes was one of three representing Austria in the 1904 Gordon Bennett at Homburg, and he finished eighth in the Vanderbilt of 1905.

Vanderbilt's cousin Elliott Shepard, whose father married Willie K.'s Aunt Margaret, raced two French cars, Hotchkiss and Clement Bayard. Although he had no major triumphs, Shepard was fourth at the end of the first day of the first French Grand Prix and was running well up on the second day until a collapsed wheel forced his retirement. He finished ninth in the 1907 GP and was running second in the 1907 Coppa Della Velocita but failed to finish. Shepard's only Vanderbilt Cup appearance was in 1906, when he retired with a broken crank shaft while in sixth place.

Lack of American participation in the Gordon Bennett series was a disappointment to its sponsor. Invitations were issued to the automobile clubs of France, Germany, the United States, Great Britain, Belgium, Italy, Austria, and Switzerland. Gordon Bennett regulations called for each country to be represented by three cars, and all parts of each car were to be manufactured in the country of its origin. Also, each race was to be staged by the club that had captured the prior year's event, and "the vehicles were to be driven by members of competing clubs." The Automobile Club of France was awarded the initial race. The lack of American entries, and their poor showing when they did race, made the Gordon Bennett Cup (the races were always referred to as "The Coupe Internationale" in the sponsor's own newspapers) strictly a European show.

The series got off to a slow start. The first Gordon Bennett—Paris–Lyon on June 14, 1900—attracted but five entries, one Belgian, three French, and Alexander Winton, whose outclassed single-cylinder Winton dropped out near Orleans with a broken wheel. In 1901 only the French team entered, and the race was combined with Paris–Bordeaux. The 1902 field was also thin, and the Gordon Bennett was run part way in conjunction with the ACF's Paris–Vienna race, the Cup cars stopping at Innsbruck. However, the 1902 entry did include two cars from Great Britain, a Wolseley and a Napier. Selwyn Francis Edge drove the Napier to victory, and Great Britain earned her first international motoring laurels and the embarrassment of staging the 1903 race in a country that considered motor racing not only illegal but blasphemous. Pressure on Parliament failed to budge England's lawmakers; the solution found was a closed course at Athy, near Dublin, Ireland.

With the 1903 race, the Gordon Bennett series came alive. Interest was high, and so many English car makers wanted to enter that Great Britain found it necessary to hold elimination trials to select their Gordon Bennett team, a procedure followed by France in the following two years. Three bright red cars represented America. Italy did not enter the Gordon Bennett until 1904, and red was the United States racing color then. The U.S. entries were an eight-cylinder Winton Bullet driven by Alexander Winton, a four-cylinder Winton Baby Bullet piloted by Percy Owen, manager of Winton's New York office, and a four-cylinder Peerless in the hands of its designer, Louis Mooers, chief engineer of Peerless. Although failing to finish the 1903 Gordon Bennett, the Peerless and big Winton both achieved fame in Barney Oldfield's hands. The Winton 8 won several races and set a fifty-five-second one-mile record, and, after rebuilding, the 80-hp Peerless became Barney's first Green Dragon.

John Warden was the only American entered in the 1904 race. It was held in Homburg, Germany, because Jenatzy had captured the 1903 Cup in his 60-hp Mercedes owned by the American industrialist Clarence Gray Dinsmore. France won at Homburg, the 1905 race going to the Auvergne Circuit near Clermont-Ferrand in the Masif-Central region of France. On July 5, 1905,

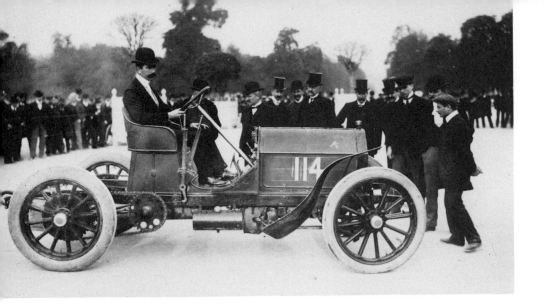

Foxhall Keene with his Mercedes before the start of the 1903 Paris–Madrid.

John B. Warden's Austrian Mercedes in the 1904 Gordon Bennett in Homburg, Germany.

Elliott Shepard's Hotchkiss in the 1906 Grand Prix of France at Le Mans.

eighteen machines represented six nations. Included were two Pope-Toledos and a Locomobile from the United States, three Italian FIATs, two Brasiers and a De Dietrich from France, three German and three Austrian Mercedes, and a Napier and two Wolseleys from England. By far the best field ever started the sixth and, ironically, the last Gordon Bennett challenge.

The three American drivers at Clermont-Ferrand were professionals with solid credentials. Irish-born Joe Tracy, who became the 1906 AAA national champion, had driven a Panhard and Brasier in New York races, a Royal in the first Vanderbilt Cup, and he had brought a Gould Brokaw's Renault home second at Havana in 1904. Bert Dingley and Herb Lytle, in untried 60-hp Pope-Toledos, were not taken seriously. But the big 17.7-liter, 90-hp Locomobile was given a chance. Unfortunately, being driven down from the port of Le Havre, the Locomobile lost second gear. With no spares, Tracy still managed two laps around the eighty-five-mile mountain circuit, limited to low and high, before the gearbox packed up.

If we overlook Charles and Frank Duryea's disputed first- and third-place finishes in the 1896 London–Brighton so-called "Emancipation Run" because it was not a proper race, the official results were considered dubious, and some historians claim the Duryeas failed to follow the official route, then the honor of being the first American car and driver to complete a European race goes to the twelfth-, and last-, place Pope-Toledo driven by Herb Lytle at Auvergne in 1905.

Unrest over several Gordon Bennett rules had been brewing. The automobile clubs, particularly the French and, for different reasons, Gordon Bennett himself, were showing signs of disenchantment with the series.

France, with its many competitive makes, took exception to the regulation that limited each nation to a single team of three cars. Bennett, who never saw one of his Cup races, was unhappy over what he considered excessive commercialism, as many manufacturers were running the races to sell their cars rather than for a love of the sport. Consequently new regulations, insisted on by the powerful Automobile Club of France, were drafted and became effective with the 1906 race. The key change resulted in turning championship racing over to the car manufacturers. In 1906 the first French Grand Prix was run over a 64.12-mile course east of Le Mans. It was to be fifteen years before Jimmy Murphy's Duesenberg won the French Grand Prix to bring the Stars and Stripes to Victory Lane in Europe.

International racing owes much to the Gordon Bennett series. They paved the way for Grand Prix racing and inspired Willie K. Vanderbilt to establish the Vanderbilt Cup. Following the 1905 Cup race, automobile racing lost Gordon Bennett. He sponsored international balloon races from 1906 until 1929, during which the United States won eight times, and the Gordon Bennett Aviation Cup, from 1909 until 1920. In 1914 when the German Army was at the gates of Paris, many citizens of the French capital, including the staff of the Paris *Herald,* had fled. However, James Gordon Bennett, then seventy-four years old, remained in Paris and personally covered the Western Front for his newspapers.

A comparison of times between the final Gordon Bennett automobile race and the first Gordon Bennett Aviation Cup shows Thery's Brasier taking the 1905 motor race with a 48.4-mph average as Glenn Curtiss averaged a slightly slower 47.65 mph to capture the 1909 air race.

America Catches Up   II

From the beginning American and European automobile makers used racing to sell cars. When Henry Ford beat the favored Alexander Winton over the Detroit Driving Club's one-mile oval at Grosse Pointe in October 1901, he won more than the $1000 prize and a cutglass bowl; he won recognition. Looking back on his racing experience, Ford said, "Winning a race or making a record was then the best kind of advertising."

As Leo Levine points out in *The Dust and the Glory,* except for record breaking, Grosse Pointe was the beginning and end of Henry Ford's career as a race driver. However, it was only the start of the Ford Motor Company's use of performance to sell automobiles. Buick, which has not, officially, been near a race track for fifty years, had a distinguished racing career. In 1906 Buicks won the Eagle Rock and Mt. Washington hill climbs; ran coast to coast in twenty-four days for a new New York–San Francisco record; won at the Empire City dirt track in Yonkers, New York; and captured their class in an endurance run in Los Angeles. By 1909 a staff of forty maintained fifteen racing Buicks, including the three that captured three first-place finishes during the 1909 first-ever race at the Indianapolis Speedway. Not only did the pioneer car makers themselves promote their racing triumphs, but industry suppliers, tire companies, makers of carburetors, shock absorbers, headlights, and even technical products such as bearings carried the part they played to a public eager for racing news.

All kinds of auto racing flourished. Races were held on city streets. Horse tracks were hastily converted, cinder and dirt ovals were built, and road racing prospered. Impromptu weekend skirmishes between handfuls of car owners became commonplace. Run over country roads, these informal contests often finished in the town square in a carnival-like atmosphere, the participants cheered on by family and friends. For a time, record-breaking, usually one-car-at-a-time flying starts over the measured mile and hill climbing rivaled the popularity of racing. Although Pike's Peak was not run officially until 1916, America's hills and mountains were being assaulted as early as 1898, when Freelan Stanley climbed Mt. Washington in one of his Steamers. Boston's annual Eagle Rock Climb began in 1901. The Chicago Motor Club staged its yearly Algonquin Climb up two hills. George Robertson, who in 1908 became the first American to win a Vanderbilt Cup race, won a 0.7-mile climb at Rockville, Connecticut, in a Stevens-Duryea.

Alexander Winton appears in the news twice in 1897 for winning a one-mile race in Cleveland and for taking only ten days to travel from Cleveland to New York. A half-mile dirt track opened in Bradford, Connecticut, with Hiram Percy Maxim's Columbia winning a five-mile race. Winton cut his time for the Cleveland–New York run to forty-seven hours and thirty-seven minutes. In May 1900 a Riker Electric won a road race from Springfield to Babylon, Long Island, and back. In Cleveland in 1901 the ubiquitous Mr. Winton ran the mile in 1:02.25. A year later the Winton Bullet captured the first Brighton Beach race over its one-mile dirt track, and Barney Oldfield twice drove Henry Ford's 999 to wins at Grosse Pointe. The following June at Indianapolis, Oldfield became the first racer to cover a one-mile oval in under a minute. By this time there was racing in Cleveland, Detroit, and at the St. Louis World's Fair.

New tracks were soon to open in Chicago, Minneapolis, and Point Breeze, Philadelphia. Morris Park, a 1.39-mile dirt track in the Bronx, gave New York City three tracks. It seemed that races, hill climbs, and "speed" runs were going on everywhere.

Record runs were being contested on public roads and beaches and over frozen lakes and rivers. In Europe, especially in France, where paved highways were in use well ahead of the United States, the arrow-straight old Roman roads were the scene of frequent record attempts. *Scientific American* of November 30, 1901, carried the account of a record run held in

Henry Ford in 999 and Harry Harkness driving a Simplex at Grosse Pointe, 1903. Ford scholars believe this to be a staged shot (note the track surface of the Simplex's right front tire). This composite was used in advertising by the G & T Tire Company.

Indianapolis Speedway, August 19, 1909. Louis Chevrolet's Buick captured the opening-day 250-mile Prest-O-Lite Trophy.

Stanley Steamer at the completion of the Mount Washington hill climb in 1904.

Henry Ford with Barney Oldfield at the wheel of 999 in 1903.

Brooklyn on November 16, 1901. The great Henri Fournier, winner of that year's Paris–Berlin and Paris–Bordeaux races, was to challenge America's best. The twenty-five thousand spectators who lined Ocean Parkway saw the sixty-second mile broken three times. Racing slightly downgrade on a specially prepared dirt strip, with the timing handled by the U.S. Army Signal Corps, Fournier's 40-hp Mors registered runs of 52 and 51.8 seconds, close to 70 mph. Bostwick's 40-hp Winton made the run in 56.6 seconds, followed by Foxhall Keene's Mors and the streamlined, sixty-cell Riker Electric, which was timed at 63 seconds.

New Jersey's beaches were being tested from Asbury Park to Cape May. The beach at Newport, Rhode Island, was tried in 1900, and a five-mile course at Denver Beach, near Galveston, Texas, was used by cars and motorcycles. Racing in Florida moved into the limelight on the sands between Ormond and Daytona Beach, where it was to flourish for thirty years. When conditions were right, just right, a low tide and little wind, Ormond-Daytona offered a 500-foot-wide, fifteen-mile-long straight stretch of hard-packed white sand. Sir Henry Segrave, on first seeing Daytona in 1927, called it "a veritable marvel of nature." In his book *The Lure of Speed* he said, "Here, if ever, was the one place in the world where a speed of 200 miles or more an hour could be attained."

Alexander Winton and R. E. Olds first tried the beach at Ormond in April 1902. Both declared that it would be fine for racing, and it was diplomatically announced that the Winton Bullet and Oldsmobile Pirate had achieved identical times of 50 mph. William K. Vanderbilt, Jr., who held the official land speed record briefly in 1902 when his Mors covered the mile in 76.08 mph, visited Ormond Beach for the first time in 1903. He returned with a party of friends early in 1904, and Ormond-Daytona became a fixture in both the social and racing world.

On January 12, 1904, Henry Ford drove his Arrow, a great buckboard of a race car, all engine and bare bones (it had been rebuilt after a crash in Milwaukee in which the driver died), over the ice of Lake St. Clair to set a new world speed mark of 91.37 mph for the mile. As with many automobile pioneers, Ford enjoyed being around race cars. For fifteen days he was recognized as the fastest man in the world by the American Automobile Association but not by the official world body, the Automobile Club of France.

Mr. and Mrs. Henry Ford had arrived at Ormond Beach just in time to see Vanderbilt improve on Ford's

25

Henry Ford, in cap, with Gaston Plaintiff (left), manager of Ford's New York office, on the New Jersey shore, 1905.

time by two-fifths of a second as Willie K. drove his 90-hp Mercedes to a 92.30-mph record for the measured mile. Vanderbilt held the record until July 1904, when it returned to Europe, the Frenchman Rigolly reaching 94.78 mph at Nice on March 31. In July 1904 Rigolly became the first officially to travel faster than 100 mph, his Gobron-Brillie being clocked over Belgium's Ostend Highway at 103.55 mph. With the exception of Barney Oldfield's 1910 run of 131.72 mph in the Blitzen Benz, world-fastest mile honors were to remain in Europe until 1928, when Ray Keech broke the overseas monopoly in the White-Triplex. Actually, Burman's Benz reached 141.73 mph in April 1911, DePalma's Packard 149.87 in 1919, and Tommy Milton's Duesenberg Special 153.10 in 1920, but these were one-way runs.

After Keech it would be another thirty-six years before America again held the land speed record. However, not being in possession of the official world title did little to thin traffic on the beach as the AAA continued to supervise runs for the American record.

It is possible that steam wagons, steam tractors, and roadgoing steam locomotives were running both in Europe and the United States a century before gasoline-propelled cars. If we accept the likely premise that the first race took place the very instant that the drivers of the first two self-propelled vehicles saw each other, devotees of steam may believe they have suffered still

another slight and insist that Paris–Bordeaux was merely the first race for gasoline power.

Steam wagons were operating in Philadelphia as early as 1805. A Thomas Blanchard drove around Springfield, Massachusetts, in a steam wagon in the 1820s, and in 1827 the Johnson brothers of Philadelphia may have had the world's first automobile accident when their steam wagons collided. In the 1830s John Gore of Vermont drove a steam wagon for at least a decade, and in 1875 the state of Wisconsin offered a $10,000 prize for "a cheap and satisfactory substitute for the horse." Inspired by the substantial prize money, aspiring motorists prevailed on the state to sponsor a race to determine who best met the self-propelled-vehicle criteria. Six steam wagons entered the Wisconsin contest, but only two began the race. Starting at Green Bay on July 16, 1878, the machines "Oshkosh" and "Green Bay" began a 231-mile run, won by Shomer and Farrand in the "Oshkosh" in thirty-three hours and twenty-seven minutes actual driving time.

The Stanley twins, Francis Edgar and Freelan Oscar, first raced one of their steam cars over a one-third-mile oval in Charles River Park, Cambridge, Massachusetts, in November 1898. Not only was the steamer fastest on the track, winning with a record average speed of 27.40 mph, but it also captured a hill climb, held in the area on the same day. After a brief period,

Alexander Winton after covering the mile in 52.2 seconds, 69 mph, in the Winton Bullet at Ormond Beach, March 28, 1903.

The first International Speed Trials at Ormond-Daytona Beach, January 1904. The twenty-two cars pictured here were owned by local residents.

during which the Stanley business was owned by John Brisbane Walker, the publisher who had staged the 1896 Cosmopolitan race, and A. L. Barker, a New York paving contractor, the Stanleys regained the firm and again participated in races and hill climbs to promote their cars. Following Frank Durbin's winning the Newton, Massachusetts, Commonwealth Avenue Hill Climb, in a stock Stanley in April 1903, F. E. Stanley began designing special racing cars—lightweight streamlined models powered by oversized boilers, usually painted red. First time out for the racing model was Memorial Day, 1903, at the Readville Track, near Boston. F. E. Stanley managed to nose out the bizarre Cannon steamer with its dual-driver controls—one in front for steering, a second driver in the rear working the throttle, brakes, and power. Stanley set a new American one-mile record at Readville only to lose it later the same day when Barney Oldfield covered the mile in 58.4 seconds driving a Ford at Yonkers, New York.

The first documented use of steam was in France, where Nicolas J. Cugnot, a lieutenant in the French Army, built a steam-driven artillery tractor which he demonstrated to a military purchasing commission in 1769. Unfortunately, Cugnot failed to make a sale, as the self-propelled gun carriage performed poorly.

Cars driven by steam, as well as electric batteries, excelled in the shorter events in the sport's early days.

In 1902 the Frenchman Leon Serpollet, who in 1888 had invented the multiflash boiler that greatly advanced the steam-car cause, set a world speed mark of 75.06 mph for the flying kilometer. Serpollet was to retain the honor only until later that same year when Vanderbilt's Mors became the first gasoline-powered record holder. Louis Ross reached 94.73 mph driving a dual-engined Stanley on Ormond Beach in 1905, quick enough to take Speed Week laurels on the beach but not fast enough to claim a new world record. The 1905 season also saw England's Arthur MacDonald drive a Napier over the sands to hold briefly the record at 104.65 mph, while a Bostonian, Herbert Bowden, managed to travel better than 109 mph in the "Flying Dutchman II," a twin-engined Mercedes. However, the American Automobile Association, under whose sanction Speed Week was held, declared the Mercedes illegal for exceeding the weight limit by four hundred pounds. Bowden, who had taken the second Mercedes engine from his boat and lengthened his race car to accommodate it, was thought to have been treated unfairly when the AAA refused to recognize his time.

The Automobile Club of France did not get around to recognizing Land Speed Records, unless held under their jurisdiction, until 1927. In somewhat the same arbitrary manner, from 1906 until 1914, the French Grand Prix was simply known as the Grand Prix. Other nations staged major races—for example, Germany's Kaiserpries and Italy's Targa Florio, using similar regulations—but there was only one Grand Prix.

The Florida beaches began attracting the great European drivers. In 1906 Vincenzo Lancia drove a FIAT, and Victor Hemery and Louis Chevrolet had Darracqs. That January, F. E. Stanley introduced the Rocket, the latest of his Wogglebugs, a narrow, streamlined single-seater that the press said resembled an upside-down canoe. Driven by Fred H. Marriott, foreman of the Stanley repair shops, the 50-hp Bug averaged

111.80 mph to beat readily the 110-hp FIAT and 80-hp Napier in the one-mile Dewar Cup. Later in the week, despite some hanky-panky on the part of the officials, who shifted the starting time for the feature thirty-mile race from 9:00 a.m. to 7:00 a.m. without notifying the Stanley team, Marriott won again by a wide margin. Speed Week's feature event was to be the Bug's record attempt on Friday, January 26. Wire-wheeled, with a razor-sharp nose, the red steamer silently gathered speed for several miles until it triggered the timing device at the start of the measured mile. Seconds later the Rocket had shattered the world speed mark by 18 mph, recording a 127.66-mph run, to become the first machine to exceed two miles a minute. Marriott went out again, registering 121.57 mph to establish a record for the flying kilometer.

Nineteen hundred and seven saw the Stanley Steamers return in force to the Ormond-Daytona Tournament of Speed. Stanley driver Frank Durbin captured the mile race for touring cars, Marriott won the five-miler in the red Bug, and F. E. Stanley established a new record for steam touring cars. By the end of the week all attention was centered on the Wogglebug's attack on the land speed mark. Record day was cool and cloudy as several thousand spectators watched Fred Marriott make his warm-up runs. Then the Bug started down the beach, obviously faster than ever before. A record seemed assured as Marriott swished past the start of the measured mile. Then Marriott hit a rough spot in the sand, and the Bug is said to have sailed a hundred feet in the air before it crashed and rolled. Marriott was hurled into the surf and seriously injured. The world's fastest race car was demolished. Marriott, who estimated he was going well over 150 mph at the time of the crash, recovered, but the Stanleys were shocked by the accident, and Stanley Steamers never raced again. Fred Mariott's 127.66-mph record withstood constant assaults until March 16, 1910, when Barney Oldfield recorded 131.72 mph on the beach in his 1311-cubic-inch, 200-hp Blitzen-Benz.

Following World War I, English drivers dominated the land speed record scene. Not until 1922 did Ormond-Daytona get back in the news when a relatively unknown American driver, Sig Haugdahl, became the first to travel three miles a minute, his Wisconsin Special reaching 180.27 mph in a one-way run. As international record rules had been revised to call for averaging the time of two runs, one in each direction, Haugdahl's one-way run was not recognized. However, Haugdahl will be remembered as probably the first race driver to balance his tires by using weights on the wheel rims. Captain George Eyston, in his book *Motor Racing and Record Breaking,* reports that Haugdahl increased his speed from 160 mph to 180 mph, solely as the result of eliminating the vibration caused by unbalanced tires.

Malcolm Campbell, a London businessman whose consuming passion was to hold the land and water speed records concurrently, had set a new world mark of 146.16 mph in his Sunbeam over the Pendine Sands in Wales in 1924. He slightly improved his time in 1925, only to have both Henry Segrave and Parry Thomas better his record. Campbell ordered a new machine with a 900-hp Napier aircraft engine and readily regained the honor. Henry Segrave then brought his 1000-hp, dual-engined Sunbeam to Daytona, where, on

Otto Nestman driving a Stevens-Duryea at Ormond-Daytona, January 3, 1904.

William K. Vanderbilt, Jr.'s, 90-hp Mercedes set a 92.30-mph mile record at Ormond-Daytona, January 27, 1904.

OVERLEAF: During the final heat of the 1905 Dewar Trophy at Ormond Beach: the W. K. Vanderbilt, Jr., Mercedes, No. 1, the A. E. McDonald Napier, No. 5, and the E. R. Thomas Mercedes, No. 6.

AAA Contest Board secretary Samuel Butler, center, inspecting new timing equipment at Ormond-Daytona in 1906.

Frank H. Marriott's Stanley Steamer covered the Ormond-Daytona mile in 28.2 seconds at 129 mph, January 26, 1906.

March 29, 1927, he reached 203.79 mph, first to break the magic 200-mph barrier. As a result of his achievement, Segrave received the honor of knighthood.

Following Parry Thomas' fatal crash at Pendine, record runs were no longer allowed in Wales, and in 1928 Campbell brought his rebuilt Bluebird to Daytona, where he regained the record with a run of 206.96 mph. Eight weeks later the record returned to America when Ray Keech flung the enormous three-engined White-Triplex over Daytona's sands at 207.55 mph. Driven by three twelve-cylinder Liberty aircraft engines, one in front and two in the rear, each rated at 1500 hp, the White-Triplex was one of the largest of all gasoline-engined racing cars. Keech went on to drive at Indianapolis in 1928 and to win the 500 in 1929, only to have a fatal crash on the boards at Altoona two weeks after Indy.

Speed Week 1928 saw America lose one of its best young drivers when Frank Lockhart crashed his Stutz Black Hawk Special. Not only was Frank Lockhart a fine driver (he won Indianapolis in 1926 when twenty-four years old), but he was also greatly respected as the designer of a device for cooling compressed air in supercharged engines. Lockhart used one of his intercoolers in the Miller Special, in which he set a new qualifying record for the 1927 Indy, as well as in his Miller-powered Black Hawk record car. His first try at the land speed record, on a windy February day in 1928, resulted in his being blown into the sea. Two months later, April 25, 1928, when Lockhart brought the repaired Black Hawk back to Daytona, Ray Keech had broken Malcolm Campbell's record. Now the land speed duel was between two determined Yanks who had learned their trade in the tough school of American track racing. Tire failure at an estimated 210 mph sent the Black Hawk

into a wild slide, followed by a series of end-over-end crashes. Lockhart's injuries were fatal.

The White-Triplex returned to Daytona in 1929 to try to better Sir Henry Segrave's recent record of 231.44 mph. The ill-handling Triplex was in the hands of Lee Bible when the huge machine went out of control *after* it had completed its run over the measured mile. Lee Bible and a photographer were killed, and there was speculation as to whether Daytona's sands had reached their limit. From 1931, when Sir Malcolm Campbell retrieved record honors, until 1935, when the final land speed run was held at Daytona, times had been pushed from 244.09 mph to 276.82 mph. Later in 1935 Sir Malcolm made his first run over the Salt Flats at Bonneville, Utah, passing the 300-mph mark the first time out.

Stock-car races came to the Beach in 1935, the beginning of an era that was to see sedan racing take its place among the most popular of American spectator sports. From December 18, 1898, when the electric-powered machines of Count de Chasseloup-Laubat and Camille Jenatzy held the first of their six meetings that were to raise the flying kilometer mark from 32.29 mph to 65.79 mph, the land speed record book reads like a series of duels—not only contests between constructors, suppliers, and nations but fiercely contested, head-to-head struggles among a special breed of dedicated men. Between 1935 and 1947 George Eyston, John Cobb, and Sir Malcolm Campbell used the Bonneville salt flats (first run by Teddy Tetzlaff in 1914) to raise the LSR chase to 400 mph. In 1964 Sir Malcolm's son Donald reached 403.01 mph, only to have the jet power of Art Arfons, Craig Breedlove, and Gary Gabelich give America supremacy as they pushed close to the speed of sound. From 1898 until 1971 official LSRs were set sixty-two times, yet only twenty-eight drivers made these runs, Sir Malcolm holding "fastest man in the world" laurels nine different times between 1924 and 1935.

•   •   •

The saga of early American touring is a literature unto itself. The first men to drive across the United States were not only courageous and resourceful but incredibly hardy. A fifty-dollar bet is said to have prompted the first successful coast-to-coast journey. Dr. Horatio Nelson Jackson, of Burlington, Vermont, bought a 20-hp, two-seater Winton touring car, hired

At the Ormond garage: the Louis Ross Stanley Steamer, No. 4, winner of the 1905 Dewar Trophy, and Herbert L. Bowden, the first American to exceed 100 mph, seated in his twin-engined Mercedes, No. 2. Bowden recorded a 109.65-mph mile, but the car was disqualified for being overweight.

John D. Rockefeller with the White-Triplex crew, Ormond Beach.

Frank Lockhart's Miller-powered Stutz Black Hawk shortly before the car's fatal record attempt, April 25, 1928.

Sir Malcolm Campbell at Daytona Beach in Bluebird II.

Sir Malcolm Campbell examining the Blue-bird's tires after its 276.82-mph record run, March 7, 1935.

Percy Megargel and mechanic Barton Stanchfield in "Old Steady" and Dwight Huss and Milford Wigle in "Old Scout," winner of the 4400-mile, 44-day race to Portland, Oregon, in New York, May 8, 1905.

Sewall K. Crocker as chauffeur, and began his west-to-east trip in San Francisco on May 23, 1903. Following a northern route by way of Sacramento and Mary-ville, California; Lake View, Oregon; Caldwell, Idaho; Granger and Laramie, Wyoming; North Platte and Omaha, Nebraska; Chicago, and Cleveland, they arrived in New York on July 26, 1903. Both men drove as they covered approximately six thousand miles in sixty-three days (of which forty-five were actual travel time), averaging a remarkable 125 miles a day.

The second car to cross the country was on its way while Dr. Jackson was still en route. On June 20, 1903, Marcus Kraup, a reporter for *The Automobile,* and his driver-mechanic, E. T. Fetch, a foreman in the Packard plant, drove "Old Pacific," a 12-hp, 1903 Packard, from San Francisco to New York, following a route slightly to the south of that taken by Dr. Jackson. Kraup and Tom Fetch reached New York on August 21, cutting three days off Dr. Jackson's time.

When Portland, Oregon, became the site of the United States Office of Public Roads convention, held in conjunction with the Lewis and Clark Centennial Exposition scheduled to open in June 1905, it was thought that a transcontinental automobile race, terminating in Portland, would dramatically demonstrate the nation's lack of highways. The Olds company agreed to participate, and two curved dash runabouts were prepared

for Dwight Huss and Percy Megargel. Huss, who drove "Old Scout" and had driven Oldsmobiles in several races, was accompanied by Milford Wigle, an Olds factory mechanic. "Old Steady" was driven by Megargel and a mechanic named Barton Stanchfield. The Olds factory posted a $1000 prize for the first driver to finish, provided that he arrived in Portland prior to the opening of the convention. The second driver was to receive his transcontinental car as his award. The two runabouts left Hell's Gate Bridge in New York on May 8, 1905. Following a harrowing trip, Huss brought "Old Scout" into Portland on June 20. Megargel arrived five days later.

In his bibliography *Transcontinental Automobile Travel, 1903–1940,* Carey S. Bliss tells of a Mr. and Mrs. John D. Davis, who left New York for San Francisco on July 13, 1899, arrived in Detroit on August 19, then disappeared, never to be heard from again.

L. L. Whitman, who in 1903 drove an Olds from California to Maine in seventy-three days, shattered the transcontinental record in 1906. Driving a six-cylinder, air-cooled Franklin (the same make that had set a New York-to-San Francisco record of thirty days in 1904), Whitman left San Francisco on August 2, 1906, and reached New York on August 17, covering 4100 miles in fifteen days, two hours and twelve minutes. Whitman drove east via Reno, Elko, Ogden, Laramie, Grand

Island, Cedar Rapids, Chicago, Cleveland, and Albany. The Franklin used 263 gallons of gasoline, one and one half gallons of kerosene (it ran on kerosene for seventeen miles when out of gasoline), twenty-one gallons of cylinder (engine) oil, and three gallons of gear and transmission oil. It had four punctures and a change of tires in Chicago. The H. H. Franklin Manufacturing Co. of Syracuse, New York, made much of the record in its advertising. So far, no one had driven an automobile across the United States in winter. It took the New York-to-Paris race to accomplish that.

Newspapers, having sponsored automobile races and exhibitions in the United States and Europe (the first was the Paris paper *Le Vélocipède* for an event that attracted only a single entry in 1887), from the beginning continued to show a lively interest in motor sports. In 1907 the largest newspaper in Paris, *Le Matin,* sponsored a race from Peking to Paris. Although it lacked any American entrants, interest in "Peking to Paris" was high in the United States, and an even more nearly impossible race was planned the following year. Sponsored by *Le Matin* in conjunction with *The New York Times,* the route was originally planned from New York to Seattle by road; Seattle to Valdez, Alaska, by boat; a drive over frozen rivers and bays to the Bering Sea; over the frozen Bering Sea to Siberia; and on to Vladivostok. From roadless Siberia the cars were to find their way to Paris, via Harbin, Manchuria; St. Petersburg; and Berlin. Complicating this outrageous idea was the need to travel in midwinter, as the route called for driving about six hundred miles over the frozen Yukon River from Fairbanks to St. Michael. A jaunt of four hundred miles over frozen snow (no roads or trails existed) was needed to reach the Yukon, followed by a three-hundred-mile drive along the Alaskan shoreline before reaching the Bering Sea crossing point. If this sounds incredible, the reading of George Schuster's fascinating account *The Longest Race* and *Round the World in a Motor Car* by Antonio Scarfoglio, a member of the Italian Zust team, makes the hardships experienced driving across the United States equally formidable.

The race from New York around the world to Paris began in Times Square on February 12, 1908. A quarter of a million New Yorkers saw Colgate Hoyt, president of the Automobile Club of America (Mayor George McClellan was prevented from reaching the grandstand by the crowd), fire a gold pistol to send the first car off at 11:15 a.m. Thirteen cars had been entered, but only six started: a German Protos, an Italian Zust, three French makes—a De Dion, a Motobloc, a Sizaire-Naudin—and the American Thomas Flyer. The machines were all open models, totally lacking protection against the elements. The De Dion had skis for its front wheels, a sail and a mast, and a huge reserve of food and cham-

Sewell Croker, at the wheel, and Colonel H. Nelson Jackson pause in Chicago, July 1903. This Winton was the first automobile to cross the American continent.

E. G. "Cannonball" Baker during his 1915 eleven-day, seven-hour transcontinental record run.

pagne. Each machine flew its national colors, many of the crews carried firearms, and all were well supplied with chains, ropes, and shovels.

Snow began falling twenty miles out of New York. The Thomas, which had been last to leave, took the lead. Before the first day ended the single-cylinder Sizaire-Naudin, smallest car in the race, had dropped out. The four-cylinder, chain-driven 60-hp Thomas changed crews as it crossed the United States. It was first driven by Edwin, then Montague, Roberts (Brighton Beach 24-Hours winner in 1907) and thereafter almost entirely by George Schuster, a thirty-five-year-old mechanic and test driver for the Buffalo firm.

Hardly a day now passed without each of the five remaining cars running into serious mechanical problems. The second night out, in Rochester, New York, the entire Italian population, doctors and bankers as well as mechanics, turned out to help the Zust. In Buffalo the Thomas factory replaced the Flyer's engine, changed the front axle, and brought up a third driver. While the machines were still in upstate New York, it became so cold that food had to be broken into edible bits by a hammer. Twelve days out the Thomas was thirty-six hours ahead of the Zust and three days in front of the Protos and Motobloc. At Cheyenne, Wyoming, the Union Pacific gave the Thomas permission to run on their tracks, not driving on the rails with special

wheels but bouncing along on the ties. By now the Thomas factory had shipped spare parts on ahead so that vital replacements were occasionally cached along the route. Linn Nathewson replaced Monty Roberts at this point, and the Thomas pushed into Utah, where they were forced to hire an Indian guide to show them the route. On March 24 the Thomas reached San Francisco, having gone 3800 miles in forty-one days.

The Zust was still in Utah, the Protos and De Dion in Wyoming. Wheels were replaced, the suspension fixed, and a new transmission installed before going to Seattle to embark for Alaska. Arriving in Valdez, the Thomas found snow so deep that the car could not leave the dock. It was the first automobile in Alaska, and there was not even a trace of a route to the Yukon. The race organizers then telegraphed the Thomas to return to Seattle and proceed to Vladivostok by boat. After spending only twenty-four hours in Alaska, the Thomas arrived back in Seattle on April 16, the organizers awarding it a fifteen-day bonus for its Alaskan excursion. The Protos, which had been shipped from Salt Lake City to Seattle on a railroad flat car, was fined fifteen days. The Zust and the De Dion were on the Pacific before the Thomas and Protos sailed.

Schuster, who was now driving and running the Thomas show, took the first boat to Japan. They reached Yokohama on May 10 but stayed on board, as the crew

Start of the New York-to-Paris race: the Italian Zust and German Protos in Times Square, February 12, 1908.

The Zust crew at the end of the first day in upstate New York: Emilio Sirtori, driving, next to a local guide, Henri Haaga (left), and Antonio Scarfoglio in the rear.

The American Thomas Flyer in trouble in Siberia.

The victorious Thomas Flyer getting help the first night out.

The Thomas Flyer being heaved out of mud in Julesburg, Colorado.

The Thomas Flyer triumphantly returns to New York.

A New Orleans Knox in New York for the 1905 Glidden Tour.

had been unable to locate the Russian consul. Docking at Kobe on May 12, the Thomas started its drive across Japan as soon as it had secured its vital Russian visas. As the Flyer was wider than many Japanese roads, the driving in Japan required much maneuvering and building of temporary bridges. Yet on May 5 it was aboard the SS *Mongolia* bound for Vladivostok. At Siberian "race headquarters," the Grand Hotel, Schuster says he found Lieutenant Koppen and two factory experts hard at work overhauling the Protos and stripping it of excess weight.

The Italian Zust team was having many difficulties, not the least of them being financial. The De Dion, the last of the French entries, was being withdrawn. After spending three days working on the Thomas and arranging for gasoline and spares to be shipped ahead on the Siberian railroad, the Thomas and the Protos began their drive across trackless Asia on May 22.

The most publicized incident of the journey took place only twenty miles out of Vladivostok when the Thomas came upon the Protos, stuck to the top of its wheels in mud. In recounting the moment in his book, Schuster says he was inclined to pass the Protos fearing damage to the Thomas, but Captain Hans Hansen, originally one of the De Dion crew who had switched to the Thomas in Chicago, suggested helping the Germans. George MacAdam, a *New York Times* photographer, who had

42

joined Schuster, George Miller, and Hansen in Seattle, shot the scene for his paper, and a painting of the incident by Peter Helck achieved wide circulation. As the Flyer pulled away, the three Germans and their Russian-Army officer guide toasted the Thomas for what Lieutenant Koppen later called "a gallant, comradely act."

By nightfall the Thomas found itself in the same fix. Fortunately, a cadre of forty Russian soldiers manhandled the Flyer back on the trail. Twice Schuster had to travel ahead for supplies. One five-day trip on the Trans-Siberian railroad to Harbin, Manchuria, put them six days behind the Protos. The Thomas was closing in fast when it just missed the once-every-twelve-hour ferry, with the Protos aboard, over Lake Baikal.

On June 29 the American car passed the Protos, Herr Koppen giving the Americans a crisp salute, only to lose the lead in the Urals when Schuster was required to make a four-hundred-mile trip by wagon to collect spares. In a journey distinguished by ingenuity and resourcefulness on everyone's part, the Italians got special kudos for replacing an engine bearing by melting down bullets, shaping a form from a cough-syrup tin, and firing it in an earthen mold. Past Gorki and St. Petersburg the weary, desperate, filthy crews rumbled on day and night without rest. The Thomas reached Berlin on July 26, the same day the Protos completed

Charles J. Glidden, in white, with Augustus Post in the 1906 Glidden Tour.

New York City Maxwell dealer celebrating the 1911 Glidden Trophy championship.

the run into Paris. After 13,341 miles in 169 days, the Thomas reached Paris on July 30, the winner by sixteen days.

It was a soft summer evening when the Flyer pulled up in front of *Le Matin* offices on the Boulevard Poisonniers. Even though the committee was to take several weeks before confirming the American victory, the delay did little to dampen the enthusiasm of the French people for the *"voiture Americaine."* Today the New York–Paris Thomas Flyer occupies a spot of honor in Bill Harrah's great car collection in Reno.

.   .   .

America's Glidden Tours achieved worldwide fame. Charles J. Glidden was an adventuresome, well-to-do New Englander who had the foresight to invest in Mr. Bell's invention. Following an early career as a reporter on a Boston newspaper, Glidden retired in 1900 at the age of forty-three to spend the remainder of his life—and a great deal of money—touring the world and promoting better driving conditions. In 1903 he covered most of Western Europe, including a trip beyond the Arctic Circle in Sweden. With Mrs. Glidden as a passenger he began an almost incredible seven-year, occasionally interrupted tour around the world in which he logged a carefully documented and photographed 50,000 miles. On the first leg, 3536 miles from Boston to Vancouver, British Columbia, Glidden's Napier covered 1800 miles of the journey equipped with flanged wheels for travel on railroad tracks. Provided with a conductor, the Napier was scheduled as a special train. After leaving his Pacific steamer at Yokohama, Glidden took a route that led him through China, the Philippines, Java, Australia, Ceylon, India, and Asia. The Napier entered Jerusalem by the Jaffa Gate and then made its way to Europe.

As paved roads were unknown outside a few large American cities, touring in groups was not only sociable; it was frequently essential. Early motorists depended on their companions to pull them out of the mud, help change tires, and fix a balky engine.

In November 1904 Charles Glidden gave the AAA a trophy to be awarded to the automobile club winning a tour of not less than 1000 miles. Eligible were all AAA member clubs "or any club in the world recognized by them." Following the 1904 New York-to-St. Louis tour, won by the trophy donor, the competition became known as the Glidden Tour. Run annually from 1905 through 1913, the original Glidden Trophy became a much sought-after prize. Percy Pierce's Pierce-Arrow won the 1905 and 1906 runs. In 1907 a team of two Pierce-Arrows, a Packard and two Thomases representing the Automobile Club of Buffalo, where the Thomas and Pierce-Arrows were made, won the 1500-mile run.

As the cars became more reliable the AAA began handing out stiffer penalties. Official observers rode in each car, and, although they were allowed to help with repairs, the infraction list extended from "one point for steam leak in line" to "500 points for broken steering rod." Newspapers started covering the tour, and in some towns cheering crowds lined the streets.

Manufacturers began to dispute results; a referee's judgment was taken to court. The tour, usually held in the autumn, became big business, and the winners were widely advertised. Several events exceeded 2500 miles, lasting from twelve to fifteen days. While obviously not a race, Glidden Reliability runs were a severe test for both man and machine. As in rallies, the old cars were known to really fly when they needed to make up time to avoid penalty points for being late.

The American tenor James Melton, an ardent and expert car buff and collector, revived the Glidden Tours in 1946, the annual junket becoming a Veteran Car Club fixture.

In 1954 the American automobile historian Henry Austin Clark led a team of ten American vintage cars to England to challenge a like number of old British makes. The Anglo-American Vintage Car Rally traveled from Edinburgh to the Goodwood Race track in the south of England, with a stop at Prescott for a hill-climbing contest. An updated version of the Royal Automobile Club's 1000 Mile Trials, the 1954 meet was typical of "old car" rallies having their roots in the early Glidden Tours. An Anglo-American Vintage Rally was held in the United States in 1957.

Great Racing, Great Men   III

In his book *The Golden Age of the American Racing Car* Griff Borgeson makes a strong case for the period between the two world wars. It was a time of superb drivers—Tommy Milton, Jimmy Murphy, and Frank Lockhart—and of magnificent cars, the Millers and Duesenbergs. Racing enthusiasts have been inclined to think of their own decade as racing's golden age. If the greatness of racing were to be measured in terms of speed or the size of the purse, then this year, or next, would be the best yet, as each season's prize money is larger than the last, and the cars go faster and faster. Formula changes, including displacement limitations devised to reduce speed, have at best a temporary effect. Should other criteria be used? If we consider the daring and hardihood of the drivers, the genius of the early builders, and public support of the young automobile industry, then the era that began in the autumn of 1904 with the first Vanderbilt Cup and ended in Savannah on Thanksgiving Day 1911 was surely too a golden age.

In 1904, when he was twenty-six, William K. Vanderbilt, Jr., had solid credentials as a race driver. He had successfully competed with the top European professionals and had twice held the land speed record. As a "millionaire sportsman," young Vanderbilt was expected to be interested in fast cars as well as yachts and horses. Unexpected was his use of wealth and influence in bringing international racing to America. The country was well behind Europe in the development of the motorcar and even more backward in the building of adequate roads. Vanderbilt was convinced that international automobile racing would help develop better American cars and highways. Influenced by his friend Gordon Bennett, he initiated a race series combining several of the Gordon Bennett regulations with those used by the mighty Automobile Club of France. The event was to be run on regular roads over a 250- to 300-mile distance. The machines were not to exceed 2204 pounds or weigh less than 880. Each car was to carry two persons, seated side by side, each to weigh not less than 132 pounds, and, as in the Gordon Bennett series, it was required that the race car and all of its components be manufactured in the country it represented.

Then, as now, American racing was not organized as it was in Europe, where each country is represented on the international ruling body by a single "Automobile Club Nationale." Established in 1899, the Automobile Club of America, the ACA, was recognized in Europe as the official sanctioning organization of American racing. With many of its well-to-do members having overseas ties, it was not surprising to find the ACA following the customs of European automobile clubs. The American Automobile Association began in Chicago in March 1902, when there were only 23,000 cars in all of America. The "Racing Committee" of the AAA, whose duties were to "supervise tours, races, hill climbs, and other trials," continued until 1907. In 1908 the AAA formed its "Contest Board," which became the sole sanctioning body of American motor sports and, with few exceptions, remained so until August 1955, when the AAA dropped all of its racing activities.

The painter Peter Helck, whose book *The Checkered Flag* brings this time so wonderfully alive, quotes the historian James Rood Doolittle as saying that the AAA, which from the beginning was a broadly based and more democratic organization than the ACA, was formed because of the failure of the ACA to bring about a national body.

Except for one-mile dirt tracks at Brighton Beach and Yonkers, the mile oval at Grosse Pointe, and the beginnings of Ormond-Daytona Beach, racing in the United States prior to the first Vanderbilt Cup was characterized by exhibitions and one-night stands. Two Cleveland-to-New York runs were made by Alexander Winton in 1897 and a third in 1899, during which he lowered his time to forty-seven hours and thirty-seven minutes. Champion bicycle rider Barney Oldfield began his sensational automobile racing career in the fall of 1902, demonstrating Henry Ford's two race cars, the Arrow and the 999. He immediately won races and broke records at Grosse Pointe, at Empire City in Yonkers, and on a new one-mile dirt track in Indianapolis. In November 1903 Oldfield switched to the Winton Bullet, traveled west, and set a 65.6-mile mark on the new dirt track in Los Angeles. In August 1904 Earl Kiser recorded a

Official program car for the 1904 Vanderbilt Cup.

68.3-mph mile driving the Winton 8 at Glenville in Cleveland. But before the year was out Barney had blasted a 70-mph lap in the Peerless Green Dragon to reclaim the mile record.

Eventually the AAA was awarded the staging of the first Vanderbilt challenge, and Mr. Vanderbilt bought a handsome thirty-one-inch-high silver loving cup from Tiffany. Over the weekend of July 4, 1904, posters announced:

Automobile Races!
Nassau County Highways!!!
Will be Held over the Superb Macadam Highways
of Nassau County on Saturday, October 8,
1904. The Distance Will be Between
250 and 300 Miles and Will Start
at Westbury at About Daylight

Reports indicate that most of the 28.44-mile course consisted of oil-soaked dirt roads. The little that was paved with "superb macadam," especially the section that lay in Queens in New York City, was in wretched condition. From Westbury the route followed the Jericho Turnpike to Jericho, south to Plainedge, over what is now Broadway and Hicksville Road, west on Hempstead Turnpike to Queens, turning east at the Jericho Pike intersection.

Scene from the Broadway musical hit, *The Vanderbilt Cup,* **starring Elsie Janis with Barney Oldfield and his Peerless Green Dragon.**

The Garden City Hotel became race headquarters, and from it came a steady stream of edicts. One of these—practice was to be held at the legal speed limit—was ignored. The Europeans claimed not to understand it, and the American drivers were happy to ignore it. It was difficult to say who was in the race on October 8 until the start. Two White Steamers were suddenly withdrawn. The French Ambassador was needed to get the three Panhards out of customs, and a "Peoples Protective Association" was formed to protest the use of Nassau County roads for racing. One editor wrote, "The spirit which approves of such an abuse of the highways is that which led the nobility into the excesses which precipitated the French Revolution." Telephones were installed around the circuit, and over a hundred police were hired to patrol the thirty-mile route.

Of the eighteen entries five were German, six French, five American, and two Italian. Although all engines had four cylinders, they ranged from the 4,500-cc Packard "Gray Wolf" to monstrous 15,400-cc engines in the Panhards and the 14,700-cc Simplex. Horsepower measurements in 1904, while not precise, do supply interesting comparisons. Each of the Panhards was rated at 90 hp. The three American machines—Joe Tracy's Royal at 35 hp, Herb Lytle's Pope-Toledo, and Charles Schmidt's Packard, each at 24 hp—were the least powerful cars. Also representing America was "Spyder"

Webb in a 60-hp Pope-Toledo and owner-driver Frank Croker (son of Boss Croker of Tammany Hall) in a much modified 75-hp Simplex. Four of the German Mercedes were 9200-cc, 60-hp touring cars, with one, a 12,000-cc, 90-hp all-out race car, owned by Clarence Dinsmore and driven by the Mercedes works driver Wilhelm Werner, who was to become Kaiser Wilhelm's chauffeur.

The two 75-hp FIATs, in the experienced hands of the American William Wallace and Paul Satori, were the first cars to leave the race. Led by Fernand Gabriel, winner of the ill-starred Paris–Madrid of 1903, the seasoned French team was favored to win. In addition to Gabriel's 80-hp De Dietrich, the three Panhards were driven by the expatriate American George Heath, George Teste, and Henri Tart. Gould Brokaw entered a 80-hp, 12,000-cc Renault to be driven by Maurice Bernin, who, with Paul Lacroix, was to capture the Morris Park twenty-four-hours in 1907. The 11,300-cc Clement-Bayard was handled by the builder's son, nineteen-year-old Albert Clement.

It was reported that before dawn an unruly crowd of 50,000 (attendance figures, usually arrived at by optimistic promoters or journalists eager to report record-breaking crowds, were no more reliable in 1904 than at present) lined the course. At 6:00 a.m. the Mercedes 60 driven by Al Campbell left the Westbury start-finish line. Gabriel followed at 6:02, and, except for Satori in

The smallest entry in the 1904 Vanderbilt Cup: the Packard Gray Wolf, which finished fourth.

Alfred Gwynne Vanderbilt's FIAT, which started two hours late, the field left in good order at two-minute intervals.

America's first international automobile race was close and exciting. However, it was marred by vandalism and the poor crowd control that was to plague future Vanderbilt Cup races and eventually contribute to their leaving Long Island. The fifteenth car to leave, Teste's Panhard, covered the first lap at 70.9 mph, the day's best lap time, and led for the first three laps. Joe Tracy, who was given the best chance among the Americans, dropped from sight for two hours during the first lap. When the Royal reappeared, Al Poole, Tracy's mechanic, dropped a note at the start-finish line explaining their absence. The Royal had broken its driveshaft. Tracy had stopped in Queens and had persuaded a black-smith to open his shop and forge a new driveshaft. Patron Vanderbilt stayed busy as an official referee, rushing around the course at racing speeds in his Mercedes 90. Werner protested violently, in vain, over being delayed by a train at Oyster Bay. Clements also objected to being held up at the Hicksville control, claiming the delay had cost him the race.

By mid-race only ten cars were running, and restless spectators began moving onto the circuit to look for approaching cars. George Teste went out with ignition trouble on lap four, with a six-minute lead. George Heath moved into first place and successfully fought off a challenge from young Clement, going on to win by a margin of one minute, twenty-eight seconds. Herb Lytle's Pope-Toledo was third and Schmidt's Packard fourth. Heath covered the 284.4 miles (the total distance was 302.4 miles, including the Hicksville and Hempstead controls) in six hours, fifty-six minutes, forty-five seconds for a 52.2-mph race average. Unfortunately the crowd swarmed onto the track after Heath and Clement finished, and the five cars still running were prevented from crossing the finish line.

In a paragraph headed "Luck Was a Factor," the October 15, 1904, issue of *The Automobile* stated:

Luck was a more important factor, however, in the winning and losing of the Vanderbilt Cup race than in probably any other international race ever held. Cut glass and nails were strewn thickly along portions of the road, and especially at the bad corners. Whether or not this was done maliciously will probably never be known. As hundreds of cars passed over the course in the days preceding the race and did not meet with more than ordinary tire troubles, the inference is that the course was planted. Veiled threats made by organized opposition to the race are still fresh in the memory.

Barring this disagreeable, if intentional, dastardly feature, the race was a remarkable success. When one considers the slight experience that most of those in charge at the start or along the course had had in such events, the results are very agreeable.

The account goes on to note, "But one unfortunate accident, the death of Carl Mensel, George Arents' riding mechanic." Arents, who had told the AAA that he knew every inch of the circuit by heart and did not need to practice, was then roasted. "This accident was due entirely to the foolhardiness of the driver in entering his car . . . previously he had made a wild entry into the Hempstead control, showing inability to handle a car at high speed."

New York got its third track when Morris Park, in the Bronx, held its first race in May 1905. Louis Chevrolet's FIAT captured the opening feature, and Walter Christie's radical front-drive machine made its New York debut by winning at Morris Park on July 4. Endurance runs began to develop a considerable following. On May 5 Charles Wridgway averaged 36.6 mph for 1000 miles as he circled Brighton Beach for close to twenty-six hours. At Empire City six weeks later, Guy Vaughn's French Decauville lowered the 1000-mile mark to twenty-three hours, thirty-three minutes. In November 1905 the Clemens and Herz National covered 1095 miles in twenty-four hours at the Indiana State Fairgrounds.

Reaction to the first Vanderbilt Cup was mostly favorable. Although France won, American cars had performed better than had been expected. Taking note of the large crowds and widespread press coverage, American builders began preparing cars for 1905. The "Good Roads Movement" used the race to publicize their cause.

Interest in the second Vanderbilt Cup was so high that the organizers were forced to hold an elimination race to determine the five cars to represent the United States. In addition to limiting each country's entry to five machines, there were several more changes in 1905. The course was shifted somewhat north. The return leg now passed over East Norwich Road, west on North Hempstead Turnpike, south on Guinea Wood Road to I.V. Willets Road and the Jericho Turnpike. Control areas, in which the cars had slowed as they passed through Hempstead and Hicksville, were abandoned, and the course now measured 28.3 miles.

Following the four-lap, 113.2-mile trials, held on September 23, the judges then ignored the results, limiting their selection to the first two finishers, Bert Dingley's Pope-Toledo and Joe Tracy's Locomobile. Passed over were Jardine-Royal, Nutt-Haynes, and Monty Roberts-Thomas, the cars that ran third, fourth, and fifth. That the Royal and Haynes were production models was said to have influenced the decision. Selected to represent the U.S., in addition to the Pope and Locomobile, were a second Pope-Toledo for Herb Lytle, a White Steamer in the hands of its builder, Walter White, and a front-drive Christie driven by Walter Christie. Although the last three machines failed to complete the elimination run, the Vanderbilt Cup Commission apparently believed they had a better potential than the three that had earned a starting berth.

As a young machinist, J. Walter Christie worked on one of the first U.S. submarines, attended night classes in engineering at Cooper Union, and in 1899, at Philadelphia's Cramp Shipyard, helped build the new battleship *Maine*. Christie's design of a special turret for the *Maine*'s big guns achieved a measure of acceptance, and, when only twenty years old, he opened his own machine shop in New York, where he began working on a front-wheel-drive automobile. It was the practice of Christie's contemporaries to promote their cars by racing. The majority hired drivers, but Christie usually drove his own. By 1904 *Scientific American* and *The Automobile* both ran pieces on the Christie's radical

Walter Christie and George Robertson, who was to win the Vanderbilt Cup in 1908, in the Christie that collided with Vincenzo Lancia's FIAT while the Italian was leading the 1905 Vanderbilt Cup.

Long Island, October 8, 1904: George Heath, the expatriate American, winning the first Vanderbilt Cup in his Panhard.

American racing came of age when George Robertson drove Locomobile No. 16 to victory in the 1908 Vanderbilt Cup. Willie Haupt's Chadwick, No. 4, was the only other car to lead the Long Island classic. The painting is by Peter Helck N.A., proud owner of old No. 16. From the Lawrence H. Greenwald Collection.

Arthur Duray supporting his poised mechanic. Their De Dietrich finished third in the 1906 Vanderbilt Cup.

Barney Oldfield in the front-wheel-drive Christie at the Speedway in 1916.

design. Christie failed to do well in the 1904 or 1905 Ormond-Daytona Beach trials, but he managed to win one heat from Louis Chevrolet's FIAT at Morris Park in July 1905. He also raced on the beaches at Cape May and at Atlantic City, where he recorded a thirty-eight-second mile. Although George Robertson failed to qualify the Christie for the 1905 Vanderbilt, it made the starting field when the judges tossed out all but the first- and second-place cars in the elimination trials. There have been successful front-wheel-drive race cars, but no one but Christie attempted a system with each front wheel being driven directly by planetary gears. Christie's refusal to incorporate some type of a differential probably prevented his machine from being a success. In many ways he was years ahead of the industry with V-4 transverse engines and the use of both rear and twin-engined race cars and cast wheels.

With his nephew, Lewis Strang, who was to become an outstanding driver, as his riding mechanic, Christie entered the 1907 French Grand Prix. An enormous 19,618-cc V-4, the 1907 Christie, the largest car ever to enter a Grand Prix, retired shortly before the halfway mark from clutch, tire, and engine failure. Annoyed by critical remarks made by other car makers who claimed the Christie had not truly represented the best in American race cars, Christie said, "I think the American manufacturers who sat comfortably on this side talking about mythical cars for a purely visionary Vanderbilt race and doing absolutely nothing show very poor taste in belittling my efforts." His testy challenge to beat any car at any track for any amount of money was not taken up.

After recording 70-mph laps on the dirt at Morris Park and Brighton Beach, Christie began barnstorming. At Pittsburgh's Brunot Island in September 1907 he crashed into a wrecked car, suffering painful but not serious injuries. Lewis Strang, apparently without his uncle's consent, borrowed a car and at the Birmingham fairgrounds set a 51.35-second one-mile record. With Christie and others driving, his cars continued to race and barnstorm. Walter Christie's match races against Oldfield and Ralph DePalma were great crowd pleasers. So, too, was a touring-car race Christie entered which called for the drivers to stop, pick up, and then discharge a load of passengers. As some drivers did not come to a full stop while discharging their occupants, spectators were treated to the spectacle of passengers rolling in the dust.

Although one of his cars reached nearly 120 mph at Daytona in 1910, Christie was soon to close out his racing career. He became a major producer of fire-engine tractor equipment and was later to pioneer, but not profit from, the building of a widely copied concept in army tanks.

The fourteen European entries in the 1905 Vanderbilt represented the cream of the world's race cars. The French returned with a new Panhard for the 1904 winner, George Heath; Victor Hemery and Louis Wagner were in Darracqs; François Szisz drove for Renault; and there was a 17,000-cc De Dietrich for Arthur Duray, a French national born in New York of Belgian parents. Mercedes were driven by John Warden, the American who had finished fifth in the infamous Paris–Madrid and had been a member of the Austrian Mercedes team in the 1904 Gordon Bennett. Filling out the German team

were young Vanderbilt's friend, Foxhall Keene, Al Campbell, and the legendary Camille Jenatzy. Three-time holder of the land speed record, builder of the historic streamlined electric "La Jamais Contente," and winner of the 1903 Gordon Bennett, Jenatzy, the Belgian Red Devil, was the star of the Mercedes team. However, FIAT was favored in 1905, with three 110-hp, 16,300-cc race cars entered for factory drivers Vincenzo Lancia, Felice Nazzaro, and Louis Chevrolet. Smaller 75-hp, 10,600-cc machines were slated for Paul Satori and Emanuel Cedrino. Chevrolet crashed his 110 in practice and drove an American-owned 75 FIAT in the race.

The crowd began gathering days before the race. Farmers, many of whom had resisted holding the event, charged fifty dollars per person to camp in their fields. New York papers estimated over 200,000 spectators on hand at 6:00 a.m., October 14, 1905, as Jenatzy's Mercedes broke the tape starting the second Vanderbilt Cup. The field followed at one-minute intervals. Satori's FIAT was the last away. Big, jolly Vincenzo Lancia took the lead on the first lap. After seven laps he was twenty-one minutes ahead of Heath, who was second, and had turned a 4:23.18—72.9 mph, fastest lap of the day. With only sixty-five miles to go Lancia pulled out of the Michelin depot, following a routine tire change, and collided with Christie. Twenty-eight minutes late at the start, Christie was intent on making up time and was hogging the center of the road. The front-wheel-drive car was out, and the FIAT lost forty-seven minutes being repaired. Now running one and two, Heath and Hemery went at it hammer and tongs, Hemery's Darracq winning with a 61.5-mph race average. Joe Tracy brought the Locomobile home third, and a heart-broken Lancia, after dominating three-quarters of the race, finished fourth. Szisz, Nazzaro, Warden, and Duray were still running, but again the race was called as the crowd swarmed over the course.

The third Vanderbilt Cup, ten laps over a 29.7-mile

Boxholders watching Felice Nazzaro's FIAT start the 1905 Vanderbilt at 6:08 a.m.

course that combined parts of the two previous circuits, was held on October 6, 1906. American car makers applied for entries in such numbers that elimination trials were run over the full 297 miles on September 22. Joe Tracy's new 16,200-cc, 90-hp Locomobile was best of the twelve American hopefuls. Tracy won the trials with a 60.4-mph average, with Le Blon's Thomas, Harding Haynes, Lytle's Pope-Toledo, and Christie filling the first five places. However, W. J. Miller filed a protest, claiming, among other infractions, that on lap six Lytle's Pope-Toledo had been towed to restart. The protest was upheld. The veteran Lytle was replaced by the Frayer-Miller driven by Frank Lawell. Once more, the French team was *très formidable.* Heath was back in an 18,300-cc Panhard; Duray in a De Dietrich; Albert Clement in a Clement; Louis Wagner drove a new 100-hp, 12,700-cc Darracq; and the American amateur Elliott Shepard was in a 130-hp, 16,300-cc Hotchkiss. Mercedes was down to two entries, 14,000-cc 120s for Jenatzy and William Luttgen. The Italians produced two strong teams. Three FIATS were driven by works drivers Lancia, Nazzaro, and FIAT engineer Aldo Weilschott, and there were new Italas for Fabry and Cagno.

The 1906 Vanderbilt was Louis Wagner's all the way, his spidery-looking Darracq leading the entire ten laps. As reported in *The Checkered Flag,* Wagner, who won with a 61.43-mph average, was quoted as saying, "The miracle was not my winning but that hundreds were not killed in my doing so." Tracy, who finished ninth, made

the day's best time, posting a 67.6-mph fastest lap, but the Locomobile, as with the other American entries, suffered far more tire trouble than the Europeans. Lancia and Duray, who finished second and third, had a furious race-long struggle, with Clement and Jenatzy, who wound up in that order, close behind.

As had been feared, the lack of crowd control resulted in spectator injuries and a fatal accident. Early in the race Joe Tracy stopped at the official's stand to warn Vanderbilt that the crowd, said to exceed 300,000, was out of control. Willie K. took off immediately in his white Mercedes to rally the police. It had been an exciting, fiercely fought race between the world's finest drivers. But it was to be the last race on Long Island to be run entirely on public roads.

Twenty-four-hour races, now so closely associated with Le Mans, were first staged in America. The earliest twenty-four-hour race began in Columbus, Ohio, on July 2, 1905, where the Soules brothers' Pope-Toledo covered 828.50 miles to win. In 1907 the one-mile dirt track in Point Breeze, Philadelphia, ran twenty-four-hour "Endurance Derbys" on May 25 and July 1. Brown and Maynes' Autocar covered 791 miles to win the May race, with Harry Michener and Ralph Mulford driving a Lozier to victory in July. Three twenty-four-hour races were run in New York between August 9 and September 28, 1907. Monty Roberts averaged 44.8 mph as he drove a Thomas to victory at Brighton Beach. At Morris Park, Lacroix and Bernin's Renault won on September 6, and

Willie K. Vanderbilt and Joe Tracy. Tracy managed the Matheson Team in 1908.

William Luttgen's Mercedes in the 1906 Vanderbilt.

Cedrino and Parker drove factory-entered FIATs to win on September 28.

Interest in the first twenty-four-hour races, as with all early racing, centered as much on the novelty of the automobile as it did on the contest, with twenty-four-hour events having the added fillip of frequently being the scene of important social functions.

New Jersey came close to holding the 1907 Vanderbilt Cup.

"Want Militia for the Vanderbilt Cup Race—Famous Event Not to Be Held Unless Soldiers Are Called Out—Rules of Contest More Liberal" read the May 16, 1907, New York *American.* For a time it seemed that the cup was to find a new home, but, according to the New York *Herald,* New Jersey state senator Joseph S. Frelinghuysen, "Father of the law that operates automobiles in New Jersey," was violently opposed, and no Vanderbilt Cup race was held in 1907. The governor of New York had again refused requests to assign troops. Vanderbilt thought one solution to the crowd-control problem would be to build a private course.

By the fall of 1908 nine miles of the Long Island Motor Parkway, part of a forty-five-mile private toll road that was to bisect Long Island from Bayside, in the New York City borough of Queens, to Lake Ronkonkomo, was finished. When the road was complete, for one dollar the motorist was invited on a trip that promised "No Speed limit . . . No Grade Crossings . . . No Dust . . . No Police Traps."

A handsome chalet, the Motor Parkway Inn, a copy of the Petit Trianon at Versailles, was built at the Lake Ronkonkomo end of the parkway. And the Paris edition of the New York *Herald* encouraged holding a Versailles benefit at the Lake Ronkonkomo Petit Trianon for the original that was desperately in need of repair.

The parkway was a failure as a race course, but it proved a popular tourist attraction. *The New York Times* of May 18, 1911, said that the rumor that the New York Central was taking over the Long Island Motor Parkway to construct an electric railroad in competition with the Long Island Rail Road was false. When questioned by the *Times* Mr. Vanderbilt replied emphatically, "There is no truth whatever in it."

In 1938 the Long Island Motor Parkway was given to New York State in return for back taxes. The Garden City tollhouse currently is occupied as a dwelling; parts of the road in Queens are used as bicycle paths; some of the parkway is in use in Suffolk County; and in 1972 ACCUS, the Fédération de l'Automobile American representative, moved its office to the Vanderbilt Motor Parkway in Hauppauge.

Although motor racing was the paramount reason for the toll road, Vanderbilt and his friends eagerly looked forward to using the parkway to commute from their Long Island estates. Speedway builder and Miami Beach developer Carl Fisher, who vigorously promoted the idea of making Montauk Point, on the eastern tip of the island, into a deep-sea port, may have tried to

At the start of the small-car race on the Long Island Motor Parkway, which ran two weeks prior to the 1908 Vanderbilt Cup. Lytle's Lancia is No. 34.

interest Vanderbilt in this never-to-be-realized dream, as Vanderbilt originally hoped to have the road run to Montauk Point.

Nine miles of the parkway were completed in the fall of 1908 in time for the running of a shakedown event, the Motor Parkway Sweepstakes, held on October 11. Herb Lytle's Isotta won the ten-lap, 234-mile trials with a 64.3-mph average.

George Robertson did not compete on Long Island that day, as he was busy winning the first of four annual Founder's Day Cup races run through Philadelphia's Fairmount Park.

Local press and police estimates said that 400,000 Quaker City fans watched Robertson's 40-hp Locomobile average 49.5 mph over the 7.8-mile course that paralleled the Schuylkill River. Cyrus Patschke's Acme was second and Mulford's Lozier third as all entrants but one finished the race without a single change of tires. At the victory ceremonies Robertson said it was the best-policed race he had ever participated in. At the close of its report the trade journal *Jobber Topics* wrote, "It was expected that the Quaker City Club would not have to forfeit any monies to the Fairmount Park commission to return the roads to their original condition, for they are now better than ever."

Herb Lytle's Isotta turning into Ellison Avenue from the Jericho Turnpike on its way to winning the 1908 Motor Parkway Sweepstakes.

Louis Chevrolet practicing in his FIAT for the 1905 Vanderbilt Cup.

The fourth Vanderbilt Cup was held on October 24, 1908, over a 23.46-mile circuit that combined nine miles of Long Island Parkway and fourteen miles of the old course, including punishing sections of the Jericho Turnpike. The seventeen entries, of which eleven were American, reflected changed regulations that permitted stock chassis, albeit stripped and race-prepared, and a weight increase from 1000 kg, 2205 lbs., to 1200 kg, 2646 lbs. Of more significance was that the ACA had granted the first American Grand Prize to Savannah, scheduled for November 26, only one month after the Vanderbilt Cup. It was Savannah that pulled the international stars and latest racing machinery.

On September 16, the ACA and AAA had stopped their bickering long enough to sign an agreement recognizing the ACA as American representatives of the AIACR, forerunners to the FIA.

The Cup crowd of 200,000 in 1908, smaller than in prior years, proved no less hard to handle. Although much of the course was far out of town and a wire fence lined the entire nine miles of Long Island Parkway, this did little to prevent the circuit from being overrun. Only after hoses were turned on the crowd in the pits could the race get started at 6:30, thirty minutes late.

Fresh from victories in both the Brighton Beach twenty-four-hour and Fairmount Park races, George Robertson was favored to bring the United States its first Vanderbilt Cup. His 90-hp, 16.2-liter Locomobile, which Joe Tracy had driven to a ninth-place finish in the 1906 Vanderbilt, expected its most severe challenge from Lytle's Isotta, Lewis Strang's Renault, and the Louis Chevrolet Matheson. But No. 16 won the day, the Locomobile covering 258 miles with a record 64.3 average. Herb Lytle was second by less than two minutes, as Willie Haupt's Chadwick, which had led laps four through six, was slowed by ignition troubles, and Joe Florida's Locomobile finished third. Emil Stricker, the only European entrant, and Foxhall Keene had their Mercedes catch fire, and Louis Chevrolet retired early with a cracked cylinder. Locomobile No. 16, which holds a special place among historic American race cars, is now owned by Peter Helck, whose art and writings have brought so much honor to automobile racing.

Lewis Strang then went on a winning streak that was to earn him a return to the French Grand Prix as driver of the Thomas, a ride originally slated for Montague Roberts. On March 19, 1908, Strang drove an Isotta-Fraschini to victory in the first Savannah race, the

George Robertson in the Locomobile, No. 16, winning the 1908 Vanderbilt Cup, the first for an American car and driver.

342-mile Challenge Trophy for stock cars. One month later Strang was in New York, where his Isotta won the Briarcliff Trophy, run for 240 miles over a hilly thirty-mile road course in Westchester County. New York newspapers gave Briarcliff considerable exposure. The *American* carried a page-one story headed "Three Noted Drivers in Briarcliff Race—Oldfield, Satori, Cedrino." Page two of the same paper had a five-column head, "Drivers Warned That Slightest Mistake Will Likely Cost Them Their Lives." The *Herald*'s ubiquitous Duncan Curry, whose by-lined auto-racing features appeared almost daily, said, "Briarcliff promised to be the greatest ever."

Strang's streak was momentarily stopped in the French Grand Prix at Dieppe in July when he retired with clutch failure after four laps, as had his uncle, Walter Christie, the year before. In September, Strang's Isotta averaged 53.6 mph to win on the new 10.6-mile road course near Lowell, Massachusetts. Lewis Strang did not win any of the three twenty-four-hour races, two on the Brighton Beach dirt mile and one on the dirt at Milwaukee, held within a three-week span in the fall, but he did become the 1908 AAA national champion.

The Savannah races, a bright chapter in American racing, were held between March 1908 and November 1911. A relatively small, out-of-the-way Southern city, Savannah lacked everything that was needed to stage international automobile races except enthusiasm. Reporting on the March inaugural in which state militia was used to guard the then seventeen-mile course, the March 26 issue of *The Automobile* said, "One thing is certain, and that is that members of the Vanderbilt

Cup Commission feel decidedly happier than they did a year ago, knowing if Long Island cannot be the scene of the race, there exists a city called Savannah in a county called Chatham, containing therein a course which will be well guarded, well prepared and most satisfactory for the great automobile race of the year."

The Savannah Automobile Club had been disappointed when they failed to land the 1908 Vanderbilt Cup. But, as Dr. Julian Quattlebaum points out in his history of the Savannah races, their grief was short-lived. From 1908 until its demise in 1916, the American Grand Prize overshadowed the Vanderbilt Cup.

The convict labor used to build the new twenty-five-mile-long and thirty-to-sixty-foot-wide Savannah course did a superb job. The course was lined with palm trees and moss-covered oak. Augusta gravel, soaked in 80,000 gallons of oil, resulted in a hard-packed, dust-free surface, and a grandstand seating 16,000 was erected at the start-finish line. Ocean liners were chartered to bring in fans, officials, and participants. Pullmans were used for living quarters, and several visitors were reported, incredulously, to have driven from New York! On November 25, the day prior to the Grand Prize, Hillard's Lancia, after a battle with Bob Burman's Buick, won the 196-mile light-car race held over 9.6 miles of the GP course.

Fifteen European and six American race cars started the fog-delayed GP. Hemery, Hanriot, and Erle each drove a 750-cubic inch Benz; Wagner, Nazzaro, and young Ralph DePalma were in FIATs. France was represented by Rigal and Hautvast in Clement-Bayards. Lewis Strang and Ferenc Szisz, the Hungarian who won

Seymour's Simplex, No. 22, at the April 1908 Briarcliff road race, Westchester County, New York. This was Ralph DePalma's first race in which he drove an Allen-Kingston.

Lewis Strang and his mechanic, Leland Mitchell, in their Thomas at Dieppe for the 1908 Grand Prix of France.

Team FIAT and friends following the 1908 Savannah races. Seated, left to right, are: third-place finisher Felice Nazzaro, Grand Prize winner Louis Wagner, and Victor Hemery, who was second in a Benz. Standing, left to right, are: Alessandro Cagno, second, Ralph De-Palma, fourth, Arthur Duray, fifth, Jack Scales, sixth, Ferenc Szisz, eighth, and Rene Hanriot, ninth.

the first French Grand Prix, drove Renaults, and Arthur Duray was in a De Dietrich. Italian champion Alle-sendro Cagno, pioneer Henri Fournier, and Piacenza drove Italas. Against this formidable overseas challenge were six different American makes: Seymour's Simplex, Harding's National, Mulford's Lozier, Zengle's Acme, Haupt's supercharged Chadwick, and Burman's Buick Special.

Although American cars were given little chance, two American drivers, Strang and DePalma, were among the favorites. DePalma led the first two laps, his FIAT earning fastest-lap honors, but the best American finish was Joe Seymour's Simplex in eleventh place. Hemery, Nazzaro, Wagner, and Hanriot all held first place, with Wagner and Hemery nipping Nazzaro on the final lap when the Italian suffered tire failure. Wagner's fifty-six-second margin over Hemery had the crowd of over 100,000 on its feet, so close a finish after six hours and ten minutes of racing having been almost unheard of.

Crowd control had been excellent, the races well run, and the hospitality outstanding. Several unruly spectators had been jabbed with bayonets, and Hanriot, driving against traffic after the finish, had his Benz tires

shot out when he ignored a captain's warning. Savannah assumed that the Grand Prize, and perhaps the Vander-bilt Cup too, would come to them in 1909. However, Robert Morrell, chairman of the ACA, and Jefferson Thompson of the AAA jointly announced that all future Grand Prize and Vanderbilt Cup races were to be held on Long Island.

Henry Ford, who attended the Savannah races as a member of the ACA Technical Committee, is reported to have said that specially built race cars were needed to win races and that he might get around to making such cars when his factory caught up with all of its orders. This attitude, apparently shared by other U.S. manufacturers, contributed to the pre-World War I dominance of European race cars in America.

Racing's westward trek began in 1909 when the Indianapolis Motor Speedway opened on August 19. The Speedway's policy of paying auto racing's largest purse, although important, has been only one factor in making the Indianapolis 500 Mile Sweepstakes America's premier event. Other tracks are and have been faster. First the boards, then Daytona and now the new 2.5-mile Indianapolis replica at Ontario, California, have equaled

The first race at the Indianapolis Speedway was for balloons.

Carl Fisher, the man who conceived Indianapolis, drives a Stoddard Dayton through a Speedway turn in 1909.

or surpassed Indy speeds. Good management has had much to do with the Indianapolis Speedway's success. Dedicated men who plowed profits back and made up losses out of their own pockets have characterized Indy owners. When the Speedway had lean years following World War II, Tony Hulman rescued it. Under his ownership the Speedway has become the best-maintained plant in the racing world. But it is continuity (Indy has missed only the war years) that gives the 500 a special place in a sport where having a place to race is a perennial problem.

New road courses were opened at Portola, near San Francisco, and at Crown Point, Indiana, where Joe Matson's Chalmers and Louis Chevrolet's Buick won opening events held in June 1909. Strang, Chevrolet, and Bill Knipper were winners at the new two-mile dirt track in Atlanta, and Barney Oldfield averaged 63.50 mph on the dirt mile in Dallas. A great driver and an even greater showman, Barney was in constant hot water with the AAA Contest Board. He was not to win an official AAA championship race until March 17, 1915, near the end of his career, when his Maxwell finished first at the 3.23-mile road course in Venice, California.

From 1902 until 1909 national champions were selected by the country's sports writers. The AAA picked

CIRKUT PHOTO BY BRETZMAN 1909

the champion from 1909 until 1916, when the point system based on the driver's finishing position in AAA championship races, a system still in use in somewhat modified form, was first tried.

Brighton Beach again staged three twenty-four-hour races in 1909, Joe Tracy's mechanic, Al Poole, sharing driver honors with George Robertson to win the July race in their Simplex. Basle and Raffalovitch's Renault were winners in August and the Mulford-Patschke Lozier in October. George Robertson, who was to earn the 1909 AAA National Championship, won the second, and last, Lowell road race on September 8. A month later Robertson's Simplex beat Ralph Mulford's Lozier to repeat his 1908 victory in Philadelphia's Fairmount Park.

The fifth Vanderbilt Cup was run on October 30, 1909, over a 12.64-mile course consisting of 5.15 miles of parkway and 7.49 miles of country roads, a short course for its time. Restricted to strip chassis, production models with engines of 301 to 600 cubic inches, only Spencer Wishart's Mercedes, Joe Seymour's Isotta, and the Hearne–Lewis Strang FIAT represented foreign makes. After leading the first lap Wishart gave way to Louis Chevrolet's Buick, which led through lap four. Chevrolet then recorded a 76.3-mph fastest lap, only to retire with a broken engine. The race fell to steady Harry

Grant, who moved his ALCO through the field to win by five minutes over Ed Parker's FIAT. The small, relatively well-behaved crowd was credited to the late, 9:00 a.m., start and lack of European drivers.

Continued bickering between the ACA and AAA had resulted in the incorporation of "The Motor Cup Holdings Company" early that year, "organized to promote automobile races for the silver cup donated by William K. Vanderbilt, Jr., and known as the Vanderbilt Cup, and the gold cup donated by the Automobile Club of America, and known as the Grand Prize. . . ." It was also stated that the formation of the company was in line with "the agreement reached by the AAA and ACA for a new company to promote these two events over the Long Island Motor Parkway." Original members were Vanderbilt, Harry Payne Whitney, Colgate Hoyt, and Mortimer Schiff, among others. William's cousin, Cornelius Vanderbilt, and Colgate Hoyt were also officers in the ACA and AAA. However, the American Grand Prize did not run on Long Island, or anywhere else, in 1909.

The Playa del Rey Motordome, first of the twenty-four board tracks that would be built from coast to coast between 1910 and 1926, opened in Los Angeles on April 8. Barney Oldfield, who three weeks before had set a 131.75-mph one-mile straightaway record at Day-

Brighton Beach, 1909. Raffalovich and Basle, Renault, covered 1050 miles to win the "New York 24 hours." The scoreboard shows the final results.

ENTRIES	1	2	3	4	5	6	7	8	9	10	11	12	13	14	15	16	17	18	19	20	21	22	23	24
RENAULT	53	97	146	197	242	289	338	382	431	478	520	568	612	655	695	743	783	829	869	910	953	995	1021	1050
PALMER-SINGER	46	85	127	174	217	237	263	283	295	342	383	424	465	509	549	593	637	672	676	701	735	779	824	870
ACME	55	60	93	146	169	188	233	268	294	345	395	442	492	539	587	636	683	732	770	774	774	785	835	883
ACME	55	90	113	161	212	251	299	343	386	424	469	512	566	577	615	626	628	659	676	679	721	746	746	760
LOZIER	46	99	123	123	123	134	176	226	274	322	324													
STEARNS	52																							
HOUPT	22	72	78	100	113	113	114	153	168	168	168													
ALLEN-KINGSTON	44	54	66	96	132	174	176	220	257	295	335	379	421	457	500	540	582	615	657	701	741	786	823	866
FIAT	53	63																						
RAINIER	52	100	151	201	246	295	336	387	401	428	436	479	526	573	621	668	712	742	776	810	841	858	899	938

tona, was the opening-day attraction. The great one did not disappoint the sell-out crowd. Barney covered the steeply banked mile in 36.22 seconds for a 99-mph closed-course record, shattering the 95-mph mark set by Strang's FIAT in Atlanta. Five days later at Playa del Rey, Ray Harroun's Marmon captured 50- and 100-mile features, a good start toward the AAA National Championship he was to earn in 1910.

Brighton Beach held its last twenty-four-hour race in 1910. Basle and Poole, two former winners, teamed up to win in May, with Poole's Stearns earning the laurels in August.

One of the best and most durable road-racing series was Elgin, which ran intermittently from 1910 until 1920 and again in 1932 and 1933. The first Elgin road race was held on August 27, 1910, over an 8.5-mile complex of country roads fifty miles west of Chicago. Ralph Mulford's Lozier, Livingston's National, Buck's Marmon, and Eddie Hearne's Benz each captured one of Elgin's four inaugural events.

The third annual Founder's Day race in Philadelphia's Fairmount Park was taken by Len Zengle's Chadwick. A Kissel, driven by Harvey Herrick, won the second annual Cactus Derby over the desert from Los Angeles to the Arizona State Fairgrounds in Phoenix. In its second year (Indianapolis would not begin its 500-mile sweepstakes until 1911) the Speedway staged race meets in May, July, and September.

The crowds returned for the 1910 Vanderbilt Cup, and so did the problems. Held on October 1, the earliest of all eleven Cup races, to allow maximum time between the Cup and Grand Prize, which was scheduled for October 15, both events were slated to run on the 12.64-mile circuit used in 1909. The sixth Vanderbilt pulled thirty challengers, the largest of all Vanderbilt Cup fields. Entries ranged from Joe Dawson's 318-cubic-inch Marmon to the 597 CI Simplex and Apperson. The fifteen voiturettes, smaller cars limited to 300-cubic-inch engines, ran their own contest.

George Robertson's brilliant career ended during practice when a reporter, seeking firsthand racing impressions, panicked and grabbed the wheel as the Benz went through the Massapequa Turn. The car overturned. Robertson was injured seriously and never raced again. The journalist was unhurt. Robertson's accident was widely reported in the New York papers. His speed through the turn, 70 mph, was noted, as was the erring journalist's name, Stephen Reynolds, but no mention was made of the reporter's foolishness. My account of the incident, taken from *The Checkered Flag,* is Robertson's own.

Except for Barney Oldfield, who was enjoying one of his many AAA suspensions, the 1910 Cup entry represented the cream of American drivers. Bob Burman, Louis and Arthur Chevrolet drove big, 594-cubic-inch, race-readied Buicks. Joe Dawson and Ray Harroun were in Marmons, and rising star Ralph Mulford was in a Lozier. Gordon Bennett veteran Bert Dingley was in a Pope-Hartford, and 1909 Cup winner—big, steady Harry Grant—raced an ALCO. The only foreign cars were two Benzes, driven by Eddie Hearne and the legendary David Bruce-Brown, and a Mercedes driven by Spencer Wishart. Much was made of Stoddard-Daytona driver Tobin De Hymel, a young Texan said to be a "pure-blooded Aztec Indian."

Averaging close to 75 mph, Louis Chevrolet led the first nine laps, with teammate Bob Burman on his tail. But Chevrolet crashed and Burman fried his engine. Joe Dawson took the lead until lap eighteen when Grant moved ahead to win his second straight Cup, beating the Marmon by twenty-five seconds.

The 1910 Vanderbilt Cup was America's Paris–Madrid. The New York *Evening Telegram* headline "Grant Wins, Three Killed; Another Dying" was typical. Two riding mechanics, Mathew Bacon of the Columbia and Chevrolet's Charles Miller, were dead and twenty spectators were injured. Final results were affected by the accidents. Joe Dawson had been leading but stopped to offer assistance after his Marmon had plowed into an errant group. An immediate result of the disaster was the cancellation of the October 15 American Grand Prize. Lack of crowd control, always a major problem since the first Cup race, finished racing on the roads of Long Island.

On October 10, 1910, after the enterprising Savannah Auto Club sent a delegation to New York, the ACA granted the Grand Prize to Savannah. As many drivers had other commitments a November 12 date was selected as one that would interfere least with driver schedules and still give the organizers time to prepare.

Start of the 1911 Labor Day 50-mile feature at Brighton Beach: No. 20 is the Sheets/National, No. 14 the Burman/Opel, No. 11 the Wishart/Mercedes, and No. 22 is Hughes in the winning Mercer.

David Bruce-Brown in Victory Lane after his Benz won the 1910 Grand Prize in Savannah.

Considerable new road work was required. New grandstands and pits were built as hundreds of convicts, later to be honored with their own enclosure at the race, again labored to make a deadline. The circuit was shortened from 25.13 to 17.3 miles, but the race became longer, as twenty-four laps, representing 415.2 miles, were covered in 1910 as opposed to sixteen laps, or 402.08 miles, around the original course. European drivers were especially pleased when they learned that the New York course was out. Dr. Quattlebaum, the Savannah historian, quotes Louis Wagner, Victor Hemery, and Felice Nazzaro, three hallowed racing names, as saying, "Not even Europe ever furnished a more perfectly patrolled course. . . . I wonder if they will give us any more of those fish dinners?" Nazzaro said, "Had it been known that the race would be in Savannah, there would have been an even dozen foreign stars over here. . . . Manufacturers and drivers had no faith in Vanderbilt Cup officials to police the course . . . it took a lot of persuasion and money to bring me over." Wagner was most enthusiastic: "I am ready to go south tonight. . . . I dreaded the race on Long Island, but now I am anxious to begin training."

Once again railroads and steamship lines prepared specials. Telegraph lines were strung, and a revolutionary electric timer was installed at the start-finish line. Two Light Car Trophy races of 190 and 277 miles, won by Billy Knipper's Lancia and Joe Dawson's Marmon, were run on November 11, the day prior to the Grand Prize. Second in the Trophy race was the Mercer of young Washington Roebling, whose family owned the Mercer factory and who was to lose his life on the *Titanic*.

Only six of the fifteen GP entries were European. Victor Hemery, David Bruce-Brown, and Willie Haupt drove for Benz, while Felice Nazzaro, Louis Wagner, and Ralph DePalma were in FIATs. Some Americans ran the same made-ready-to-race stripped chassis stock cars as in the October Vanderbilt. The Marmon team had their regulars, Joe Dawson and Ray Harroun. Bob Burman, in a 593.7-cubic-inch Marquette-Buick, was joined by Arthur Chevrolet. Twice a Vanderbilt winner, Harry Grant again drove an ALCO; Lou Disbrow switched from his National to join Charley Basle in a sleek Pope-Hartford. Ralph Mulford and Joe Horan drove Loziers. Several American entries, including Louis Chevrolet's Buick, failed to make the field due to pre-race accidents and transport failures.

At 9:00 a.m. Fred Wagner, then the starter for almost all major American races, got the Grand Prize under way with a slap on the back of Arthur Chevrolet, a procedure he followed at thirty-second intervals for the entire field. The contest was primarily between FIAT and Benz. Hemery, Nazzaro, Wagner, Haupt, and De-Palma each held the lead until lap twenty-three, when young David Bruce-Brown slipped ahead of teammate Hemery to win by 1.42 seconds. This was an incredibly close finish for its day and for the distance covered. Bruce-Brown's Benz averaged 70.55 mph as Nazzaro's FIAT recorded a 75.7-mph lap to earn him the fastest-lap honors. American cars driven by Burman, Mulford, Horan, and Harroun, several with engines half the size of the winning Benz, filled the next four places.

Although all entries used Michelin tires, it is interesting to note that Bob Burman, who took third place, changed fifteen tires on his Buick, while Ralph Mulford, who came in fourth, ran the entire 415 miles without replacing a single tire. Meticulous Mulford, in his immaculate white driving outfit, including a white tie, and "Wild" Bob contrasted in many ways.

The night following the 1910 Grand Prize, the Savannah Automobile Club contacted the ACA's Robert Morrell regarding next year's race. Later Savannah also requested the Vanderbilt Cup. Both sanctions were granted, and in 1911 Savannah staged the two premier road races in America.

The year 1911 opened with "Terrible Teddy" Tetzlaff averaging 80.6 mph in a 100-mile match race on the boards at Playa del Rey. In April, Bob Burman drove his Benz to a 141.7-mph one-mile record at Daytona Beach. A few months later Burman established new dirt-track marks at Brighton Beach at half his Daytona speed. A National, manufactured by Arthur Newby, one of the Indianapolis race founders, and driven by Len Zengle, earned the Elgin Trophy. Herr's National, Hughes's Mercer, and Roberts' Abbott-Detroit also won preliminary races. That year Eddie Hearne drove his FIAT to victory in the main event at the new 7.9-mile Cincinnati road course.

Lee Oldfield in his Abbott-Detroit at the 1910 Massapequa Sweepstakes.

That year also one of American auto racing's most tragic accidents occurred at the New York State Fair in Syracuse. On Saturday, September 16, eleven died and many were seriously injured when Lee Oldfield crashed into the crowded grandstand on lap forty-three

Bob Burman's Peugeot during the 1915 San Diego Expo race.

Ruckstell/Mercer and Gabel/Tabis at the start of the 1915 San Diego Exposition race.

Hughie Hughes's Mercer at Point Breese, Philadelphia.

Fairmount Park races ran near this section of Philadelphia, known as Brewerytown.

of the fifty-lap feature race. Lee Oldfield had been running second to Ralph DePalma when the right front tire on his Knox let go. Originally scheduled to drive the old Jenatzy Mercedes, young Oldfield switched to the Knox that had been assigned to Fred Belcher. The crowd of 65,000, largest in the fair's history, had included President Taft, who left the fairgrounds shortly before the start of the last of the day's six races.

Bob Burman, who earlier in the day had set a new, 48.82 seconds, track record in the Blitzen Benz, and Ralph DePalma, who won the fair's three-mile "Free for All" in his Simplex, had argued with the track officials over the condition of the track. At first they had refused to race but finally consented. Eyewitness reports claim that both DePalma, the leader, and Oldfield had tire trouble. According to one account, "part of the shoe . . . could be seen revolving and beating the track . . . efforts were made to get him to stop and replace the bad tire, but his [Oldfield's] manager was seen to urge him onward and to motion to him to increase his speed." According to newspaper reports, at about 5:30 p.m., when Oldfield's car was almost touching DePalma's, "Spectators saw Oldfield's machine leap into the air for a few feet, then settle back on its four wheels, continue its mad pace, and then crash squarely into the fence. . . ." Lee Oldfield, who had been incorrectly identified as Barney's younger brother, was reported hospitalized. Lee said, "I don't know what happened. I heard my tire blow up, then I went through the fence. After that everything was a blank. When I came to, I was being lifted from the top of a man on whom I had landed."

DePalma, unaware of the accident, as were most of the crowd, went on to complete the race. When he heard of Oldfield's arrest he changed his travel plans, staying in Syracuse overnight to help secure young Lee's release. Next day he went on to Hartford and Philadelphia, where he raced on Thursday and Saturday.

Lee Oldfield became a test driver and research engineer for E.M.F., Amplex, Marmon, and Nash and was chief engineer for Stutz. He then became a petroleum-products consultant and was an active member of the AAA Contest Board, where in the early 1950s he served as chairman of its Technical and Certified Testing Com-

mittees. In 1973 Lee Oldfield, then a hearty eighty-four, described his Syracuse accident to the historian Charles Lytle:

President Taft had been asked to the New York State Fair and promised a ride about the track in a race car. But the track was very dusty, so two sprinkling watering carts were driven about the track, to lay the dust. Then it became too wet, and one cart was allowed to stand at the gate off the track, at the back stretch entry, and dripping water made a puddle and mud formed. . . . To the best of his knowledge, as he was held incomunicado until his release. Even his team left town. He suffered only a cut under one eye, although he was bandaged tightly from hips to armpits, although never in any pain such as would seem to demand such bandaging. Ralph DePalma and the Secretary of the Contest Board did return to Syracuse, to act as character witnesses, and he was ultimately released with no punishment whatever meted out. . . .

Following the Syracuse disaster, the AAA Contest Board attempted to reduce spectator and driver hazards, but increased speeds outran what, for the most part, were makeshift measures. Drivers were disciplined

Fairmount Park, Philadelphia, October 9, 1911: Erwin Bergdoll's Benz, No. 8, the overall winner, and Louis Disbrow's National, No. 16.

for appearing at "outlaw" (other than AAA-sanctioned) events. Among those chastised were T. S. Duby, who was suspended for two years for competing in an unsanctioned race in DeWitt, Iowa, under the name of Bliss; C. B. Kent, who lost his AAA license for six months for appearing in an unsanctioned meet in Madison, Wisconsin; and the irrepressible Barney, whose habitual rule-bending cost him his AAA privileges for all of 1911.

Although criticism of the sport, particularly road racing, grew, so did the number of events. By 1912 professional races were being held from San Diego to Tacoma in the West and from Florida to New England in the East and in almost every state in between.

October 1911 saw the finish of a fine road-racing series in Philadelphia and the beginning of another in Santa Monica. For four years the Quaker City Motor Club had staged annual Founders Day races in Philadelphia's Fairmount Park. Spectators, estimated by the Philadelphia police and local newspapers to have exceeded 400,000, were well behaved, but Mayor Reyburn, after first supporting the project, mounted vigorous opposition. The last Fairmount Park race was won by Erwin Bergdoll, whose Benz averaged 60.80 mph for 202 miles to earn "big car" honors. Races for smaller-engined cars that day were captured by Hughie Hughes's

Mercer and two Nationals. The Bergdoll brothers, Erwin and Grover Cleveland, were soon to achieve a less pleasant sort of fame: Sons of a millionaire Philadelphia brewer, Grover Cleveland Bergdoll became the most publicized draft dodger of World War I.

The first Santa Monica road race was run on October 14, 1911. The 8.4-mile course, along the shores of the Pacific, was one of the most picturesque in America. It started on Ocean Avenue, continued through Death Curve, where it joined Nevada Avenue, near Wilshire Boulevard, then on to Old Soldiers Home at Sawtelle, returning via San Vicente to Ocean Boulevard. A three-mile straight helped make Santa Monica one of the fastest road courses of its day. The opening 202-mile "Free for All" on October 14 was won by Harvey Herrick's National with a 74.60-mph average. In the heavy and Medium car races, Merz in a National and Keene in a Marmon were first.

On November 30, 1911, *The Automobile* headline read "Lozier Smashes Vanderbilt Record." The Cup race, held on the 17.14-mile Savannah GP course on November 27, was staged only three days before the Grand Prize. Two new stars, Ralph Mulford and Ralph DePalma, waged a race-long battle. Winner Mulford, in his semistock Lozier, came in two minutes, eleven seconds ahead of DePalma's Grand Prix Mercedes. Spencer

Wishart finished second in a car similar to DePalma's, and two-time Cup winner Grant was fourth, in a Lozier. DePalma's 77.9-mph lap was the day's fastest. Bruce-Brown retired on the sixth lap when his FIAT broke a wheel.

At 9:00 a.m. on a bitter cold Thanksgiving morning Fred Wagner performed his back-slapping ritual on Caleb Bragg to start the third American Grand Prize. Favored among the sixteen starters were Eddie Hearne, Victor Hemery, and Erwin Bergdoll, each in a 928-cubic-inch Benz, wealthy Caleb Bragg and former GP winners Louis Wagner and David Bruce-Brown in FIATs. Of the American cars only Mulford's Vanderbilt Cup-winning Lozier and Burman's Marmon were given a chance. It was one of the coldest days in Savannah history. The track surface had frozen solid, and the sale of whiskey, passed through the crowd by appropriately garbed waiters, flourished at fifty cents a glass.

First-lap speeds, from a standing start, ranged from Caleb Brown's 79 mph to 61.7 mph for Mitchell's Abbott-Detroit. The great Hemery, after third-lap engine troubles put him hopelessly behind, blazed an 81.6-mph fastest lap of the day, and then retired.

Following Bragg's early lead, the Grand Prize became a contest between DePalma, Hearne, Bruce-Brown, and Mulford. Cyrus Patschke's Marmon held the lead on laps nine and ten, the first time an American car had been in first place in any of the Grand Prize races. But Patschke's effort destroyed his engine, the Marmon retiring on lap ten.

Racing the same machine that had won him the Vanderbilt only three days earlier, Mulford stayed with the leaders and held second place only two laps from the finish when his white Lozier broke its driveshaft going over trolley tracks that crossed the course.

Bruce-Brown moved out front for the first time on lap twenty-one. He then lost the lead to Hearne but recaptured it on the next to last lap to win the Grand Prize for the second straight year. The best finish by an American car was Disbrow's Pope-Hartford in fourth, followed by Mitchell's Abbott-Detroit. The gap between European race cars and the semistock American specials was closing.

Savannah had come up with another well-run race meet. Hospitality had been outstanding. The two giants of French racing, Louis Wagner and Victor Hemery, remained in Savannah to go on a fishing trip. Several manufacturers held farewell parties for their hosts. The Abbott Motor Company generously presented their four race cars to their drivers, GP entrants Mitchell and Limberg, and to Mort Roberts and Hartman, who had run in the Tiedeman Trophy.

Following the 1911 races, Savannah's enthusiasm ran thin. Officials were criticized for using convict labor to build the course and the state militia to patrol it. Many of the growing motoring public expressed annoyance on being denied the use of local roads while the race cars practiced. Even those who had supported the events were somewhat overwhelmed when they thought of trying to organize another international meet. They declined to bid for the Cup or Grand Prize in 1912. The Savannah combination of rigid crowd control and gracious hospitality had set a standard unique in American automobile racing.

Bruce-Brown brings FIAT the 1911 Grand Prize.

The always immaculate Ralph Mulford stops to fill his Lozier with gas on the way to winning the 1911 Vanderbilt Cup.

Eddie Pullen in Hudson, No. 4, being pursued by "Cockeyed" Brown, Santa Monica, 1919.

America Builds Real Race Cars　　　　　　IV

Marmon engineer–race driver Ray Harroun was successful at the Indianapolis Speedway from the day it opened, August 19, 1909. After he captured several short events, Harroun finished third behind the winning Buicks in the 100-mile trophy race. At the Speedway in 1910, after winning races in Atlanta and Los Angeles, he had four firsts, two seconds, and three thirds. Harroun came out of retirement to drive a single-seater 427-cubic-inch Marman Wasp in the first 500 in 1911, the only one of the forty starters to ride solo. His winning average was 74.59 mph, and he was less than two minutes in front of Ralph Mulford's Lozier.

By 1912 the United States was building a number of thoroughbred race cars. Where only a single Stutz and two Mercers made the 1911 Indianapolis field, in 1913 Mercer, Stutz, and Mason accounted for nine of the twenty-seven starters. In 1912 the 351-cubic-inch Mason, built by the Duesenberg brothers but named after their benefactor, a Des Moines attorney, won races at Brighton Beach and Milwaukee. Mercer and Stutz began finishing ahead of larger-engined stripped-chassis stock models.

In 1914 Duesenbergs appeared under their own name; the Mason became the Maytag and moved its factory to Waterloo, Iowa. Maxwell, with encouragement from Speedway president Carl Fisher, was soon to prepare a team of 298-cubic-inch, four-cylinder race cars designed by Ray Harroun. The displacement trend at the 500 was toward smaller engines. Indianapolis winners from 1913 through 1916 show 448 cubic inches for Goux's Peugeot, Rene Thomas' Delage 380, and 274 for DePalma's Mercedes and Resta's Peugeot. There are many who believe the 90-cubic-inch, supercharged Miller and Duesenberg eights of the late 1920s were the ultimate American race car.

Joe Dawson's National won the 500 in 1912, but it would be 1920 before Gaston Chevrolet's Frontenac brought America another home-grown, albeit French-accented, victory.

The AAA Contest Board encouraged the trend to smaller-capacity engines. The 600-cubic-inch limit of 1911 was reduced to 450 for 1913. It was not until 1930

that Eddie Rickenbacker, then owner of the Speedway, attempted to reverse the trend. In a futile effort to get the nation's car makers to go racing, Rick banned superchargers and increased engine size to 366 cubic inches (5981 cc.). This was not one of Rick's better ideas. Until Wilbur Shaw's Maserati won in 1939, Miller or Offenhauser engines were in each winning car. The best showing by any of the stock-block-based "Junk Formula" entrants was a third by Cliff Bergere's Studebaker in 1932.

The second Santa Monica road race, held on May 4, 1912, saw Teddy Tetzlaff capture the feature. Joerman's Maxwell and Ralph DePalma's Mercer won shorter preliminary events. The average winning speeds for the three races show an 8-mph difference between each event—62 mph for the Maxwell, 70.20 mph for De-Palma's Mercer, with the FIAT, in the feature, averaging 78 mph.

Tacoma, Washington, held its first Montamara Speed Carnival in 1912. Evans, Pullen, and Cooper took the shorter races, and Tetzlaff's FIAT won both the heavy-car race and the 250-mile Free-for-All. The first Tacoma Montamara, or Monta Marathon, as it was sometimes called, was run on a 3.5-mile road course. In 1914 the switch was made to a two-mile dirt track, and from 1915 until 1922 the race was held on a two-mile planked-board speedway. Ralph DePalma, winner of the AAA driving title in 1912, drove the Schroeder Mercedes to win over a thirty-four-car field in the Elgin Free-for-All. Hughes's Mercer, Merz's Stutz, and Endicott's Mason won shorter Elgin events. That year was a good one for Lou Disbrow, who won firsts on the dirt at Galveston and San Diego. It also saw an air-cooled Franklin win the fourth Cactus Derby from Los Angeles to Phoenix and the Vanderbilt Cup find a new home. Help from Pabst Beer and the Milwaukee Auto Dealers Association brought the Vanderbilt Cup and American Grand Prize to Milwaukee, Wisconsin, in 1912.

Following the announcement that the Greenfield circuit would be the site of both races, the Milwaukee organizers abruptly changed to one in Wawautosa Township. The September 28, 1912, issue of *The Club*

Journal explained: "Immediately the Greenfield circuit was announced, hold-up men and speculator sharks went down there and bought up all the parking space, grandstand sites, and other right of way." The *Journal* went on to say that work on the new course was to proceed for ten days before an announcement of the site change was made. Described as a 7.88-mile parallelogram, it had been shortened from 8.2 miles by taking out some bad corners. The course included the old Fond du Lac trunk highway from the northwest corner of the Milwaukee city limits.

The eighth Vanderbilt Cup was run on October 2, 1912, again three days prior to the Grand Prize. Its eight-car field was the smallest in Cup history, but it

was not lacking in class. DePalma had his Elgin-winning Mercedes, and Spencer Wishart and George Clark also raced the German car. Gil Anderson drove a Stutz; England's Hughie Hughes entered a 309-cubic-inch Mercer, the smallest car to compete; and Teddy Tetzlaff again drove his big FIAT. Only two stock cars were entered. Nineteen-eleven Cup winner Mulford had switched to a Knox, and Milwaukee amateur Harry Nelson drove a Lozier. The 1912 Vanderbilt was all Tetzlaff, until he ran out of road on the twenty-sixth of thirty-eight laps. DePalma and Hughes then raced wheel to wheel until DePalma pulled out to finish forty-three seconds in front of the Mercer. After seven tries, Mercedes had won its first Vanderbilt Cup.

Front row at the first 500 in 1911: Johnny Aitken, National No. 4; Harry Endicott, Inter-State No. 3; Ralph DePalma, Simplex No. 2; and Lewis Strang, Case No. 1 and the pace car.

The Marmon Wasp driven by Ray Harroun to a surprise win in the 1911 500.

The Speedway grandstands in 1913.

Shortly after the start of the 1911 Indianapolis, Lou Disbrow's Pope-Hartford, No. 5, goes under Joe Jagersberger's Case, No. 8, and the Case driven by Will Jones, No. 9.

Although he raced for less than five years, many rate David Bruce-Brown among the best of all American drivers. While still at Harstrom Preparatory School he won the amateur class in the 1908 Shingle Hill Climb and in 1909 drove a Mercedes to win it outright. When it neared time for the 1908 Ormond-Daytona Speed Week, young Bruce-Brown sought out New York AAA officials and asked for an introduction to someone at FIAT. He met E. R. Hollander, FIAT's American agent. Liking Bruce-Brown's enthusiasm and good manners,

Hollander allowed him to accompany the team as a mechanic. Bruce-Brown made the trip contrary to family wishes, having borrowed enough money from his school's boxing coach for a one-way train ticket to Florida.

According to Fred Wagner, who was on board the train that carried the FIAT team and other AAA officials to Daytona, young Bruce-Brown had everyone charmed before they got there. Except for once riding with Cedrino on the meet's final day, Bruce-Brown had not

Ralph DePalma and mechanic Tom Alley as their Mercedes wins the 1912 Vanderbilt Cup in Milwaukee.

Joe Dawson's National, winner of the 1912 500.

been in a car. However, following the professional races, he was given permission by Hollander to enter the amateur mile, provided AAA gave approval. It did, and David Bruce-Brown went on the books with a thirty-six-second amateur record. On hearing the news, his socially prominent mother, who had been bombarding the FIAT camp with telegrams forbidding David to drive, wired congratulations—and money. He returned to Daytona in 1909 to come in second to Barney Oldfield and to win the Dewar Trophy, awarded for the best combined performance in three one-mile heats and a ten-mile race, beating out Ralph DePalma.

When Bruce-Brown nosed out teammate Hemery to win the 1910 Grand Prize, the truculent French champion said that he had been beaten by a young master. Leaving the Benz team, Bruce-Brown raced a FIAT in the first 500 in 1911, qualifying twenty-fifth and finishing third. He drove a National in the 500 of 1912 but retired early with a broken engine. In 1911 he had become the only American to twice win the American Grand Prize.

As members of the FIAT team, the two great American drivers DePalma and Bruce-Brown competed in Europe for the first time in 1912, joining the veteran Louis Wagner at Dieppe for the French Grand Prix. After the first day Bruce-Brown was in first place. He had set the fastest lap, 78.02 mph, beating George Boillot in his Peugeot by two minutes after ten laps around the 47.8-mile circuit. On the second day he was disqualified for taking on gasoline on the course after he had repaired a broken fuel line. However, he pressed on to finish an unofficial third. Jules Goux and DePalma, incidentally, had suffered disqualification on the first day for the same reason.

Nine weeks later in Milwaukee, while practicing for the 1912 American Grand Prize, Bruce-Brown's FIAT blew a tire with fatal results. AAA Contest Board member, starter Fred Wagner, tells of how he was about to close the course so that regular traffic could resume when Bruce-Brown asked for two or three more laps. Hard rains had resulted in both the Cup and Grand Prize having been set back a week, and, although the track was damp in spots, Bruce-Brown said he needed a few more laps to adjust the FIAT's timing. As one of the favorites—he had recorded an 80-mph lap in practice—Wagner let him out. When Bruce-Brown pulled in and requested still more time Wagner said he then saw that the FIAT's tires were worn to the fabric and ordered Bruce-Brown to return to the garage. Bruce-Brown may not have heard the warning as he roared off on his last lap. Tony Scudelari, his mechanic, died a week after Bruce-Brown. Following the fatal accident, an inquest was held, and a coroner's jury returned a verdict that the road was too narrow for safety.

A field of twelve cars, three American and nine European, ran the fourth American Grand Prize. Amateur

Teddy Tetzlaff in his FIAT S61 at Santa Monica, 1912.

Teddy Tetzlaff.

Starter Fred Wagner with his hand on Bob Burman's arm at the 1912 Milwaukee Grand Prize.

David Bruce-Brown and his mechanic in the 1912 French GP at Dieppe.

Caleb Bragg, Barney Oldfield (making his first start in a major road race), and Teddy Tetzlaff drove FIATs. Erwin Bergdoll, Bob Burman, and Joe Horan drove for Benz, and Spencer Wishart, George Clark, and DePalma raced Mercedes. Two American cars, Anderson's Stutz and Hughes's Mercer, along with Fountain's Lozier represented the United States.

"Terrible Teddy" again took an immediate lead and again broke down while in first place. On lap thirty-one his suspension collapsed. DePalma, closing fast in the final laps, lost the Mercedes as he attempted to pass Bragg, whose FIAT went on to win with a 68.5-mph race average. Both DePalma and Tom Alley, his mechanic, were hospitalized. Bergdoll finished second, with Anderson's Stutz twenty-four seconds behind. Oldfield, a creditable fourth, was next to the last car running at the finish.

A three-year option to hold the Cup and Grand Prize was offered to the Milwaukee promoters. However, in spite of 60,000 spectators at each race, it was not accepted.

An effort was then made to return the race to Long Island, the New York *World* of November 17, 1912, heading a story: "Race Has Lost in Prestige on Every Running Away from Native Territory."

Following Milwaukee, professional road racing in the United States, with the exception of Elgin, was now concentrated on the West Coast. More than twenty-five years after the Vanderbilt Cup left Long Island, when it did return it was to Roosevelt Raceway in Old Westbury, near the original Vanderbilt Cup circuit.

Although Indianapolis remained the premier American event, Los Angeles became the nation's racing capital. During the board-track era and the 1930s more first-class racing was held in California than in the Midwest and East combined. Perhaps Westerners

Emanuel Cedrino, winner of the 300-mile beach race, the longest ever, at Daytona Beach, March 5, 1908. Ralph DePalma was to have driven this FIAT.

Spencer Wishart's Mercer finished second at the Speedway in 1913. Ralph DePalma drove it in relief after his Mercer ran a bearing.

Buick, No. 14, approaching the Brisbee control in the Los Angeles–Phoenix Cactus Derby.

became more involved with machinery because of California's greater dependence on the automobile for personal transportation; or it may have been that the open spaces of the West attracted a breed of men that found expression by building and driving race cars.

The first board tracks were built in California in 1910. At their peak, six of the country's twenty-four wooden bowls were in the West. California tracks—Ascot, Gilmore, Atlantic Boulevard, and Balboa—were the training ground for the country's best oval-track racers. The first midgets of the early 1930s held nightly shows on a dozen ovals from Sacramento to Los Angeles' Loyola Stadium. Championship cars raced at Oakland and San Jose, and, a little later, the midgets ran in the Rose Bowl and Los Angeles Coliseum. By 1950, watching midget racing in California was like going to the movies. The Los Angeles area became the home of many Indianapolis builders and drivers; each spring saw them take the pilgrims' trail to Indianapolis.

Neither the Vanderbilt Cup nor the Grand Prize was held in 1913. Cross-country races remained popular in the West with runs from Los Angeles to Sacramento, Los Angeles to Phoenix, and El Paso to Phoenix. Victories in these 500-mile desert derbies were registered by Frank Verbeck's FIAT, Orin Davis' Locomobile, and Newkirk's Simplex. At Indianapolis, the victory of Jules Goux's Peugeot triggered the 1914 invasion that saw French cars and drivers capture the first four places. Earl Cooper, who relieved Charley Merz to bring Stutz a third in the 500 of 1913, went on to win the Tacoma, Santa Monica, and Corona road races.

A small, quiet man, Earl Cooper had a reputation for being a smart driver who showed concern for his car. In addition to winning the 1913 AAA national championship he also captured the AAA title in 1915 and 1917 to become the first three-time national champion.

Caleb Bragg's FIAT, winner of the 1912 Grand Prize, leaving Milwaukee's grandstand turn.

Bob Burman, Peugeot No. 7, Earl Cooper, Stutz No. 8, and Eddie Pullen, Mercer No. 4, at the old Ascot, April 1915.

Gil Anderson's Stutz in the 1912 Milwaukee Vanderbilt Cup.

75

Midgets in Los Angeles' Gilmore Stadium.

**Barney Oldfield's Stutz after winning the 1914
Los Angeles–Phoenix Cactus Derby.**

He enjoyed a distinguished driving career that did not end until his Marmon finished third at Monza in the 1927 Italian Grand Prix. In later years Cooper acted as a racing consultant for Union Oil and served on the AAA Contest Board.

In the Midwest, Ralph Mulford, now driving a Mason, won on the dirt at Columbus as Anderson's Stutz and DePalma's Mercer captured feature events at the 1913 Elgin races.

Although not on so grand a scale as Savannah, Corona is another example of a small community that managed to stage races of national importance. In April 1913 the Corona Auto Club decided it would be a good thing for their town to observe California's Admission Day, September 9, with an automobile race. Corona was known as the "World Lemon Capital," and its orange and lemon packing plants supported the

staid community of magnolias, pepper trees, and palm-lined streets. A city of 6,000, fifty miles east of Los Angeles, Corona appeared an unlikely site for a major auto race, except for one factor. As its name suggests, the Corona city plan was a circular one, the entire town being encompassed by Grand Circle Boulevard, a 2.77-mile long, seventy-foot-wide perfect circle of an avenue. The AAA, having lost many of its road courses, granted Corona a sanction. John Flagler, an Eastern industrialist, donated a $5000 trophy, and the promoters guaranteed $11,000 in prize money. At the time, only Indianapolis carried a larger purse.

Grandstands seating 30,000 were built on lawns between the curb and pepper trees. Churches and homes were thrown open to serve as ladies' rest rooms. Visitors' accommodations were arranged for in nearby communities, including Riverside, which was to have its own race-crowd housing problems fifty years later.

Official tryouts were scheduled for September 1, but race cars, driven into town by their mechanics and drivers, were already arriving by mid-August. One of the first to try the new circuit was Earl Cooper, who, without pushing, lapped the giant circle at 88 mph. Tetzlaff's 120-hp FIAT did two consecutive laps at over 100 mph, and Frank Verbeck from nearby Pasadena, who was something of a local hero for having recently won the Panama-Pacific road race, also pushed his FIAT close to the 100-mph mark. The practice times went out over the press wires, and the nation's newspapers talked of new world records.

Ralph DePalma, fresh from winning Elgin, hired a boxcar so that his crew could rebuild his Mercer during the 2,000-mile journey west. A grudge between Oldfield and DePalma (who had always beaten Barney

up to this time) was played up by the press. Always a superb showman, Barney held court at Riverside's Mission Inn, which was later to serve as race headquarters for the Los Angeles *Times'* Grand Prix. He bragged that his Mercer would run the competition off the course.

Special trains, some from as far as San Francisco, helped bring a crowd of over 100,000 to Corona. Admission was fifty cents, and no one was allowed access to the Grand Boulevard area unless he wore a tag showing that he had paid. The first day began with a thirty-seven-lap race for light stock cars with engine displacements up to 231 cubic inches. A Buick, Reo, and Studebaker won the first three places.

Two races were combined for the feature, a 252-mile race for cars with engines up to 450 cubic inches and the 302-mile unlimited Free-for-All. Drivers in the me-

Joe Thomas, Eddie O'Donnell, and Eddie Pullen at Ascot, 1916.

A classic front row for the opening of Ascot's mile oval, April 1916: Jimmy Grant in the No. 10 Stutz, Eddie Pullen's No. 4 Mercer, and the winner, Eddie O'Donnell's No. 12 Duesenberg.

Goux, mechanic Biguin, and Major Sedgwick. The Peugeot design was the beginning of the modern American race car.

The Peugeot team in 1913: the Speedway's Major Sedgwick, second from left, who was instrumental in bringing the French cars to Indianapolis; Jules Goux, with camera case and cap, winner of the 500 of 1913; and Goux's mechanic, Biguin, to the right of the flag.

dium class were eligible for the feature purse if they covered the fifty additional miles.

Oldfield's Mercer, the Stutz driven by Italy's Felix Mangone, Tony Jeannette's National, and DePalma's Mercer made up the front row as sixteen cars, four abreast and four rows deep, started the day's big event.

Oldfield set the early pace, but repeated stops for fresh tires allowed Cooper to take the lead. Hard-chargers Tetzlaff and DePalma were among the early retirements. On lap fifty-nine, roaring back from a pit stop, Barney came on a small boy who had darted onto the track. Oldfield took heroic avoiding action, and the Mercer flew into the trees. Frank Sandhoffer, Barney's mechanic, suffered head injuries. A spectator's leg was broken, but Oldfield was unhurt. Earl Cooper screeched to a stop when he saw the overturned Mercer, only to have Barney yell, "Get going, damn it. I'm O.K.!" Cooper later said, "Had Barney been killed in the wreck, I could not have finished." Tetzlaff, who had passed the Stutz when Cooper had stopped, broke an oil line with twenty laps to go, and Cooper won with a 74.7-mph average. Taylor's Marmon, fifty minutes behind, was second and the National third. Only three cars finished.

In 1914 Grand Boulevard's dirt and oil surface was repaved with asphalt, the race date moved to Thanksgiving Day, November 26, and a high-wire fence encircled the entire track.

The nineteen cars that lined up before an even larger crowd than in 1913 were among the world's finest—Peugeots in the hands of Eddie Rickenbacker and Bob

Billy Chandler driving a Mercer in the 1913 Elgin road race.

Georges Boillot and Jules Goux in Gasoline Alley with their 1914 Peugeots. Mechanics stand by Boillot's entry.

Burman (who had reached 110 mph in practice), Sunbeams driven by Harry Grant and Harry Babcock, De-Palma's Elgin-winning Mercedes, and Oldfield's new Maxwell. Eddie Pullen headed the Mercer team, and defending champion Earl Cooper was back in a Stutz.

New records were assumed. The track surface was faster, each machine carried sufficient fuel to go the distance, and tires showed much improvement over the past year. Two English Sunbeams had recently completed Santa Monica without a change.

Pullen's Mercer won the second Corona. Eddie averaged 87.76 mph and earned $4000 for winning and $2000 for establishing a new world record. Oldfield finished second without making a single pit stop, and Eddie O'Donnell's Duesenberg was third as seven of nineteen starters completed the 301 miles.

Corona failed to hold a race in 1915. By the time a new organization, the Citrus Belt Racing Association of Corona, was formed, the initiative was lost. The 1916 race, held on April 8, had ominous beginnings. Earl Cooper and Sterling Price were injured in pre-race accidents, and a plane dropping leaflets advertising the race had crashed. Favored in the twelve-car field were Bob Burman's Peugeot, Pullen's Mercer, Oldfield's Delage, and O'Donnell's Duesenberg. Following an early scramble, O'Donnell's Duesenberg took the lead and held it to win with an 85.60-mph race average.

Burman had been closing fast when, with twelve laps to go, a broken rear wheel sent the Peugeot into a three-block slide that ended as the French machine

Tommy Milton in the Detroit Front-Drive Special, driven by Leon Duray, C. W. Van Ranst, Ralph Hepburn, and Milton to eighth place at the Speedway in 1927. General Electric super-charging wizard Sanford Moss stands behind Milton.

Start of the 1915 American Grand Prize at the San Francisco World's Fair: Newhouse/Delage, No. 15; Ruckstell/Mercer, No. 6; and Cooper/Stutz, No. 8. Dario Resta, in No. 9 Peugeot, won.

The Mercer Team at Elgin. England's Hughie Hughes behind the wheel with mechanic Eddie Pullen, who was to become a great Mercer driver. Mercer chief engineer Finley R. Porter, holding hat, stands next to Mrs. Hughes.

The start of the 1916 Corona road race.

crashed into a pole. Mechanic Erick Schroeder died in a nearby emergency hospital, a guard was killed instantly and five spectators injured. Bob Burman died later that afternoon.

Corona was finished. More than the fatal accident caused its demise. There had been fewer paying spectators. Corona residents objected to the litter and destruction of property and the unruly crowds. Youngsters climbed the high-wire fence, while adults used wire cutters to make holes in it. Revivals, tried in the early 1950s, failed. The town has grown well beyond its Corona, but the Great Circle is as it was over sixty years ago.

Following the 1913 hiatus, the Vanderbilt Cup and American Grand Prize found a new home in Santa Monica. The 8.4-mile circuit bordering the Pacific on the edge of Los Angeles had been staging first-class road races since 1910, but the Cup and Grand Prize represented something special. One statement read, "The granting to Southern California of the privilege of running the W. K. Vanderbilt, Jr., and International Grand Prize races is the highest honor ever paid the Pacific Coast by New York City. It also is the best advertisement since Mayor Alexander wore knee pants." On safety, the program read, "The only reason we are enjoying the Vanderbilt Cup and International Grand Prize is because the crowd cannot be controlled on Long Island. Mr. Shetter (race chairman) wishes to make a personal appeal to every spectator to assist the police in keeping order should any accident occur."

The event was postponed for a week due to heavy rains that isolated the Los Angeles area. Local newspapers used the time to build up the coming duel between Ralph DePalma and Barney Oldfield. DePalma

had been captain of the Mercer team but resigned in a huff when the Mercer management hired Barney without consulting him. Unable to locate a good new race car, DePalma fell back on the venerable Schroeder Mercedes he had first driven in 1911 and had used to win the Elgin race and the Vanderbilt Cup in 1912. With a smaller engine, the Mercedes had been DePalma's ride in the 1912 Indy. The same car brought Ralph Mulford a seventh-place finish in the 500 of 1913 and, with a Peugeot engine, an eleventh place in the 500 of 1914. Based on the 1908 Mercedes Grand Prix car, the chain-driven old beast was in need of an almost complete rebuilding.

The ninth Vanderbilt was more than a match race between these two giants of American racing. The Stutz team of Earl Cooper and Norwegian-born Gil Anderson could run with the best, as could Eddie Pullen and Spencer Wishart in their Mercers.

Not until mid-race did DePalma and Oldfield become front-runners as Pullen and Anderson set the pace for the first eighteen laps. During the final laps of the first Santa Monica one of motor racing's favorite tales was acted out. In *The Checkered Flag,* Peter Helck wrote, "DePalma swung wide on the Nevada Avenue turn and, looking back observed the crucial state of his opponent's rubber. Virtually together, both cars thundered past the pits when DePalma signalled for a stop next time around. As hoped, the signal was observed by Oldfield and obviously welcomed by the old master. At lap end, with the German car trailing guilelessly, the Mercer scooted in for replacements, while DePalma, successful in the ruse, never paused." DePalma won his second Vanderbilt by eighty seconds, a good start for one of his best years.

The American Grand Prize was held on February 28, 1914, only two days after the Vanderbilt Cup. More than 250,000 spectators, many of them hoping to see a repeat of the Oldfield-DePalma fireworks, saw an American car and driver win their first Grand Prize. Tetzlaff

English Sunbeam spills driver Marquis and his mechanic during the 1914 Grand Prize in Santa Monica.

Ralph DePalma and mechanic Jeffkins push their Mercedes past the pits as the 1912 Indy winner, Joe Dawson, looks on.

DePalma and Louie Fontaine winning the 1915 Indianapolis 500 in a Mercedes.

Earl Cooper bringing his Stutz to victory in the 1913 Corona road race.

followed his regular routine by storming off, setting the fastest lap, 86.6 mph, then breaking. Wishart moved his yellow Mercer out front and stayed there until mid-race, when he was sidelined with engine trouble. The only English car ever to contest the Grand Prize, Marquis' Sunbeam, crashed on lap thirty-three while in the lead. Anderson's Stutz moved up only to expire three laps from the finish with a broken piston. Having averaged 77.2 mph for 403 miles, Pullen's Mercer took the checker forty minutes ahead of the second-place Marmon.

French drivers Réné Thomas, Arthur Duray, Albert Guyot, and Jules Goux had a picnic at Indianapolis in 1914. Oldfield, with relief from Gil Anderson, the first American to finish, came in fifth. Two outstanding Americans, DePalma and Pullen, had withdrawn after qualifying. DePalma's Mercedes was handling poorly, and Pullen also realized that he had little chance against the Delage and Peugeot. The next American car to win the 500 was Chevrolet's Frontenac in 1920. In 1913 and 1914 American builders were still going to school at the Speedway.

The 1914 championship year was made up of twelve events, of which five were road races. Eddie Rickenbacker's Duesenberg won the 300-mile inaugural at Sioux City, Cooper captured the Tacoma main event, and at Elgin on August 24 both features fell to DePalma's Mercedes. Two weeks later 15,000 fans packed Brighton Beach to see the Mercedes win fifty- and 100-mile sprints, insuring DePalma of his second AAA national championship.

Entries for the 1915 Vanderbilt Cup and Grand Prize were almost identical. Burman, Hall, and Tomasini appeared in the Cup race but not the Grand Prize, as Taylor's ALCO and Cooper's Stutz ran only in the latter. The distance—400 miles for the GP, 296 for the Vanderbilt—as well as prestige, slightly favored the Grand Prize.

The Vanderbilt was originally scheduled for Washington's Birthday, February 22, but bad weather delayed it until March 6. The Grand Prize ran on February

27 as planned, despite continued rain and high winds.

The 1915 field of thirty cars was the largest ever to start a Grand Prize, raced over 3.84 miles of paved and boarded streets within the grounds of San Francisco's Panama-Pacific Exposition. The setting was bizarre. A quarter of a century later it was to be duplicated, on a smaller scale, at the New York World's Fair.

Among the favorites at San Francisco were the Maxwell and Mercer teams with Rickenbacker, Oldfield, Carlson, and Pullen. Stutz had many backers for its strong entry of Anderson, Wilcox, and Cooper. And there was DePalma with his Mercedes. France, who since 1908 had ignored both the Cup and Grand Prize, fielded cars by Bugatti, Delage, and Peugeot.

Resta and his Grand Prix Peugeot had an amazing impact on American racing. Despite his Italian name and swarthy good looks, Dario Resta actually was an Englishman, having migrated to Great Britain with his parents as an infant. He was born in Livorno in 1885, worked in the London shops of Panhard as a mechanical engineer before racing, and first raced in 1907, driving a Mercedes owned by F. R. Fry, the English chocolate maker. He won three races at Brooklands and was awarded a place on the Austin team for the 1908 French Grand Prix, where he finished nineteenth. Fry had bought the Grand Prix-winning Lautenschlager Mercedes, and for several years Resta drove it to frequent victories at Brooklands. Resta joined Sunbeam in 1912 and came to the United States early in 1915. Although Peugeots were favorably regarded in America (Jules Goux had won the 500 of 1913 with a Peugeot,

and Arthur Duray and Goux had driven the French car to second and fourth places at the Speedway in 1914), Resta was unknown until the California races of 1916.

Resta won both San Francisco races. Howdy Wilcox's Stutz was second by more than seven minutes in both events. The Grand Prize, run before the Vanderbilt for the first time because of miserable weather, was regarded as a lucky win for Resta. Conditions were so bad for the GP that most of the stars dropped out, and Resta led all but a few laps. Good weather for the Vanderbilt Cup, run on March 6, a week following the GP, enabled Resta to win with a 66.45-mph average, 10 mph faster than his GP time.

After driving the 345-cubic-inch car in San Francisco, Resta switched to a 4.5-liter, double-overhead cam, four-weel-brake Grand Prix model. After a race-long struggle he finished second to DePalma at Indianapolis; won the inaugural 500 on the Chicago Board Speedway; in June returned to Chicago to record the first 100 miles with better than a 100-mph winning time; and closed the year in November by winning the Harkness Cup at Sheepshead Bay.

A soft-spoken, quiet man, respected by his fellow drivers, Resta made few close friends. In 1916 he won the Indianapolis 500, was victorious on the board speedways at Omaha and Chicago, and again won the Vanderbilt Cup. In two years Resta won nine of the nineteen championship events he entered. He was the 1916 AAA national champion, an honor earned by only one other European, Victor Hemery, who received the title in 1905 on the basis of his Vanderbilt Cup victory.

Dario Resta earned more than racing gold in the United States. He married the sister of Spencer Wishart, the talented amateur who lost his life in 1914 while his Mercer was leading the Elgin Trophy. He disagreed with Peugeot and drove a Frontenac at Sheepshead Bay in 1917 but failed to finish. With a successful business in both London and New York, he drove his own special at Sheepshead Bay and Chicago in 1918 and in 1919 at Sheepshead Bay, his favorite American track, and in Tacoma. Several seconds and thirds came his way but no wins. Resta returned to the United States in 1923 to drive a Durant Special at Beverly Hills and a Packard Special at the Speedway, where he qualified third and retired on the eighty-eighth lap with a blown head gasket. Back in England, he joined the Sunbeam-Talbot-Darracq group. In September, 1924, Dario Resta lost his life when his Sunbeam crashed at Brooklands.

Following a futile bid from Corona for the 1916 Vanderbilt Cup and American Grand Prix, the two road-racing classics returned to Santa Monica. Held on November 16 and 18, Cup entries totaled nineteen, with twenty-one cars for the Grand Prix. As in 1915, the field for the two events was almost the same. Even the prize money—$4000 first, $2500 second, and $1000 third—was identical.

For the first time AAA 300-cubic-inch engine-displacement limits applied to both events. Up to 450-cubic-inch engines were allowed in the Grand Prize, but none was used, as such entrants would not be eligible to receive AAA championship points. Johnny Aitken joined Resta in a Peugeot for the Cup race. Cooper was back in a

Stutz, Rickenbacker headed a Duesenberg team sponsored by William Weightman, who also drove, and the formidable Pullen led a team of three Mercers.

After leading most of the first half, Aitken's Peugeot retired with engine trouble, and Resta, who had been turning 90-mph laps, eased off to win with an 86.98-mph average for the 294 miles. Cooper's Stutz was second, eight minutes behind Resta, with the well-to-do amateur, Weightman, a distant third.

Two days later the seventh and final Grand Prize was won by Howdy Wilcox, although he was relieved by Johnny Aitken, who drove Wilcox's Peugeot from lap twenty until the finish on lap forty-eight.

In contention with Resta for the AAA title, Aitken had started to look for a substitute ride immediately after he had broken his engine on the first lap. Rickenbacker also jumped cars, switching Duesenbergs with patron Weightman, eventually to finish fifth. Leading from the start until lap eighteen, when he was sidelined by ignition failure, Resta began an aggressive but fruitless search for another car. Aitken, driving the Wilcox car for better than half distance, was first awarded the GP points, which gave him the national championship. Resta protested in vain until Rickenbacker sought out AAA officials and backed Resta's protest on the ground that he had not received points at Indianapolis when he had driven the Henderson Maxwell for more than half the 300-mile race. The AAA reversed itself, giving the points to Wilcox and the championship to Resta. Cooper's Stutz, the car that Resta had so desperately tried to buy during the race, saying that "price was no object," came in second, six minutes behind Aitken. Less than half the field finished. Two days between races of 294 and 403 miles had not been enough to make repairs.

It was a dismal finish for so great a series. Lew Jackson, a comparative novice, lost control of his old Marmon on San Vincente Boulevard, hit a concession stand, then plowed into a tree. Jackson, a cameraman, and two occupants of the stand were killed.

The 1916 Santa Monica had been ill-starred before an engine was fired. Richard Kennerdell, AAA Contest Board chairman, and Vanderbilt aired sharp differences over race regulations. The Cup donor accused the AAA of violating the spirit of the events and objected strongly to running the GP only two days after the Cup race. Vanderbilt said that the American Grand Prize belonged to the ACA, not the AAA, and that he was considering the withdrawal of both trophies.

There are photographs of Willie K. in the stands at Santa Monica, watching the end of what he had so gloriously started.

The 1916 Indy winner, Dario Resta, in his Peugeot at Sheepshead Bay, New York.

T. E. "Pop" Myers with Howdy Wilcox (left) and Johnny Aitken at the 1916 Indianapolis.

Proper Drivers and Magic Machines   V

During World War I American automobile racing did not come to a full stop. In 1917 it had barely slowed. Indianapolis did not run in 1917 or 1918, and there was a scramble to get the Speedway's Memorial Day date.

In 1917 the championship season consisted of fourteen AAA-sanctioned oval-track races. For the first time not a single road race was on the championship schedule. In 1916 there had been two and in 1915 ten.

It is doubtful that the Vanderbilt Cup or American Grand Prize would have been held in 1917 even if the United States had not been at war. The climate for road racing was poor. It was in trouble politically for safety reasons and because some citizens considered the noise, the mischief, and, when a road race was held nearby, the loss of their driving privileges a nuisance. Of more importance, perhaps, promoters preferred to hold races on oval tracks. Whether dirt, brick, paved or board, an oval track is usually fenced in. Thus enclosed it gives the promoter a reasonable chance to collect admissions. Also there were fans then, as now, who preferred to sit in a grandstand where they could see the entire race course. However, road racing in America did not die; it hibernated.

After announcing that no championship points would be awarded for the war's duration, the AAA reversed itself. Earl Cooper, who acquired his points by mid-season with wins on the dirt at Ascot, on the boards in Chicago, on cement at Minneapolis, and over Tacoma's planks, won his third national championship. Barney Oldfield set a slew of one- to fifty-mile records in his Miller-powered "Golden Submarine" at St. Louis, and Louis Chevrolet's Frontenac captured the 250-mile Memorial Day feature in Cincinnati. Lou Disbrow, Oldfield, and, for a short time, Eddie Hearne were suspended by the AAA for joining the International Motor Contest Association, which had been founded in 1915 (and still thrives today) by Mid-West State Fair Operators as a protest against it. Ira Vail and Ralph Mulford did surprisingly well racing their stock Hudsons, and Eddie Rickenbacker journeyed to England to pick up a new Sunbeam race car. But the popular Rick never had a chance to drive it, as shortly after his return he joined the Army with the intention of becoming General Pershing's driver. Rick never drove the general but apparently pestered him, with success, for a transfer to the Air Corps.

Driver millionaires now are routine, but none of today's superstars come close to matching Eddie Rickenbacker's accomplishments, wealth, or prestige. It would be difficult to find a more typical American folk hero than Rickenbacker (the first "h" became a "k" during the First World War). Rick's family had been poor, and he swept floors at the Firestone-Columbus Motor Buggy garage, where his diligence was rewarded when he was given a chance to race his employer's car. His racing career, from 1912 until November 30, 1916, lasted less than five years. His lifetime driving record shows seven wins in forty-one championship races, a good but not sensational achievement.

Rickenbacker was an obvious leader; owners sought him, and he usually had a choice of cars. His victories were made in Duesenbergs (2) and Maxwells (5), but he also drove Masons and, in two races, a Peugeot. The individualism that was to characterize his life asserted itself early when he turned "outlaw" and received an AAA suspension. He was reinstated with fanfare and later served as chairman of the AAA Contest Board.

His magnificent war record, accounting for twenty-six German planes in eight months, earned him the Congressional Medal of Honor, the Croix de Guerre, and the Legion of Honor. As captain of the 94th Squadron, with their famed "Hat in the Ring" symbol, Rick returned to an unmatched hero's welcome. He never raced again, but he remained active in the sport.

Rick was an auto maker from 1922 until 1927, when the "Hat in the Ring" trademark graced the Rickenbacker car. It was well made, said to have been priced too low for its quality, and when Rickenbacker closed his plant some of the design features of the Rickenbacker were sold to Audi in Germany.

Although he never won the 500—a tenth in 1914 was his only Indianapolis finish—as with most American race drivers, Rickenbacker looked to the Speedway as does a pilgrim to a sacred place.

After first approaching Tommy Milton, who was not interested, Carl Fisher sold the Indianapolis Motor

Examples of the 1930-38 Indianapolis "Junk" Formula that permitted production engines of up to 366 cubic inches. Cliff Bergere is in No. 28, a Reo-engined special that finished ninth in 1931, and Phil Shafer, No. 26, who drove his Buick-powered Special to a fifteenth-place finish in the 1934 500.

Eddie Rickenbacker with future driving star Eddie O'Donnell at the Speedway in 1914, where Rick's Duesenberg qualified twenty-third and finished tenth.

Speedway to Eddie Rickenbacker in August 1927. Of the original Speedway owners, Fisher, who had squandered several fortunes in his Miami Beach and Montauk Point land-development schemes, survived until 1939; Frank Wheeler, weary of ill-health, took his life in 1921; James Allison, whose plant is now a part of General Motors, died in 1928; and Arthur Newby passed on in 1933. The combination of hardheaded Hoosier businessmen and Fisher, a flamboyant visionary, had provided the American automobile with a showplace unmatched in the world of motor racing.

Rickenbacker's Speedway period was troubled first by the Depression following the Wall Street crash and, later, by World War II. Beginning with the sophisticated 91.5-cubic-inch supercharged Millers and Duesenbergs, Rick, in an attempt to broaden the appeal of the 500, in 1930 introduced the "junk formula" and, briefly, the return of the riding mechanic. As hoped for, American car makers responded with semistock race cars powered by non-supercharged 366-cubic-inch engines. The crowd-pleasing but hazardous business of reinstating the riding mechanic, banned from 1922, lasted from 1930 until 1937. Buick, Studebaker, Chrysler, Reo, Hudson, and others raced at the Speedway during the "junk formula," but none of them came close to winning the 500. Sadly, this period saw specialized European race cars pull farther ahead. There was little incentive during the Depression for a budding Duesenberg or Miller to build a thoroughbred American race car.

An Offenhauser engine first graced the Speedway's Victory Lane in 1935. A direct descendant of the Miller eight, the four-cylinder "Offy" stems from the supercharged four-cylinder hydroplane engine built by Miller in 1929. Shorty Cantlon had finished second in the 1930 Indianapolis driving a Miller four in a Stevens chassis, and Leo Goosen soon started his lifelong career of wringing more horses out of the venerable Miller-Offenhauser.

Fred Offenhauser, Miller's plant foreman, had bought the business from his boss in 1933, and in 1946 the engine plant was acquired by Dale Drake and the revered, three-time 500 winner Lou Meyer.

Rickenbacker ran the Speedway until 1946 with expert help from Wilbur Shaw. It was Shaw who arranged the sale of the then rundown Brickyard to its present owner, Tony Hulman. Rick's ordeal at sea during World War II and the iron-fisted, autocratic way he ran his major airline give the Rickenbacker legend the proportions of a Paul Bunyan.

Board speedways began their lethal reign in 1915. Two California tracks—the mile at Playa del Rey, which was destroyed by fire in 1913, and the half-mile at Elmhurst—were the first. But both were out of business before the board-track boom began.

Fred Moskcovics fathered the board idea. In a distinguished career that started on a drawing board at the Daimler works in Germany and saw him become president of Stutz, Moskcovics never lost his zest for racing.

During a trip to the Pacific Coast Moskcovics interested a group of Californians in building a race track in the Los Angeles area. Thinking of the speeds reached by bicycles as they whirled around their sharply banked wooden saucers, Moskcovics sold his associates on retaining former bicycle champion Jack Prince to build a board speedway. As a bicycle enthusiast Frederick E. Moskcovics had become friendly with Prince and knew that the Englishman was in America building bike-racing ovals.

Grant's Stutz leading Dave Evans out of the boarded Elks Tooth Turn in the 1917 Venice Grand Prix.

OVERLEAF: Stutz drivers Gil Anderson and Howdy Wilcox on the Chicago Board Speedway, June 1915.

Henry Ford (left) with the Speedway founders. From left to right, Arthur Newby, Frank Wheeler, Carl Fisher, and James Allison.

Barney Oldfield with the Miller "Golden Submarine."

Ralph Mulford's Frontenac, No. 9, and Tommy Milton's Duesenberg, No. 7, at the Uniontown boards, May 16, 1918.

Opening day at the new 1¼-mile Beverly Hills Board Speedway, February 29, 1920, with Ralph Mulford in the Duesenberg-Meteor, No. 12, and Jimmy Murphy and Tommy Milton in Duesenbergs Nos. 10 and 9. Murphy won the 250-mile inaugural with a 103-mph race average.

Ralph Mulford, No. 9, and Dario Resta, No. 19, both Peugeots, on the boards at Sheepshead Bay, Brooklyn, May 1916. Resta won with an 83.26-mph average for 300 miles.

The 1925 Indy 500 winner, Ralph DePalma's nephew Peter De-Paolo, on the boards at Culver City.

Three-time national champion Earl Cooper in Gasoline Alley at the wheel of Cliff Durant's Junior 8 (supercharged Miller) Special, which was driven to a second-place finish by Dave Lewis and Benny Hill in the 500 of 1925. Stutz's president, Fred Moskovics, is on the extreme right.

Typical of the damage suffered by board tracks, Atlantic City Speedway, 1928.

Al Rogers winning the 1949 Pikes Peak hill climb. The 12.5-mile run has 165 turns in total.

The start of the inaugural race at the Speedway, while it was still unpaved, August 19, 1909.

With their turns banked as sharply as 45 to 52 degrees (Daytona, for example, is 31 degrees), the majority of the twenty-three board tracks that opened between 1915 and 1926 measured between 1.25 and 2 miles. Constructed of sixteen-foot-long two-by-fours laid edge to edge, a mile-and-a-quarter track required over one million board feet of lumber.

Prince, a seat-of-the-pants designer, was later joined by Art Pillsbury, a trained engineer who served on the AAA Contest Board for many years.

The speedway era was truly launched at the opening of the two-mile Chicago Board Speedway on June 26, 1915. Dario Resta and DePalma, who had dueled for 500 miles at Indianapolis before DePalma won, drew an enormous crowd, eager to see the Mercedes and Peugeot renew their struggle. DePalma was sidelined, and Resta won the Chicago 500. The Peugeot's winning average was 97.58, almost 10 mph faster than DePalma's winning average at Indianapolis four weeks earlier.

Chicago, with its modest 19- and 29-degree banks, was only a beginning. Speeds soared as the bankings became sharper. Both Miller and Duesenberg began to make sleek, narrow, high-revving, small-engined race cars, the riding mechanic being dropped to improve the silhouette.

Rickenbacker won a 300-miler on the dirt at Sioux City with a 74.70-mph race average on July 3. Two days later he opened the board track at Omaha by winning over the same distance as Sioux City with a 91.74-mph average, and he drove the same Maxwell. Resta returned to Chicago on August 7, after DePalma's Packard had taken a 100-mile stock-car test on July 10, and he became the first driver in America to complete 100 miles in less than sixty minutes. His Peugeot averaged 101.86 mph.

Conventional paved tracks opened at Fort Snelling, Minnesota, and Narragansett Park in 1915, but racing fans could not get enough of the boards. Sheepshead Bay, in the New York City borough of Brooklyn, opened its parabolic two-mile bowl on October 9 and held another race on November 2. Anderson's Stutz averaged 102.60 mph to capture the 350-mile inaugural, and Resta recorded a 105.39-mph winning average. During World War I board-track construction halted, but Sheepshead Bay and Chicago each held two major meets in 1917 and 1918.

The one-mile Ascot track that opened in Los Angeles on April 15, 1915, and the five-eighths-mile Legion Ascot speedway that followed it may have trained more top-flight drivers than the flat-out racing over board tracks. Wooden ovals went up in Uniontown and Altoona, Pennsylvania, in Cincinnati and Kansas City. Fresno, Beverly Hills, Cotati, San Carlos, and Culver City opened board tracks in California. Board tracks opened in Charlotte, North Carolina, Rockingham, New Hampshire, Laurel, Maryland, and Miami. The fastest board track of all, and the last, was the Atlantic City Speedway, built in 1926.

Located midway between Philadelphia and Atlantic City in Hammonton, on the edge of New Jersey's Pine Barrens, the speedway was not in "Speedway," as the organizers said, nor in "Amatol," as shown in AAA records. And it surely was not in Atlantic City, twenty-eight miles east.

A foreword in the May 1, 1926, inaugural program states, "In six weeks five million feet of lumber have been converted into the world's greatest board speedway . . . the world's kings of speed introduce a sport new to this section of the country." Opposite the foreword is an advertisement for a Duesenberg sedan with coachwork by Charles Schutte under the headline "Out of the Crucible of Racing Has Come Commercial Perfection." And on the back cover is pictured a Stutz with the statement "The first lap of this race will be paced by the New Stutz Four-Passenger Speedster." On another page of the program Philadelphia's finest hotel, the Ritz-Carlton, tells of a special bus terminal provided for service "to and from the Speedway during trials, qualification and day of race." The track's major backer, Charles M. Schwab, president of Bethlehem Steel and a director of the Speedway Association, rode in the Stutz pace car with Fred Moskcovics.

Under "Foreign Drivers" are pictures of two handsomely dressed gentlemen, Count De Marguenat and Baron Vladimir de Rachewesky, "the two most famous drivers in all Europe." The reader is also informed that in 1923 the count "carried off the honors in the coveted French Grand Prix," that he and the baron were selected to represent France and Russia, and that "the Bugatti cars which these noblemen will pilot are owned by Charles M. Ward, assistant general manager of the Speedway who for many years has been a bosom friend of the two famous drivers."

Not only did the count not win the 1923 French Grand Prix—Segrave did—his name does not show as a starter, and neither De Marguenat nor Rachewesky appear in standard reference books on motor sport. On race day the Frenchman's Bugatti retired after eighteen laps, and the baron did not start at all. Harry Hartz's Miller earned $12,000 of the $40,000 purse after averaging 135.2 mph to win the 300-mile opener.

The May race, which had been a sellout, was followed by four shorter races on July 17, the day Earl Cooper drove a front-wheel-drive Miller to win the 200-mile feature at Rockingham. The Atlantic City Speedway continued to be busy. Four major events, including a twenty-four-hour Studebaker Stock Car Endurance Run and Frank Lockhart's 147.7-mph record-smashing 1.5-mile lap, were staged in 1927. Lockhart's Miller made Atlantic City the fastest of all speedways. Indianapolis

Louis Chevrolet driving a FIAT, New York, 1905.

did not reach Lockhart's speed for thirty-three years, when Jim Hurtibise qualified for the 500 of 1960 at 149.56 mph.

In 1928 at Atlantic City Fred Winnai's Duesenberg won on July 4; a Studebaker driven by Bergere, Gulotta, and Kreiger averaged 68.37 mph for 30,000 miles in August; and a 100-mile race was run in September. Then Amatol-Atlantic City-Hammonton, the world's fastest race track, closed for good.

It was difficult and expensive to maintain a board track in raceworthy condition. Constant exposure to the elements combined with the pounding of race cars shredded the surface. Splintered fragments of lumber and gaps in the planking became routine hazards. Many remedies were tried, but nothing worked except regularly scheduled major repairs. During the Depression money was tight, crowds fell off, and the era ended with the Roaring Twenties. The boards were deprived, by less than a half mile an hour, of the closed-course, one-mile record when Lockhart's mark fell in June 1928 as Leon Duray, born George Stewart, turned a 148.17-mph lap with his front-wheel-drive Miller over the 2.5-mile Packard proving ground, a concrete oval.

None of the Chevrolet brothers ever won the national championship, although in 1917 Louis Chevrolet was only fifty-four points behind Earl Cooper. Louis was born in Switzerland in 1878. His younger brothers, Arthur and Gaston, were born in France in 1886 and 1896, in the pleasant village of Béaune, the wine capital of Burgundy. After working in the shops of several early car builders, including that of De Dion-Bouton, Louis migrated to Montreal in 1900. In France he had invented a pump for Vintners and, prophetically, made and raced bicycles, which he called Frontenacs. Louis stayed in Canada a few months, then came to New York and worked at the De Dion branch in Brooklyn. Two years later he joined E. R. Hollander, FIAT's American agent, as a mechanic. In May 1905 he drove a 90-hp FIAT in the one-mile time trial and three-mile Free-for-All at Morris Park in the Bronx, winning both races. Then Hollander entered him in the 1905 Vanderbilt Cup. Chevrolet crashed the big FIAT during practice. A customer's smaller 75-hp model was found as a replacement, but after moving up through the field a wheel failed, and he wrecked the second FIAT.

In 1906 Louis left FIAT for Walter Christie, where he helped build a front-wheel-drive Christie powered by a Darracq engine. At Ormond Beach the following year he, Victor Hemery, and Victor Demogeot raced the Christie-Darracq, achieving near record-breaking times of 120 mph. Then W. C. Durant, founder of General Motors, hired both Louis and Arthur Chevrolet to race and contribute their mechanical talents to the newly acquired Buick division.

In the same year Louis raced a Buick in the Vanderbilt Cup. He set the fastest lap, 76.3 mph, and was leading when a cracked cylinder forced him to retire. The 1910 Vanderbilt saw Louis again earn the fastest-lap honors, but again he failed to finish.

In 1909 Louis Chevrolet drove a Buick at the Indianapolis Speedway. On August 19, following a one-mile demonstration by Barney Oldfield's Benz, and Lou Schweitzer's win with Stoddard-Dayton in a five-mile dash for under 230-cubic-inch engines, Chevrolet captured the ten-mile sprint. He also entered the inaugural-day feature event, the 250-mile Prest-O-Lite Trophy race, which he led until a stone shattered his goggles and injured an eye.

After Durant lost control of General Motors in 1910 he retained Louis Chevrolet to design a new car that was to use his name. The first Chevrolet, the 1912 model, was a quality touring car. Durant is said to have put pressure on Chevrolet to produce a smaller, lower-priced machine to compete with Ford's Model T. Durant regained control of General Motors in 1916, but before that he and Louis Chevrolet had parted, Chevrolet selling his interest to Durant for a fraction of what the stock was soon to be worth.

Chevrolet then became associated with Albert Champion, the fiery French-born founder of the Champion and AC Spark Plug companies, who backed Louis in the building of his Frontenac race cars. Following poor showings in mid-season, Louis drove the Frontenac to the first of its many major triumphs, on December 2, 1916. By this time, however, Chevrolet had quarreled with Champion and was on his own.

Seven Frontenacs qualified for the 1920 Indianapolis. Four of these cars were entered as Monroes (William Small of Monroe having paid a large enough sum for them to enable Chevrolet to make three for himself). Five fell out with identical steering-arm failures, but Gaston Chevrolet drove his Frontenac to a win after race leader DePalma ran out of fuel.

The year 1920 was a successful but tragic one for the Chevrolet brothers. Arthur was seriously injured during practice for the 500. Then on Thanksgiving Day Gaston and Eddie O'Donnell touched on the boards of the elaborate new Beverly Hills Speedway. Behind Sarles's Duesenberg by five laps, O'Donnell, Chevrolet, and Joe Thomas were tightly bunched as they swept into the east turn. Eyewitness accounts say the Frontenac ticked O'Donnell's Duesenberg as Chevrolet swung wide to pass Thomas, who was on the inside. The twenty-eight-year-old Gaston Chevrolet was killed instantly. Eddie O'Donnell died the following day. Roscoe Searles, who drove without a stop, had gone on to win the race.

Six Frontenacs were in the twenty-three-car field for the 1921 Indianapolis. Two of the six were new eight-cylinder models entered by Louis Chevrolet for Ralph Mulford and Tommy Milton. Four-cylinder Frontenacs had won the prior year, but Louis Chevrolet realized that the Ballot and Duesenberg eights were potentially faster. Milton won the 500 with an 89.62-mph average. Percy Ford, Andy Burt, and Jules Ellingboe took turns driving a Frontenac four to a third-place finish, and Mulford finished ninth in the second eight.

Attracted by the Frontenac's success, A. A. Ryan, a Stutz director, engaged Louis Chevrolet to build a deluxe Frontenac touring car to compete with the Duesenberg passenger models. Louis, working with Cornelius Willett Van Ranst, the young engineer responsible for the four- and eight-cylinder Frontenac engines, started building the passenger car in a new plant in Indianapolis. Business was bad, however. The corporation papers made him financially responsible, and in April 1923 Louis Chevrolet was forced into bankruptcy.

Van Ranst's idea to build special cylinder heads for Model-T Fords gave Louis Chevrolet his most sustained success. Beginning late in 1920 and for the next four-

The Louis Chevrolet Cornelian. The only one made, it ran in the 1915 500 as No. 27.

teen years, the small Chevrolet brothers' plant in Indianapolis produced thousands of the most widely used heads in the history of racing.

Fronty-Fords dominated dirt-track racing. Several, including one driven in 1924 by Alfred Moss, father of Stirling Moss, raced at the Speedway. As late as 1930 a Fronty-Ford, prepared by Arthur Chevrolet and driven by Chet Miller, finished thirteenth in the 500 in spite of a forty-one-minute pit stop to replace a broken spring.

In *The Golden Age of the American Racing Car* Griff Borgeson states that in 1933, when work was hard to find, Louis Chevrolet was said to have taken a mechanic's job in a Chevrolet plant. We do know that Louis Chevrolet failed to prosper in his later years. He did some work on marine and aircraft engines, but he was in poor health for some time prior to his death in 1941.

The first one-mile dirt track built specially for automobile racing was Langhorne. In 1926 a group of Philadelphians calling themselves the National Motor Racing Association paid $27,000 for eighty-nine marshy acres on the old Lincoln Highway between Pendel and Langhorne, fifteen miles north of Philadelphia. For many years the fastest dirt track in the country and always

one of the most hazardous, Langhorne passed through several ownerships until Ralph Hankinson, a showman famed for promoting state-fair auto racing, took over.

The first major race at Langhorne was won by twenty-year-old Fred Winnai, an unknown who later became a national star. Winnai may have had an unusual advantage at Langhorne: He had driven the bulldozer that carved the track.

Hankinson sold the track to Lucky Teter, who planned to use it as headquarters for his "Hell Drivers" as well as for racing. Teter died in 1942 when he failed to complete one of his ramp-to-ramp jumps, after which the track lay idle until 1946, when John Babcock bought it for his sons. Langhorne was then sold to its final owners, Al Gerber and Irv Fried, two competent businessmen who had run the concessions at the Yellow Jacket Stadium, the defunct Philadelphia Shrine of Midget Racing. Gerber and Fried promoted every type of racing, refurbished the twenty-year-old plant, and prospered.

Although many Indianapolis winners raced at Langhorne, prominent drivers, including Wilbur Shaw, Rodger Ward, and A. J. Foyt, all former winners at the Horne, refused to return to the oddly shaped, rutted mile. Lang-

Henry Ford in Fred Harder's Barber-Warnock Frontenac, seventeenth-place finisher in the 500 of 1924. In the photo: Louis Chevrolet, third from left; Barney Oldfield stands behind Ford, next to helmeted driver Harder; the AAA's Kennerdell in cap; Edsel Ford; and, in the flat top hat, Harry Stutz.

horne was paved in 1965, but the new surface managed to retain the dirt's strange humps and hollows.

By the time Bobby Unser won Langhorne's 1969 and 1970 championship-car races, lap times were reaching 130 mph, and drivers said it was like racing on ice. USAC championship drivers boycotted the 1971 race, twenty of their mates having earlier ended their careers there. In 1972 the Horne began its descent into a shopping center.

The end of board speedways and the almost total extinction of road racing made dirt tracks the standard race course of the 1930s. With the conspicuous exception of Indianapolis, AAA national championships were decided at state fairgrounds on tracks designed for horse racing. The Wisconsin State Fairgrounds near Milwaukee, first used by race cars in 1903, is the nation's oldest operative automobile race track. It was not used continuously, however, that honor being claimed by Indianapolis alone. Milwaukee began as a horse-racing oval in 1891. It had been the home of exhibitions, match races, and time trials, and in 1907 and 1908 twenty-four-hour races were staged there. Barney Oldfield set a fifty-six-second-mile record in 1905 and twelve years later returned in his Miller-powered Golden Submarine to beat Ralph DePalma's Packard Special.

There was little action on Milwaukee's dirt during the board-speedway boom, but from 1930 until now it has remained a fixture on the championship trail. The track was paved in 1954.

No one knows how many dirt tracks there were in the Thirties, nor for that matter how many there are now. It's a good guess that a thousand dust-filled, quarter-mile or less bullrings pock the earth near small towns of the Midwest alone. Chris Economaki, whose *National Speed Sport News* each week reports the best of oval-track racing, says, "Any summer weekend when the sun shines, at least 1800 meets are held on 1230 tracks. And that does not include drag racing."

At the top of the dirt-track race-car hierarchy are the "Big Cars" used in USAC-sanctioned events. Similar to the front-engined Indianapolis roadster, championship dirt-track cars have a slightly shorter wheel base and a higher center of gravity. A good number of sprint-car championships are run on dirt, as are a majority of midget races. Once away from the national championships, modified and supermodified, two terms subject to a bewildering array of definitions, cover the majority of cars raced on the smaller tracks by less prestigious sanctioning bodies.

The supermodified racers of the 1970s are usually open, although they have recently sprouted roll cages. Modified cars are sedans, usually lightened, strengthened, older models with improved handling, housing a finely tuned, sophisticated V-8 engine. What appears to be a shabby jalopy most often is a quite sanitary race car.

Racing on dirt tracks is the most hazardous form of a hazardous sport. It takes more stamina, an equal amount of talent, and more guts than driving on a paved surface that is often three times faster. It is a kidney-jarring, dust-filled nightmare, yet many top drivers will tell you that it is fun to drive and that the dirt is their favorite surface.

Tommy Milton, Jimmy Murphy, Frank Lockhart, Duesenberg, and Miller: Proper heroes and magic machines, the most evocative names in American racing.

Born in 1893, Milton overcame a sightless left eye (he passed driver physicals by memorizing eye charts) and a near fatal crash to live a rewarding life.

Two years Milton's junior, Murphy's tragically brief career was highlighted by two national championships, victories at Indianapolis and in the French Grand Prix. Frank Lockhart started racing in California in 1924. He won the 1926 Indianapolis 500 on his first visit to the Speedway, set several new speed records, invented a cooling device that greatly improved the performance of supercharged engines, and was killed during a record attempt at Daytona in April 1928.

Tommy Milton first raced in 1913, driving his own Mercer in an Alex Sloan barnstorming tour. Following several seasons of "arranged" finishes, during which he was obliged to let the better-known drivers "win," young Tommy lost patience, stormed to an unscheduled victory, and was fired.

After World War I Milton captained the Duesenberg team and in August 1919 won the 301-mile Elgin road race. A week later, at Uniontown, he crashed and burned on the boards and was hospitalized for five months.

The winner of the race in which Milton was injured was Joe Boyer, one of the best and, as heir to the Burroughs Adding Machine fortune, one of the wealthiest drivers of his time. With Slim Corum, Boyer won the 1924 Indianapolis, but two months after winning the 500 he lost his life on the boards at Altoona.

While mending, Milton helped to design a twin-engined Duesenberg record car. On April 27, 1920, he set a one-mile straightaway record of 156 mph at Daytona. That year Milton captured the first of his two consecutive national driving titles, finishing third in the 500, one place ahead of his protégé and former riding mechanic, Jimmy Murphy. Milton's Frontenac won the 1921 Indianapolis. He dropped out of the 1922 classic with a loose gas tank, but in 1923 he won the 500 again driving the HCS Miller Special.

Milton's overseas venture almost matched that of Murphy's when, despite a balky gearbox that kept his Miller stuck in top gear, he led the 1925 Italian Grand Prix at the halfway mark. A twenty-minute pit stop to repair a broken oil line ruined his chance of winning, but he finished fourth. In 1927 after a period of semi-

Start of the July 4, 1939, AAA stock-car race at Langhorne Speedway.

OVERLEAF: Action on the one-mile Langhorne dirt track.

Master builders (left to right) Louis Chevrolet, Harry Miller, Fred and Augie Duesenberg at the Speedway, 1923.

The five-eighths-mile Ascot dirt track, 1927.

retirement, Milton drove Cliff Durant's Miller-powered front-wheel-drive Detroit Special at the Speedway. Relieved in turn by Leon Duray (during his barnstorming days Alex Sloan changed George Stewart's name to Leon Duray to cash in on Arthur Duray's popularity), Cornelius Van Ranst, and Ralph Hepburn, the Miller finished eighth. A clear-thinking, articulate man, Tommy Milton remained in automobile racing as an official, ran a successful business, and then worked as a consultant to several car makers.

The story of Jimmy Murphy is another of racing's "rags to riches" tales. In the best Alger tradition, orphan Jimmy made himself useful around a racing garage in California, where he was born in 1895. Following rides as a mechanic with Eddie O'Donnell and Tommy Milton, Murphy first drove at Uniontown on Labor Day 1919. The following year he won his first major victory at Beverly Hills, in February, when his Duesenberg averaged 103 mph for 250 miles.

In 1921 Murphy's triumph in the French Grand Prix became a milestone in American racing. Not until Dan Gurney and his All American Racers' Eagle (Anglo American was the name used by Gurney in Europe until 1968, when he closed his shop in England) did an American car and driver combination capture a championship Grand Prix.

That the Duesenberg team raced in the French GP was largely the work of W. F. Bradley, the French-based English journalist who clearly rated his "dean of motor racing writers" laurels. A reporter for English and American publications, onetime staff member of Gordon Bennett's Paris *Herald,* overseas representative for American racing organizations, and, conversely, a

frequent manager of European racing teams at Indianapolis, Bradley played a role in motor sports on both sides of the Atlantic for fifty years. He witnessed the start of the 1903 Paris–Madrid and, with Paris as his base, covered Europe during racing's formative years.

In 1913 the Indianapolis Speedway appointed Bradley its European agent. During World War I he worked for the U.S. Army aircraft supply mission in France and in 1919 began acting as the AAA Contest Board representative to the Association Internationale des Automobile Clubs Reconnus. The AIACR was the forerunner of the post-World War II Fédération Internationale de l'Automobile (FIA).

Bradley's first job for the Speedway was to round up European machines and drivers for the 1913 Indy. The Speedway fathers had the right idea. The addition of first-class overseas talent is a sports-writer's bonanza and traditionally has helped to build record-breaking gates.

Much of the advance made by American race cars following World War I can be credited to the Speedway's wisdom in acquiring two 1914 Peugeots. Concerned over a possible lack of competition due to the war, the Speedway spirited the Grand Prix Peugeots to Indianapolis, where they served as models for the three Premier race cars, precise replicas of the 4.5-liter, 274.59-cubic-inch DOHC French racer. Of the GP Peugeots raced by Dario Resta and Bob Burman, says Griff Borgeson, "engine and chassis were the textbooks for Harry Miller and Fred Offenhauser."

It was Bradley who had convinced Georges Boillot to send the Peugeots to Indianapolis in 1913, where Jules Goux won and Zuccarelli finished twenty-second.

Frank S. Lockhart, winner of the 1926 rain-shortened 500 on his first trip to the Speed-way, in the Peter Kries Miller Special.

Touring circus at Brighton Beach for the night racing, 1915.

The three Speedway-owned Premiers that were driven in 1916 by (left to right) Tom Rooney, Howdy Wilcox, and Gil Anderson. These Peugeot copies were painted green, a color that was to be shunned in later years. In the 1916 500 Wilcox finished seventh, Anderson broke an oil line, and Rooney was in an accident.

It was also he who made arrangements for the four Duesenbergs in the 1921 French Grand Prix. Two of the slim, straight eights were intended for French drivers Guyot and Inghibert, the remaining two for Joe Boyer and Murphy. Rated at 183 cubic inches—three liters—the same displacement limitations applied to both Indianapolis and Grand Prix cars in 1921. Where the gleaming blue and white Dusies may have had an advantage was in their hydraulically operated four-wheel brakes, said by some historians to have been among the first to be seen on a European circuit.

In spite of the Duesenberg's late entry (for which Albert Champion advanced Fred Duesenberg an astronomical 86,500 francs) the American team was the best prepared in the 1921 French GP. Managed by 1908 Vanderbilt Cup winner George Robertson, who had served in France as a lieutenant colonel, with Augie Duesenberg himself looking after the cars, the Americans had a formidable crew.

The seven Anglo-French Sunbeam-Talbot-Darracq cars were in such a state of unpreparedness that the factory withdrew them. Four drivers, however—André Boillot, Réné Thomas, Lee Guinness, and Henry Segrave, who was appearing in his first major race—bought or "borrowed" the cars, and they became private entries.

During practice Murphy damaged himself and Inghibert, who was riding with him, more severely than he did the Duesenberg, after a brake locked and he crashed. Murphy had his ribs taped. However, Inghibert could not drive, so his Duesenberg went to André Dubonnet, who is said to have offered substantial inducements to get the ride. As Dubonnet was one of the original Sunbeam drivers and as another, Count Zborowski, withdrew when his machine was not ready for practice, the only Sunbeam-Talbot-Darracq driver to miss

the French Grand Prix was one of the most deserving, Dario Resta. The favored team was the Ballots, driven by Ralph DePalma, Jules Goux, Louis Wagner, and Jean Chassagne.

At 9:00 a.m. on July 26, 1921, paired cars began leaving at thirty-second intervals to cover thirty laps over the 10.75-mile "short" Le Mans circuit. Ralph DePalma, with his nephew Peter DePaolo as his riding mechanic, and Joe Boyer's Duesenberg recorded identical eight-minute, twenty-one-second fastest first laps. But it was to be Jimmy Murphy's day. He led for twenty-three of the thirty laps, set the fastest race lap—seven minutes and forty-three seconds, 83.40 mph—and after four hours and seven minutes finished fifteen minutes ahead of DePalma with a 78.22 race average. As the winning Duesenberg crossed the finish line, the large crowd in the grandstand sat on their hands. Lautenschlager had won the last Grand Prix run at Lyon in 1914, and the French were bitter over another foreign victory.

Murphy returned home after the race, and DePalma journeyed to Brescia to drive the Ballot in September. Murphy bought the French GP winner from Duesenberg, switched to a Miller engine, and entered the Duesenberg-Miller at Indianapolis as the Murphy Special. He qualified for the 500 at 100.50 mph and won with a 94.48-mph race average, breaking the Speedway record set by DePalma in 1915 by almost 5 mph. Murphy clinched the AAA 1922 national championship with a win on the boards at Beverly Hills in December and in 1923 captained a team of six Miller-engined Durant Specials.

Murphy won again at Beverly Hills and at Fresno and finished behind Tommy Milton and Harry Hartz at Indianapolis. In September Jimmy returned to Europe to drive a new car for Harry Miller in the Italian Grand

Start of the 1920 Elgin road race: DePalma is in the Ballot, No. 2, and Jimmy Murphy in the Duesenberg, No. 12.

Front row at the 1922 Indianapolis: Jimmy Murphy, No. 35 (on pole), Harry Hartz, No. 12, and Ralph De-Palma, No. 17. Murphy finished first, Hartz second, and DePalma third.

Starting grid for the 1921 French Grand Prix at Le Mans; Jimmy Murphy is in Duesenberg No. 12.

Ernie Olsen, seated next to Jimmy Murphy, waves for the Ballot to give way as Ralph DePalma grins. The Americans finished first and second.

Murphy gets the checkered flag, becoming the first American to win the French Grand Prix in an American car.

Prix at the recently opened Monza Autodrome. As the Monza track, a 6.2-mile combination of what was then a modestly banked oval and road course, was constructed within a high-walled former royal park, the Italian organizers were able to collect admissions from all who watched the races, not only those who sat in the grandstand, as was the almost universal European custom. With large crowds expected from nearby Milan, substantial prize money, equal to that paid in the United States, was offered in Europe for the first time.

Driven by Murphy, Count Louis Zborowski (an English citizen whose mother and wife were American), and an Argentine millionaire, M. Alzaga, the Millers were two-liter, 122-cubic-inch DOC straight eights with four valves per cylinder. At half distance Murphy lay fourth, four minutes behind Bordino's FIAT; Zborowski had retired and Alzaga was last. However, Monza was not to be Le Mans, and the best Murphy could do was pick up one position to finish third. Murphy was nosed out of the 1923 driving title by Eddie Hearne. He had finished third at Indianapolis and had won three broad-track features at Altoona, Kansas City, and again at Altoona. Racing with "Cowboy" Phil Shafer for the lead in a 100-mile championship at the Syracuse Fairgrounds in September 1924, Murphy flipped and was injured

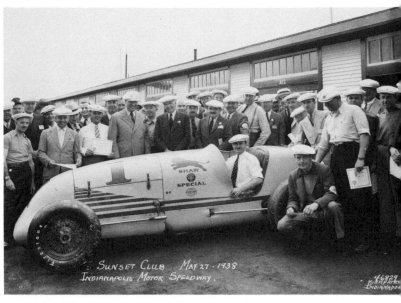

Sunset Club, May 27, 1938. Wilbur Shaw at the wheel of his 1937 500-winning Gilmore Special, as Peter De Paolo, Colonel Harrington of the AAA, Speedway owner Eddie Rickenbacker (in stiff straw), and Harry Hartz form part of one of the group's annual meetings in Gasoline Alley.

Jimmy Murphy in the Miller-Durant Special that finished third in the 1923 500.

fatally. He had acquired sufficient points to win his second national championship without Syracuse.

Lou Meyer and Wilbur Shaw, the first and second members of the superselect society of three-time Indianapolis 500 winners (Mauri Rose and A. J. Foyt are the others), had an impact on American racing that went well beyond their racing years. Meyer was born in 1904, and the first contest in his twelve-year racing career was at the Speedway in 1927, when he drove forty laps in relief for Wilbur Shaw. He earned the first of his three national championships in 1928, the second in 1929, and the third in 1933. Reversing the usual career pattern, Meyer did not race on dirt until 1930, following his first two national titles. His 1928 and 1933 Indianapolis victories were in Miller eights, but in the 1936 race, which he captured with a record-smashing 109.069-mph average, he prophetically won in a four-cylinder Miller.

Meyer retired in 1939, after smacking the wall at Indy, and, with Dale Drake, purchased the rights to manufacture the Offenhauser engine. Meyer severed his partnership in 1964 to supervise the Indianapolis engine-building program of the Ford Motor Company.

A native Hoosier, Wilbur Shaw was born near Indianapolis in October 1902. His first racing was on the dirt in 1920, and his initial appearance at the Speedway was in 1927. With few AAA-sanctioned events during the Depression, Shaw turned "outlaw" and was refused an entry for the 1929 Indianapolis. The 91.5 supercharged single-seater formula was abandoned in 1929, and the riding mechanic briefly returned. Shaw introduced the crash helmet in 1933 and began to concentrate on the Indianapolis 500. His first Indy victory came in 1937, driving an Offenhauser-powered special he had helped to build. Shaw had back-to-back wins at the Speedway in 1939 and 1940, driving a supercharged Maserati. While aiming for his third straight Indy win in 1941, a wheel collapsed and Shaw hit the wall on the 151st lap, still in contention.

Shaw, keenly interested in road racing, had gone to Monza with Leon Duray in 1932. He raced in the 1936 and 1937 Vanderbilt Cup revivals at Roosevelt Raceway, Long .Island, near the site of the original course. Although he failed to finish in 1936 and his Maserati wound up eighth in 1937, Shaw's Roosevelt Raceway experience was to reshape his career. Admiring a late-model Maserati after the race, Shaw told Chicago sportsman Mike Boyle that he thought he could win the 500 in such a car. A deal was made, and Shaw's double 500 winner, the Boyle Special, occupies an honored spot in the Speedway Museum.

Disturbed over the condition of the Speedway following World War II, Shaw was instrumental in persuading Tony Hulman to buy the then rundown plant. He was appointed Indianapolis Motor Speedway president in 1946, and, until his death in 1954, he traveled constantly as a spokesman for the Speedway and racing in general. He had been a pilot for twenty-five years when he and his two companions, pilot Roy Grimes and auto racing artist Ernest Roose, crashed in a cornfield near Decatur, Indiana, on October 30, 1954. The fatal accident occurred one day before Shaw's fifty-second birthday.

Following World War II new men turned the sport around. Bill France shaped the crowd-pleasing popular world of stock-car racing. Road racing was to enjoy a postwar boom, and drag racing would find respectability and popularity as it moved from the streets to the strips.

The Road Racing Renaissance

VI

Although road racing in the United States came close to a complete stop in the 1920s and early 1930s, a few American cars and a trickle of American drivers continued to appear in Europe.

A French-owned Chrysler ran in the 1925 Le Mans, and French owners drove a 3.9-liter (238-cubic-inch) Willys Knight and two smaller-engined Overlands in the 1926 twenty-four-hours. One Overland was damaged in practice, and the remaining Toledo cars broke down during the race.

However, the 1928 Le Mans came close to being an American show. A 4.9-liter Stutz, in the hands of Edouard Brisson and R. Bloch, finished a close second to the winning Bentley as French drivers brought Chryslers home third and fourth.

In the 1929 Le Mans, one of three Stutzes was fifth, with Chryslers sixth and seventh. The sixth-place Chrysler, with its 4.1-liter engine, also earned third in that year's "index of performance" category.

Stutz and Chrysler made occasional appearances at Le Mans during the 1930s, as did a Duesenberg, in the royal hands of Rumania's Prince Nicholas, in 1933 and 1935.

Zborowski continued to campaign his 1923 Miller in European Grand Prix until his death in a Mercedes at Monza in 1924. In 1925 the Monza promoters again attracted that year's winner of the 500, Peter DePaolo, as well as Tommy Milton and Peter Kries. To DePaolo went the honor of driving the Alfa Romeo originally slated for Antonio Ascari. After a long pit stop DePaolo finished fifth, with Milton's Duesenberg fourth. Kries withdrew early, but not until he had set a 103.2-mph fastest lap. Milton, who had stalled at the start and was forced to fight a balky gear box, and DePaolo had both been serious threats. The 1927 Italian Grand Prix saw 1927 Indianapolis winner George Souders bring his Duesenberg 8 to Monza accompanied by Cooper and Kries in Miller-powered Cooper Specials. Fresh out of Purdue University, Souders won the 500 on his first trip to the Speedway. It rained at Monza on September 4, 1927, and the American's performance, although Souders ran in second place for the first twelve laps,

seemed to reflect their uneasiness over racing in the wet.

In 1929 Leon Duray (George Stewart) a showman in the Oldfield tradition, as well as one of the fastest men of his time, took with him to Europe two front-wheel-drive Millers, the Packard Cable Specials. Pole winner of the 1925 Indianapolis, in which he finished sixth, Duray was at his best setting flat-out records over sharply banked ovals. Partially subsidized by Cord to popularize the front-wheel-drive principle in Europe, the big, black-suited Duray and his slim 91-cubic-inch, 1500-cc, supercharged Millers caused a sensation. Duray set new five- and ten-mile records at Montlhery, outside Paris. A month later at Monza for the Italian Grand Prix he made the fastest lap and led in each of the two heats, driving different cars in each heat, only to retire with suspension and other ailments.

European constructors were beside themselves. The French and Italian press ridiculed them for being humiliated by a tiny-engined American car, but race fans overseas were enthralled by the flamboyant Duray and his handsome machines.

Ettore Bugatti did something about it. He gave Duray three type-43 Bugattis and cash for the two Millers. Duray returned to the United States and became a Bugatti dealer just long enough to sell the three cars. Bugatti went to school on the Millers, and Bugatti's type 50, which appeared in 1930, was Molsheim's first with double overhead cams. Duray had helped American builders repay their debt to the 1914 Peugeot; it was American racing's "Lafayette, we are here."

The occasional European junket of Indianapolis drivers became increasingly rare. Phil Shafer, a consistent front-runner in the 500, brought his Buick 8 Special to the Nurburgring for the 1931 German Grand Prix. It rained, the Buick had suspension troubles, and Shafer retired at the two-thirds mark.

Peter DePaolo kept his family tradition alive (Uncle Ralph had raced in three French Grand Prix) with frequent overseas appearances. National champion in 1925 and 1927, winner of the 1925 Indianapolis with a record 101.13-mph average, the diminutive DePaolo

109

came out of retirement in 1934 to drive a Miller in the Grand Prix of Tripoli. He was joined by Lou Moore, whose Indy record included two 3rds and a 2nd, and by Ernie Olsen, who had been Jimmy Murphy's mechanic when he won the French Grand Prix. The Americans, singled out by General Balbo, the Governor of Tripoli and Italian Air Minister, were lavishly entertained. After taking Balbo for a ride around the Grand Prix course, DePaolo, in his amusing autobiography, *Wall Smacker,* tells how the Governor challenged him to a race, and won, when he flew around the circuit just a few feet over the top of DePaolo's car. From Africa the touring Yanks went to Berlin and raced at Avus, where De- Paolo's Miller lost its engine at the halfway mark while running in second place. DePaolo then made arrange- ments, through Bradley, to drive a Maserati in the Grand Prix of Spain. During practice at Barcelona DePaolo hit a curb. He avoided the spectators, but the accident ended his racing career. Seventy-five on April 15, 1973, Peter DePaolo remembered how he had told his famed Uncle Ralph that he had better switch to Barney Oldfield's tires if he wanted to start winning again. But DePalma's feelings toward Barney were too strong, so young DePaolo quit as his uncle's riding mechanic to race his own cars. Asked if he would like

to race one of today's cars, DePaolo, looking as trim and handsome as in his championship days, said, "If I was racing now I'd concentrate on the 500-milers and run road races the rest of the time."

During the Duesenberg–Miller era Great Britain al- most ignored American race cars. It was extremely rare to find an American car competing in the English events. In the late 1920s a Stutz raced at Brooklands and in the Tourist Trophy. A Graham-Paige finished second in another meet at Brooklands, and in 1935 Gwenda Hawkes pushed her Derby-Miller to new ladies' records both at Montlhery and Brooklands.

American-born, English-educated Whitney Straight interrupted his Cambridge years to participate in and to form a professional racing team that included such outstanding drivers as Dick Seaman and Buddy Feather- stonehaugh. Straight himself won and placed well in several Grand Prix, but increasingly he devoted his energies to flying. Following a distinguished career in the RAF, he became managing director of BOAC and later joined Rolls-Royce. Although his driving was largely in Maseratis and MGs at Brooklands, in 1933 Straight raced the 4376-cc Duesenberg Special that had been built for Count Trossi.

It was the mid-1950s before Yank drivers began show-

Leon Duray (George Stewart) in the Packard Cable Special, a front-wheel-drive Miller, that qualified second for the 1929 Indy at 119.087 mph.

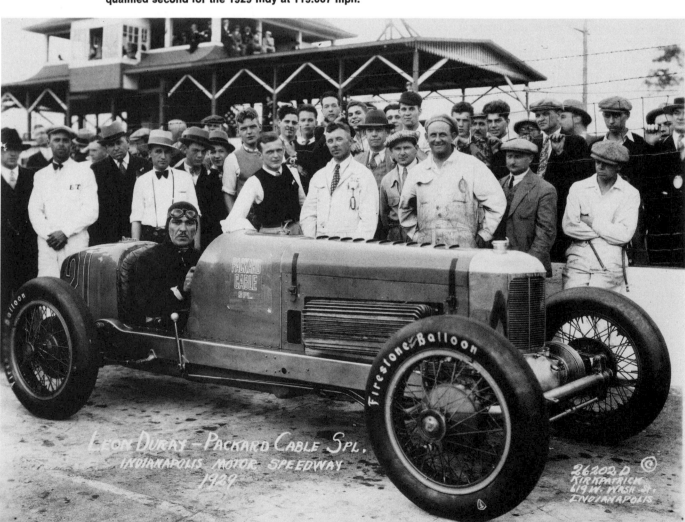

The DeVere/Mangin Chrysler which finished second in the 1928 24 Hours at Spa, Belgium.

ing any sign of the force they were to become in European racing.

A ripple of road-racing interest appeared in widely separate parts of America in the early 1930s. Fred Frames's Ford and Phil Shafer's Buick Special each won 203-mile features at Elgin when the Midwest classic enjoyed a revival in 1932 and 1933. In California, Stubby Stubblefield's Ford took a 250-mile road race for stock cars held in February 1934 over a 1.9-mile course in Long Beach. And in December of that year, 50,000 spectators watched Kelly Petillo win a 200-mile road race held at the Los Angeles airport, then known as Mines Field. The following year Petillo won the 500.

A far-reaching event took place at Daytona Beach on March 8, 1936. Disturbed by the exodus of land speed record challengers to the Salt Flats of Utah, the city fathers turned for help to a former Beach record holder, Sig Haugdahl. What was needed, they said, was a race that would continue to attract visitors and keep Daytona's cash registers jingling. Haugdahl's solution was wonderfully simple. He measured off 1.5 miles on the beach, a corresponding 1.5 miles of the narrow blacktop that paralleled the beach, U.S. Route A-I, and joined them by cutting two one-tenth-mile connecting roads through the sand.

The AAA sanctioned a 250-mile road race for stock automobiles, and a $5000 purse helped to pull a good, although uneven, entry to Daytona. Led by 1934 Indianapolis winner Bill Cummings, the field included dirt-track stars Doc Mackenzie and Bob Sall, midget champion Bill Schindler, and England's Major Goldie Gardner. Also entered were two young sports-car drivers, Sam and Miles Collier, and a tall twenty-seven-year-old Virginian who was working in a Daytona gas station. It was 1938 before the lanky young mechanic became one of the Daytona promoters, but what Bill France learned on the beach was to reshape American automobile racing.

Bill Cummings' Auburn qualified fastest with a respectable 70.39-mph lap, but times fell sharply in the race itself as the two connecting chutes were churned into impassable quagmires. When the overworked tow trucks could no longer keep the course open, the race was stopped at 200 miles with Milt Marion the winner. The first five finishers drove Fords, including Bill France, who came in fifth. Course conditions improved for the 1937 Daytona race when marl, a clay and calcium fertilizer, was spread in the chutes. Another popular attraction, the 200-mile motorcycle race that was to become a Daytona fixture, began that year. By 1959, when

Milt Marion's Ford winning the 250-mile beach and road race, Daytona Beach, March 1936.

Big Bill France, now the czar of stock-car racing, moved the beach races to his spectacular Daytona International Speedway, the late-model stock car had begun to rival traditional Indianapolis machines as the American race fan's favorite.

The October 12, 1936, and July 5, 1937, Vanderbilt Trophy races held at Roosevelt Raceway, Westbury, Long Island, were *not* revivals of the 1904–1916 series. The Roosevelt Raceway promoters, who included George "Wet Wash" Marshall, owner of the Washington Redskins professional football team, located George Vanderbilt, a distant kin of Willie K.'s, in order to cash in legitimately on the prestigious reputation of the original Vanderbilt Cup series. Also the award was to be known as the Vanderbilt Trophy, not the Vanderbilt Cup, and it came from Cartier rather than Tiffany.

Substantial prize money—$20,000 for first, $10,000 for second, $5000 for third, down to $1400 for the tenth prize, plus lap-leader awards, pulled the best of European and American cars and drivers. In 1936 the immortal Tazio Nuvolari, even then considered the greatest of all drivers, was teamed with Antonio Brivio and Giuseppe Farina in the supercharged Alfa Romeos of Scuderia Ferrari. From France came Raymond Sommer's Alfa and Jean-Pierre Wimille's type-59 Bugatti. Earl Howe, Major Goldie Gardner, and Pat Fairfield represented England.

The cream of American drivers accepted the 1936 Vanderbilt Trophy challenge in cars pitifully unsuited to racing on a tight, sixteen-turn road course. Among the Americans were three Indianapolis winners—Wilbur Shaw, Mauri Rose, and Bill Cummings—as well as Rex Mays, Shorty Cantlon, Ted Horn, Red Schafer, Henry Banks, Billy Winn, George Connor, Chet Miller, and Babe Stapp. Although Nuvolari's Alfa recorded 70.1 mph to be fastest in practice, starting positions were determined by draw, the front row consisting of Brivio's Alfa, Billy Winn's four-cylinder Miller, and Shaw's Offy-powered Gilmore Special.

Billy Winn's short-wheel-base, high-bodied Miller, with its four-wheel brakes, was not only fastest of the Americans but also managed better lap times than all the European road racers except the factory Alfas. Although Nuvolari won, it was little Billy who provided the excitement with his hard-charging, broad-sliding tactics. Winn ran in second place for much of the race and was never lower than fourth until his rear axle packed up on lap sixty-four of the seventy-five-lap, 300-mile event. Except when he stopped to change plugs on lap twenty-five, Nuvolari led all the way. Wimille, Brivio, Sommer, and the Australian McEvoy followed the little Italian master. Mauri Rose's Miller-Offy, which came in eighth, was the best finish for an American. Nuvolari's 65.998-mph winning average disappointed the

112

1932 Indy winner Fred Frame, No. 10, won the Ford V-8-dominated 200-mile 1933 Elgin stock car road race with an 80.22-mph average.

George P. Marshall, famed owner of the Washington Redskins football team, George Vanderbilt (center), and Eddie Rickenbacker (right), with the 1936 Vanderbilt Trophy.

Gene Haustein driving a Hudson-powered Martz Special in the 1932 Elgin road-race revival.

Some of the forty-five entries in the 1936 Vanderbilt Trophy race round the first turn.

Vanderbilt revivals were held at Roosevelt Raceway, Long Island, near the site of the original Cup series, in 1936 and 1937. The four-mile circuit was shortened to 3.3 miles and "straightened out" for the 1938 race.

New York motorists try the new Roosevelt Raceway.

crowd of 50,000. Departing spectators were heard to say that they had gone faster than the winner driving to Westbury.

In an effort to provide a faster if not more spectacular show, the track was considerably altered for the 1937 Vanderbilt Trophy. Several curves were removed, a close to 4000-foot straight was created, and the final turn leading to the main straight was more steeply banked. The course now measured 3.33 miles, and, as the organizers retained the 300-mile distance, ninety laps were required. Prize money remained the same, except for an additional $10,000 for the first three American drivers. In 1937 Hitler made the Mercedes-Benz and Auto Union racing teams a part of the Nazi propaganda machine. The Germans were given the funds and the talent and told to win. They did. Two Mercedes-Benz W125s and two Type C Auto Unions were the 1937 show-stoppers. Rudolf Caracciola and Dick Seaman drove the supercharged 8-cylinder, 5.6-liter, 650-hp Mercedes, with Bernd Rosemeyer and von Delius trying to harness the 600-hp V-16, rear-engined Auto Unions. Already feeling Hitler's heat, France and England stayed away. Except for the two German teams the only other Europeans were Alfa Romeo drivers Nuvolari and Farina. Americans, in an attempt to beat the Europeans with their own cars, acquired a Maserati and several Alfa Romeos. The fastest of this group was the supercharged Alfa Romeo eight that Scuderia Ferrari had used as a practice car in 1936. Bill White had bought the Alfa for Rex Mays, and the 1940–41 national champion had worked hard getting it ready. During practice it had been faster than the factory Alfas, but this was a German year. Mays was clearly the outstanding American in 1937, running third as the swastika-bearing silver cars alternated in holding the first two spots. Caracciola retired on lap twenty-two with a broken supercharger, and Nuvolari blew his engine in a vain attempt to catch Seaman. Billy Winn started where he had left off in 1936, mixing it up with the leading Europeans until the halfway point when his engine let go. Rosemeyer's Auto Union averaged 82.5 mph to win, as Seaman, slowed by a falling fuel supply, brought the Mercedes home second. Rex Mays finished third. The older Alfa's strong finish at Roosevelt Raceway was no fluke. It was to run in seven straight 500s, a fifth in 1939 being its best Indianapolis finish.

The second Roosevelt Raceway was responsible for Wilbur Shaw's interest in his famed Boyle Special, the Maserati that carried him to two of his three 500 crowns. The Vanderbilt Trophy races of 1936 and 1937 had given a needed boost to the fledgling, somewhat self-conscious, sport of road racing, just getting under way.

George Rand and Charles Moran, who were to become influential statesmen in American racing, began their careers in sharply different ways. George Rand first raced in 1930, on the half-mile dirt track at Deer Park, New Jersey, where he drove a Chrysler-60. Charles Moran received most of his education in French schools. He ran in the French Bol D'Or 24 Hours (limited to cars with up to 1100-cc engines) through the forests of St. Germain. He also drove a 5.3-liter du Pont at Le Mans in 1929, where he retired when the du Pont's ballast shifted, fell through the floorboards, and bent the driveshaft. Moran raced a du Pont in the 1930 Indianapolis in which

Hard-charging Billy Winn's Miller at Roosevelt Raceway, June 1937.

Rex Mays at Roosevelt Raceway in the Alfa Romeo he later raced at Indianapolis.

Rear-engined Auto Union driven by Bernd Rosemeyer to victory in the 1937 Vanderbilt Trophy.

Miller Collier in the ex-Freddy Dixon Riley 9 in 1935.

he qualified nineteenth and finished twenty-seventh after being involved in a wreck on the twenty-second lap. Moran never returned to Indy as a driver, but he did race a Ferrari at Le Mans in 1951 and 1952 and, with John Gordon Bennet, a Cunningham in 1953.

In 1955 he won the SCCA B-sports racing national championship, and, as a gesture to those who might believe that ACCUS was "out of touch," Moran and George Rand completed the 1959 Sebring 12 Hours in a Lotus.

In 1956 an FIA committee came to the United States to determine who would act as the nation's Automobile Club Nationale. They first approached Art Pillsbury, as the former senior steward of the AAA Contest Board, but were turned down. The committee then discussed with Charles Moran the need for American representation on such vital matters as race-car specifications, driver exchange privileges, and race dates. ACCUS, the Automobile Competition Committee of the United States, was formed in 1957 as the American arm of the FIA.

George Rand, a resident of Paris in the mid-thirties, entered voiturette races at Albi and, with Sam Collier, raced Maseratis at Picardie and, with Collier, shared the driving of a K3 Magnet at the County Down Trophy race in Belfast. It was Rand who, after returning from Europe to stay, brought a maturity to the ARCA, the Automobile Racing Club of America.

The ARCA usually gets credit it does not deserve for being the pre-World War II founding father of the Sports Car Club of America. However, the ARCA rarely gets the recognition it should have for the part it played in the American road-racing comeback.

From 1929 until 1933 the three sons of Barron Collier, the American car card advertising czar, owner of resort hotels and holder of Florida lands larger than some of our smaller states, used the driveway of Overlook, their Pocantico Hills, New York, home, to play race driver. With their close friend Tom Dewart, whose family owned the New York *Sun,* Miles, Sam and Barron Jr., whose ages in 1929 ranged from sixteen to twenty-two, formed the Overlook Automobile Racing Club and began driving low-powered home-made specials on the driveways of the estate.

As documented in John Rueter's history of the ARCA, the Collier boys, all avid followers of motor sports since childhood, named the narrow driveway turns "Home Corner and Member Straight," terms connected with England's Brooklands. By 1933 the group had outgrown the home grounds, and the club became known as the ARCA. Miles Collier, the youngest and most dynamic of the brothers, started a club journal and kept race records. In 1934 a Boston region was formed, and the club located a new race track, a 0.7-mile strip of land in the corner of an abandoned farm. This they named the Sleepy Hollow Ring. The club was incorporated, under Delaware laws, in June, and in July they held a six-hour evening race at Sleepy Hollow, starting at 7:30 p.m.

General Motors styling chief Bill Mitchell, then working for the Collier Advertising Company (as was George Rand and the author), designed the ARCA club badge. Later that summer two Philadelphians—Frank Griswold, whose Alfa coupe was to capture the first Watkins Glen, and Bob Harrison—both set new 35-mph, Sleepy Hollow Ring lap records. The Boston region of the

The ARCA car badge.

Richard Wharton's Alfa Romeo winning Alexandra Bay in 1940. Wharton and Frank Griswold both entered cars in the 1939 Indianapolis.

1912 American Grand Prize winner Caleb Bragg awards the trophy to George Rand for winning the Montauk GP, July 1940.

Joel Thorne finished ninth in No. 22, one of four Indianapolis entries made by the young New Yorker in 1938.

ARCA held races at Wayland on October 7, 1934, 1500 spectators paying to see Langdon Quimby's Willys 77 win. M. Ivanovitch (Sam Collier) was second in a J2 MG with Simeb Nola (Alan Bemes) third in an Austin.

The autumn of 1934 saw the ARCA revisit an historic racing scene as they staged races on the public roads around Briarcliff in New York's Westchester County. As George Rand recalls, the ARCA gave little thought to Briarcliff having been raced by DePalma and the early giants. The membership was preoccupied with getting permission to race from the property owners whose homes bordered the 3.3-mile circuit. As a single refusal was enough to lose the course, it was not surprising that Briarcliff was run for a second and last time in 1935.

The senior Barron Collier, a native of Memphis, was not without influence in his home town. In May 1936 the ARCA staged the Memphis Cotton Carnival Road Race, an eighty-mile dash over public roads, which Sam Collier won in an Auburn Speedster. In July 1937 the second of six annual ARCA Mount Washington Hill Climbs was won by Barron Jr.'s Alfa in 14:50.5, a record time that stood for years. In August the ARCA ran another of its "Round the Houses Races" at Alexandra Bay, where Ladd's Ford V-8 Special, which enjoyed a one-lap handicap, nosed out George Rand's Maserati, the scratch car.

The ARCA had come of age. The Collier brothers became American agents for Morris Garages, importing as many as 125 MGs annually. Miles Collier would say that he knew every American MG owner personally and that they had pledged not to sell their cars before first offering them to the American MG Car Company. Working at the Collier garage in Long Island City was John Oliveau, whose father had left his native France to work for Peugeot in New York, then for Mercer. Oliveau is a key figure in ACCUS, as are Rand and Moran. John first served as technical director and is now executive director of the organization.

At its peak the ARCA had 136 members. Although the atmosphere remained casual, its members were getting experience and their machinery was getting hotter. Miles raced a Frazer-Nash at Le Mans in 1935 and an 847-cc MG in 1939, retiring both times with mechanical problems. Sam and Miles were to drive Briggs Cunningham entries in the post-World War II 24 Hours, as were George Rand, Moran, and a new generation of American road racers.

Joel Thorne, who was to concentrate his considerable talent and money on Indianapolis, acquired a Ford V-8 Special and ran it in ARCA events. A couple of Bugattis and Maseratis, an Alfa, the latest MGs, of which two were supercharged, a "junk formula" Indy Studebaker and some potent specials, including John Rueter's famed "Old Gray Mare," made for interesting ARCA fields.

ARCA races were held over a 1.87-mile section of Roosevelt Raceway in September 1937, at Montauk Point in 1939 and 1940, and, as had their racing ancestors in 1915 at the San Francisco Exposition, the ARCA raced through the grounds of the New York World's Fair in October 1940. Although he was not active in the beginning, George Rand became ARCA president in its later years. Through his friendships with European drivers, particularly Raymond Sommer, Rand imported several of the Alfa Romeos and Maseratis that

Grand Prix cars rumble through New York streets on their way to the World's Fair.

Rand's Maserati leads Frank Griswold's Alfa Romeo through a narrow stretch of the 1940 New York World's Fair Grand Prix.

Griswold receives the trophy from the fair president, Harvey Gibson, as Ralph DePalma looks on.

National Hot Rod Association founder Wally Parks, with Vic Edlebrock, one of the largest makers of high-performance components, at the 1972 NHRA Nationals at Indianapolis Raceway Park.

Dick Landy in a Dodge Pro Stock at the NHRA Winternationals. This class is popular, as fans can readily identify dragsters with their own cars. Note the "wheelie bars," in rear between tires, doing their job.

not only altered the tone of ARCA racing but, as in the case of the Maserati driven by Wilbur Shaw (whom Rand knew through their mutual interest in flying), influenced Indianapolis.

Joel Thorne, whose Ford Special finished second to the winning Willys at Briarcliff in 1935, was an early ARCA member. Following the 1936 Vanderbilt, Thorne bought the eight-cylinder Alfa Romeo Sommer had driven to fourth place. In 1937 Thorne gave it a good drive to wind up sixth at Roosevelt Raceway. Before Thorne's erratic behavior attracted a hostile press, the Bergen, New Jersey, *Herald* singled out the young New Yorker in its Roosevelt Raceway report. "To Joel Thorne, the American racing public owe the credit and honor that the United States attained in this race. . . . Joel Thorne owns a string of race cars, many of which he drives himself, promised that the United States would be represented by a car capable of giving the foreign drivers better competition, and he lived up to his word. To such sportsmen go all the plaudits. . . . Joel drove a car in Chicago a few weeks ago and had the baptism of going through his first fence, although his car was badly wrecked he came through with only minor injuries and his driving at this track ranks him as one of the premier drivers of American raceways."

In the 500 of 1938 Thorne entered three specials—for himself and for Jimmy Snyder and Ronny Householder. Thorne, who had a two-way radio in his car, finished ninth. Snyder, after leading the race, had supercharger trouble and finished fifteenth, with Householder fourteenth. In the 1939 Indianapolis Snyder was second, Thorne seventh, Rex Mays sixteenth and Mel Hansen nineteenth, all but Hansen driving six-cylinder Thorne Specials. In 1940 Thorne ran only one car, for himself, and finished fifth. This was the year at Indy that fellow ARCA member Frank Griswold, Jr., entered an Alfa Romeo for Al Miller, and Rene Dreyfus and Rene Le Begue raced the Lucy O'Reilly Schell Maserati Special. The French pair did not win the 500; they were tenth. However, in view of Rene Dreyfus' subsequent success as a New York restaurateur, the results are being felt, gastronomically, to this day. Thorne was in a fifth-lap wreck in 1941, but an eight-year-old Thorne Special, with George Robson driving, won the 500 in 1946.

The DOHC six-cylinder engine built by Art Sparks was the last non-Offenhauser-engined car to win at the Speedway until 1965. The only other six-cylinder engine ever to win Indy powered Ray Harroun's Marmon in 1911. The German ace Rudolf Caracciola, after failing to get a Mercedes for the 1946 Indianapolis, accepted a ride in a Thorne Special. The Grand Prix star crashed in practice and was so seriously injured that he did not race again for six years. Three months after winning Indy in the Thorne Special, George Robson was killed in Atlanta on the dirt. Thorne entered cars in the 500s of 1947 and 1948, but they failed to qualify. In 1955 Thorne, a veteran pilot, died when his plane crashed into an apartment house in Los Angeles.

A pair of Funny cars blast off after the electronic Christmas tree has flashed the green "Go." Both the Mustang (left) and Vega (right) are powered by supercharged Chrysler engines producing 1800 hp. The photograph was taken during the NHRA Winternationals at Pomona.

Rand recalls getting a firm turn-down in 1938 when he approached Commissioner Grover Whalen for permission to hold a race meet at the New York World's Fair. The following year Tom Dewart, whose family connections with the New York *Sun* were well known, reopened negotiations, and the ARCA proposal was accepted. Rand says he does *not* believe that tradition played any part in selecting the exhibition site. The majority of ARCA members may not have been aware of the Vanderbilt Cup and American Grand Prize having been held at the San Francisco Fair. The ARCA, Rand said, "was simply looking for a place to race." The "World's Fair Grand Prix," run at 10:30 on the morning of October 6, 1940, was the last and probably the best of all ARCA race meets. The Fair management agreed to hold the race in the least crowded international section of the fairgrounds, to place barricades around the .75-mile circuit, and to police the area for the seventy-five-minute contest. The course was bumpy, but a good-sized crowd saw good racing from a field that included two GP Alfas, two Bugattis, George Rand's Maserati, Miles Collier in the Bu-Merc (Briggs Cunningham's Buick-powered Mercedes), several BMWs, an Aston-Martin, a Delage, several Specials, and a handful of MGs. Griswold's Grand Prix Alfa won. The rough surface resulted in several split gas tanks. George Weaver retired with ignition failure, and there was a spectacular crash, without injuries, when the Delage plowed into the wood fence. Following the World's Fair

race, Ted Allen, secretary of the AAA Contest Board, wrote George Rand relative to ARCA members racing without AAA licenses and to object to the race being held without AAA supervision.

Earlier in 1940 the American Automobile Association had invited the ARCA to join the AAA, but the offer was declined. Looking ahead, one wonders if the AAA would have been so eager to use the Le Mans disaster of 1955 to get out of racing and, if the Sports Car Club of America would have become a 20,000-member-strong road-racing giant, if the ARCA had become an AAA member club.

Too many ARCA members were in the armed forces in 1941 to stage any events. On December 9 George Rand, as club president, sent the membership a letter suspending the ARCA for the war's duration. The Automobile Racing Club of America was never reactivated. However, it was former ARCA members such as the Collier brothers, the two Georges, Weaver and Rand, together with such racing enthusiasts as Alec Ulmann and Cameron Argetsinger, who pointed the Sports Car Club of America toward road racing.

The SCCA was formed by seven vintage sports car enthusiasts in Boston on February 26, 1944. Although the ARCA had thirty-six members in the Boston area, not a single one of them was among the SCCA founding fathers. The gentlemen who started the SCCA were motivated by a laudable passion to preserve old American sports cars. They were not interested in racing.

As Ted Robertson, founder and first SCCA president, wrote in *Sports Car:*

Road racing with late model sports cars had been well handled for several years prior to the war by the ARCA. This club suspended activities in December 1941, but we anticipated that it would resume operations after the war; consequently we had never given any thought to this type of activity when we formed SCCA.

The beginning might best be summarized by quoting from the original constitution: "Article II—Purpose. The purpose of the club shall be to further the preservation of sports cars, to act as an authentic source of information thereupon, and to provide events for these cars and their owners."

We succeeded in preserving them all right. They're now museum pieces, valued at up to twenty times their list prices, and practically never run on the road any more.

Early SCCA events, held between 1944 and 1948, were largely vintage-car meets, occasionally combined with an acceleration run. Individual members entered the 500. Bill Milliken raced his Bugatti up Pikes Peak, and Briggs Cunningham organized a hill climb in Connecticut near Fairfield. But it was Watkins Glen, first held on October 2, 1948, that put American road racing back on the map.

If you classify dragsters as race cars—and you should—consider the post-World War II race fan who, the numbers say, prefers hot rods to Indy roadsters or to sports cars or Daytona stockers. The hot rod was born on Muroc Dry Lake in the Mojave Desert, a hundred miles north of Los Angeles, now the site of Edwards Air Force Base. This ten-mile-wide, twenty-mile-long and one-mile-high plateau was where the early California car nuts, strange inventive creatures, ran their home-made bombs in the moonlight.

Tommy Milton brought Muroc a measure of fame on April 14, 1924, when his three-liter (183-cubic-inch) Miller turned the mile in 151.3 mph. Three years later Frank Lockhart followed with a supercharged Miller, half the displacement of Milton's, and ran a 164.00 mile. Stubblefield and Wilbur Shaw also tried Muroc. But it really belonged to the kids—kids who were to become the movers and shakers of the postwar high-performance boom.

"Big Daddy" Don Garlits at the New England Dragway, Epping, New Hampshire, where he recorded 6:08 seconds, 241.28-mph, and 6:08 seconds, 237-mph runs. Garlits pioneered the rear-engined AA Fuel Dragster and is one of a select few to cover the quarter mile in the five-second range.

Ab Jenkins' Mormon Meteor at the Bonneville
Salt Flats, where its twenty-four-hour run established eighty-seven AAA records, September 1938.

Engine wizard Bud Winfield and Ab Jenkins
(left) examining Jenkins' 1946 Bonneville challenger.

**Art Arfons' Green Monster at the Bonneville
Salt Flats. Arfons held the Land Speed Record
on three occasions during his 1964–65 duel
with Craig Breedlove.**

Breedlove, the first man to exceed 400, 500, and 600 mph, held the Land Speed Record four times.

Craig Breedlove (left) surveying the scene of near disaster at Bonneville.

Gary Gabelich, a former drag racer and power-boat champion, guiding the Blue Flame to a 622.407-mph two-way average to become the world land record speed holder, October 23, 1970.

Not all drag racing was being done at Muroc Lake or on the salt flats at Bonneville. The wide streets of Los Angeles were a constant temptation, and it wasn't long before the rods were getting the wrong kind of attention. Wally Parks, who became editor of *Hot Rod Magazine* and founder and president of the National Hot Rod Association, was one of those who realized that for drag racing to survive it needed to improve its image and be self-policed. In 1937 the Southern California Timing Association was formed. Within a year the SCTA had its own paper, the predecessor of *Hot Rod Magazine.* With Muroc, an air base, and Bonneville 800 miles away, drag racing, to stay in business, was forced to move from streets to private strips. The first drag strip opened in Goleta, California, in 1948.

Within twenty years this uniquely American form of automobile racing became the fastest-growing and, by certain measurements, the most popular type of competition in the United States. Each year three sanctioning organizations—the NHRA, the American Hot Rod, and International Hot Rod Associations—stage over five thousand drag meets for more than eight million paying fans to watch. Unlike other forms of racing, drag meets are two-at-a-time, side-by-side, standing-start contests between evenly matched cars. They are run over one-quarter-mile-long and at least four-lane-wide drag strips, and the timing and starting are handled by sophisticated electronic equipment.

There are drag classes for everything on wheels, but the three "pro" categories—top fuel, funny cars, and pro stock—pay the largest purses and pull the biggest crowds. Pro meets with their "heads-up" even starts (other classes use a system of handicaps) routinely produce speeds of 230 mph for top fuelers and funny cars. In twenty years top speeds have gone from 110 mph to over 250 mph. Of more importance, because elapsed time decides the winner, is the fact that ETs are now under the six-second mark. With NHRA opening its meets to rocket power, 300-mph top speeds are likely.

Drag racers rarely drive other types of race cars, but pioneer hot-rod mechanics and builders Ed Winfield, Phil Remington, and Fran Hernandez played vital roles in the Ford racing program. Frank Coon too is one of road racing's leading engine tuners. Veteran Don Garlits, three times a national champion, first to surpass 180 mph and first to build a rear-engined top-fuel dragster, is the biggest name and leading money winner in this branch of the sport. Although California is its capital, ACCUS has designated the NHRA National, held each Labor Day weekend at Indianapolis Raceway Park, as drag racing's national championship.

Stock cars, dragsters, sport cars, Grand Prix racing, Indianapolis cars, sprints and midgets: post-World War II American automobile racing was to have it all.

Racing Politics   VII

The polarization that troubles American automobile racing is frequently blamed on the nation's size and the variety of its racing interests. These are factors, but the primary reason for friction between NASCAR, USAC, and SCCA, three of the four ACCUS members that dominate professional auto racing in the United States, is the issue of driver exchange privileges.

Although ACCUS usually presents a united front to the FIA on vital issues such as car specifications, schedules, and safety measures, the business of driver exchange—allowing the driver of a rival sanctioning organization to enter races put on by other clubs—restricts ACCUS members when working together.

Drivers are allowed to appear in events sanctioned by other clubs provided such events are listed on the FIA calendar as "Full International." Such listings are hard to come by, however. They are granted on a limited basis and, more to the point, require the consent of a majority of ACCUS members. All this might not have mattered if auto racing had not become an entertainment industry with a star system as vital to its success as Hollywood's or Broadway's.

The racing spectators' interest seems to have passed through three stages. In the beginning a large part of the attraction was the novelty of the automobile. Between the two world wars race cars, the machines themselves, appeared to capture the enthusiast's fancy. Today's promoter depends on "name" drivers to bring in the crowd. Having the current Indianapolis winner at your mile oval can mean the difference between meeting the minimum guaranteed purse and making a profit. Trenton promoter Sam Nunis said that Jim Clark's appearance at his September 1964 Trenton 200 added better than 10,000 paying spectators to his 26,500 gate, a figure that remains a New Jersey State Fairgrounds record.

Because Indianapolis is a part of its Championship Trail, USAC is blessed with the largest number of prominent drivers and is most sensitive to the issue of driver exchange. The racing public might be better served if the driver were free to choose where he races. Even so it is easy to understand USAC's concern. If a road racer, or other non-USAC driver, wins the 500 and, after pocketing Indy's gold, returns overseas or to his American road racing campaign, the majority of USAC tracks are without the 500 winner, their star attraction. Such reasoning helped to shape USAC's thinking in 1972 when they refused to permit their superstar, A. J. Foyt, to run in a NASCAR 500-mile stock car race in his native Texas. It was not on the calendar as a Full International.

The complicated issue of multiple sanctioning organizations exists only in the United States. Elsewhere, FIA members are represented by their ACN—Automobile Club Nationale.

The reasons for America's multiple sanctioning arrangement are buried in the country's racing history. Run by dedicated, albeit conservative, men, the AAA Contest Board worked within an organization that gradually became hostile to racing. Slow to accept new ideas, the AAA took until 1950, long after Bill France had demonstrated the popularity of stock cars, to form its own stock car division. And the association's early moves to establish a road racing division were halfhearted gestures at best.

When the AAA, using the Le Mans disaster as an excuse, abandoned the Contest Board in 1955, the United States Auto Club was formed to fill the breach. Operating very much as had the AAA Contest Board, USAC concentrated on the Indianapolis 500 and other established programs. These covered product certification tests; land speed record supervision; twelve to fifteen national championship races for Indianapolis or "dirt" cars; a non-championship "big car" series; and the stock car division. It was a broad program, and it kept the new Indianapolis-based organization busy. But it was not enough. NASCAR, sports car, and drag racing were beginning to roll, but not in USAC's direction. Ironically, for its first fifteen years USAC was led by Tom Binford, who, largely in vain, worked to give USAC a less conservative posture.

Following World War II, Daytona Speed Week started to reclaim some of its former greatness. Motorcycle and stock car races were being held on a 4.1-mile combination beach and highway course a few miles south of the 1936 circuit. Time trials again were held on the

129

Start of the 1955 stock car race. NASCAR moved from the beach to Daytona International Speedway in 1959.

Lee Petty, a three-time NASCAR champion, takes the checker in 1954.

beach, and running the measured mile against the clock with your hot Olds or imported sports car became a part of many enthusiast's winter holiday.

By the mid-1950s Speed Week had become a NASCAR showcase. Tim Flock won the 1955 Grand National over the beach course, his Chrysler 300 winning over Lee Petty's entry of similar make. A Buick Century was third, and Oldsmobile 88s rounded out the first five. Flock, who had finished first in 1954 only to be disqualified, was behind Fireball Roberts at the end of the one-hour-and-forty-three-minute contest. NASCAR officials declared Roberts' Buick "illegal" because its push rods had been "altered," and Flock had the win he missed the year before. Banjo Mathews' Ford captured the wreck-shortened Sportsman race, and Bob Said, a young sports car driver, manhandled a Formula I Ferrari to a "straightaway" record for the mile. Said reached 174.334 mph going south and 166.743 on his return to average 170.538 mph.

The sports car and Grand Prix class was peppered with prominent road-racing names. Phil Walters won the Paul Whiteman Trophy in a Briggs Cunningham "D" Jaguar with a 164-mph two-way average. SCCA president "Gentleman" Jim Kimberly and three-time Le Mans winner, U.S. Ferrari importer Luigi Chinetti, drove Marenello cars; Briggs Cunningham ran one of his C-4Rs, and Bill Frick, builder of the hybrid Fordillac and Studillac, drove the big 4.9 Ferrari in which Umberto Maglioli had won the 1954 Mexican Road Race. Ford Thunderbirds, led by Big Bill Spear, proved fastest in Class 3, comprising cars costing less than $4000. The Thunderbirds beat out XK120 Jaguars and several Corvettes.

Following the "formal" straightaway runs, tourists had their big moment. For twelve dollars NASCAR sent you down the hallowed sands on an officially timed run, and if you recorded better than 100 mph you became a member of the Century Club.

Bill France, displaying the single-mindedness that has marked his career, stopped working as an automobile mechanic in 1938 so that he could devote his talents to promoting and driving in stock car races. Concerned with the uncertainties and gypsylike atmosphere that characterized stock car racing, he began his struggle to regulate car specifications and improve driver benefits. Sitting on the pit wall at Indianapolis prior to the 1973 drivers' meeting, Bill told how NASCAR became a formal sanctioning body. "In 1946 I planned a 100-mile championship stock car race in Charlotte. When I talked to a local sports writer about publicity for the race in his newspaper, he said if I wanted to call it a national championship I should have it sanctioned by a national association that kept track of the drivers' points. I told Jim Lamb, the secretary of the AAA Contest Board, of my plans and asked to have the AAA sanction the race. Lamb said he would check on it. Three weeks later, I presume after he talked with Art Pillsbury, chairman of the AAA Contest Board, I asked Lamb if he had an answer and he said, 'We decided we were only interested in the big stuff.'" France grinned. "Well, we had to start our own organization."

In December 1947 a group led by Bill France met in the Streamline Motel in Daytona Beach to form the National Association for Stock Car Auto Racing. NASCAR was to change the face of automobile racing in the United States. With the perennial exception of Indianapolis, Grand National races, 500-mile or longer events for late-model sedans on NASCAR's superspeedways—Darlington, Daytona, Charlotte, Rockingham, Atlanta, and Talladega—usually draw the biggest crowds and pay the largest purses in American racing. Two new USAC events—500-mile races for Indianapolis cars at Ontario, California, and at Pocono, in Pennsylvania—have reported crowds of over 100,000. However, as noted before, racing attendance figures are suspect. As of this writing, the faltering Ontario track has gone under the management of a group headed by Tony Hulman and Parnelli Jones.

NASCAR racing is not truly national, although it opens its season by sending its premier attraction, Grand National late-model sedans, to the Riverside, California, road course. It is in the Southeast, its heartland, where the popularity of stock car racing surpasses that of professional baseball and football. Its storied stars such as the late Fireball Roberts, former champion Lee Petty, and his even more talented son, Richard, are more than folk heroes. They are revered.

For many racegoers the Detroit family sedan, albeit in appearance only, has replaced the thoroughbred American race car. United States builders have shown themselves capable of making some of the world's finest-designed and best-performing cars. In place of Duesenbergs and Mercers, stock car races of the 1950s

Trenton promoter Sam Nunis, in hat and pointing, stands with (right to left) Jim Clark, A. J. Foyt, and Rodger Ward. The most successful of all Speedway chief mechanics, George Bignotti, stands with hands on hips next to Foyt's No. 2.

The former French champion René Dreyfus, now an American restaurateur, being honored at Sebring by (left to right) ACCUS president Tom Binford; FIA representative H. Schmitz of Germany; John Oliveau, executive director of ACCUS; André Surmain; Sebring promoter Alec Ulmann and Jerry Reigel.

Jim, Bill Sr., and Anne France with Ford's 999 in 1955.

Glenn "Fireball" Roberts and Bill France at the 1962 Le Mans. The stock car ace finished sixth as co-driver of Bob Grossman's Ferrari.

The 1965 drivers meeting at Indianapolis. In the front row of the grid are A. J. Foyt, Jim Clark, and Dan Gurney (sitting on extreme left of each row). Speedway owner Tony Hulman (with dark glasses) is in the foreground.

featured Hudson Hornets and Olds 88s. And stock car fans loved it.

A handful of American sports cars appeared in the early 1950s. Briggs Cunningham opened a plant in West Palm Beach for the building of expensive Italian-bodied, usually Chrysler-powered Cunninghams. Indianapolis chassis builder Frank Kurtis began selling a sports car in 1948, and by 1953 his 500 K series was a frequent SCCA winner. Brooks Stevens' Excalibur enjoyed some popularity, but it was not until the autumn of 1953, when Chevrolet introduced the Corvette, that an American manufacturer got back to producing a true sports car.

Almost as if it were above racing's day-by-day problems, the Indianapolis 500-Mile Sweepstakes rolled serenely on. Following Shaw's death in 1954, Tony Hulman, one of that small band of worldly Hoosiers who, after the best of Eastern schooling and much travel, return to Indiana to live an almost baronial life, took over the running of the Speedway. Thanks to Clabber Girl Baking Powder, a Terre Haute brewery, and other interests, Hulman was able to plow his 500 profits back into the Speedway plant. You may question such hyperbole as the "Greatest Race Course in the World"; nevertheless the track and its towering grandstands are an imposing sight, and they are superbly maintained. And Indy may be the racing world's only track with adequate and clean toilet facilities.

In a business that puffs up attendance figures to where they have become meaningless, the estimated 275,000 to 300,000 quoted by the Speedway may err on the low side. The grandstands actually hold 230,000, according to a count made by a team of Boy Scouts hired by a curious Indianapolis newspaper, and the parking area within the giant 2.5-mile oval has been said to hold 25,000 cars. Only the Speedway staff and perhaps the tax men know, but they are not making statements. Should the 300,000 attendance figure, largest to see a sports event in the world, appear impressive, the additional 600,000 or so who pay to watch the two weekends of time trials must not be overlooked. The drama of some seventy cars struggling to qualify for Indy's thirty-three sacred starting spots is enjoyed by some fans more than the race itself.

Mauri Rose, an engineer who raced on a selective basis during his entire twenty-four-year driving career, won the AAA National Championship in 1936, the same year he had been the highest finishing American at Roosevelt Raceway. Rose earned the pole at Indianapolis in 1940 but went out on lap sixty when his supercharged Maserati 8 developed plug trouble. In 1941 he took over teammate Floyd Davis' Offy, then in fourteenth place, and went on to win. He drove former driver Lou Moore's front-wheel-drive Offenhauser-powered Blue Crown Specials to victories in 1947 and 1948 to become one of the Speedway's rare three-time winners.

"Wild Bill" Holland, who won the 500 in 1949 with a record 131.32 mph race average and finished second to Rose in 1947 and 1948, earned a place in Indianapolis folklore with the hell he raised at the Speedway in 1947. A mild-mannered rookie in 1947, poorly fitting his "Wild Bill" nickname, Holland believed he had been getting misleading signals from his pit.

Carroll Shelby, Birdcage Maserati, at Riverside, October 1960.

Chuck Daigh drives Lance Reventlow's Scarab in the 1958 *Times* Grand Prix, Riverside.

1963 U.S. road racing champion Bob Holbert, No. 14, in his Porsche RS61 at the 1961 Nassau Speed Week.

Start of the Corvette race in the 1962 Cumberland Nationals.

Roger Penske in the Zerex Special wins the 1962 *pro* race at Laguna Seca.

Phil Hill, No. 69, in a 4.9 Ferrari, Walt Hansgen's No. 60 D-Type Jaguar, and Masten Gregory's No. 4 Maserati V-8 at Riverside, October 1957.

Phil Hill's Ferrari gets on the marbles at the Thillois hairpin during the 1959 French Grand Prix at Reims.

CLOCKWISE FROM BOTTOM LEFT:

Ken Miles takes a Shelby Cobra through the esses at Sebring, March 1963.

Cobra and Ferrari coupes about to pass the hulk of a Navy amphibian plane at Sebring.

The Le Mans start at the 1969 Sebring. Mario Andretti, nearest to the camera, dashes for Ferrari No. 25 as Mark Donohue goes for Lola No. 9. Ford GT-40 of Jackie Oliver and Ickx traveled 1242.8 miles to win.

A Sebring driver gets his time during the 1963 12 Hours.

Sebring sunsets signal the closing stages of the 12-hour endurance race.

Some of the 300,000 spectators watch Bobby Unser, in the white car, and Peter Revson lead the 1972 field into turn one at the Speedway. The race was won by Mark Donohue, No. 66, immediately behind Revson.

Parnelli Jones came within 10 miles of winning the 1967 Indy in the Granatelli Turbine.

Al Unser wins the 1971 Indianapolis, his second in a row.

OVERLEAF: With lights blazing to warn slower cars of its approach, A. J. Foyt slams the big Ford MK IV through the esses at Le Mans. Dan Gurney and Foyt covered 3247 miles to win the 1967 24 Hours.

Eddie Sachs, No. 6, the fastest qualifier, and 1952 500 winner Troy Ruttman, No. 28, at the 1960 Indy.

CLOCKWISE FROM LEFT:

Pace car brings the 1973 24 Hours field past the Daytona grandstand.

Start of the 1973 Daytona 500 stock car classic.

Aerial view of Daytona International Speedway. In addition to the 2.5-mile banked tri-oval, the speedway includes a 1.31-mile road course.

The Mark Donohue/David Hobbs Ferrari, No. 6, passes No. 64 Corvette during the 1971 Daytona 24 Hours. The Penske-owned Ferrari 512M led for two hours but was involved in a minor accident as the Porsches took the four top places.

Richard Petty's Dodge, No. 43, passes A. J. Foyt's Chevelle. Petty won the 1973 Daytona 500 with an average speed of 157.2 mph.

CLOCKWISE FROM LEFT:

Parnelli Jones and Vel Meletich with their new championship car, conceived by former Lotus designer Maurice Philippe. On October 4, 1973, Mario Andretti drove this car to a world record 214.158 mph lap on the Texas World Speedway banked oval.

Parnelli Jones driving the No. 51 white Fike Plumbing Special at Funk's Winchester Speedway, May 1960. The next day Parnelli joined the U.S. Auto Club and raced at Indy the following year.

1966 U.S. road racing champion Chuck Parsons, No. 10, and Masten Gregory in the October 1966 Laguna Seca Can-Am, where Gregory's McLaren finished fifth.

Skip Barber in an English March Formula 5000 powered by a highly tuned Chevrolet engine. The single-seater road racer was partially sponsored by the U.S. Navy during 1973.

Mark Donohue in a Penske's Porsche 917/10 at Laguna Seca in 1972, where Mark and teammate George Follmer finished 1–2.

Swiss Grand Prix driver Jo Siffert's Porsche 917/10 leads Denny Hulme's McLaren through Laguna Seca's turn nine. Siffert's Porsche was the forerunner of the model that broke the five-year McLaren stranglehold on the Can-Am series.

Vic Elford driving the "ground effects" Chaparral 2J in practice for the 1970 Monterey-Castrol Can-Am at Laguna Seca.

Denis Hulme signals his intention of entering the pit lane during the 1971 Monterey Can-Am. Between 1967 and 1972 Hulme won twenty-one Can-Am races and more than $660,000.

The Motown Shaker, Vega-bodied Funny Car, is driven by Detroit's Al Bergler.

Seventeen-year-old high school student John Stewart, who began his drag-racing career by downing the veteran Don Garlits in his first championship run. Stewart's fuel dragster is powered by a Donovan engine.

Drag-racing news was made in January 1973 when the NHRA approved of hydrogen-rocket power for exhibition runs. Since this dragster is propelled rather than driven through the rear wheels, there is no need for huge rear tires. Driving the Pollution Packer is Dave Anderson, who has reached 322 mph in 4.97 seconds. A special class of rocket dragsters appears imminent.

According to Speedway press director Al Bloemker, Holland had a two-mile lead over Rose at the 400-mile mark and had enough fuel and sufficient tread on his tires to finish without a stop. However, Mauri Rose, who was never known to let up, was closing in on his teammate at a second a lap. Lou Moore, with his life savings in the two cars, visualized a closing duel in which his two jewels would be wrecked or driven to destruction.

No other car was near enough to catch the two Blue Crown Specials, so Moore gave each of them the EZ sign. Holland promptly slowed down by about three miles an hour. But Rose kept charging and passed Holland on lap 193. Thinking he still had a one-lap lead, Holland moved over and cheerfully waved Rose by. On the next lap, with his rookie now 400 feet behind the veteran, Moore gave both cars the O.K. sign. Later Rose's pit held up the P-I signal while Holland was shown the O.K. Mauri Rose went on to finish twenty-eight seconds ahead of a shocked and furious Holland, who, on stopping outside Victory Lane, is reported to have shouted, "Who the hell can a driver rely on if his own pit crew won't keep him informed of his position?"

Controversial finishes are not new at Indianapolis. The results of the very first 500 in 1911, officially won by Ray Harroun's Marmon, have been questioned by prominent automobile-racing historians, some of whom believe the victory belonged to Ralph Mulford. A letter from Mulford appearing in *Speed Age* magazine supports this theory.

. . . Didn't you overlook the multiple crash in front of the official stands which eliminated four cars, threatened for a few wild moments to end the race and caused some of the scoring difficulties? Naturally the Lozier manager, Mr. C. A. Emise, and the pit crew as well as Mrs. Lozier and our friends in the grandstand, knew that number 33 was due and were greatly relieved when it came safely through the accident area.

The Lozier protest was based on the claim that this lap was not scored and their records showed I drove 201 laps before getting the checkered flag. However, with the timing and scoring hopelessly muddled up, there was no way to prove this claim, so we accepted second place. . . .

Finishing third in the 1947 Indianapolis was Ted Horn, one of the few American oval track drivers to have achieved greatness without ever having won the 500. National AAA champion for an unprecedented three consecutive years, from 1946 through 1948, Horn lost his life when a spindle broke during a 100-mile dirt-track race at the DuQuoin Fairgrounds. At the Speedway, Horn drove Millers six times before running an Art Sparks six in 1941. He then used the former Wilbur

Richard Petty racing through the California fog to win the 1973 Riverside 500.

Shaw Maserati for three years beginning in 1946. During this period, 1936 through 1948, Horn posted a record of one second place, four thirds, and four fourths. We are indebted to Al Bloemker's *500 Miles to Go* for the following tribute to Ted Horn. At the 1947 Indianapolis victory banquet Tommy Milton interrupted his introduction of the winner, Mauri Rose, to ask Rose who he thought drove the day's best race. Without hesitation Rose replied, "Ted Horn drove the best race this year and I guess we all know it. . . . He made four pit stops, I made only one, but he finished third and drove the fastest laps of the race to do it."

By 1950 the AAA, apparently sensitive to its role in racing, was making an effort to publicize "the race track's contribution to the cars we drive." In his address to the forty-eighth annual AAA meeting in New York's Waldorf-Astoria, Ray Sherman, vice-chairman of the Contest Board, made a point about racing-inspired automobile improvements. Beginning with the chestnut of Ray Harroun's first use of the rear-view mirror in the first 500, Sherman also spoke of knee action, lower radiators, streamlining, high-speed engines, four-wheel brakes, better shock absorbers, balanced crankshafts, aluminum pistons, better bearings, better spark plugs, balloon tires, ethyl gasoline, and wheel balancing.

The FIA granted the Indianapolis 500 Championship Grand Prix status between 1950 and 1960. Any points now earned at the Speedway would count toward the drivers' and constructors' world championships. However, only three top Grand Prix drivers came to the Speedway during that time—Alberto Ascari, Juan Manuel Fangio, and Giuseppe Farina. In 1952 Ascari qualified a Ferrari 12 in the nineteenth spot but retired on the fortieth lap with a broken wheel. Fangio visited the Speedway in 1959 but, after saying he did not believe his car to be competitive, left without attempting to qualify. From 1946 until 1961, the year John Cooper triggered the rear-engine revolt that made all existing Indianapolis machinery obsolete, Luigi Villoresi was the only European to make a good showing in the 500, his 3-liter Maserati finishing seventh in 1946.

The Offenhauser engine and two chassis builders, Frank Kurtis and A. J. Watson, ruled the Speedway from 1950 until 1964. Kurtis began building race cars on the West Coast in the early 1930s. His midgets, the first racers to use full torsion-bar suspension, dominated their class, and as early as 1936 Kurtis utilized offset engines, an idea that did not become accepted at Indianapolis until 1952. Kurtis built the original Novis, big, fierce, front-wheel-drive, hard-to-handle race cars that became the battle cry of the Indy underdog. And he built successful sports cars too. Johnny Parsons gave Kurtis his first Indianapolis victory in 1950, and in 1951 Kurtis won again with Lee Wallard. The Cummins Diesel Special in which Freddie Agabashian

Bill Vukovich in his Kurtis-Offy in 1953, on the way to the first of his two consecutive 500 victories.

earned the pole in 1952 was another Kurtis car. The great Bill Vukovich, a hard-charging, taciturn and sometimes surly man, yet far from being the "mad Russian" of his legend, drove Kurtis-Offys to win the 500 in 1953 and 1954. Vukovich died early in the 1955 Indianapolis while trying for his third straight 500. Second-generation Indianapolis drivers include Gary and Merle Bettenhausen, Duane Carter, Johnny Parsons, and Billy Vukovich. Speaking of his father, young Vuky says, "My father was a very intense man, a loner. When I started racing I was a little that way myself, but I've changed. That 'mad Russian' stuff about my father was a gimmick." Bob Sweikert, who was to lose his life on the high banks at Salem in 1956, won the 1955 Indianapolis. It was Sweikert who took Frank Kurtis on his fifth and final trip to Victory Lane. Each year for six consecutive years, 1952 through 1957, more than twenty of the 500's thirty-three starters had run Kurtis cars.

Pat Flaherty then won the 1956 500 in John Zink's Watson-built Special (it was the first Indianapolis race sanctioned by USAC), and young, prematurely gray, crew-cut A. J. Watson became the darling of Gasoline Alley. Starting with single entries in 1956 and 1957, Watson had four cars at the Speedway in 1959, including Rodger Ward's and Jim Rathmann's, in the first two places.

Rathmann and Ward reversed the finishing order in 1960 when eight Watson-built roadsters qualified. A. J. Foyt earned the first of his three 500s in a Watson chassis in 1961 when eleven Watson-Offenhausers and many Watson copies were on hand. Repeat wins for Ward and Foyt in 1962 and 1964, with Parnelli Jones's controversial victory in 1963, saw Watson cars earn the checker at Indianapolis seven times before he was shut out by rear-engined machines.

Some Speedway builder-chief-mechanics, such as George Bignotti and Clint Brawner, not only improved on the Brabham, Lola and Lotus chassis; they built their own rear-engined cars, and they were winners. Ward brought Watson a second in the 1964 Indianapolis with a rear-engined Ford, but Watson was never to regain his roadster popularity.

Only three times between 1950 and 1964 was the Kurtis-Watson string interrupted—in 1952 when Troy Ruttman, aged twenty-two, the youngest driver ever to win the 500, drove the Eddie Kuzma-built Agajanian entry, and in 1957 and 1958 when the George Salih-designed and Quinn Epperly-built radical twenty-one-inch-high roadster with a laydown engine brought victories to the veteran Sam Hanks and to Jimmy Bryan.

Headlines read "The Race of Two Worlds," "500 Miglia di Monza," "Indy Challenged by European Drivers." It wasn't quite that way, but there was good racing, especially the second year. And it was fun. Following a 100-mile championship on the dirt in Detroit on June 23, 1957, ten of USAC's better cars and drivers flew to Italy for a 500-mile race at Monza on June 29. Tony Bettenhausen, Jimmy Bryan, Ray Crawford, Andy Linden, Pat O'Connor, Johnnie Parsons, Troy Ruttman, Paul Russo, Eddie Sachs, and Bob Veith represented a USAC team that included three Indianapolis winners and three national champions. Unfortunately the Grand Prix challenge did not materialize in 1957. The only Europeans to race the visiting Yanks were three Ecurie Ecosse D-Type Jaguar

Four-time Indy pole winner Rex Mays stands behind Joe Garson at a 1946 indoor midget meet.

Three-time Indianapolis winner Mauri Rose being escorted by young Andy Granatelli, in dark coveralls, and Carole Landis after Rose won his second 500 in 1947.

Grand Prix champion Alberto Ascari, whose Ferrari broke a wheel on lap forty, with his crew at the Speedway in 1952.

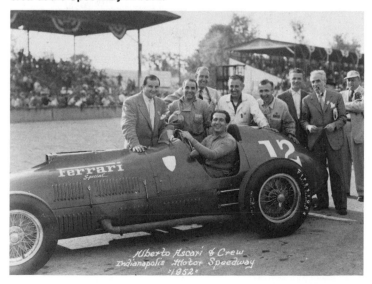

Start of the 1955 Indy. Jerry Hoyt, right, Tony Bettenhausen, and Jack McGrath make up the front row. Vukovich, in the center of the second row, lost his life in an accident on the fifty-sixth lap.

At Victory Lane in 1954. The famed Borg Warner Trophy stands behind Vuky.

sports cars. Jean Behra did qualify a Maserati, but it failed to start, and a Ferrari driven by Mario Borniggia was too slow to make the field.

Led by the genial David Murray, who had brought Jaguar a 1-2 finish at Le Mans over the prior weekend, the D-types were no match for the Indianapolis roadsters on Monza's steep, thirty-nine-degree banks. And no amount of talking would convince the organizers to incorporate the road course, where the Jags would have been at home. Practice showed the American cars to be a good 15 mph faster than the Jags (Bettenhausen's Novi earned the pole with a closed-course record lap of 176.818 mph), but the trials also revealed that the bumpy, 2.4-mile oval was a car killer. Between the concrete paving were one-inch-high tar strips!

The race was run in three equal heats of sixty-three laps, and the Americans led every lap but one when the English veteran Jack Fairman took advantage of the D-type's four-speed gearbox to get a good start and capture first-lap honors. Sachs, O'Connor, Linden, and Crawford dropped out with broken fuel tanks, Bettenhausen was sidelined with engine trouble, and teammate Russo's Novi failed to make the starting grid. Jimmy Bryan won the first two heats and finished second to Ruttman in the third to take overall honors. The cigar-chomping dirt-track expert—the Italian press dubbed Bryan the "Churchill of the Speedways"—

earned $34,679 of the $92,000 purse and promised to return. Ecurie Ecosse's chief mechanic Wilke Wilkenson fiddled with the outclassed Jags' suspension, and they finished a surprising fourth, fifth, and sixth.

The 1958 Race of Two Worlds was again held on June 29, only this time the Europeans put on a good show. Jim Rathmann, Rodger Ward, Johnny Thomson, Don Freeland, and Jim Reece made their first trip, as did Indianapolis rookie A. J. Foyt, who was not an "official" member of the party although he did get to drive.

The European challenge not only included Luigi Musso, Mike Hawthorn, Phil Hill, and Harry Schell in Ferraris, but it also had 1957 Le Mans winner Ivor Bueb and Masten Gregory in D Jaguars, Jack Fairman in a Lister Jaguar, and, most spectacular of all, the Eldorado Ice Cream Italia, a monstrous Maserati Special driven by Stirling Moss.

For added interest two Indianapolis roadsters were loaned to the Auto Club of Milan for assignment to two European drivers. One machine, the Dean Van Lines Special that Bryan had used to win the 1957 Monza, was given to Juan Manuel Fangio, who had earned his fourth consecutive World Drivers Championship in 1957. The second roadster, owned by Sclavi and Amos, was to be assigned to a European driver selected by the organizers. They picked the little Frenchman, Maurice Trintignant, a Grand Prix veteran, owner of vineyards, mayor of the village of Vergeze, a greatly respected driver with a reputation for being easy on race cars.

Unfamiliar with the characteristics of an Indianapolis roadster's clutch (it's either in or out) or gearbox and unable to understand Bernard Cahier, an English-speaking European journalist who, as a latter-day Bradley, was acting as liaison between car owner Fred Sclavi and his driver, Trintignant was less than his effective self while being screamed at, especially by Mrs. Sclavi, for slipping the clutch.

One heat was enough for the distraught car owner as well as the driver. Before the second heat started, Sclavi said, "I think I'll give that nice-looking skinny kid from Texas a chance." Foyt, "that skinny kid," drove to sixth-place finishes in the two final heats.

The Dean Van Lines car never went to Fangio's satisfaction. Although he did qualify it third fastest at 171.400 mph, Fangio ran only two desultory laps during the third heat.

Fastest of all second-year qualifiers was Luigi Musso, whose record 174.653 mph spoke more for his courage than his Ferrari. Musso led for the first ten laps, with Hawthorn relieving him midway through the first heat. Phil Hill then drove the Musso-Hawthorn car for most of heats two and three and was able to move the Ferrari from dead last, when he left the pits, to a third-place finish. Rathmann and Bryan finished one-two overall, with Rathmann's Leader Card Special out front for 179 of the 189 laps. Musso, Sachs, and Bryan were the only other lap leaders. Stirling Moss put on a good show with the ill-handling Ice Cream Wagon. Running third for most of the day, Moss stayed in contention until the steering broke in the final heat, and the big Maser destroyed itself along the top guardrail.

It had been a good, friendly race meet. American announcer Chris Economaki was on the Monza public-address system more than his Italian counterpart. There

A. J. Foyt winning his first 500 in 1961.

had been excessive restrictions placed on American journalists and photographers, but there was a "journalists' revolt," and Monza manager Ing. Bacciagaluppi instructed the *carabiniere* to ease off.

The Italians were good hosts. The American party was lavishly entertained. Count Johnny Lurani invited the visitors to see his collection of old race cars. The Firestone tire distributor for northern Italy, a member of the illustrious Visconti family, opened his magnificent palazzo on the shores of Lake Como to the Americans, and every man in the party fell in love with the count's beautiful daughters.

At the Brussels World's Fair, ten days after Monza, American car owner Jim Robbins met one of the American journalists who had made the Monza trip. Robbins, who was to lose his life a decade later when a jet he was piloting crashed on take-off, said he had been so impressed with Musso at Monza that he was going to have the young Italian drive a Robbins entry in the next Indianapolis. Only then did Robbins learn of Musso's death at the French Grand Prix at Reims the week following Monza.

During the second Race of Two Worlds, pleasant Italian girls wandered about the pits selling large silk scarves. The scarf shows three colorful single-seater race cars, the emblem of the Auto Club of Italy, and along its borders in large blue letters are the names of twenty-five American and European personalities who had been at Monza. Ten of those listed—Jean Behra, Luigi Musso, Peter Collins, Jo Bonnier, Wolfgang von Trips, Ivor Bueb, Harry Schell, Jimmie Bryan, Tony Bettenhausen, and Eddie Sachs—have since perished

in racing accidents. Two more, Ron Flockhart and Jim Robbins, lost their lives flying their own planes, and one, the 1958 world champion Mike Hawthorn, died on the highway near his Surrey home.

The first Watkins Glen was a watershed in American racing. Prewar ARCA events had shown that a good many young Americans were interested in becoming road racing drivers, but there was nothing to indicate widespread spectator interest. Little more than a decade had passed since the poorly supported Vanderbilt Trophy races at Roosevelt Raceway, and several subsequent road racing revivals had met with lukewarm receptions.

Watkins Glen became a reality only because young Cameron Argetsinger, who had recently attended law school at nearby Cornell and was a summer regular at his grandparents' home on the shores of Lake Seneca, convinced the village elders that a European-style road race would bring fame and fortune to their upstate New York hamlet.

Alec Ulmann, the SCCA's first Activities Chairman (who soon was to promote Sebring), helped Cam Argetsinger, who had accomplished the Herculean job that included getting state and local authorities to close the roads and having the New York Central Railroad stop its trains where its tracks crossed the race circuit. The SCCA's first director of competition, Bill Fleming, recalls that Argetsinger retained Henry Valent, a local attorney who later became president of the Grand Prix corporation, and that Valent found an obscure clause in New York state laws permitting the closing of public roads for the purpose of road racing. There was a

American expatriate Harry Schell stands between two world champions, Alberto Ascari and Mike Hawthorn (shading his eyes), at the Ferrari drivers' meeting at Monza, 1953.

Eddie Sachs in Jim Robbins' Special in the 1958 Monza Race of Two Worlds.

suspicion that the favorable clause may have been arranged by Willie K. Vanderbilt prior to the running of the first Vanderbilt Cup in 1904.

The following item from the April 9, 1948, Elmira *Star-Gazette* indicates the enthusiastic, if somewhat distorted, support given the project:

Watkins Glen—Directors of the Chamber of Commerce are endeavoring to attract the most unusual convention to this village. They hope to hold a meet in July or August of the Sports Car Club of America. Watkins Glen may originate the only "American Grand Prix." Such an annual event would draw tremendous crowds, it is believed. The events would include hillclimbs, acceleration and braking trials and match races.

On October 2, 1948, Frank Griswold won both inaugural-day events, the 26.4-mile "Junior Prix" and the 52.8-mile "Grand Prix." His 2.9-liter prewar Alfa Romeo coupe averaged 63.7 mph for eight laps to win the feature over 6.6 miles of village streets, linked to paved and unpaved country roads above the town. Briggs Cunningham drove his Buick-powered Mercedes into second place, with Haig Ksayian bringing a Cunningham-owned TC-MG home third. Watkins' crowds grew rapidly. By the third year it was estimated that 100,000 spectators (there were no admission charges) jammed the little resort.

As the crowds grew, so did the hazard of racing on public roads, particularly through the village streets. A young spectator died in 1952; he was sitting too close to the curb. The driver of the car that struck him was unaware of the accident. The course was moved to the crossroads village of Dix, a few miles from Watkins Glen, where 4.6 miles of township roads were converted into a makeshift circuit.

It was a difficult time for the young promoters. The SCCA opposed the move, saying that the Dix course would not be ready in time, and, if it were, it would first have to pass inspection before they would grant a sanction. The New York state police opposed the move, as they were beginning to frown on all racing on public roads. However, the Dix course was entirely on township and private land, and the organizers went gamely ahead. The circuit was completed in forty days, and the "outlaw" sixth Watkins Glen was held as scheduled, with Walt Hansgen driving his XK120 Jaguar Special to win by an eyelash over the George Harris Allard.

Although the Dix circuit was doomed from the start —famed English driver George Eyston, acting as an honorary steward in 1953, told the organizers he admired their spirit but they had better move to a race course free of so many odd dips and strange turns— it did enable the Grand Prix group to begin collecting much needed admission charges.

The present Grand Prix circuit site was first used in 1956 when George Constantine's D Jaguar won with a 71.4-mph race average. Before the course was altered for the 1972 U.S. Grand Prix, Formula I and Can-Am sports cars were lapping the rolling 2.3 miles at nearly double Constantine's winning time.

Before professional road races began to attract European drivers to the United States on a regular basis, the Watkins Glen nationals and fall Formula Libre races

Road racing returned to America at Watkins Glen on October 2, 1948, when fifteen amateurs raced over the upstate New York village streets and nearby roads. Tying his shoe on the wheel of his Buick-powered Mercedes is Briggs Cunningham. Right is Mike Vaughn's Lagonda, and car No. 35 is the Alfa Romeo Coupe in which Frank Griswold won the eight-lap, 52-mile Grand Prix.

were among American road racing's few star attractions. Fans turned out in large numbers to see Jo Bonnier's Maserati win over Dan Gurney's Ferrari and to watch Stirling Moss run away from the field in Rob Walker's tiny Cooper-Climax. When the prestigious U.S. Grand Prix moved to Watkins Glen in 1961, after false starts at Sebring and Riverside, Watkins was ready.

Road racing began to flourish. SCCA-sanctioned races were held on an abandoned airfield near Fort Lauderdale and at Palm Beach Shores in Florida. Bridge-hampton, Long Island, the scene of road races thirty years earlier, staged sports car races on a four-mile course that combined village streets and nearby lanes. On the West Coast, Torrey Pines, near San Diego; Paramount Ranch, near Los Angeles; Pebble Beach, on the Monterey peninsula; Golden Gate Park, in the heart of San Francisco; and Santa Barbara, all sprang into existence in the early 1950s. In July 1950 the Chicago region of the SCCA staged races over a 3.35-mile public road course in the resort village of Elkhart Lake, Wisconsin, with Jim Kimberly winning in his Ferrari. The circuit was extended to 6.5 miles in 1951 and 1952, so that it circled the lake before cutting back through the village, and crowds estimated at 100,000 saw John Fitch successfully withstand challenges from Phil Walters, Briggs Cunningham, and a young Californian named Phil Hill.

Watkins Glen founder Cameron Argetsinger stands beside his Bugatti (No. 3) prior to the start of the 1949 race. Charles Moran, Jr. is in Bugatti No. 20.

Sam Collier in Cunningham's new Ferrari prior to the start of the 1950 Grand Prix. Standing to the left is Sam's younger brother, Miles, and to the right, Alfred Momo, wearing glasses, and Ed Hall. Sam Collier was killed on the second lap of the Grand Prix when the Ferrari left the road.

1950 Seneca Cup winner Phil Walters, who was also to win the 1951 Watkins Glen Grand Prix, behind the wheel of Cunningham's Cadillac-Healy. The young man directly behind Walters is the future driving star Walt Hansgen.

The starting grid of the 1970 U.S. Grand Prix at Watkins Glen. Jochen Rindt, No. 2, won the first of the six Grand Prix races he was to win during his tragically short career.

The usual crowd-control problems contributed to the passing of a Wisconsin state law, which in part said, "There will be no racing or speed contests on the State's public roads." Cliff Tufte opened the parklike Road America circuit a few miles outside of Elkhart Lake in September 1955, and this time Phil Hill's Ferrari won by inches over Sherwood Johnston's D Jag.

There were drivers and there were cars, but state after state was cracking down, and there were precious few places to race. Fred Wacker and Charles Moran persuaded U.S. Air Force General Curtis Le May (on occasion he would slam on a helmet, clamp a cigar between his teeth, and go racing) to permit the SCCA to use Strategic Air Command fields. General Le May not only granted the request; he encouraged it, and fourteen race meets were held under joint SAC and SCCA auspices. By the end of the SAC agreement in 1955, enough closed courses and abandoned airfields were in use to keep road racing alive. Two years later Riverside and Laguna Seca, two first-rate circuits, opened in California as Bridgehampton and Lime Rock went into business within a hundred miles of New York. Thompson, Connecticut, had been holding SCCA races since 1951, when George Weaver built a 1.56-mile road course around the existing Thompson oval. As with Marlboro near Washington, D.C., Thompson was at its best when used for drivers' schools and club meets.

The doyen of American road courses is Sebring. Sam and Miles Collier had been looking for a place to race

in Florida when Sam flew over to the old bomber base where he had trained during World War II. Before arrangements could be completed, Sam's Ferrari went off the road during the third Watkins Glen in October 1950, and he succumbed to his injuries.

Alec Ulmann, who says his interest in racing goes back to his childhood in Russia when he witnessed the start of the 1908 St. Petersburg–Moscow race, had an aircraft-parts warehouse on the base, and, as a friend of the Colliers and an SCCA officer, he stepped in. The first Sebring on December 31, 1950, the six-hour Sam Collier Memorial, was won by a Crosley Hot Shot (the results were decided on a handicap basis) driven by Fritz Koster and Ralph Dishon. The SCCA sanctioned the first Sebring, but Ulmann wanted a race with international status, and he sought AAA support. The second Sebring, held in March 1952, was the first to go twelve hours. The Manufacturers Championship was introduced by the FIA in 1953, and Sebring began to pull the famed European drivers whose factory-supported teams were seeking precious world-championship points—and sunshine.

Although Phil Walters and John Fitch drove a Cunningham to win in 1953, Sebring soon became a European show. It would be 1965, when the Jim Hall and Hap Sharp Chaparral survived a cloudburst, before an American car won again. It was incongruous to accept the dreary central Florida retirement village as the U.S. home of international auto racing. But it was. The great names of the 1950s raced over the 5.2 miles of abrasive airport runways and abandoned development streets. And they all complained.

But the March weather could be magnificent, the scent of orange blossoms filled the soft night air, and there always was an abundance of pretty girls lying about the pools at Harder Hall and the Kenilworth. The Florida police did develop a regrettable tendency to abuse visiting drivers. Is it possible that some deep-seated antipathy is at work between race drivers and policemen? New York's finest roughed up and jailed the great Louis Wagner for three days in 1908 for speeding on Broadway, and an Indianapolis patrolman man-handled mild-mannered Bobby Unser after the 1968 Indy winner committed a minor traffic violation.

Sebring's Golden Age began in the mid-1950s—Mike Hawthorn and Phil Walters racing Phil Hill and Carroll Shelby for twelve hours in 1955; Juan Manuel Fangio and Eugenio Castellotti in 1956; Fangio and Jean Behra in 1957. The long string of Ferrari victories saw Olivier Gendebien and Phil Hill win three times. Hardly a great driver of this time had not blasted past the rotting old mammoth seaplanes and weatherbeaten hangars—usually hating every minute of it.

Colin Chapman and Mario Andretti at Watkins Glen. A 500 winner, Mario Andretti set a lap record to earn the pole in the 1968 Grand Prix, his first Formula I race.

Phil Hill winning at Pebble Beach, April 1955. All four wheels on his Ferrari Monza are off the ground. The narrow, tree-lined public-road circuit was abandoned in 1956, but road racing was saved on California's Monterey peninsula when nearby Fort Ord provided the Laguna Seca course.

Sprite drivers Stirling Moss and Steve McQueen (left) at Sebring in 1962. In the 1970 Sebring, McQueen and Peter Revson finished second overall in the screen star's Porsche 908.

Although the Ulmanns may have been slow in bringing Sebring up to modern standards, they played a key role in America's road racing renaissance. Beyond staging America's first international sports car races in modern times, in December 1959 Sebring held the first United States Grand Prix since the American Grand Prix series of 1908–1916. As the final Formula I championship event of the year, and with Stirling Moss still in the running for the world driver's title, there was a good deal of interest, at least in the pits. But the gallant Englishman retired with engine trouble, and a sweet-natured young New Zealander, Bruce McLaren, went on to win his first Grand Prix.

Alec Ulmann took the U.S. GP to Riverside on November 20, 1960. Stirling Moss won this one, but the crowd was, if possible, as thin as at Sebring. The twelve hours at Sebring still was the place to be that third weekend in March. Ford began making its presence felt. Miles and McLaren won seconds in 1965; Miles and Ruby won firsts in 1966, with Fords filling the first three places. In 1967 Andretti-McLaren won a first in the Ford MK4, the first to finish the grind with a better than 100-mph race average.

Sebring began to run into trouble as race averages soared. Safety-conscious officials displayed an increasing reluctance to grant Sebring race dates. In 1966 it was engulfed in criticism when a Porsche left the track and killed four VIP spectators standing in a non-spectator area. The infield crowd (Sebring is usually held over the third weekend in March to capture college students who flock to Florida during spring recess) was getting out of hand. A newspaper circulated stories of infield orgies, and pictures went out showing a state policeman jabbing a photographer with an electric cattle prong. Alec Ulmann made several unsuccessful attempts to move the circuit, and in 1973 he did not renew his arrangement when the SCCA refused to grant Sebring its regular March date.

But the battered old course—it has had more reruns than a John Wayne Western—wasn't ready for obscurity. Reggie Smith, Ulmann's perennial right-hand man, negotiated a new lease, and IMSA, the International Motor Sports Association, the sanctioning body headed by former SCCA executive director John Bishop, granted Sebring its usual March race date. No legendary Maseratis, Ferraris, or Chaparrals roared through the long

The John Fitch/Phil Walters Cunningham C5 roadster, third in the 1953 Le Mans, recorded 154.8 mph on the Mulsanne Straight, the fastest time in the race.

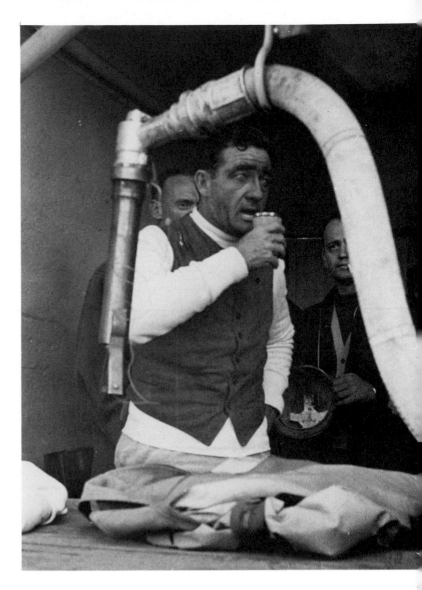

Florida twilight, but the large field of Porsches and Corvettes put on a good show as the Gregg-Haywood Porsche Carrera covered 1175 miles to win.

In March 1951 George Rand, one of the few ARCA drivers to remain active after the war, acted as captain for a group of eight Americans invited to participate in a race that was being staged as part of the Pan American games in Buenos Aires. South American junkets played an important role in the careers of several young American drivers. John Fitch believes his winning of the General Peron Grand Prix brought him to Briggs Cunningham's attention; Carroll Shelby first met John Wyer in the Argentine in January 1954 and was racing for Aston Martin that spring; and Phil Hill began his fruitful association with Scuderia Ferrari in Buenos Aires in January 1956.

Rand drove the Cunningham Ferrari in which Sam Collier had suffered his fatal accident at Watkins Glen in 1950; Fred Wacker, the Anglo-American Tom Cole and Fitch had Allards, with Bill Spear and Jim Kimberly driving Ferraris. Fitch, who drove Cole's old Cadillac-Allard to a full-lap win over Wacker, was made an honorary member of the Peronist Party by the dictator

and launched himself as the first professional U.S. road-racing driver.

In 1950 Briggs Swift Cunningham first tried to bring a Le Mans victory to an American team. An internationally known salt-water sailor, Cunningham raced six-meter yachts as a member of the American team prior to World War II, and in 1958 he was to captain the winning *Columbia* in the American Cup races against Great Britain. While still at Yale, Cunningham met Ralph DePalma and became interested in auto racing. With the help of Buick chief engineer Charles Chayne, Cunningham built the Bu-Merc, a Mercedes-Buick Special that Miles Collier drove in the 1940 New York World's Fair GP and in which Cunningham finished second in the first Watkins Glen.

Late in 1949 Cunningham bought one of the Fordillacs —Ford coupes with tuned Cadillac V-8 engines in a modified Ford chassis—that were being made by the new firm of Frick-Tappett Motors in Freeport, Long Island. Phil Walters, who successfully raced midgets at the Freeport stadium under the name of Ted Tappett (young Dan Gurney was one of Tappett's most ardent fans), had teamed with local engine-tuning wizard Bill

John Fitch, right, and his 1955 Le Mans driving partner, Pierre Levegh. The crash of Levegh's Mercedes the following day took the largest toll in racing history.

Frick in the building of Walters' all-conquering stock car. The pair had an eye on the then beginning market for hopped-up specials, and Cunningham was one of their first customers.

Pleased with his Fordillac, Cunningham asked Phil Walters to help him build three cars in which he could tackle Le Mans. Walters had never heard of Le Mans or seen a sports-car race, but he liked the idea and joined Cunningham in West Palm Beach, where Cunningham cars began production. As time did not permit new cars for the 24 Hours in 1950, Cunningham bought two type-61 Cadillac sedans. An enormous open body was put on one, and, except for a little work on the brakes, the second car was raced almost as it came out of the showroom.

Frick-Tappett were now a part of Cunningham enterprises, and Phil Walters, with Miles and Sam Collier, joined Cunningham at Le Mans. The open Cadillac, affectionately called "Le Monstre" by the French, lost all but high gear but was still driven to eleventh place by Walters and Cunningham. Sam and Miles Collier brought the blue and white coupe home tenth.

Cunningham had used the Cadillacs to find out what it would take to win the 24 Hours. One of Walters' and Cunningham's experiments was to stuff a big Cadillac engine into an Austin-Healey. The hybrid took a first (Walters) and a second (Cunningham) at Watkins Glen. Cadillac then refused to sell Cunningham more engines, so he turned to Chrysler, whose engines were to power all Cunningham race cars but one. The last Cunningham

A meeting of the drivers in the Cunningham pits at the 1960 Le Mans: Briggs Cunningham (left), Bob Grossman, Fred Windridge, Dr. Dick Thompson, and Chevrolet's Zora Arkus-Duntov. John Fitch, with his back to the camera, stands on Cunningham's right.

built before the plant closed in 1955, the open C-6R, used an Offenhauser engine. Briggs returned to Le Mans in 1951 with three C-2Rs and a little 726-cc Crosley Hot Shot in roadster form. Driver pairings were Fitch-Walters, Cunningham-Huntoon, Rand-Wacker with Schraft-Stiles in the Crosley. Three Cunningham entries retired, but after eighteen hours the Fitch-Walters car was in second place. Then a bearing began to go, and they were lucky to nurse the Cunningham to its eighteenth-place finish. Back home the blue and white C-2Rs cleaned up.

Two lighter C-4Rs and a C-4RK coupe ran the 24 Hours in 1952, but only the Spear-Cunningham machine, in which the patron himself drove for twenty-two of the twenty-four hours to finish fourth, completed the race.

In many ways 1953 was Cunningham's best at Le Mans. Two refined C-4s and a new slippery-shaped, open C-5 with huge seventeen-inch brakes were entered for Fitch-Walters, Cunningham-Spear, and Moran-Bennet. The Cunninghams finished third, seventh and tenth. *If* the C-type Jaguar had not had its sensational new disc brakes (they raised the Le Mans record by a staggering nine mph), Fitch and Walters, whose car finished third with a race average seven mph faster than the 1952 winner, *if* the C types had not been able to go so deep into the Sarthe circuit's many turns, *if* . . .

Two weeks later Fitch flipped the C-5 in the Reims 12 Hours as he barreled through the long sweeping bend past the pits. The car was written off, but Fitch came out of it with minor injuries. Two weeks later he

Wives of the drivers Thompson and Windridge brighten the Cunningham pits, 1960.

After running as high as fourth in the 1960 Le Mans, the Grossman/Fitch Corvette is nursed home with the aid of ice packs.

The Grossman/Fitch Corvette took an eighth-place finish at Le Mans, 1960.

was driving a Sunbeam in the Alpine Rally. The 1954 Le Mans saw Cunningham enter two C-4Rs for Bill Spear–Sherwood Johnston and Cunningham-Bennet. Walters-Fitch was assigned Cunningham's new Ferrari. The Ferrari failed to last as the Cunninghams finished third and fifth. Cunningham tried a new combination in 1955, the Offy-engined C-6R for himself and Sherwood Johnston and a D-type Jaguar for Phil Walters and Bill Spear. Neither car finished.

Following a good season in America and in Europe, John Fitch became a technical adviser for the 20th Century-Fox film *The Racers,* based on a novel by driver-journalist Hans Reuch. The author had been injured in a racing accident, so Fitch, with the Swiss champion Baron de Graffenreid, drove in the race scenes, made certain that the various locales were authentic, and acted as the liaison between Hollywood and the racing world.

After coming in fifth overall and winning the Grand Touring class for Mercedes in the Italian classic, the grueling Mille Miglia, Fitch was given a ride in a Mercedes-Benz 300 SLR for the 1955 Le Mans. His co-driver was the veteran French ace Pierre Levegh, who, in 1952, had battled the mighty Mercedes team single-handed until the twenty-third hour when his Talbot failed while he was in the lead. Fitch was never to drive the Mercedes at Le Mans. It was Levegh, on the forty-second lap, nearing the end of his first driving turn, whose car crashed into the packed stands as he vainly sought to slip between an Austin-Healey and a Jaguar that had suddenly changed direction.

The 300 SLR's magnesium skin and its shattered engine sprayed the crowd across from the pits with lethal, shrapnel-like fragments. Levegh and more than eighty spectators died in a disaster that shocked the world. Many safety measures, especially those related to circuit hazards, were taken as auto racing fought to survive the storm of criticism that followed the holocaust.

Soon after the 1955 season Phil Walters stopped racing. He had won close to a hundred midget and stock-car races as Ted Tappett, and, as Phil Walters, he enjoyed an outstanding career as a sports car driver, including double victories at Sebring and Watkins Glen.

Mercedes retired from racing after 1955, and Fitch briefly drove again for Briggs Cunningham. In 1957 Fitch became team manager-driver-consultant for the Corvette challenge at Sebring. For several years he managed the Lime Rock circuit near his Connecticut home, where in September 1958 Fitch staged one of the first professional sports car races in the modern era. This was sanctioned by USAC and outlawed by the SCCA.

When Cunningham returned to Le Mans in 1960 it was with a team of three Corvettes and a Jaguar. Fitch was with him as Bob Grossman's partner in one of the Corvettes. Grossman's Le Mans record shows six consecutive finishes in the twenty-four-hours in the top ten, including a sixth place in 1962 when he was driving a 3-liter Ferrari coupe with stock-car star Fireball Roberts as his co-driver. In 1960 Cunningham drove with young Bill Kimberly, a pair of SCCA regulars—Fred Windridge and Dr. Dick Thompson—drove the remaining Corvette, and Dan Gurney and Walter Hansgen were assigned the Jag. Only the Fitch-Grossman car survived. After running as high as fifth, the big Chevrolet engine lost its water. Alfred Momo, Cunningham's longtime *chef d'affaires,* packed the Corvette's engine compartment with ice, and Grossman and Fitch nursed the big blue and white coupe to an eighth overall and first in Grand Touring.

The Briggs Cunningham–Walt Hansgen era, from 1956 until 1964, was to see some great racing, with Cunningham himself occasionally driving at Sebring during the 1960s. Cunningham opened a fine automobile museum in Costa Mesa, California, but seems to have given up on ever bringing a blue and white car home first at Le Mans.

The Young Masters

VIII

Five drivers—Phil Hill, Ritchie Ginther, Dan Gurney, Masten Gregory and Carroll Shelby—were the young masters of postwar American racing. Three Californians, a music-loving Kansan, and an affable Texan went overseas and carved out places for themselves as members of the tradition-encrusted European factory teams. They carried American colors into victory lane from the Nurburgring to Monza, and when they came home they set American racing on its ear. After two of them, Shelby and Gurney, stopped driving, they became builders—and made race cars that won Indianapolis and the Manufacturers World Championship.

Some very good Yanks stayed home. Others made brief overseas forays, and a few, particularly Bob Bondurant, who drove for Shelby in 1964 and 1965, and Ronnie Bucknum, as part of Honda's Formula I effort, earned lasting fame. Some American drivers did not take to Europe. Bob Holbert was thoroughly unhappy at Le Mans in 1961, when he and Masten Gregory finished fifth overall in a factory Porsche. Walter Hansgen, who rarely had a bad day, did poorly at Le Mans, frequently winding up in the sandbank at Tertre Rouge.

In 1963 Jim Hall worked hard to make his mark in Grand Prix racing, and Harry Schell, an expatriate American, was already in the forefront of international racing in the 1950s. Schell, who was raised in Paris by enthusiast parents, both of whom raced and rallied with considerable success, made his Paris bistro, L'Action Automobile, European racing's unofficial headquarters. He was a good driver—he won the Caen Grand Prix in a Maserati and shared the 1956 winner in the Ring's 1000 K's—but he was not a great one, and his outlandish off-track escapades overshadowed his racing accomplishments. In 1960 Schell was killed practicing in the wet at Silverstone.

The trek to Le Mans became commonplace. California Lotus dealer Jay Chamberlain had a ninth overall and a second in the 1957 Index of Performance. He also had a serious crash in the rain at the 1958 Le Mans. Triumph expert Mike Rothchild enjoyed several factory rides. Motoring journalist John Bentley, a small-car specialist, raced a 1100-cc Cooper and several Oscas at

Le Mans. His co-driver in 1956, when the Cooper finished eighth, was Ed Hugus, who racked up an eighth in 1957 driving a Porsche with Ernie Erickson. In 1960, the year twenty-four Americans drove in the 24 Hours, Hugus, co-driving with brewery heir Augie Pabst, finished seventh.

Before the 1960s, road racing in the United States was almost entirely in sports cars. An occasional vintage Grand Prix single-seater appeared in Formula Libre races (George Weaver's Poison Lil, an ancient GP Maserati, was a perennial first-lap leader at Watkins Glen). But until the December 1959 U.S. Grand Prix, sports cars, those, in theory, that carry two passengers and operate on public roads, were the standard American road racer.

By 1960 sports car racing had become the almost exclusive domain of the Sports Car Club of America. The U.S. Auto Club ran a thin, four-event, championship road racing series from 1958 through 1961. The USAC venture into sports car racing helped to convince the SCCA it had better develop its own professional program. Until 1961 the SCCA had resisted strong pressures to introduce professional racing which would allow SCCA drivers to collect cash rather than a trophy. USAC still sanctions an occasional race for Indianapolis-type cars on U.S. and Canadian road courses and says it retains an interest in forming a road racing division. However, before 1969, when former SCCA executive director John Bishop founded IMSA, the International Motor Sports Association, the SCCA had road racing all to itself.

The U.S. Road Racing Championship, first of the pro series that now dominate the club's activities, got under way in 1963. If you wanted to make a career out of road racing, if you drove well enough and were a good enough salesman, you found yourself a patron, or bought your own car. Phil Hill did both.

Philip Hill was born in Miami and raised in Santa Monica, where his father was the postmaster. He bought his first sports car, a supercharged MG-TC, in 1947, and three years later, with Ritchie Ginther as his crew chief, drove an XK120 Jaguar to win his first race. This

The start of a Volkswagen-based Formula Vee event at Vineland, New Jersey, 1964. Vees are the most popular of all Sports Car Club of America racing classes.

was at Pebble Beach. In 1952 Hill drove the former Ascari Ferrari to a sixth overall in the Pan American road race, and in 1954 he made his first trip to Le Mans, where the Osca he shared with Fred Wacker dropped out while leading its class. Hill and Ginther went off the road in the 1953 Mexican Road Race, but in 1954, with Ginther again as Hill's passenger, Hill drove Alan Guilberson's Ferrari into a second-place finish twenty-four minutes behind Maglioli's works Ferrari.

Hill, paired with Carroll Shelby (it was their only major race together), finished a disputed second to the Walters-Hawthorn, Cunningham-owned Jaguar at Sebring in 1955. Only after Cunningham's own scorer, the respected Joe Lane, was consulted were the results announced. Following the 1955 confusion, Joe Lane became Sebring's official scorer. Hill captured the SCCA 1955 "D" Sports racing championship, and in January 1956 he joined the Belgian racer Olivier Gendebien, in the Argentine, as a member of the Ferrari sports-car team. Hill and Gendebien, beginning their long and successful partnership, were second to the Stirling Moss–Carlos Menditeguy Maserati in Buenos Aires. The same year Hill and Gendebien scored wins for Ferrari in Sweden and Sicily, and in 1958, again paired with Gendebien, Hill captured Le Mans, becoming the first American to win that twenty-four-hour classic.

Paired with Peter Collins, Hill was first in the 1958 Buenos Aires 1000 K's, and then, again with Gendebien,

he won Sebring the same year. Hill's performance in sports cars earned him a place on the Ferrari Formula I team. He was at the top. Following 1958 late-season third-place finishes at Monza, where he recorded the fastest lap, and at Casablanca, in 1959, Hill drove to fourths at Silverstone and Monaco, finished second in the French Grand Prix at Reims (on a day the track temperature soared to 110 and melted the tar surface), earned a third in the German Grand Prix at Avus (with Gurney's Ferrari second), and at Monza he had a popular second in the Italian Grand Prix.

In the 1960 Monza, Phil Hill won his first Grand Prix, the first to be taken by an American since Jimmy Murphy's victory in 1921. Phil went into the 1961 season, the first for the new 1500-cc Grand Prix formula, apprehensive over the reliability of the small, superlight cars, commenting testily, "Anyone can now drive these fool things." It was to be a bittersweet year for the sensitive young Californian. Seconds at Zandvoort in the Dutch Grand Prix and at Aintree in the British, third-place finishes over the Nurburgring and at Monte Carlo, with a first at the bullet-fast Spa circuit in the Ardennes, set the stage for Monza, where Phil Hill's victory in the 1961 Italian Grand Prix made him the first American to win the World Drivers Championship. But Hill's friend and rival, the brilliant young German Wolfgang von Trips, lost his life at Monza and Phil's triumph was edged with tragedy.

Phil Hill and the Belgian star Olivier Gendebien after winning the 1958 Le Mans, the first
of three for this pair of Ferrari drivers.

Dan Gurney crouches to make himself appear
smaller than his quite tall father.

Dusk at Le Mans as Phil Hill takes his Ferrari Testa Rosa down the pit straight on his way to
winning the 1961 24 Hours.

Hill, with Gendebien, had maintained his winning ways with Ferrari sports cars, in 1962 capturing Le Mans for the third time and winning the Nurburgring's 1000 K's. However, relations between the cantankerous Commendatore and his outspoken American champion had begun to deteriorate. During seven years as a factory sports car driver, Hill had won Ferrari six manufacturers' world championships. He had won thirty major races since starting to drive Ferraris in 1952, and he had earned the world drivers championship in Ferrari Grand Prix cars. But in 1962 Phil Hill had fallen from grace, and that year was his last with Enzo Ferrari.

Hill then joined two former Ferrari men, engineer Carlo Chiti and team manager Romolo Tavoni, at ATS. However, the new Formula I machine never became competitive, and Hill concentrated on sports cars for the remainder of his career. Between 1964 and the close of the 1967 season, when he retired, Hill won the Daytona 2000 K's, driving a Ferrari with Pedro Rodriguez; the 1966 Nurburgring 1000 K's, with Jo Bonnier in Jim Hall's Chaparral; and in July 1967, with Mike Spence, he brought the winged Chaparral home ahead of the Jackie Stewart–Chris Amon Ferrari in the BOAC six-hours at Brands Hatch. He also drove a Chaparral in the 1966 Can-Am series, where he won at Laguna Seca, and was fourth in season points.

Today Phil Hill, the single Yank ever to hold the world drivers title, and with Dan Gurney the only American to achieve top rank in Grand Prix racing, is sought as a TV commentator, listens to his unique collection of classical player-piano rolls, putters with vintage cars, and recently has begun to raise a family. Journalist-race driver Denise McCluggage said it best when she titled her piece on Phil Hill "Hamlet in a Helmet."

Dan Gurney's parents (his father was an opera singer) moved from Long Island to Riverside, California, shortly after Dan finished high school. An ardent race fan, young Gurney was one of the group that had cheered midget star Ted Tappett from their special seats behind the pits at Freeport Stadium. He first raced a

TR-2 at Torrey Pines in 1955, moved up to a Porsche Speedster, a Corvette, and then a short-wheel-based 4.9 Ferrari in which he ran second to Carroll Shelby at Riverside in 1957. Gurney won at Palm Springs the following spring and headed for Europe.

It was a wet Le Mans, and Bruce Kessler crashed the 3-liter Ferrari he was sharing with Gurney. Two weeks later Gurney had a ride with the Belgian Andre Pilette in the twelve-hour sports-car race, then held at Reims as a preliminary to the French GP. Pilette flipped the Ferrari coupe but not before Gurney had demonstrated his talent.

Gurney returned to Europe in 1959 to drive sports cars for Ferrari, but in mid-season, with the French Grand Prix, he became a member of the Formula I team. He was second in the German GP on the high banks at Avus and, with co-driver Chuck Daigh and the Hill-Gendebien team which "relieved" them, shared in winning the 1959 Sebring 12 Hours. He was lured to BRM in 1960 but had a poor year in Formula I while sharing the winning Maserati with Stirling Moss in the Nurburgring's 1000 K's.

In 1961, the lanky Californian moved to Porsche, driving their new Formula I car to seconds at Reims, Monza, and Watkins Glen to finish second in the World Drivers Championship. Although he had yet to win his first Grand Prix, Gurney's 1961 standing was the highest of his career. He won the 1962 French GP at Rouen for his first and Porsche's only Grand Prix victory.

Earlier in 1962 Dan won the Daytona Continental inaugural in a climax that caused a change in the rules of racing. With his Lotus-Ford showing signs of failing, near the end of the race Gurney, while well in the lead, pulled up high on the banks just short of the start-finish line. As the checkered flag came out Gurney got his roadster going with its starter motor, coasting down the banks and over the finish line. Crossing the finish line under your own power is now required.

Indianapolis attracted Gurney for the first time in 1962 when he tried John Zink's experimental turbine

Jack Brabham's Cooper-Climax leads Lloyd Ruby through one of Indy's shallow turns. The rear-engined car was slower on the straights, but it pulled away from the Indy cars on the four turns and finished ninth.

Car builder John Cooper, Grand Prix champion Brabham, and Jim Kimberly, right, a former sports-car champion whose backing made possible the 1961 Cooper entry at the Speedway.

Car owner J. C. Agajanian, rarely seen without his white cowboy hat, and Colin Chapman, a dedicated cap wearer, trade headgear at the Trenton Speedway.

Ralph Liquori's solid-axle front-engined Dirt car contrasts sharply with Jim McElreath's rear-engined Ford.

but switched to one of Mickey Thompson's Harvey Aluminum Specials. He qualified Thompson's rear-engined Buick at 147.886 mph, good enough for eighth on the grid, but fell out on the ninety-second lap with transmission failure and was credited with a twentieth-place finish.

Gurney was doing graduate work at the Speedway. In 1961 John Cooper, who in 1946 built the 500-cc rear-engined Formula III cars that were forerunners of today's rear-engined racers, brought a 2.7-liter Cooper Coventry-Climax to the Speedway. With financial help from Jim Kimberly and a cool drive from world champion Jack Brabham, the little green car had an enormous impact on Indianapolis and on Gurney. Indy drivers found that Brabham, who learned to race in Australia, where he was "Speedway" champion from 1948 to 1951, was not inclined to back off in a tight situation. The Cooper, while giving away more than 30 mph on the straights, sailed through Indy's four shallow 9-degree turns without slowing down, and Brabham, to the surprise of Speedway regulars, did not find it necessary to stay in the hallowed groove. The Cooper qualified thirteenth at 145.144 mph against pole-sitter Eddie Sachs's 147.481 mph. It finished a creditable ninth, and the Speedway was never again to be the same.

Convinced that a well-designed rear-engined car could win the 500, Gurney asked the brilliant English builder Colin Chapman to see the 1963 Indianapolis. Gurney, who paid for Chapman's trip, also introduced him to Ford executives.

"I'd watched the Indy cars at Monza in 1958 in that Race of Two Worlds," said Gurney. "I'd seen how Brabham did at Indy in the little 265-hp Cooper. In 1962 I qualified eighth in Mickey Thompson's rear-engined Buick—you know that was a good car. I had seen what a rear-engined car could do in Grand Prix racing. Chapman, along with Cooper, were the best rear-engined car builders, and Chapman is a very creative guy. I knew what the rear-engined car could do at Indy and I wanted to be in on it."

Out of these Gurney-inspired meetings came the rear-engined Lotus-Fords that broke the Offenhauser roadster's long reign. Between 1965 and 1973, Ford won the 500 five times. Jim Clark and Dan Gurney first drove Lotus-powered-by-Ford entries in the 1963 Indianapolis. Gurney, accidentally, did much to assure the old guard that lightweight rear-engined monocoque machines were sturdy when he crashed his Lotus into the wall during practice and walked away unhurt. Had he been driving a heavy front-engined, solid-axle roadster, the results may not have been so fortunate.

Although Ford's more sophisticated DOHC engine was still a year away, the 255-cubic-inch V-8 pushrod powered Clark to a second and Gurney to a seventh-

172

Parnelli Jones pits on his way to winning the 1963 Indy. Taking on a full load of fuel and a change of tires in twenty seconds is not at all unusual.

OVERLEAF: Gurney drove his Gurney-built Formula I Eagle to win the 1967 Grand Prix of Belgium with a record 148.818-mph average.

Fire, following a fifty-fifth-lap pit stop, puts Parnelli out of the 1964 500.

Winning the 1966 *Motor Trend* 500 late-model sedan race. Gurney won a total of five NASCAR Grand Nationals on the Riverside road course.

Ford paired two of America's best to win the 1967 Le Mans: A. J. Foyt (left) and Dan Gurney in Victory Lane.

place finish. Had the chief steward, Harlan Fengler, been more severe with Parnelli Jones for his aggressiveness under the yellow caution light (the rules require that a driver hold his position), Parnelli would not have continued to charge through the field. Of more importance, if Fengler had instructed starter Pat Vidan to use the black flag Vidan had curled in his hand, Clark would have won in 1963 as well as in 1965. Jones's venerable No. 98 had developed a crack in its oil tank late in the race and was spraying the track with oil. Parnelli's supporters say Fengler did the proper thing. The crack was horizontal, and once the oil level got below it, about ten laps from the finish, it stopped leaking. And, how the hell can you black-flag a guy when he's in the lead and about to win Indy?

Clark and Chapman took the setback graciously, although Chapman and Agajanian, Parnelli's car owner, had had a heated discussion with Fengler at the start-finish line during the final minutes of the race. Several drivers, including Eddie Sachs, who got punched in the nose when he insisted on reminding Parnelli Jones that he had won unfairly, and Roger McCluskey, who spun in Jones's oil, were openly critical of the officials.

Following Porsche's withdrawal from Grand Prix racing, Gurney joined Jack Brabham's Formula I team. Gurney won his second French GP at Rouen in 1964, again bringing a new car its first-ever Grand Prix victory. Gurney, a member of the Indianapolis Lotus team in 1964, was withdrawn after 110 laps as a safety precaution when teammate Jim Clark's Lotus developed tire failure. Winner of five 500-mile NASCAR races at Riverside, Gurney's success at Indianapolis and in sports car and Grand Prix racing had earned him the reputation of being America's finest all-round driver. He formed All-American Racers with Carroll Shelby

Two giants of American racing: diminutive Ritchie Ginther (left) and Mario Andretti, at Riverside.

late in 1964 but in 1965 continued to race for Jack Brabham in Grand Prix. Gurney had two bad years at the Speedway, falling out with timing-gear failure in 1965 and in 1966, being unable to restart his new Eagle-Ford after it was damaged during that year's infamous first-lap melee.

In sports cars Gurney's Lola-Ford won the Bridge-hampton Can-Am, the only non-Chevrolet-powered car to win a Can-Am during its first four years. Gurney made racing history by winning the 1967 Grand Prix of Belgium in his AAR Eagle, becoming the first American driver to win a Grand Prix in an American car in forty-six years. Co-driving with A. J. Foyt, Dan Gurney set a 135.48-mph twenty-four-hour race average to bring Ford its second Le Mans victory, and, until Andretti went faster, he had a 167.942-mph qualifying record at Indianapolis. He finished the 1967 season by winning the Rex Mays 300 Championship car race at Riverside to become the first driver to win Grand Prix, stock car, sports car, and Indianapolis championship car races in one year.

Gurney acquired full ownership of All-American Racers in 1967. In the 500 of 1968 Gurney-built Eagles finished first, second, and fourth. Bobby Unser's first-place Eagle was powered by a turbocharged Offen-hauser, while Gurney's second-place Eagle used a stock-block Ford. When Gurney and Shelby formed All-American Racers their big objectives were the two plums of single-seater racing, Indianapolis and Formula I. Shelby, who was spending more and more time on Ford projects, withdrew from AAR, but it did fulfill its promise.

Gurney, No. 48, passing rookie Mike Mosley during the 1970 Indianapolis. The most versatile and, to many, the finest of modern American drivers, Gurney's best at the Speedway were second-place finishes in 1968 and 1969.

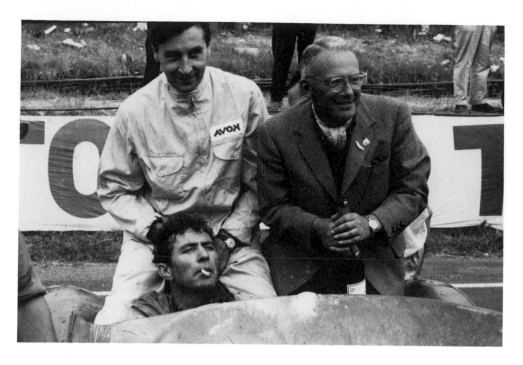

Carroll Shelby, behind the wheel, and co-driver Roy Salvadori with David Brown, owner of Aston Martin, following their victory in the 1959 Le Mans.

Masten Gregory and his Austrian co-driver, Jochen Rindt, being toasted after winning the 1965 Le Mans in a North American Racing Team Ferrari.

In 1968, after abandoning Formula I, Gurney closed his Anglo American Racers plant in England. He continued to build AAR Eagles at his Costa Mesa shop and began cutting down his personal racing schedule. In the 1969 Indianapolis, second place earned him $68,000. In 1970 he ended his long association with Ford when he fielded a team of two Plymouth Barracudas for himself and young Swede Savage in the Trans-Am championship. Following a third for his Eagle-Offy in the 1970 Indianapolis, Gurney joined his friend Bruce McLaren as a member of the McLaren Formula I and Can-Am teams. After victories at Mosport and St. Jovite in the Can-Am, Gurney finished no higher than sixth in a series of Grand Prix races. Sponsor conflicts resulted in Gurney leaving Team McLaren in mid-season. In September 1970 he qualified second in the Ontario 500 and was leading at the halfway mark when he was forced to retire. His final race as a driver was the October Riverside Trans-Am. Dan Gurney's fifteen-year career had established him as one of the most versatile

drivers of all time, and to many he was the best American driver of his age.

Although Ritchie Ginther and Masten Gregory never reached the Phil Hill–Dan Gurney class, their accomplishments helped make American drivers a force in international racing. Following rides as Phil Hill's mechanic in the Mexican road races, Ginther drove Aston Martins, a Porsche Spyder, and Ferraris on the West Coast before going to Le Mans in 1957, where his two-liter Ferrari failed to finish. He shared a Ferrari Testa Rosa with his employer, Johnny von Neumann, in the 1958 Sebring, became manager of Ferrari of California, and in 1960 finished second in the Argentine 1000 K's and was offered a factory ride.

A small man, with a sensitivity that includes but goes beyond race cars, Paul Richard Ginther became chief test driver for Ferrari. His Formula I debut was the 1960 Grand Prix of Monaco, where he had the distinction of being the first driver of the new rear-engined Formula I Ferrari. Ginther was sixth at Monte

178

Ken Miles, left, and Carroll Shelby hold their trophy after the Double 500 at Bridge-hampton, September 1964. Shelby's manager, Al Dowd, stands on right.

1963 U.S. road-racing champion Bob Holbert's Porsche leads Harry Heuer's Chaparral at Watkins Glen.

Carlo and second to his friend Phil Hill at Monza. In 1961 he finished fifth in Grand Prix drivers' standings, but the next two seasons were to be his best.

After switching to BRM in 1962 Ginther had seconds at Monaco and Monza and a third in the French GP. With BRM teammate Graham Hill, he gave the Rover-BRM turbine a brilliant ride in the 1963 Le Mans. Placed in a special category, the green 00 coupe covered 2583 miles, enough to have won the twenty-four-hours up to 1958.

Ginther's 1963 record included repeat seconds at Monte Carlo and Monza and a 3rd at the Ring in the German GP, saw him tied for second place with BRM teammate Graham Hill in the World Drivers Championship. His BRM was the only Grand Prix car to complete all championship Formula I races in 1964, and Honda selected the diminutive Californian when the Japanese firm entered Grand Prix racing. Ginther brought the raucous Honda 12 two sixths and a seventh-place finish before winning the 1965 Mexican Grand

Prix for his own as well as Honda's sole Grand Prix victory. Ginther left Honda and Grand Prix racing after the 1966 Mexican GP, in which he finished fourth. With his racing savvy and test-driver experience, Ritchie Ginther is a sought-after team manager.

Although it called for courage and a special talent, Masten Gregory's habit of jumping out of rapidly moving, accident-bound race cars may have made it difficult for the slight, spectacle-wearing basso to find good rides. He won his first race in 1953 at Golden Gate Park in San Francisco. Later that summer, following a string of wins in SCCA races, he entered his C-type Jaguar at Floyd Bennett Field, New York, where it caught fire during practice. Spotting another, almost new C Jag in the pits, he bought it on the spot for $5000.

In 1954 Gregory failed to finish the Argentine race but bought the winning Ferrari and took off for Europe, where, in sports car races, he was fourth at Reims, third at Lisbon, and a winner at Aintree and Nassau. He drove a 250 Maserati for Centro-Sud, and his first full

179

Carroll Shelby in the Cobra roadster, Ken Miles in the chassis of the first Cobra Daytona coupe, and designer Pete Brock.

year in Formula I, 1957, was his best. He finished every race he started and had a third at Monaco and a fourth at Monza to finish fifth in the year's world driver standings.

A series of accidents slowed Gregory's career, but in 1959 he joined John Cooper and earned a third at Zandvoort and a second in the GP of Portugal. Co-driving with Camoradi U.S.A. promoter Lloyd "Lucky" Casner in sports cars, their Maserati won the 1961 Nurburgring 1000 K's. Gregory also won the 1963 Mosport 200 and in 1965, with Jochen Rindt, was first at Le Mans in the North American Racing Team Ferrari 250 LM coupe, which was entered by three-time Le Mans winner Luigi Chinetti. Gregory qualified thirty-first in the 1965 Indianapolis 500 and electrified the crowd by moving up to fifth place by the forty-third lap only to fall out on the fifty-ninth lap when his rear-engined Ford lost its oil pressure. In 1970 at Sebring, Gregory's and the Dutchman Toine Hezeman's Alfa Romeo T-33 completed 247 laps, one less than the winning Ferrari, to finish third.

The oldest and most colorful of America's young masters was Carroll Shelby. Son of a rural mail carrier, Carroll was born in the village of Leesburg, Texas, in 1923 and was raised in Dallas. Shelby drove a friend's MG TC to his first victory in 1952. He was soon a regular winner, first in an XK 120 Jaguar, then in a Cadillac-Allard. In January 1954, with Phil Hill, Bob Said, and Masten Gregory, Shelby represented the U.S. in the Argentine 1000 K's.

In South America Shelby met John Wyer, who became Shelby's team manager at Aston Martin and his associate in Shelby's Cobra and Ford ventures. Following South America—where Shelby and Masten Gregory's

brother-in-law, Dale Duncan, drove a Cad-Allard into tenth place, the only American entry to finish—Shelby and Charley Wallace, a Washington, D.C., hairdresser, raced a Wyer-managed works Aston Martin at Sebring but retired early.

With encouragement but no commitment from John Wyer, Shelby went to England in the spring of 1954. The Aintree track in Liverpool, home of England's annual madness, the Grand National Steeplechase, had built an automobile race course within the horse track, and Wyer entered an Aston Martin, painted blue and white, in honor of its American driver. After a heady race on a wet track, Shelby beat a host of English drivers to finish second to Duncan Hamilton's C Jaguar. Shelby joined Captain George Eyston, Donald Healey, and Roy Jackson-Moore at the Bonneville Salt Flats in August, where the group's two Austin-Healeys set more than seventy land speed records.

With Phil Hill, Shelby had a close second in the 1955 Sebring, and he became a consistent winner of major SCCA nationals, driving a 4.9 Ferrari supplied by John Edgar, one of Shelby's many patrons. Shelby was injured at Riverside in September 1957, but recovered to win a classic race from Gurney, Walt Hansgen, and Gregory at Riverside in November.

The high point of Shel's career was winning the 1959 Le Mans with Roy Salvadori in a factory Aston Martin DBR-I. Shelby's Formula I record was uniformly dismal. He was limited to less than first-class machinery, Centro-Sud Maseratis and the heavy, front-engined Aston Martin GP car that was obsolete before it was raced. A fourth at Monza in 1958, when he shared a ride with Masten Gergory, was Shelby's best Grand Prix finish.

Dave MacDonald, Bob Holbert, and Carroll Shelby (left to right), with Daytona coupe.

Ken Miles' Cobra, No. 50, leads Bob Johnson's, No. 33, at Laguna Seca.

The laconic Texan of the striped farmer's overalls and railroad engineer's hat had been looking ahead. Carroll Shelby sports cars, with Jim Hall and Jim's brother Dick as partners, had opened in Dallas in 1956. Shelby's last season as a driver was 1960. Recurrent chest pains had been diagnosed as angina pectoris, and, following wins at Riverside in May and Castle Rock in June, Shelby quit.

A popular man with a knack for getting along with men on the business side of racing, Shelby withdrew from his Dallas garage and moved to California, where he became a racing tire distributor and opened the Shelby School of High Performance Driving. He had the good fortune to hire the many-talented Peter Brock to run his driver's school, first located at Riverside, and to begin his adventure of building the Cobra (Shelby says the name Cobra came to him in a dream), an American sports car that was to meet, and beat, the Europeans.

The first Cobras were Anglo-American hybrids with Ford engines, with body and chassis supplied by England's AC Car Company. Unsuccessful in getting General Motors to supply him with their lightweight V-8, Shelby talked Ford's Dave Evans into sending him two 221-cubic-inch Fairlane engines, which, after tuning, were shipped to the AC works at Thames Ditton, near London. Later Ford came through with several larger, 260-cubic-inch, high-performance engines, and Shelby went to England to help build the first car. The CSX00 arrived in California early in 1962 and soon was in Detroit being evaluated. Donald Frey, who was to become president of the Ford Division, liked what he saw. Shelby moved into the Scarab plant, recently vacated by Lance Reventlow, and, with help from bright young Ford men such as Evans, Ray Geddes, and Jacque Passino, began production. Working on the engineering side was Phil Remington, whose solid credentials went back to the days at Muroc Lake.

Shelby sold seventy-five Cobras in 1962, although only a small percentage of the first year's production was used for racing. In January 1963 Dave MacDonald and Ken Miles (both were to die in racing accidents, MacDonald at the Speedway and Miles testing the Ford "J" car at Riverside) finished 1-2 at Riverside to bring Shelby his first Cobra victory.

By the end of 1963 Bob Johnson's Cobra had replaced Dr. Dick Thompson's Corvette as SCCA national A Production champion, a title Cobra was to hold until 1969, when it was reclaimed by Corvette. Shelby moved into a giant plant next to the Los Angeles air-port. Peter Brock designed the sleek Daytona coupe, and competition Cobras started coming through with lightweight 427-cubic-inch engines delivering close to 500 hp. Veteran Porsche driver Bob Holbert, a four-time SCCA national champion, drove for Shelby in 1963, the first year for the U.S. Road Racing Championship, the SCCA's first professional series. Using his Porsche RS-61 on the short courses and the Cobra where its power counted, Holbert became the first U.S. road racing champion, bringing Cobra the unofficial SCCA manufacturers' title as well.

In 1964 Cobras won six of the eight USRRCs they entered—at Augusta, Pensacola, and Laguna Seca they ran first, second, and third—but Shelby was after bigger game. He had his eye on the FIA world manufacturers' championship, an almost private preserve of Enzo Ferrari; and Shelby came close to winning it in the Cobra's first year of international racing. By the time Ferrari became aware of the Texan's charge, the snake had its fangs in the tail of the prancing black horse. Ferrari retained the manufacturers' title in 1964, but it was close, 84.6 points to Cobra's 78.3. In events counting toward the world title, MacDonald-Holbert had been first GT and fourth overall at Sebring; Gurney-Grant second GT in the Targa Florio; Gurney-Bondurant first GT and fourth overall at Le Mans; Bondurant first GT in the Freiburg Hillclimb; Gurney first GT and third overall in England's Tourist Trophy; and at Bridge-hampton in the final Grand Touring Championship race of the season, Miles, Bucknum, Johnson, and Parsons finished one through four in the GT class.

But the Cobras had been skunked by Ferrari at Spa, the Nurburgring, Reims, and in the Tour de France, and they just missed. At Bridgehampton, when Shelby heard they had not placed well in the Tour de France, he just grinned and drawled, "Just you all wait till next year." What a "next year" it was! In 1965 Cobras won seven world-championship events, were twice second and scored 90.3 points. An American car had earned the FIA International Manufacturers' Championship.

Shelby now turned his attention to making the GT-350 and later the Shelby GT-500, both highly tuned versions of the Ford Mustang. The Cobra racing program was gradually turned over to private entrants. When Cobra production stopped, Shelby had produced 1140 of his stark, gutsy sports cars. In his book *The Cobra Story,* Shelby isn't far off when he said, "The American car, as far as international road competition was concerned, was the Cinderella. And I don't think I'm too wrong in saying it was the Cobra that saved the act."

Acceptance

IX

The Ford Motor Company won almost everything in sight during the 1960s. They led NASCAR's Grand National Division in total stock-car victories in 1963, 1964, and 1965. After second-place finishes at Indianapolis in 1963 and 1964, Ford supplied engines for three consecutive 500 winners. They dislodged the Corvette and the Ferrari Coupe from the SCCA's big production-class national championships, and, through Ford of England, in 1965 they began working with Cosworth Engineering on the engine that was to rule Grand Prix racing.

More than anything, Ford wanted the rewards of winning Le Mans, the most publicized, with Indy, of all races, and the satisfaction of beating Ferrari, the most prestigious name in racing. Shelby's Cobras had finished ahead of Ferrari in the manufacturers' championship for production cars. Now Ford challenged the Italian master in his own back yard, with his own kind of sports racing car.

In Leo Levine's *Ford: The Dust and the Glory,* one of racing's very best books, he tells of Ford's cloak-and-dagger negotiations to buy or merge with Ferrari. Led by Donald Frey, Ford brass traveled to Maranello during 1963 but eventually despaired of ever reaching an understanding, as the capricious Commendatore kept changing the ground rules, and Ford decided to go it alone.

With Henry Ford II and Ford president Lee Iacocca pushing the project, Roy Lunn, a former Aston Martin engineer working for Ford in Detroit, was quickly transferred to a newly formed high-performance division. With Carroll Shelby and Ray Geddes, Lunn was soon on his way to England to shop for a car builder. The United States had skilled Indianapolis car builders and talented sports car designer-builders such as Joe Huffaker, Bob McKee, and Troutman and Barnes. But Ford was after an advanced design and, at that time, was probably correct in thinking it would find it more readily in Europe.

Colin Chapman, already known to Ford through Indianapolis, and Eric Broadley, whose Lola was outstanding among smaller English race cars, had the inside track. Broadley had entered an extremely low, slippery-shaped, Ford-powered, mid-engined coupe in the 1963 Le Mans. Although it failed to finish the twenty-four hours, it ran well and obviously was a very advanced car. Also, as Levine points out, if the venture was a success, Broadley, a pleasant, reserved man, would be less inclined than Chapman to seek personal recognition. Shelby's friend, Aston Martin racing manager John Wyer, was hired to run the Ford team and to work with Broadley, Lunn, and Shelby. Bruce McLaren tested the prototype, and two GT-40s—so named as they were forty-inch-high Grand Touring cars—were ready for the Le Mans trials in April 1964.

Phil Hill and Bruce McLaren ran the Nurburgring 1000 K's in May. It was the GT-40's debut, but it failed to finish as Ferraris ran 1-2-3. Three cars, driven by Gregory-Ginther, Attwood-Schlesser, and Hill-McLaren, also failed in their first Le Mans, and two weeks later the same drivers suffered the same fate in the Reims 12 Hours. Two GT-40s entered Nassau Speed Week, an informal, loosely handled annual bash over an abandoned airport's rough runways, and both retired with suspension failure.

In February 1965 a Shelby-prepared GT-40 brought Ford their first win. Driven by Indy veteran Lloyd Ruby and the British-born California sports car ace Ken Miles, and Ginther-Bondurant, GT-40s placed first and third in the Daytona 2000 K's, run over the difficult 3.81-mile combination of Daytona's high banks and infield runways. GT-40s earned a second at Sebring and a third at Monza but were blanked in the Targa, at the Ring, and in the 1965 Le Mans. In 1965 Ford began using the MK II, an improved machine powered by a 427-cubic-inch (7-liter) engine.

Although John Wyer, Ford of France, Alan Mann, and Holman-Moody all prepared Ford entries, cars entered by Carroll Shelby accounted for all six victories earned by the Ford prototypes during the four years of Ford factory involvement. Miles-Ruby, Gurney-Grant, and Hansgen-Donohue were first, second, and third at Daytona in 1966; Miles-Ruby and Hansgen-Donohue first and second at Sebring; and Gardner-Whitmore second at Spa. Ford's first Le Mans was won by Amon-McLaren in a closing-lap snafu that embarrassed Ford and

Eric Broadley's Lola Coupe at Le Mans in 1963. The forerunner of the Ford GT-40 series, the low, mid-engined coupe was bought by John Mecom, Jr., and written off by Augie Pabst during practice for the 1964 *Times* GP at Riverside.

robbed Ken Miles and Denis Hulme, who had led most of the twenty-four hours, of victory. Leo Beebe, the Ford executive then in charge of the racing program, planned to have the Miles-Hulme and McLaren-Amon machines finish in a dead heat, only to find, after signals had been given, that the cars' starting position made such a result impractical.

Ford won only two major races in 1967, but they were ones that counted. Mario Andretti and Bruce McLaren captured Sebring as Ruby and Foyt finished second, and two American idols, Foyt and Gurney, brought Ford another victory at Le Mans. The Ford factory program was phased out after 1967. In four years Ford entered fifty-nine GT's in seventeen races, emerging the winner six times. If this appears a meager return for so enormous an effort, consider the caliber of competition—Ferrari—and that two of the six wins were the 24 Hours of Le Mans. Private entries kept Ford in road racing's victory lanes. The Skip Scott–Peter Revson GT-40s helped Ford earn the 1966 sports-car championship, and John Wyer led a team of Gulf Oil-sponsored GT-40s (new regulations called for five-liter engine limits on sports cars and three-liter for prototypes) to many major wins, including the 1968 and 1969 Le Mans.

Ford assumed manufacturing responsibilities for Shelby's GT line in 1968 and stopped production early in 1970 after 14,810 GT-350 and GT-500s had been built. The hotted-up Mustang had earned SCCA B production honors in 1965, 1966, and 1967, and in 1966 and 1967 Jerry Titus, a driver-journalist who worked

with Shelby on his Cobra and sedan projects, helped to bring Ford the Trans-Am sedan championship.

More important to the Detroit factories than to the racing public, the Trans-American series for over and under two-liter "sport" sedans became a showplace for the then popular "pony cars." With imports, certain winners of the small sedan class, Ford, Plymouth, Dodge, Chevrolet, and American Motors all supplied factory help. For a time, while the manufacturer remained interested, the Trans-Am series, frequently staged at second-rate tracks in out-of-the-way places, featured such superstars as Parnelli Jones, Dan Gurney, George Follmer, Mark Donohue, and Peter Revson.

General Motors, Chevrolet Division, had its Texan too. Aside from similar accents and the fact that both were lean and tall, taciturn Jim Hall and congenial Carroll Shelby had little in common. Heir to an oil-based fortune, Hall graduated from the California Institute of Technology as a mechanical engineer. He lost both parents and a sister in a plane crash in 1953 when he was eighteen and since that time has helped his brothers run the family business. Beginning with an Austin-Healey in 1954, Hall raced a succession of cars, including Ferraris, a Birdcage Maserati, and a Lister-Chevrolet.

Impressed with Lance Reventlow's Scarab, Hall commissioned its builders, Troutman and Barnes, to build the first Chaparral, a front-engined, space-frame sports car named after a raucous West Texas bird, commonly known as a road runner. The Chaparral's first win was

Sole survivor of an eleven-car Ford-Cobra entry in the 1964 Le Mans was this Doc Thompson/Jack Sears Cobra Coupe, which finished in eighth place.

Ford executives Leo Beebe and Roy Geddes (who worked with Shelby) in the Ford garage a few miles from the circuit in Le Mans.

The Ford J car at the April 1966 Le Mans trials. The experimental coupe became the successful Mark IV.

in the 1962 Road America 500. Later Hall was to say, "The first Chaparral was obsolete by the time it had been sufficiently developed to be reliable." Six of the "Scarab type" Chevrolet-powered Chaparrals were built by Troutman and Barnes. One was driven by Harry Heuer to 1962 and 1963 C Sports racing national championships, but big front-engined machines were being beaten by rear-engined Birdcage Maseratis and Cooper-Monacos as sports cars followed the lead of Formula I and embraced the rear-engined principle. Rear-engined Porsches had long been leading contenders among smaller-displacement cars.

James "Hap" Sharp joined Hall, and the Chaparral shop was set up near Midland, Texas, with Rattlesnake Raceway, Hall's own two-mile test track, in its back yard. The first "real" Chaparral, the white fiberglass, rear-engined sports car, qualified fastest its first time out at Riverside in October 1963, but it failed to finish. Hall won at Pensacola in April 1964 and a month later introduced the radical Chaparral automatic transmission. Although he suffered a broken arm from going off the road at Mosport and missed the final three races, Hall had piled up enough points to become the 1964 U.S. Road Racing Champion.

Sharp and Hall survived a cloudburst to take the 1965 Sebring 12 Hours for the first American victory at the Florida course since 1953. Following a successful 1965 season, in which Chaparrals won sixteen of the twenty-one events they entered, Hall shocked the racing world by introducing a large, driver-actuated, airfoil on the Chaparral 2E at the September 1966 Bridgehampton Can-Am. Rising fifty-four inches above the ground, thirty-one inches from the cowl, the wing was supported by vertical struts attached to the rear suspension, not to the chassis. Quickly adopted by the world's leading Formula I and sports car builders, as it greatly improved tire adhesion and general road holding, the wing concept was used universally until banned by the FIA in 1969.

Hall raced a British Racing Partnership Lotus-BRM during the 1963 Grand Prix season, but, unlike Shelby, this Texan was not entirely comfortable in the European milieu. Although his Formula I BRP machine was somewhat less than competitive, Hall had a fifth in the German GP at the Ring and a sixth at Silverstone in the British Grand Prix. Hall returned to Europe in 1966 with Jo Bonnier and Phil Hill as his drivers and won the 1000 K's at the Nurburgring in the Chaparral 2D coupe which had been introduced at Daytona.

Hill drove for Hall again in Europe in July 1967 when he and Mike Spence won at Brands Hatch. For the 1966 Can-Am, Hill teamed with Jim Hall to give the winged Chaparrals a first, three seconds, a fourth, and a fifth in the six race series. The slightly smaller, aluminum-skinned Chaparral 2B was introduced at Road America in September 1967. Hall had several seconds in the 2G, but the McLaren-Hulme juggernaut was beginning its five-year winning streak, and Hall finished the Can-Am year behind McLaren, Hulme, Surtees, and Donohue.

Jim Hall's second at Bridgehampton was his best 1968 finish. This was the single Can-Am in which American drivers—Donohue, Hall, Motschenbacher, Savage, Brown, and Gurney, in that order—shut out overseas drivers, filling all top six, point-earning spots. Ten laps from the end of the year's final Can-Am at Stardust Raceway, Motschenbacher's McLaren, forced to make an unexpected move, was struck from the rear by Hall. Hall's injuries included two broken legs, burns, and a dislocated jaw. The Chaparral was destroyed. Hall completely recovered, but he never raced big sports again, although he did run two Camaros in the 1970 Trans-Am for himself and the veteran Ed Leslie.

Chuck Daigh's F/I Scarab at Spa during the 1960 Belgium Grand Prix.

Actress Jill St. John with husband Lance Reventlow, who is in his new Scarab sports car, at Riverside, 1959.

OVERLEAF: Phil Hill in Chaparral No. 65 and Jim Hall in No. 66. The winged Chaparral, introduced at the Bridgehampton Can-Am in September 1966, was to be widely copied until banned by the FIA in 1969. John Surtees, in car No. 7, won the six-race 1966 Canadian American Challenge Cup series as well as the Las Vegas Can-Am, shown here.

The ultimate Chaparral was the "ground effects" model 2J. Two rear-mounted two-stroke engines sucked air from under the car as flexible thermoplastic skirts formed a seal with the track surface. Incredible road holding was the result, and many track records were broken but few races completed. This principle was outlawed by the FIA following the 1970 season. Chaparral driver Vic Elford clowns with the car's removable steering wheel at the 1970 Laguna Seca Can-Am.

Jim Hall, No. 9, drives the first rear-engined Chaparral at Sebring, March 1964. FIA regulations required the addition of last-minute bodywork over doors and rear fenders.

Jim Hall stands by the Chaparral 2C at the 1965 Riverside as the McLaren manager, Teddy Mayer, in dark glasses, gestures.

John Surtees drove the new, narrow anti-drag 2H Chaparral in 1969, but it was not a good owner-driver marriage and, apparently, not one of Hall's best cars.

What next came out of Midland made Hall's prior innovations—fiberglass body and chassis members, an automatic transmission capable of handling giant engines at racing speeds, and the revolutionary airfoil—appear conservative. Hall introduced the ground-effects Chaparral 2J at Watkins Glen in July 1970.

Powered by a Chevrolet engine, the incredible 2J was pulled toward the road surface by two rear-mounted, 50-hp, two-cylinder, two-stroke engines, each with sixteen-blade fans that sucked air from beneath the car. To achieve an effective seal, the sides of the boxlike car, except for the front-wheel wells, scraped along the road surface. Special skirts of Lexan, a General Electric thermoplastic, made it possible to form the required track surface seal.

As the season wore on changes were made in the rear-mounted sucker fans, but the vacuum cleaner–Hovercraft in reverse, the clumsiest and most unlikely-looking of race cars proved blinding fast.

Being fast is what racing is all about. But equally obvious is another old saw—you have to finish to win. World champion Jackie Stewart, who drove the 2J in its first race, setting a 125.85-mph fastest lap in the Glen Can-Am, said he could go deeper into the turns and come out of them faster in the new Chaparral than in any car he had driven. English driver Vic Elford took over from Stewart and established new lap records at Road Atlanta, Laguna Seca, and Riverside. But the 2J was plagued with problems, many of them simple items not related to the ground-effects principle. And there was a great deal of talk, particularly by Team McLaren's Teddy Mayer, as to the 2J's legality.

The year 1970 had been a difficult one for Jim Hall. Not as strong as before his accident, in mid-season he stopped driving in the Trans-Am to concentrate on the 2J but was unable to give it the reliability that had been a Chaparral trademark. At the close of the 1970 season the FIA declared the ground-effects principle illegal, and Hall was forced to shelve the most bizarre of modern race cars.

A report of the 1961 Canadian Winter Rally in the May 1961 Issue of *Car and Driver Magazine* in part reads: ". . . But it was the Corvair team, entered officially by the Chevrolet Division of General Motors, that provided the most pre-rally interest. Here for the first time GM was putting it on the line in a competitive motoring event. No hiding behind a dealer's skirts, no patty cake with a patron, just a simple straightforward entry, acknowledging a pride and interest in seeing how their three superbly prepared, well-driven machines would do against a strong field."

Unfortunately, the factory Corvair's victory following a disputed finish did not precipitate a change in GM's no-racing policy. It wasn't for a lack of racing interest in GM's ranks. Zora Arkus-Duntov, the Corvette Shepherd, a European driver-designer whose Ardun-Mercury engine was used in some early Allards, became General Motors' "house" racer. Racing enthusiasts were to be found through GM, particularly in Chevrolet research and development. Top brass, such as Ed Cole, now GM president, and John de Lorean, then a GM group VP, went out on limbs to encourage GM racing participation.

Hall's Chaparral and Lother Motschenbacher's McLaren, No. 11, made contact during the final Can-Am of the 1968 season at Las Vegas. Jim Hall was hospitalized for nine weeks; the Chaparral was destroyed.

A departure from prior Chaparral design was the narrow-track 2H, driven in 1969 with little success by former world and Can-Am champion John Surtees.

The Dave Heinz/Bob Johnson Corvette Stingray at the 1973 Sebring.

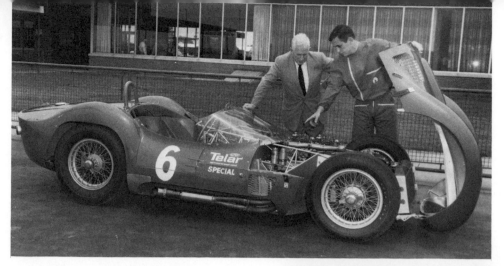

Roger Penske showing the new Bird-cage Maserati to his sponsor, Marshall Stephens of DuPont. Roger switched to a rear-engined Cooper-Monaco before the 1961 season was over.

Eighth-place finish by Penske's Formula I Cooper in the 1961 U.S. Grand Prix at Watkins Glen was the highest of all independent American entries.

John Fitch helped to get the Chevrolet factory involved in the 1956–57 Corvette Supersport program, and Daytona stock car builder Smokey Yunick had a factory-supported fling at NASCAR Grand Nationals prior to the 1957 Automobile Manufacturers Association no-racing edict. Sports car drivers began winning SCCA production car championships in Corvettes as early as 1956, when Dick Thompson, a Washington, D.C., dentist, earned the first of his six titles. What Chevrolet did have and took little trouble to hide was a V-8 engine on which tuning specialists could work wonders.

Ford enjoyed the fruits of winning Indianapolis as well as several international titles, but from 1964 until 1972 Chevrolet had an absolute lock on engines for big-bore, all-out sports cars. In the hands of engine builders such as Traco—Jim Travers and Frank Coon—highly tuned Chevrolet engines became the standard power for Chaparral and for the Anglo-American hybrid, such as Lola and McLaren, that dominated the U.S. Road Racing Championship from 1964 until 1968 and the Canadian-American Challenge Cup series.

Only in 1972, after Porsche introduced its turbocharged 917, was other than a Chevrolet-powered car a consistent Can-Am winner. Formula 5000 single-seaters, popular in both Europe and America, adopted tuned 305-cubic-inch Chevrolet engines as their standard. With Cobra-Corvette contests now history, one of the few head-on meetings between Chevrolet and Ford was in the Trans-Am sport sedan series, where the results are almost a standoff. Ford, with factory support, won in 1966 and 1967. Chevrolet, with Penske-entered Camaros driven primarily by Mark Donohue, earned the title in 1968 and 1969. Mustangs won again in 1970, and Penske-entered American Motors Javelins took the title in 1971 and 1972, but without Ford or Chevy factory opposition.

Small specialist builders—for example Canada's Bill Sadler, Troutman and Barnes, and Bob Carnes—long ago had found the compact, relatively light Chevrolet V-8 the best U.S. production engine to work with, but it was Jim Hall and, later, Roger Penske who starred in the mystery "How Much of That Stuff Comes from Detroit?"

Chevrolet-Racing . . . ? Fourteen Years of Raucous Silence!! by Paul van Valkenburgh was published early in 1973. A former Chevrolet research-and-development employee, he relates an interesting story of what took place during more than a decade of avoiding GM's official no racing policy. Jim Hall's laurels, if slightly askew, remain intact. The Texan's use of fiberglass and his revolutionary airfoil appear as largely his. Chevrolet seems to get the lion's share of the credit for the Chaparral's automatic transmission and the radical 2J ground-effects car.

Reporters covering the 1968 Can-Am at the Bridge found the following note tacked on the news board of Bridgehampton's primitive press room: "Sunday A.M. —Roger Penske, owner of Mark Donohue's Lola-Chev, had a close call while taking his morning walk when he was almost run down by a speeding motorboat." A tired gag, but revealing.

After leaving Lehigh University in 1959, where he had earned a B.S. degree in industrial management, Penske joined Alcoa and for the next four years combined careers of selling aluminum and driving race cars. Although he came from a comfortable background—his father was vice-president of a large Cleveland metals distributor—young Penske was encouraged to work to support his hobbies. He attracted national attention in 1960 by winning the SCCA F-sports racing championship in a Porsche RSK he bought from Bob Holbert. Penske then teamed with Holbert to capture the 1961 Index of Performance at Sebring and won professional road races at Laguna Seca and Riverside in 1962.

Before finishing his driving career in 1965 Penske ranked with Hansgen, Holbert, and Ken Miles, the best stay-at-home road racers of their time. Had he had more overseas experience Penske might have challenged Dan Gurney and Phil Hill. One of the first sports-car drivers to acquire substantial sponsor support, Penske has become better known for his ability to organize and sell a winning race team and for his meteoric rise as a businessman than for his driving record.

Paul P. Porter, Jr., of DuPont, who was advertising manager of the Wilmington firm's anti-freeze division, worked closely with Roger Penske during the time he drove the Telar and Zerex Specials. Porter recalls that shortly after he became anti-freeze advertising manager he was surprised to find that he had inherited a race driver.

Early in his career, about the time he bought a front-engined Birdcage Maserati, Penske convinced the proper people in Wilmington that it would be a good thing to paint Telar, the name of a new DuPont anti-freeze, on his race car. The fee, Porter recollects, was piddling, about $1500. A car buff with a keen sense of what might help publicize his new brand with the auto racing-conscious garage trade, Porter, when advised

Briggs Cunningham inspects his new Maserati in Modena, 1962. From the left: Alfred Momo, Roger Penske, Cunningham, Walter Hansgen, and Bruce McLaren.

Penske, car owner John Mecom, Jr., and co-driver Augie Pabst with the Sebring race queen after winning the 1963 Grand Touring class in Mecom's Ferrari.

The Donohue/Hobbs Ferrari, No. 6, challenged by the Pedro Rodriquez/Jackie Oliver Porsche 917 coupe. Although in the pits for one and a half hours, the Porsche won the 1971 Daytona 24 Hours. Ferrari No. 23, driven by Ronnie Bucknum and Tony Adamowicz, came in a close second.

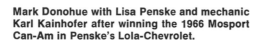

Mark Donohue with Lisa Penske and mechanic Karl Kainhofer after winning the 1966 Mosport Can-Am in Penske's Lola-Chevrolet.

that Penske had good prospects, went to his management with a racing-based product promotion and more money for Penske.

Porter said it wasn't long before Roger was making ten times his original fee. "We liked Roger, although we had to watch him like a hawk. He was a personable, well-mannered young man with a lot of drive, but our arrangement was strictly business. If Penske won, and Telar or Zerex got enough publicity to justify our investment, then it was a good deal. Of course some of our people enjoyed going to the races, getting pit passes and having Roger make a fuss over them, but that was icing on the cake. Roger's Zerex Special was a good proposition for us, and it did not hurt Penske's career to have the kind of exposure we arranged for him. We had him call his new Cooper Monaco the Zerex Special. Then he used the Zerex name on his controversial former Formula I car, and the Zerex Special came close to becoming a household word."

Porter went on to say, "There weren't many guidelines for sports car sponsorships then, as there were for Indy, and Roger was always hustling additional sponsors. We weren't keen on watering down our identity, but strange names still would appear on his cars. When Roger sold his cars and went to race for John Mecom,

Donohue (right) with the crew of his 1972 Indianapolis-winning, Penske-owned McLaren. Mark earned a record $218,767.90 in prize money.

Roger still wanted to collect the fee. As I remember it, he and young Mecom had quite a discussion about that." In 1962, Briggs Cunningham invited Penske to join Bruce McLaren and Walt Hansgen on a trip to Italy, where they shook down Cunningham's new Maseratis.

Following driving spells for John Mecom, Jr., and Chaparral, Penske joined McKean Chevrolet in Philadelphia and soon was running the dealership. However, Penske's insider status with General Motors began before he was one of their dealers. He was an adviser on the Corvair GT program and, with Jim Hall, was given several experimental engines which he helped to evaluate.

Penske gave up driving when he went into business, but he did not give up racing. His first experience as a car owner–team manager was the February 1966 Daytona, where his Corvette won its class. Sun Oil was now Penske's major sponsor, and in 1966 Mark Donohue became Penske's driver, beginning a relationship that has carried Penske cars to victories at Indianapolis and in major stock car and road racing events.

A graduate engineer whose considerate manners belie the fierceness of his driving, Donohue had earned several national championships but had failed to gain recognition until guided into professional racing by Walt Hansgen. Donohue-Hansgen first drove together at Sebring in John Mecom's Ferrari and then joined Ford, where they opened the 1966 season with a third at Daytona and a second at Sebring.

Following Hansgen's fatal accident during the April 1966 trials at Le Mans when his big MK II aquaplaned and failed to make the turn out of the pit straight, Donohue became Penske's driver. It was the first year of the Canadian-American Challenge Cup, and it gave American road racers a chance to match themselves and their machinery against the best. World champion John Surtees, Bruce McLaren, Chris Amon, Denis Hulme, Phil Hill, Dan Gurney, and Jim Hall were a part of the cast.

Delighted to be in such fast company, Donohue drove Penske's Lola to an outright win at Mosport and finished the highest of any American in the six-race series. He captured the U.S. Road Racing Championship, which used the same unlimited engine, anything-goes Group 7 sports cars, in 1967 and 1968, but, in a 1968 interview, said, "The Can-Am is the greatest. The USRRC is fine, but it was like playing tennis with your wife. When you run with those international guys and they smoke you off, you really try harder."

American road racing now had a championship that rivaled the forty-year-old world-driver series. In place of ultra sensitive Grand Prix single-seaters, the epitome of engine and chassis refinement, Can-Am sports cars, with engines of more than twice the capacity of GP cars, depended on raw horsepower.

Forerunner of the Can-Am were the pro sports car races held in Canada and California each autumn, so timed to permit entry of Formula I drivers in America for the U.S. GP and, after 1965, the Canadian Grand Prix. With purses far larger than those overseas, Can-Am grids were soon studded with world-famous names. Although lacking finesse, the 200-mph Can-Am roadster was as fast as Formula I and, to many Americans, more exciting to watch.

Mark Donohue won twice—at Mosport, Ontario, and Bridgehampton, Long Island—during the Can-Am's first three years. This was more than any other American, but it was not enough for Penske or Donohue, although Donohue had earned $47,000 in Can-Am prize money in 1968.

In 1969 Penske concentrated on Indianapolis and the Trans-Am sedan series. SCCA discontinued the USRRC in 1969 and that year increased the number of Can-Ams from six to eleven. After John Surtees won the 1966 Can-Am championship, Bruce McLaren and Denny Hulme dominated the Can-Am and made it look so easy that American drivers despaired of ever beating the two Kiwis. Following Team McLaren's 1969 season, they pocketed over $300,000 in Can-Am awards, sold their McLaren-Chevys to eager American buyers, and returned to Surbiton to build next season's cars. This had been the pleasant pattern until June 1970, when Bruce McLaren died at Goodwood while testing his new M-8D Can-Am car. The team carried on, with Denny Hulme winning another Can-Am title and $162,000.

Peter Revson joined Team McLaren, becoming the

Denny Hulme, No. 5, and Mark Donohue, No. 6, lead the September 1968 Bridgehampton Can-Am. The race was won by Donohue, with Jim Hall, No. 66, coming in second.

Sports car races with international fields, held each autumn when European drivers were in America for the U.S. Grand Prix, were forerunners of the Can-Am series. Here Parnelli Jones, No. 94, winner of the 1964 *Times* GP, lights up the tires of his Cooper-Ford.

1971 Can-Am champion after a series of near faultless drives. The United States now had a winning Can-Am driver as well as a winning engine. In 1972 Revson dropped the Can-Am to concentrate on driving Formula I for Team McLaren. Following a number of well-placed finishes, he won the prestigious Grand Prix of England in July 1973.

Revson, an early rival of Mark Donohue in SCCA club racing, in 1963 had moved overseas to gain experience in the tough school of European Formula III racing. Rated with Donohue and George Follmer as best of the current American road racers, in the 1969 Indy Revson had moved his Repco-Brabham from thirty-third, last on the grid, to a fifth-place finish. This was the year Donohue finished seventh in Penske's 4-WD Lola-Offenhauser and was named Indy's "Rookie of the Year."

Penske found the ultimate Can-Am weapon and the sponsor to support it and in 1972 returned to the Can-Am after a three-year absence.

Porsche of Germany, long a power in small-car, small-engine-capacity road racing, began going after the big sports cars in 1968 when the FIA reduced Prototype category limits to 183 cubic inches, three liters.

So as not to obsolete big-engined sports cars such as the Ford GT-40 and Lola-Chevrolets, the FIA created a Group 4 class for sports cars with five-liter, 305-cubic-inch engine limits, produced in quantities of twenty-five within a one-year period. Up to this time the 305-cubic-inch Porsche 908 (in which Yorkshireman Tony Dean won the 1968 Road Atlanta Can-Am on the rare occasion of a Team McLaren failure) had been the largest Porsche. But the Stuttgart firm, with encouragement from its American branch, who are said to account for over half of all Porsche sales, now wanted outright victories, not class wins.

Porsche had won major American races with its smaller cars—Sebring in 1960 and 1968—but this usually happened only after the Ferraris or Fords broke down. Leading American Porsche drivers Bob Holbert, Scooter Patrick, Joe Buzzetta, and Peter Gregg had raced for the factory both in America and Europe. In production racing Porsche sedans had earned twenty-four SCCA national titles between 1954 and 1970, and the Porsche 911 sedan was under two-liter Trans-Am Champion in 1968 and 1969.

Jo Siffert, the Swiss GP star, brought a 917, first of the "big" Porsches, to the 1969 Can-Am, where he

Parnelli Jones takes the lead at the start of the 1963 500, followed by Don Branson and Rodger Ward. Jim Clark, on the left of Foyt's No. 2, was second to Jones in a disputed finish.

frequently finished third or fourth, a good showing for a 300-cubic-inch engine against McLarens, Lolas, and Chaparrals driven by half-again-larger-engined Chevys. Racing in FIA events against 305-cubic-inch limits, 917s won the 1970 and 1971 Daytona 24 Hours, the Watkins Glen 6 Hours in 1970, Sebring in 1971, and a host of international events, including Le Mans. However, from 1969 until 1972, 917s raced in seventeen Can-Ams without a win. They were giving away too many cubic inches.

Early in 1972 Penske completed arrangements to run a turbocharged 917 in the 1972 Can-Am. As fine a test driver as he is a racer, Donohue worked closely with Porsche factory engineers, and the 917-10K made its debut at Mosport. Donohue qualified fastest and was leading the race when forced to pit for a minor adjustment. However, he regained most of his lost time and finished second.

During tests at Road Atlanta prior to the second Can-Am, Donohue was injured when the 917 lost some of its body work and was wrecked. The veteran George Follmer, who had helped Penske's AMC Javelins win the Trans-Am Championship, was rushed to Atlanta to substitute for Donohue. Driving the strange, 900-hp turbocharged Porsche for the first time, Follmer beat the McLarens into the first turn to lead from start to finish. In a vain attempt to catch Follmer, Hulme went off the road, and Revson blew his engine.

Searching for more horsepower cost McLaren engines

their reliability, and by the end of the Can-Am season Penske's team was toying with the opposition. After five years of ruling the Can-Am, Team McLaren found it difficult to be a loser, and rumblings, similar to those over Jim Hall's vacuum-effect Chaparral, were heard about the cost and legality of turbocharging. However, the Can-Am engine formula is a free one, and turbocharging restrictions appear unlikely. After Follmer became 1972 Can-Am champion, Penske sold one 917 for $125,000, and Follmer went to the new owner as its driver. Following the 1973 season, in which he added the Can-Am title to his long list of laurels, Mark Donohue retired as a driver.

Donohue, Revson, and Follmer, as did Penske, came up through the Sports Car Club of America, going first to its driver schools, doing well in regional races, then moving on. But they are the tip of the iceberg. Of the SCCA's 20,000 members, about 4000 hold some form of competition license. Three professional series—the Can-Am, Trans-Am, and Formula 5000 championships— are the SCCA's showpieces, but the rank-and-file SCCA member races in near anonymity. For every Revson or Donohue there are thousands of members—teachers, students, professional men and women, clerks and salesmen—who devote their spare hours to working on and racing their cars. Track owners permit club racing, for a fee, but no spectators are allowed, as they run up the insurance costs, and too few fans show up to make it worthwhile. Newspapers rarely report amateur events,

Jim Clark and American transmission expert Pete Weisman discuss use of the pneumatic jack. Clark's Lotus-Ford finished second at the 1963 Indy.

On its way to Victory Lane after winning his second 500 in 1964, Foyt's Watson roadster was the last front-engined car to win Indianapolis.

unless there is a tragedy, yet club racing is usually spirited and close.

The 1961 edition of Bloemker's *500 Miles to Go* carries a prophetic comment by Speedway owner Tony Hulman: "By 1970 we will have turbine-powered racing cars in the '500.' The conquest of space will develop new fuels, new metals and new methods of transmitting power to land vehicles." What Hulman may not have anticipated was the storm raised by Indianapolis car owners who saw millions of dollars in piston engines being sucked into the turbines' ravenous inlet annulus.

Turbine-powered race cars were not new in 1967 when Andy Granatelli so upset Speedway traditionalists. General Curtis Le May had stuffed a U.S. Air Force Boeing turbine in an old (by coincidence) Granatelli Indy roadster, which had been demonstrated at the Fairchild SCCA races in 1955. John Zink entered his rear-engined Trackburner in the 500 of 1961, where it failed to go fast enough, and in 1966 Jack Adams installed a GE turbine in a Watson roadster that also failed to qualify.

In his twenty years at the Speedway Andy Granatelli's brashness had rubbed many of the Indy establishment the wrong way. But Andy was a showman, and he went first class. He built an advanced chassis, installed a Pratt and Whitney of Canada turbine, utilized four-wheel-drive, and hired one of the best drivers in Speedway history, Parnelli Jones.

For 196 laps of the rain-interrupted 1967 Indianapolis 500 Parnelli Jones made keeping the red four-wheel-drive turbocar out front look so easy that Foyt, who was to win, said, "I was just racing for second place." A six-dollar gearcase bearing that shattered less than ten miles from the finish ended Andy's dream.

USAC had seen enough and soon began proceedings to reduce the effectiveness of turbine-powered race cars and restrict the use of four-wheel-drive. It appeared that the U.S. Auto Club was going out of its way to live up to its reputation for being reactionary. Actually the turbine four-wheel-drive issue was two-sided. You could get a good argument going on the turbine on several counts. One, the effect of its eerie silence on the racing fan. Would 300,000 spectators pay to watch thirty-three vacuum cleaners glide quietly by? And four-wheel-drive could prove so costly that it might price owning race cars beyond all but millionaires. Granatelli took USAC to court—and lost. But he was back in 1968 with three wedge-shaped turbines built by Colin Chapman. The 1968 turbine had a sixteen-inch annulus, in contrast to the twenty-two-inch air inlets for the 1967 cars. The new cars were lighter, and they were faster.

Carroll Shelby also entered turbines for the 1968 Indy but withdrew just prior to qualifying when he found a difference of opinion among his own crew regarding the legality and performance potential of

One of three wedge-shaped, rear-engined turbines built by Colin Chapman for Andy Granatelli. No. 70 was driven by Graham Hill, the 1966 500 winner and former world driving champion, who was joined by Indy veterans Joe Leonard and Art Pollard in 1968. After strong showings all three of the new turbines failed to finish.

Parnelli Jones's side-mounted turbine, No. 40, was running away with the 1967 Indy until ten miles from the finish when a minor part failed.

Car owner Andy Granatelli and 1969 Indy winner Mario Andretti in Victory Lane.

his entry. The turbines, driven by Joe Leonard, Art Pollard, and Graham Hill, were obviously still a threat to the old order.

For Granatelli 1968 at the Speedway was almost a repeat of 1967. Joe Leonard qualified with a record four-lap average of 171.559 mph; Graham Hill sat next to him on the front row, and Art Pollard put the third turbine on the fourth row. At mid-race Hill hit the wall, but Leonard and Pollard were running well. On lap 191 Joe Leonard was in the lead after a race-long battle with Bobby Unser. Following a long yellow-light slowdown, both Leonard and Pollard broke parts in their drive mechanisms when they accelerated.

The remainder of the 1968 season was a saga of epic frustration. Parnelli Jones bought one of the 1968 turbines and with Granatelli's pair went on the championship trail. The turbocars set lap records; they earned the pole, but they never won a race. Joe Leonard's fourth at Hanford was their best finish. For the Mosport road race Granatelli brought Graham Hill over from England. When the world champion wrecked his turbine during practice, he went to Granatelli to say he was sorry about the accident and would waive his considerable fee. Moved by so unusual a gesture, Granatelli could hardly speak as he declined, saying, "No, Graham, that's racing luck."

What happened at Riverside, California, during the last race of the season on December 1, 1968, makes

prior turbine history appear tame. Locked in a yearlong duel with Bobby Unser for the USAC national championship, Mario Andretti needed to finish only fifth at Riverside to earn his third national title. When Andretti's car failed him on lap sixty-one of the 116-lap, 300-mile race, he switched to the Parnelli Jones turbine being driven by Joe Leonard. Both Andretti and Leonard were Firestone drivers, and the tire maker was eager to have another national champion. Unfamiliar with turbocar handling, Andretti tried to pass Pollard going through Riverside's sweeping turn nine. When the gutsy little Italian lost it, he destroyed both his own and Pollard's turbine. Mario jumped in Lloyd Ruby's car on lap seventy, but the share of points from his third-place finish left him eleven points behind Bobby Unser, who drove all the way in his own car to finish second to race winner Dan Gurney. Andretti made up for his miscue when he brought Granatelli his longsought 500 laurels in 1969. But he had closed out one of racing's most bizarre chapters on an appropriate note.

The racing public knows little of the auto clubs that write the rules of racing and conduct the events. Two personalities, NASCAR's Bill France and the National Hot Rod Association's Wally Parks, so influenced their branches of the sport that it is difficult to picture stock car or drag racing without them. The uneasy truce existing between the U.S. Auto Club and the other sanctioning organizations was broken in May 1973 when USAC announced its intention to resign from ACCUS. USAC contended that the "Full International" listing, which allows free driver interchange, was being abused. They claim it was intended to allow a foreign driver to race in FIA-listed events when they were in the United States, that it was not designed to encourage NASCAR and the SCCA indiscriminately to have events listed as Full Internationals so they could cash in on the popularity of USAC's Indy stars. However, in December 1973, USAC withdrew its resignation when ACCUS limited its driver participation rules to international events. Under today's "right to work" laws, whether or not the sanctioning body can deny a driver's right to race where he pleases may be the real issue. Historically the better drivers are eager to try all types of racing.

A handful of USAC veterans—A. J. Foyt, Mario Andretti, and the Unser brothers (Bobby and Al)—are probably the biggest drawing cards in American racing. They have won seven 500s in the past twelve years, but Andretti and Foyt have visited victory lane in other than USAC events, and road racers have had considerable success at Indianapolis. Since 1963, when Jim Clark finished second, the 500 has been won by Clark, Graham Hill, and Mark Donohue.

Mario Andretti and his twin brother, Aldo, came to the United States when they were thirteen but still managed to take part in an Italian Formula junior training program before migrating. National champion in 1965, 1966, and 1969, the year he won the 500, Mario Andretti has an outstanding record in other racing fields. He teamed with Bruce McLaren to win Sebring in 1967 for Ford. Three years later he captured the 12 Hours again after taking over the factory Ferrari 512 S in third place only a few hours from the finish.

Andretti's stock car record is brief but impressive, as it includes winning the 1967 Daytona 500. Eager to make the most of both worlds, Andretti, who stands second only to Foyt in total USAC championship victories, added Grand Prix racing to his already full schedule. In October 1968, at Watkins Glen for the U.S. Grand Prix, he drove Colin Chapman's spare Lotus-Ford to a record 1:04.20 qualifying lap to earn the pole in his first Formula I race, and in 1971 he drove a Ferrari to win the Grand Prix of South Africa.

Bobby Unser, another road racing enthusiast among Speedway veterans, also made his Formula I debut in the 1968 U.S. GP, but Bobby, who drove for BRM, had car trouble the entire weekend.

No active driver comes close to matching the oval track record of A. J. Foyt. Five times the national champion, winner of three 500s, and, with forty-four wins, the all-time leader in total championship race victories, A. J. continues to race with only one thought —to become Indy's first four-time winner. The outstanding oval track star of his era, Foyt, for many, is the best of all American drivers. Pulling into his Speedway garage after finishing second in a championship dirt-car and in a championship "big car" race, held on consecutive days, a considerable accomplishment, Foyt replied to a bystander's "You had a pretty good weekend, A. J." by saying, "What the hell was good about it? I lost both times."

Some drivers are spooked by the Speedway. Stock car champion Lee Roy Yarbrough, accustomed to drafting—hanging his sedan within inches of the car

A. J. Foyt with the Ford Motor Company 1967 "Man of the Year" trophy and Ford racing director Jacque Passino. Car No. 1 is the Ford MK IV driven to victory by Foyt and Dan Gurney at Le Mans, and No. 14 is a Foyt-designed Coyote-Ford Indianapolis machine.

in front—at 200 mph, was replaced in the 1971 Indianapolis time trials by Jim Malloy, who immediately had Gurney's Eagle going ten mph faster. Malloy, who finished fourth that year, lost his life during the 1972 Indy trials, becoming the thirty-fifth driver to die at the Speedway, which also had claimed the lives of fourteen riding mechanics, nine spectators, and a guard.

The tragic, twice-delayed, rain-interrupted 1973 Indianapolis 500 raised the number of drivers killed at the Speedway to thirty-six. Art Pollard, at forty-six the oldest of all championship car drivers, died as a result of a practice crash. Two young drivers, David "Salt" Walthers and David "Swede" Savage, were badly hurt during the race, Savage later succumbing to his injuries. And a young member of the Savage crew was run down and killed by a fire truck as it raced through the pit lane in the wrong direction. Also seriously injured when fuel and parts of Walther's car pierced the heavy wire mesh protecting grandstand occupants were two teenaged spectators.

Following the disaster, USAC passed regulations de-signed to improve safety and reduce speeds. Significant was a fuel-load reduction from seventy-five to forty gallons and a cut in the aerodynamic wing width from sixty-four to fifty-five inches.

Accustomed to a crisis-studded existence, in 1973 American racing was plagued by a showdown on the driver-exchange issue, rising speeds, and soaring costs. Responsible owners of Indy cars, Grand National sedans and Can-Am sports cars agree that it takes around $300,000 to buy and run one car for a single season. Prize money and manufacturers' awards have increased but not enough to meet increased costs.

All too often the ability to race a competitive car depends on having a generous sponsor. Seldom actually owner of the race car, the ubiquitous sponsor pays from $10,000 to $200,000 to have anything from a small sticker on the side of a car to having the entry—for example, "The Olsenite Eagle"—named after his product or service. Commercial tie-ins are as old as racing. Two of the six machines in the 1895 Chicago *Times-Herald* contest, America's first, were the De la Vergne Refrig-

Jim McElreath bails out on lap twenty-four of the 1969 Indy, but quick action on the part of the Speedway safety crew saved the car. The engine fire was said probably to have been caused by the turbocharger.

erating Machine Co.-Benz and the R. H. Macy-Benz. The sponsor may be an automotive product, an apparel manufacturer, a brand of beer or cigarettes, a land developer or hotel chain.

Successful teams such as Parnelli Jones's (a California Firestone distributor) and Penske's (who owns Goodyear outlets) could not operate effectively without their tire company relationships. From a dollar-and-technical-assistance viewpoint, Larry Truesdale of Goodyear and Firestone's Bill McCrary are the two most powerful men in American automobile racing.

Car owners—and, if they are well known, the driver and chief mechanic—spend almost as much time looking for sponsors as they do on their race cars. Should the driver be a champion or have good prospects, chances are, as in show business, he will be represented by an agent.

Automobile racing has been called "an industrial bullfight." The drivers, racing's matadors, are among the world's finest athletes. Race drivers not only require stamina and strength, good vision, instant reflexes, and superb coordination; they must also be intelligent. A dumb race driver is a dead race driver. The tiny cockpit of an Indy or Formula I car, in which the driver lies on his back; the stock car driver in his cage of steel tubing and the slightly more comfortable bucket seat of a sports car—the office in which a race driver works is the loneliest place in the world.

Although accidents can be caused by happenings over which the driver has no control, and pieces can fall off race cars, most accidents are the result of driver error, mistakes in judgment, judgments made and carried out so quickly that the time involved cannot be measured.

Greatly improved aerodynamics and superwide tires with new compounds are two reasons for 200-mph speeds becoming routine. Not 200 mph on the straights, but in April 1973 Bobby Unser's 1000-hp Eagle earned the pole at Texas International Speedway with a closed-course record lap of 212.766 mph.

Stock car drivers began lapping over 200 mph at Talladega in 1970. Some of the best drivers, including Foyt and Andretti, have had the courage to say top speeds are getting out of hand.

An indication of automobile racing's broad acceptance came on September 21, 1971, when President Nixon invited close to 200 race drivers, officials, and car owners to a White House reception "to acknowledge the sport of motor racing." During his off-the-cuff remarks the President commented, "Not only is racing recognized for its enormous spectator appeal and the furthering of automotive equipment but also because we are a competitive country and you represent that spirit."

The reasons usually given for automobile racing's popularity—there are studies showing that only horse racing attracts more spectators—range from modern man's empathy with the automobile to the macabre attraction of potential tragedy. What is seldom said is obvious. Watching automobile racing, compared to the ball sports, is more exciting.

President Richard M. Nixon honors racing at a White House reception, September 1971. The President is seen with importer Carl Haas and world champion Jackie Stewart, with a Can-Am car in the foreground and AA Dragster in the background.

Appendix

Auto Racing Winners, 1895–1972
Charles L. Betts

Winner's elapsed time given in hours, minutes, seconds, and hundredths of seconds. For example: 12:16:24:87

1895

Nov. 2 Exhibition Run sponsored by *Times-Herald*
92-mi. Chicago to Waukegan & return
Oscar Mueller "Mueller-Benz" 9:30:00.0
9.7 mph

Nov. 28 First Automobile Race in America
Sponsored by *Times-Herald*
52.4-mi. Chicago to Evanston & return
J. Frank Duryea "Duryea" 10:23:00.0
5.1 mph

1896

May 30 New York City to Ardsley Country Club
15-mi. Road Race sponsored by *Cosmopolitan*
J. Frank Duryea "Duryea"

Sep. 7 Rhode Island State Fair,
Providence, Rhode Island
First Track Race in America
"Duryea" cars won several races, being beaten in short heats by a "Riker" electric.
1-mi. 26.8 mph

1897

May 30 Cleveland, Ohio
1-mi. "Winton" 01:48.0 33.8 mph

July 28 Cleveland to New York City
"Winton" 10 days

1899

May 22 Cleveland to New York City
Alex Winton "Winton" 47:37:00.0

Branford ½-mi. Dirt Track
Branford, Connecticut
5-mi. Race
Hiram Percy Maxim "Columbia"

Aug. 30 Climb to the Clouds
Pinkham Notch, Mt. Washington, N.H.
8-mi.
Freelan O. Stanley "Stanley" 2:10:00.0

1900

Apr. 18 First Road Race on Long Island
Springfield to Babylon & return
50-mi.
A. L. Riker "Riker Electric" 2:03:30.0
24.3 mph

1901

Cleveland 1-mi. Dirt Track
Cleveland, Ohio
1-mi. Record
Alexander Winton "Winton Quad"
:01:02.25 57.8 mph

Nov. 16 Coney Island Boulevard
Kings County, Long Island, New York
1-mi. Straightaway Record
Henri Fournier "Mörs" :51.8 69.5 mph

1902

Aug. 10 Brighton Beach 1-mi. Dirt Track
Kings County, Long Island, New York
10 mi. Race
Alexander Winton "Bullet" :10:50.0
55.4 mph

Oct. 23 Grosse Pointe 1-mi. Dirt Track
Detroit, Michigan
5-mi. Manufacturer's Challenge Cup
Barney Oldfield "999" :05:20.0 56.2 mph

Dec. 1 Grosse Pointe 1-mi. Dirt Track
Detroit, Michigan
1-mi. Track Record
Barney Oldfield "999" :01:01.2 59.0 mph

1903

Mar. 28 First Beach Trials
Daytona Beach, Florida
1-mi. Straightaway Records
H. T. Thomas "Oldsmobile Pirate"
:01:06.2 54.5 mph
Alex Winton "Bullet" :52.2 69.0 mph

May 23–July 26 First Transcontinental Record
San Francisco–New York City

Col. H. Nelson Jackson and Sewell Crocker
"Winton" 64 days

May 30 Empire City 1-mi. Dirt Track
Yonkers, New York
5-mi. Race
Barney Oldfield "999" :05:31.0
54.2 mph

June 19 First Circular Mile under 60 seconds in America
Indiana Fairgrounds 1-mi. Dirt Track
Indianapolis, Indiana
1-mi. World's Record
Barney Oldfield "999" :59.6 60.4 mph

June 20 San Francisco to New York
Tom Fetch "Packard 'Old Pacific'"
61 days

July 4 Driving Park 1-mi. Dirt Track
Columbus, Ohio
5-mi. Exhibition
Barney Oldfield "999" :05:00.6 60.0 mph

July 6–Sep. 17 Transcontinental Run
San Francisco to New York
L. L. Whitman & E. I. Hammond
"Oldsmobile" 73 days

July 18 Jackson ½-mile Dirt Track
Jackson, Miss.
1-mi. Exhibition
Barney Oldfield "999" :01:16.0 47.5 mph

July 25 Empire City 1-mi. Dirt Track
Yonkers, New York
1-mi. Track Record
Barney Oldfield "999" :55.8 65.0 mph

Sep. 29 Cross-Country Run
1137-miles, Chicago, Ill., to New York, N.Y.
B. B. Holcomb & Lawrence Duffie
"Columbia" 77:00:00.0 14.7 mph

Nov. 22 Los Angeles 1-mi. Dirt Track
Los Angeles, California
1-mi. Track Record
Barney Oldfield "Winton Bullet" :54.6
65.6 mph

Climb to the Clouds
Pinkham Notch, Mt. Washington, N.H.
8-mi.
L. J. Phelps "Phelps" 1:46:00.0 4.5 mph

1904

Jan. 3 Daytona Beach, Florida
Chas. Schmidt "Packard Gray Wolf"
1-mi. :46.4 77.8 mph
5-mi. :04:21.6 68.8 mph
Otto Nestman "Stevens-Duryea"
1-mi. :57.2 62.9 mph
5-mi. :04:57.6 60.1 mph

Jan. 12 Lake St. Clair, Detroit, Michigan
1-mi. Straightaway Record over frozen lake
Henry Ford "Arrow" :39.4 91.4 mph

Jan. 27 Daytona Beach, Florida
1-mi. Straightaway Record
William K. Vanderbilt, Jr. "Mercedes"
:39.0 92.30 mph

June Climb to the Clouds
Pinkham Notch, Mt. Washington, N.H.
8-mi.
Otto Nestman "Stevens-Duryea" :48:30.0
9.8 mph

July 25–Aug. 10 1st Glidden Tour
New York to St. Louis–1964 miles
Chas. J. Glidden "Napier"

July Climb to the Clouds
Pinkham Notch, Mt. Washington, N.H.
8-mi.
F. E. Stanley "Stanley" :28:19.4
15.2 mph
Harry Harkness "Mercedes" :24:37.6
19.5 mph

Aug. 1–Sep. 3 Transcontinental Run
4500-mi. San Francisco to New York
L. L. Whitman & C. S. Carris "Franklin"
32 days, 23 hr., 20 min.

Aug. 8 Grosse Pointe 1-mi. Dirt Track
Detroit, Michigan
1000-mi. Non-stop Run
Chas. Schmidt "Packard" 29:53:37.6
33.5 mph

Aug. 9 New York to St. Louis & return
3400-mi. Motor Non-stop Run
F. A. La Roche "Darracq" 15 days, 2 hr.

Aug. 22 Glenville Track Meet
Cleveland 1-mi. Dirt Track
Cleveland, Ohio
1-mi. Record
Earl Kiser "Winton Bullet #2" :52.8
68.3 mph

Aug. 28 World's Fair 1-mi. Dirt Track
St. Louis, Missouri
Louisiana Purchase Trophy
Barney Oldfield crashed and destroyed
"Peerless Green Dragon"

Oct. 8 Vanderbilt Cup Road Race
Nassau County, Long Island, New York
284.4-mi. Road Race over 30-mi. Course
George Heath "Panhard" 5:26:45.00
52.2 mph

Oct. 29 Empire City 1-mi. Dirt Track
Yonkers, New York
10-mi. Standing Start Record
Barney Oldfield "Peerless Green Dragon II"
:09:12.6 64.9 mph

Nov. 24 4th Annual Eagle Rock Hill Climb
Boston, Massachusetts
1-mi.
Maurice Bernin "Renault" :01:20.0
45.0 mph

1904 World's Records Made by Barney
Oldfield in "Peerless Green Dragon"

1-mi.	:00:51.2	70.0 mph
5-mi.	:04:30.0	66.5 mph
10-mi.	:09:12.0	65.0 mph
15-mi.	:14:05.0	63.7 mph
20-mi.	:18:45.4	64.0 mph
25-mi.	:23:38.6	63.2 mph
30-mi.	:28:38.8	62.9 mph
35-mi.	:33:36.6	62.2 mph
40-mi.	:38:31.6	62.4 mph
45-mi.	:43:29.0	62.4 mph
50-mi.	:48:39.2	62.0 mph

1905

Jan. 25 Daytona Beach, Florida
1-mi. Straightaway Records
H. L. Bowden "Mercedes" (Flying
Dutchman II) :34.2 102.7 mph
Louis S. Ross "Ross" (Steamer) :38.0
94.5 mph

May 5 Brighton Beach 1-mi. Dirt Track
Coney Island, Long Island, New York
1000-mi. Non-stop Run
Chas. G. Wridgway "Peerless" 25:50:01.0
38.6 mph

May 8–June 21 Transcontinental Run
New York to Lewis & Clark Exposition,
Portland, Oregon
3890 miles
Dwight Huss & Milford Wigle
"Oldsmobile" (Old Scout) 44 days

May 20 Morris Park 1.39-mi. Dirt Track
(Inaugural)
The Bronx, New York, New York
1-mi. Time Trial
Louis Chevrolet "Fiat" :52.8 68.3 mph
5-mi. Race
Chas. Basle "Mercedes" (Flying
Dutchman I) :05:34.6 53.9 mph
3-mi. Free-for-all
Louis Chevrolet "Fiat" :02:51.8 62.9 mph

May 30 Chicago 1-mi. Dirt Track
Chicago, Illinois
10-mi. Race
Webb Jay "White" (Steamer) :09:49.0
61.0 mph

June Climb to the Clouds
Mt. Washington, N.H.
8-mi. Hill Climb
F. E. Stanley "Stanley" (Steamer)
:22:17.6 21.7 mph

June 24 Empire City 1-mi. Dirt Track
Yonkers, New York
1000-mi. Track Record
Guy Vaughan "Decauville" 23:33:20.0
42.4 mph

July 4 Morris Park 1.39-mi. Dirt Track
The Bronx, New York, New York
1 lap, 1.39-mi.
Webb Jay "White" (Steamer) :01:43.6
48.2 mph
4 laps, 5.56-mi.
Walter Christie "Christie" :05:14.8
63.1 mph

July 8 Minneapolis 1-mi. Dirt Track
Minneapolis, Wis.
1-mi. Record
Webb Jay "White"(Steamer) :55.8
64.7 mph

5-mi. Race
B. Oldfield "Peerless" :04:44.6 63.1 mph
10-mi. Race
Earl Kiser "Winton" :10:33.0 56.8 mph

July 11–22 2nd Glidden Tour
New York, Boston, Plymouth, Bretton
Woods, Concord, Worcester, Lenox, New
York
870-mi. Reliability Run
Percy Pierce "Pierce-Arrow" 7 days

July 18 Climb to the Clouds
Mt. Washington, N.H.
8-mi. Hill Climb
Wm. Hilliard "Napier" :20:58.4 23.0 mph

July Driving Park 1-mi. Dirt Track
Columbus, Ohio
First 24-hr. Race in America
Soules Brothers "Pope-Toledo"
828.5 miles 34.5 mph

Sep. 23 Elimination Trial for Vanderbilt
Cup Race
Nassau County, Long Island, New York
4 laps, 28.3-mi. course
113.2-mi. Road Race
B. F. Dingley "Pope-Toledo" 2:00:50.0
56.2 mph

Oct. 14 Vanderbilt Cup Race
Nassau County, Long Island, New York
10 laps, 28.3-mi. course
283-mi. Road Race
Victor Hemery "Darracq" 4:36:08.0
61.5 mph

Nov. 17 Indiana Fairgrounds 1-mi. Dirt
Track
Indianapolis, Indiana
24-hr. Trial Run
F. W. Clemens & Chas. Merz "National"
1094.75-miles 45.7 mph

1906

Jan. 21–28 Daytona Beach, Florida
1-mi. Straightaway Record
Fred Marriott "Stanley" (Steamer) :28.2
127.6 mph
5-mi. Straightaway Record
Fred Marriott "Stanley" (Steamer)
:02:47.2 108.0 mph

July 12–28 3rd Glidden Tour
Buffalo, Saratoga, Montreal, Quebec,
Bretton Woods
1134-mi. Reliability Run
Percy Pierce "Pierce-Arrow" 12 days

Aug. 2–17 Transcontinental Run
San Francisco to New York–4100 miles
L. L. Whitman & L. S. Carris "Franklin"
15 days, 2 hr., 12 min.

Sep. 22 Elimination Trial for Vanderbilt
Cup Race
Nassau County, Long Island, New York
10 laps, 29.71-mi. course
297.1-mi. Road Race
Joseph Tracy "Locomobile" 5:27:45.0
54.4 mph

Oct. 6 Vanderbilt Cup Race
Nassau County, Long Island, New York
10-laps, 29.7-mi. course
297-mi. Road Race
Louis Wagner "Darracq" 4:50:10.0
61.4 mph

Oct. 26 Empire City 1-mi. Dirt Track
Yonkers, New York
100-mi. Race
H. J. Koehler "Buick" 2:05:00.6
47.8 mph

Nov. 6 Empire City 1-mi. Dirt Track
Yonkers, New York
100-mi. Race
C. H. Embleton "Packard" 2:00:55.0
49.6 mph

1907

May 25 Point Breeze 1-mi. Dirt Track
Philadelphia, Pa.
24-hr. Endurance Derby
J. L. Brown & Robert Maynes "Autocar"
791 miles 33.0 mph

June 29 Point Breeze 1-mi. Dirt Track
Philadelphia, Pennsylvania
24-hr. Endurance Derby
H. Michener & Ralph Mulford "Lozier"
717 miles 30.0 mph

June 29 Hamline 1-mi. Dirt Track
St. Paul, Minn.
24-hr. Race
Ralph Mongini "Locomobile" 1037 miles
43.2 mph

June Detroit 1-mi. Dirt Track
Detroit, Mich.
24-hr. Race for Stock Cars
Frank Kulick & Bert Lorimer "Ford"
(Model K) 1135 miles 47.29 mph

July 4 St. Louis 1-mi. Dirt Track
St. Louis, Mo.
24-hr. Race
Bob Burman "Jackson"

July 11 Harlem 1-mi. Dirt Track
Chicago, Ill.
24-hr. Race
Charles A. Coey "Thomas Flyer"

July 10–24 4th Glidden Tour
Cleveland, Chicago, Indianapolis,
Columbiana, Pittsburgh, New York
1570-mi. Reliability Run
Buffalo Automobile Club team, comprising
two "Pierce-Arrow," two "Thomas" &
"Packard" 15 days

Aug. 9 Brighton Beach 1-mi. Dirt Track
Coney Island, Long Island, New York
24-hr. Race
Montague Roberts "Thomas" 997 miles
41.5 mph

Sep. 6 Morris Park 1.39-mi. Dirt Track
The Bronx, New York, New York
24-hr. Race
Paul Lacroix & Meurice Bernin "Renault"
1079 miles 44.8 mph

Sep. 28 Morris Park 1.39-mi. Dirt Track
The Bronx, New York, New York
24-hr. Race
Cedrino & Parker "Fiat" 984 miles
41.0 mph

1908

Mar. 19 Savannah Challenge Trophy
Savannah, Ga.
20 laps, 17.1-mi. course

342-mi. Road Race
Lewis Strang "Isotta" 6:21:30.0
50.7 mph

Apr. 24 Briarcliff Trophy
Westchester County, New York
8 laps, 30-mi. course
240-mi. Road Race
Lewis Strang "Isotta" 5:14:13.2
46.2 mph

May 30 Giant's Despair 1½-mi. Hill Climb
Wilkes-Barre, Pa.
Willie Haupt "Chadwick" :01:49.0
49.5 mph

July 9–28 5th Glidden Tour
Buffalo, Pittsburgh, Philadelphia, Albany,
Boston, Portland, Saratoga
1669-mi. Reliability Run
E. A. Renting "Pierce-Arrow" 14 days

July 30 'Round the World Race
New York to Paris, 13431 miles
Montague Roberts & George Shuster
"Thomas Flyer" 170 days

Sep. 7 Lowell Road Race
Lowell, Mass.
24 laps, 10.6-mi. course
254.4-mi. Race
Lewis Strang "Isotta" 4:42:34.0
53.6 mph

Sep. 11 Brighton Beach 1-mi. Dirt Track
Coney Island, Long Island, New York
24-hr. Race
Mulford & Cobe "Lozier" 1107 miles
46.5 mph

Sep. 26 Milwaukee 1-mi. Dirt Track
West Allis, Wis.
24-hr. Race,
Drach & Leiser "Locomobile" 993 miles
41.4 mph

Oct. 3 Brighton Beach 1-mi. Dirt Track
Coney Island, Long Island, New York
24-hr. Race
Robertson & Lescault "Simplex"
1177 miles 49.0 mph

Oct. 10 Long Island Motor Parkway
(Inaugural)
Nassau County, Long Island, New York
23.46-mi. course
10 laps, 234.6-mi. Motor Parkway
Sweepstakes
Herbert Lytle "Isotta" 3:39:10.0
64.3 mph
9 laps, 211.14-mi. Meadow Brook
Sweepstakes
H. Hughes "Allen-Kingston" 4:00:47.0
52.6 mph
8 laps, 187.68-mi. Garden City Sweepstakes
W. H. Sharp "Sharp-Arrow" 3:19:34.0
56.4 mph
6 laps, 140.76-mi. Jericho Sweepstakes
W. R. Burns "Chalmers" 48.7 mph
4 laps, 93.84-mi. Nassau Sweepstakes
Hugh Easter "Buick" 2:07:52.0 44.1 mph

Oct. 10 1st Founder's Day Cup Race
Fairmount Park, Philadelphia, Pa.
25 laps, 7.8-mi. course
195-mi. Road Race
George Robertson "Locomobile"
4:02:30.0 49.5 mph

Oct. 24 Vanderbilt Cup Race
Long Island Motor Parkway

Nassau County, Long Island, New York
11 laps, 23.46-mi. course
258.06-mi. Road Race
George Robertson "Locomobile"
4:00:48.2 64.4 mph

Nov. 9 1st Cactus Derby
Los Angeles, Cal., to Phoenix, Ariz.
511-mi. Desert Road Race
F. C. Fenner & H. D. Ryus "White"
(Steamer) 30 hr., 20 min. 17 mph

Nov. 25 International Light Car Race
Savannah, Ga.
20 laps, 9.8-mi. course, 196-mi. Road Race
W. M. Hilliard "Lancia" 6:43:33.0
52.6 mph

Nov. 26 American Grand Prize
Savannah, Ga.
16 laps, 25.13-mi. course, 402.08-mi. Road
Race
Louis Wagner "Fiat" 6:10:31.0
65.1 mph

1909

Jan. 6 Chanslor-Lyon Challenge Cup
Los Angeles to San Diego & return
330-mi. Road Test
"Rambler" 10:32:00.0 31.4 mph

May 30 Giant's Despair 1½-mi. Hill Climb
Wilkes-Barre, Pa.
Willie Haupt "Chadwick" :01:38.4
55 mph

June 12 Portland 14.6-mi. Road Course
Portland, Oregon
First race sanctioned by the A.A.A.
3 laps, 43.8-mi. Road Race (Stock Chassis
$1600)
H. Covey "Cadillac" :47:08.0 55.7 mph
3 laps, 43.8-mi. Road Race (Stock Chassis
$3000)
C. Arnold "Pope-Hartford" :45:53.0
57.4 mph
7 laps, 102.2-mi. Road Race (Free-for-all)
Wemme Cup
Bert Dingley "Chalmers-Detroit"
1:44:18.0 58.6 mph

June 18 Indiana Trophy (under 300 cu. in.)
Crown Point, Indiana
10 laps, 23.27-mi. course
232.74-mi. Road Race
Joe Matson "Chalmers-Detroit" 4:31:21.0
51.5 mph

June 19 Cobe Trophy (over 300 cu. in.)
Crown Point, Indiana
17 laps, 23.27-mi. course
395.65-mi. Road Race
Louis Chevrolet "Buick" 8:01:39.0
49.3 mph

June 1–22 The "Great Race"
New York to Seattle, Washington—4106 miles
Bert Scott & Jimmy Smith "Ford"
(Model T) 22 days, 55 min.

June 28 Point Breeze 1-mi. Dirt Track
Philadelphia, Pa.
100-mi. Track Race
Harry Lorimer "Chalmers-Detroit"
2:02:06.8 49.4 mph
50-mi. Track Race
Ralph DePalma "Fiat" :57:43.0
52.0 mph

July 5 Denver 14.5-mi. Road Course
Denver, Colorado
20 laps, 290-mi. Stock Chassis Free-for-all
Road Race
E. McMillian "Colburn" 7:26:24.0
39.0 mph

July 10 Santa Monica 8.417-mi. Road
Course
Santa Monica, Cal.
Ferris Trophy, 24 laps, 202 miles
H. Hanshue "Apperson" 3:08:03.0
64.4 mph
Shettler Trophy, 24 laps, 202 miles
Bert Dingley "Chalmers-Detroit"
3:38:40.0 55.4 mph

July 31 Brighton Beach 1-mi. Dirt Track
Coney Island, Long Island, New York
24-hr. Race
Robertson & Poole "Simplex" 1091 miles
45.9 mph

July 12–30 6th Glidden Tour
Detroit, Chicago, Minneapolis, Denver,
Salina, Kansas City
2636-mi. Reliability Tour
W. Winchester "Pierce-Arrow" 15 days

Aug. 19 Indianapolis 2½-mi. Macadam
Motor Speedway (Inaugural)
Indianapolis, Indiana
1-mi. Speed Trial
Barney Oldfield "Benz" :43.0 83.1 mph
10-mi. Race
L. Chevrolet "Buick" :08:56.4 67.1 mph
250-mi. Prest-o-lite Trophy
R. Burman "Buick" 4:38:57.4 53.9 mph
100-mi. G. & J. Trophy
L. Strang "Buick" 1:32:40.8 64.9 mph
10-mi. Stock Car Race
L. Zengle "Chadwick" :08:32.4 70.0 mph
300-mi. Wheeler-Schebler Trophy
(Declared "No Contest" at 235-mi. due to
accidents Lee Lynch "Jackson"
4:13:31.4 55.8 mph)

Aug. 27 Brighton Beach 1-mi. Dirt Track
Coney Island, Long Island, New York
6-hr. Race
Woltman "Hupmobile" 226 miles
37.5 mph

Aug. 28 Brighton Beach 1-mi. Dirt Track
Coney Island, Long Island, New York
24-hr. Race
Basle & Raffalovitch "Renault" 1050 miles
43.7 mph

Sep. 8 2nd Lowell Road Race
Lowell, Mass.
30 laps, 10.6-mi. course, 318-mi. Road Race
for Lowell Trophy
George Robertson "Simplex" 5:52:01.4
51.4 mph
Vesper Club Trophy, 20 laps,
10.6-mi. course, 212-mi. Road Race
Bob Burman "Buick" 3:49:08.0
55.5 mph

Sep. 29 Long Island Stock Chassis Derby
Riverhead, Long Island, New York
10 laps, 22.75-mi. course, 227.5-mi. Road
Race
Ralph DePalma "Fiat" 218:38.6
62.35 mph

Oct. 9 2nd Founder's Day Road Race
Fairmount Park, Philadelphia, Pa.
25 laps, 8.1-mi. course, 202.5-mi. Road Race

George Robertson "Simplex" 218:58.8
55.4 mph

Oct. 15 Brighton Beach 1-mi. Dirt Track
Coney Island, Long Island, New York
24-hr. Race
Mulford & Patschke "Lozier" 1196 miles
49.6 mph

Oct. 24 Portola Road Contest
San Francisco, Cal.
12 laps, 21.18-mi. course, 254.16-mi. Road
Race
J. Fleming "Pope-Hartford" 3:19:18.0
63.72 mph

Oct. 30 Vanderbilt Cup Race
Long Island Motor Parkway
Nassau County, Long Island, New York
22 laps, 12.64-mi. course, 278.08-mi. Road
Race
Harry Grant "Alco" 265:42.0 62.77 mph

Nov. 6 2nd Cactus Derby
Los Angeles, Cal., to Phoenix, Ariz.
480-mi. Desert Road Race
Joe & Louis Nikrent "Buick" 19:13:30.0
25.0 mph

Nov. 9 Atlanta 2-mi. Motordrome
Atlanta, Ga.
200-mi. Track Race
L. Chevrolet "Buick" 2:46:48.5
72.0 mph
100-mi. Track Race
Wm. Knipper "Chalmers-Detroit"
1:40:46.8 59.5 mph
1-mi. Speed Trial
L. Strang "Fiat" :37.7 95.0 mph

Dec. 9 Dallas 1-mi. Dirt Track
Dallas, Texas
50-mi. Speed Run
Barney Oldfield "Benz" :47:18.0
63.5 mph

Dec. 18 Indianapolis 2½-mi. Brick Motor
Speedway
Indianapolis, Indiana
5-mi. Record
L. Strang "Fiat" :03:17.7 90.8 mph

1910

Mar. 16 Daytona-Ormond Beach, Florida
1-mi. Straightaway Record
B. Oldfield "Blitzen Benz" :27.33
131.724 mph
5-mi. Straightaway Record
B. Oldfield "Blitzen Benz" 128.88 mph

Apr. 8 Playa del Rey 1-mi. Motordrome
(Inaugural)
Los Angeles, Cal.
1-mi. Speed Trial
B. Oldfield "Benz" :36.22 99.0 mph

Apr. 13 Playa del Rey 1-mi. Motordrome
Los Angeles, Cal.
50-mi. Race
R. DePalma "Fiat" :39:55.3 75.1 mph
100-mi. Race
R. Harroun "Marmon" 1:16:21.80
78.8 mph

May 7 Atlanta 2-mi. Motordrome
Atlanta, Ga.
200-mi. (301-450 cu. in.) Race
R. Harroun "Marmon" 182:31.24
66.0 mph

200-mi. (451-600 cu. in.) Race
J. Aitken "National" 182:24.21
66.1 mph
50-mi. Free-for-all Race
H. Lytle "American" :40:20.02 74.2 mph

May 14 Brighton Beach 1-mi. Dirt Track
Coney Island, Long Island, New York
24-hr. Race
Basle & Poole "Simplex" 1145 mi.
47.7 mph

May 29 Indianapolis 2½-mi. Motor
Speedway
Indianapolis, Indiana
200-mi. Wheeler-Schebler Trophy Race
Ray Harroun "Marmon" 166:32.0
72.0 mph
100-mi. Prest-o-lite Trophy Race
T. Kincaid "National" 1:23:43.12
71.80 mph
10-mi. Race
J. Aitken "National" 08:25.9 71.5 mph
50-mi. Remy Grand Brassard Race
Ray Harroun "Marmon" :42:31.33
70.5 mph

June 14–30 7th Glidden Tour
Cincinnati, Louisville, Fort Worth, Omaha,
Chicago
2851-mi. Reliability Tour
MacNamara "Premier" 16 days

July 1 Indianapolis 2½-mi. Motor
Speedway
Indianapolis, Indiana
50-mi. Race
R. Burman "Marquette-Buick" :40:03.10
74.1 mph
10-mi. Speedway Helmet Race
Eddie Hearne "Benz" :07:13.0 83.1 mph
100-mi. Remy Brassard Race
R. Burman "Marquette-Buick" 1:20:35.63
74.5 mph
1-mi. Speed Trial
R. Burman "Marquette-Buick" :38.30
94.0 mph
200-mi. Cobe Trophy
J. Dawson "Marmon" 2:43:20.14
73.52 mph

Aug. 8 Point Breeze 1-mi. Dirt Track
Philadelphia, Pa.
6-hr. Race
Barney Oldfield "Knox" 261 miles
43.5 mph

Aug. 25 Brighton Beach 1-mi. Dirt Track
Coney Island, Long Island, New York
24-hr. Race
Al Poole & Cyrus Patschke "Stearns"
1253 miles 52.0 mph

Aug. 26–27 1st Elgin Road Races
Elgin, Illinois
36 laps, 8.5-mi. course
305-mi. Elgin National (600 cu. in.)
R. Mulford "Lozier" 292:29.84 62.5 mph
24 laps, 8.5-mi. course, 203-mi. Illinois Cup
(450 cu. in.)
Livingstone "National" 201:08.53
60.6 mph
20 laps, 8.5-mi. course, 170-mi. Kane County
Trophy (300 cu. in.)
David Buck "Marmon" 184:45.79
55.1 mph
16 laps, 8.5-mi. course, 136-mi. Fox River
Trophy (230 cu. in.)
Eddie Hearne "Benz" 150:49.00
54.0 mph

Sep. 3 Indianapolis 2½-mi. Motor
Speedway
Indianapolis, Indiana
100-mi. Free-for-all Race
Eddie Hearne "Benz" 1:19:58.09
75.0 mph
100-mi. Remy Grand Brassard Race
Howdy Wilcox "National" 1:23:03.56
72.0 mph
200-mi. (up to 600 cu. in.) Race
J. Aitken "National" 2:47:54.74
71.2 mph
50-mi. Free-for-all
Eddie Hearne "Benz" :38:02.8 79.4 mph

Sep. Transcontinental Run
New York to San Francisco
3557 mi.
L. L. Whitman "Reo" 10 days, 15 hr.,
13 min.

Oct. 1 Vanderbilt Cup Race
Long Island Motor Parkway
Nassau County, Long Island, New York
22 laps, 12.64-mi. course, 278.08-mi. Road
Race
Harry Grant "Alco" 255:58.60 65.2 mph

Oct. 1 Massapequa Sweepstakes
Long Island Motor Parkway
10 laps, 12.64-mi. course, 126.4-mi. Road
Race
W. Endicott "Cole" 2:18:04.0 55.0 mph
Wheatley Hills Sweepstakes
15 laps, 12.64-mi. course, 189.6-mi. Road
Race
H. Gelnau "Falcar" 3:14:39.0 58.4 mph

Oct. 8 3rd Founder's Day Race
Fairmount Park, Philadelphia, Pa.
25 laps, 8-mi. course, 200-mi. Road Race
Len Zengle "Chadwick" 209:57.88
57.8 mph

Nov. 5–7 3rd Cactus Derby
Los Angeles to Phoenix
480-mi. Desert Road Race
Harvey Herrick & O. M. Kern "Kisselkar"
15:44:00.0 26.0 mph

Nov. 7 Atlanta 2-mi. Motordrome
Atlanta, Ga.
250-mi. Race
Joe Horan "Lozier" 206:15.00 73.0 mph
200-mi. Race
J. Dawson "Marmon" 171:12.72
68.4 mph
100-mi. Race
Gelnau "F.A.L." 86:17.6 69.6 mph

Nov. 12 American Grand Prize
Savannah, Ga.
24 laps, 17.3-mi. course, 415.2-mi. Road
Race
David Bruce-Brown "Benz" 353:05.35
70.6 mph
Savannah Challenge Trophy
16 laps, 17.3-mi. course, 276.8-mi. Road
Race
Joe Dawson "Marmon" 263:39.98
62.6 mph
Tiedeman Trophy
11 laps, 17.3-mi. course, 190.3-mi. Road
Race
Knipper "Lancia" 199:22.67 57.4 mph

Nov. 24 Santa Monica 8.417-mi. Road
Course
Santa Monica, Cal.
Free-for-all, 24-lap, 202-mi. Road Race
Teddy Tetzlaff "Lozier" 3:04:07.0
70.8 mph

301-600 cu. in. Ferris Cup, 18-lap,
151.506-mi. Road Race
Teddy Tetzlaff "Lozier" 2:04:10.0
73.27 mph
231-300 cu. in., 12-lap, 101.004-mi. Road
Race
Tom McKeague "Duro" 1:41:04.0
60.7 mph
Up to 231 cu. in., 12-lap, 101.004-mi. Road
Race
Fancher "Maxwell" 1:42:31.0 59.1 mph

1911

Feb. 22 Oakland Road Races
Oakland, Cal.
Light Car Race—98.3 mi.
C. Bigelow "Mercer" 1:42:54.0 57.2 mph
Heavy Car Race—152.9 mi.
C. Merz "National" 2:17:20.0 66.8 mph
Free-for-all—163.8 mi.
Bert Dingley "Pope-Hartford" 2:29:30.0
65.6 mph

Mar. 19 Playa del Rey 1-mi. Motordrome
Los Angeles, Cal.
100-mi. Match Race
Teddy Tetzlaff "Lozier" 1:14:29.0
80.6 mph

Mar. 28 Pablo Beach Race
Jacksonville, Fla.
100-mi. Race
Louis Disbrow "Pope-Hartford" 1:15:25.0
78.5 mph

Mar. 31 Pablo Beach Race
Jacksonville, Fla.
300-mi. Race
Louis Disbrow "Pope Hummer"
3:53:33.50 77.0 mph

Apr. 10 Playa del Rey 1-mi. Motordrome
Los Angeles, Cal.
24-hr. Race
F. Verbeck & V. Hirsh "Fiat" 1491 miles
62.12 mph

Apr. 23 Daytona Beach, Florida
1-mi. Straightaway Record
Bob Burman "Blitzen-Benz" :25.40
141.7 mph

May 30 Indianapolis 2½-mi. Motor
Speedway
Indianapolis, Indiana
500-mi. Race
Ray Harroun "Marmon" 6:42:08.00
74.9 mph

July 4 Bakersfield Road Race
Bakersfield, Cal.
13 laps, 11.15-mi. course, 145-mi. Road
Race
Harvey Herrick "National" 2:58:58.0
48.5 mph

Aug. 25 2nd Elgin Road Races
Elgin, Illinois
36 laps, 8.5-mi. course
305-mi. National Elgin Trophy
Len Zengle "National" 275:39.08
66.4 mph
24 laps, 8.5-mi. course
203-mi. Illinois Trophy
David Herr "National" 185:55.00
65.6 mph
20 laps, 8.5-mi. course
169-mi. Kane County Trophy
Hugh Hughes "Mercer" 157:21.00

64.6 mph
16 laps, 8.5-mi. course
135-mi. Aurora Trophy
Mort Roberts "Abbott-Detroit" 151:11.32
53.8 mph

Sep. 2 Brighton Beach 1-mi. Dirt Track
Coney Island, Long Island, New York
2-mi. Time Trial
Bob Burman "Blitzen Benz" :01:37.89
73.9 mph
1-mi. Time Trial
Bob Burman "Blitzen Benz" :48.62
74.0 mph

Sep. 3 Driving Park 1-mi. Dirt Track
Columbus, Ohio
200-mi. Race
Harry Knight "Westcott" 3:45:00.0
53.2 mph

Sep. 9 Cincinnati Road Races
Cincinnati, Ohio
25 laps, 7.9-mi. course
200-mi. Cincinnati Trophy
Eddie Hearne "Fiat" 209:03.20
57.8 mph
19 laps, 7.9-mi. course
150-mi. Hamilton County Trophy
Jenkins "Cole" 166:29.00 53.9 mph

Oct. 9 4th Founder's Day Races
Fairmount Park, Philadelphia, Pa.
Division 6C (601-750 cu. in.)
25 laps, 8.1-mi. course, 200-mi. Road Race
Erwin Bergdoll "Benz" 198:41.35
60.8 mph
Division 5C (451-600 cu. in.)
25 laps, 8.1-mi. course, 200-mi. Road Race
Ralph Mulford "Lozier" 201:52.78
59.3 mph
Division 4C (301-450 cu. in.)
25 laps, 8.1-mi. course, 200-mi. Road Race
L. Disbrow "National" 208:22.0
57.5 mph
Division 3C (231-300 cu. in.)
25 laps, 8.1-mi. course, 200-mi. Road Race
Hugh Hughes "Mercer" 209:45.3
49.5 mph
(Note: above races run simultaneously)

Oct. 14 Santa Monica 8.417-mi. Road
Course
Santa Monica, Cal.
Up to 230 cu. in. 12 laps, 101-mi. Road Race
L. Nikrent "Buick" 1:42:21.0 59.2 mph

Oct. 14–26 8th Glidden Tour
New York, Atlanta, Jacksonville
1460.6-mi. Reliability Tour
Tarrytown Team "Maxwell" 12 days

Oct. 14 Santa Monica 8.417-mi. Road
Course
Santa Monica, Cal.
Free-for-all Race
24 laps, 202-mi. Road Race
H. Herrick "National" 162:24.60
74.62 mph
Heavy Car Race (301-450 cu. in.)
18 laps, 151.5-mi. Road Race
Charles Merz "National" 122:08.45
74.4 mph
Medium Car Race (231-300 cu. in.)
18 laps, 151.5-mi. Road Race
B. Keene "Marmon" 132:09.95 68.7 mph

Nov. 7 4th Cactus Derby
Los Angeles to Phoenix
542-mi. Desert Road Race
Harvey Herrick "National" 20:22:00.00
23.0 mph

Nov. 27　Vanderbilt Cup Race
Savannah, Ga.
17 laps, 17.1-mi. course
291.38-mi. Road Race
Ralph Mulford　"Lozier"　236:00.67
74.08 mph
Savannah Challenge Trophy
13 laps, 17.1-mi. course
222.81-mi. Road Race
Hugh Hughes　"Mercer"　195:37.22
70.0 mph
10 laps, 17.1-mi. course
171.40-mi. Tiedeman Trophy
Frank Witt　"E.M.F."　176:23.34　58.1 mph

Nov. 30　American Grand Prize
Savannah, Ga.
24 laps, 17.1-mi. course, 411.36-mi. Road
Race
David Bruce-Brown　"Fiat"　331:29.13
74.45 mph

1912

Feb. 17　Lake St. Clair (Frozen Surface)
Detroit, Mich.
1-mi. Speed Trial
Frank Kulick　"Ford 999 II"　:33.4
107.78 mph

Mar. 31　San Diego 1-mi. Dirt Track
San Diego, Cal.
1-mi. Speed Trial
L. Disbrow　"Jay-Eye-See"　:38.62
93.3 mph

May 4　Santa Monica 8.417-mi. Road
Course
Santa Monica, Cal.
Unlimited Class Race
36 laps, 303-mi. Road Race
Teddy Tetzlaff　"Fiat"　230:57.0
78.72 mph
Light Car Class (161-230 cu. in.)
12 laps, 101.04-mi. Road Race
Joerman　"Maxwell"　97:57.0　61.86 mph
Medium Car Class (231-300 cu. in.)
18 laps, 151.50-mi. Road Race
R. DePalma　"Mercer"　130:43.0
69.54 mph

May 30　Indianapolis 2½-mi. Motor
Speedway
Indianapolis, Indiana
500-mi. Race
Joe Dawson　"National"　6:21:06.0
78.7 mph

July 5　1st Montamara Fiesta Road Races
Tacoma, Wash.
3.5-mi. course
100-mi. Light Car Race
Evans　"Flanders Spl."　1:38:05.20
61.0 mph
150-mi. Medium Car Race
Ed Pullen　"Mercer"　2:25:13.0　62.1 mph
150-mi. Medium-heavy Car Race
Earl Cooper　"Stutz"　2:15:00.0　66.9 mph
200-mi. Heavy Car Race
Teddy Tetzlaff　"Fiat"　2:52:31.65
68.4 mph
250-mi. Free-for-all Race
Teddy Tetzlaff　"Fiat"　3:47:00.45
65.8 mph

July 25　Driving Park 1-mi. Dirt Track
Columbus, Ohio
200-mi. Race
Spencer Wishart　"Mercer"　3:28:04.50
58.0 mph

Aug. 30　3rd Elgin Road Races
Elgin, Illinois
36 laps, 8.5-mi. course,
305-mi. Free-for-all
R. DePalma　"Mercedes"　265:36.25
68.9 mph
18 laps, 8.5-mi. course,
152-mi. Aurora Trophy
Hugh Hughes　"Mercer"　140:40.00
65.0 mph
30 laps, 8.5-mi. course,
254-mi. Elgin National
R. DePalma　"Mercedes"　223:06.00
68.4 mph
24 laps, 8.5-mi. course,
203-mi. Illinois Trophy
Charles Merz　"Stutz"　184:32.25
66.1 mph
12 laps, 8.5-mi. course,
101-mi. Jenks Trophy
H. Endicott　"Mason Spl."　100:42.90
60.6 mph

Sep. 7　Brighton Beach 1-mi. Dirt Track
Coney Island, Long Island, New York
1-mi. Time Trial
Bob Burman　"Blitzen Benz"　:47.85
75.4 mph

Oct. 2　Vanderbilt Cup Race
Wauwatosa Course, Milwaukee, Wis.
38 laps, 7.88-mi. course,
299-mi. Road Race
R. DePalma　"Mercedes"　260:31.54
68.9 mph

Oct. 3　Milwaukee Road Races
Wauwatosa Course, Milwaukee, Wis.
Pabst Trophy
28 laps, 7.88-mi. course,
220.64-mi. Road Race
M. Roberts　"Mason"　225:08.71
58.8 mph
Wisconsin Motor Challenge Trophy
22 laps, 7.88-mi. course,
173.36-mi. Road Race
W. Endicott　"Mason"　186:44.79
55.6 mph

Oct. 5　American Grand Prize
Wauwatosa Course, Milwaukee, Wis.
52 laps, 7.88-mi. course, 410-mi. Road Race
Caleb Smith Bragg　"Fiat"　359:27.44
68.4 mph

Oct. 28　5th Cactus Derby
Los Angeles to Phoenix
511-mi. Desert Road Race
R. Hamlin　"Franklin"　18:10:22.00
28.1 mph

Nov. 5　Brighton Beach 1-mi. Dirt Track
Coney Island, Long Island, New York
100-mi. Race
Ralph Mulford　"Mason"　1:42:11.00
58.4 mph

Dec. 23　San Diego Beach
San Diego, Cal.
1-mi. Time Trial
Bob Burman　"Blitzen Benz"　:28.00
128.6 mph

9th Glidden Tour
Detroit, Indianapolis, Louisville, Memphis,
Baton Rouge, New Orleans
1272-mi. Reliability Tour
"Maxwell"　12 days

1913

Jan. 1　San Diego Road Race
San Diego, Cal.
2 laps, 91.7-mi. course,
183.4-mi. Road Race
G. Hill　"Fiat"　3:58:12.0　46.4 mph

March 2　San Diego Road Race
San Diego, Cal.
34 laps, 5.9-mi. course,
200.6-mi. Road Race
Billy Carlson　"Benz"　3:23:09.0　59.1 mph

May 30　Indianapolis 2½-mi. Motor
Speedway
Indianapolis, Indiana
500-mi. Race
Jules Goux　"Peugeot"　6:35:05.0
76.9 mph

July 4　Panama-Pacific Road Race
Los Angeles to Sacramento
443.6-mi. Road Race
Frank Verbeck　"Fiat"　11:01:16.0
40.0 mph

July 4　Driving Park 1-mi. Dirt Track
Columbus, Ohio
200-mi. Race
Ralph Mulford　"Mason"　3:21:48.0
59.2 mph

July 7　2nd Montamara Race Meet
Tacoma, Wash.
57 laps, 3.5-mi. course,
200-mi. Potlatch Trophy
Earl Cooper　"Stutz"　2:49:37.0　71.1 mph
72 laps, 3.5-mi. course,
250-mi. Montamarathon
Earl Cooper　"Stutz"　3:32:08.20
70.7 mph

July 11–19　10th Glidden Tour
Minneapolis to Glacier Park, Montana
1245-mi. Reliability Tour
"Metz"　8 days

July 28　Galveston Beach Race
Galveston, Texas
20 laps, 5-mi. course,
100-mi. Beach Race
Louis Disbrow　"Simplex"　1:23:59.0
71.5 mph

Aug. 9　Santa Monica 8.417-mi. Road
Course
Los Angeles, Cal.
53 laps, 445.258-mi. Road Race
Earl Cooper　"Stutz"　6:01:52.0　73.8 mph

Aug. 30　4th Elgin Road Races
Elgin, Illinois
36 laps, 8.5-mi. course,
301-mi. Elgin National
Gil Anderson　"Stutz"　253:38.97
71.4 mph
Chicago Automobile Club Trophy
36 laps, 8.5-mi. course,
301-mi. Road Race
Ralph DePalma　"Mercer"　271:56.90
66.3 mph

Sep. 9　1st Corona Road Races
Los Angeles, Cal.
3-mi. course
301.81-mi. Free-for-all Race
Earl Cooper　"Stutz"　4:02:38.00
74.7 mph
251.97-mi. Medium Car Race
Earl Cooper　"Stutz"　3:21:29.50
75.0 mph
102.45-mi. Light Car Race
Waterman　"Buick"　1:37:20.00　67.7 mph

Nov. 4 6th Cactus Derby
Los Angeles to Phoenix
564-mi. Desert Road Race
Orin Davis "Locomobile" 18:50:00.0
29.9 mph

Nov. 5 Cross-country Race
El Paso to Phoenix
517-mi. Desert Road Race
Newkirk "Simplex" 17:10:00.0 33.3 mph

1914

Feb. 26 Vanderbilt Cup Race
Santa Monica 8.417-mi. Road Course
Santa Monica, Cal.
35-lap, 294.035-mi. Road Race
Ralph DePalma "Mercedes" 3:53:41.0
75.49 mph

Feb. 28 American Grand Prize
Santa Monica 8.417-mi. Road Course
Santa Monica, Cal.
48-lap, 403.24-mi. Road Race
Ed Pullen "Mercer" 5:13:30.0 77.2 mph

May 30 Indianapolis 2½-mi. Motor
Speedway
Indianapolis, Indiana
500-mi. Race
Rene Thomas "Delage" 6:03:45.00
82.5 mph

June 20 Indianapolis 2½-mi. Motor
Speedway
Indianapolis, Indiana
29 laps, 72.5-mi. Stock Car Speed Run
W. R. McCulla "Packard" (Twin Six)
:52:04.08 70.4 mph

July 4 Sioux City 2-mi. Speedway
(Inaugural)
Sioux City, Iowa
300-mi. Race
E. V. Rickenbacker "Duesenberg"
3:49:02.00 78.6 mph

July 4 3rd Montamara Speed Carnival
Tacoma, Wash.
2-mi. Dirt Track
100-mi. Intercity Trophy Race
Parsons "Frantz" 1:21:29.40 73.6 mph
200-mi. Potlatch Trophy Race
Hugh Hughes "Maxwell" 2:41:32.40
74.3 mph
250-mi. Montamarathon Trophy Race
Earl Cooper "Stutz" 3:24:34.80
73.4 mph

Aug. 1 Galveston Beach Race
Galveston, Texas
10 laps, 5-mi. course,
50-mi. Beach Race
Ralph Mulford "Peugeot" :33:59.6
88.4 mph

Aug. 12 Bonneville Salt Flats
Wendover, Utah
½-mi. Straightaway Speed Run
Teddy Tetzlaff "Blitzen Benz" :12.60
142.85 mph

Aug. 21–22 5th Elgin Road Races
Elgin, Illinois
Chicago Automobile Club Cup
36 laps, 8.5-mi. course,
301-mi. Road Race
R. DePalma "Mercedes" 4:05:01.00
73.9 mph
Elgin National Trophy
36 laps, 8.5-mi. course,

301-mi. Road Race
R. DePalma "Mercedes" 4:06:18.00
73.5 mph

Sep. 7 Detroit 1-mi. Dirt Track
Detroit, Mich.
1-mi. Time Trial
Louis Disbrow "Simplex Zip" :50.4
71.5 mph
10-mi. Race
Louis Disbrow "Simplex Zip" :09:16.6
64.6 mph

Sep. 7 Brighton Beach 1-mi. Dirt Track
Coney Island, Long Island, New York
50-mi. Race
R. DePalma "Mercedes" :50:42.40
52.2 mph
100-mi. Race
R. DePalma "Mercedes" 1:40:15.00
59.5 mph

Sep. 26 Kalamazoo 1-mi. Dirt Track
Kalamazoo, Mich.
100-mi. Race
Bob Burman "Peugeot" 1:34:29.4
63.5 mph

Oct. 22 Galesburg 1-mi. Dirt Track
Galesburg, Ill.
100-mi. Race
Ralph Mulford "Duesenberg" 1:32:54.5
64.5 mph

Oct. 24 Minneapolis 1-mi. Dirt Track
Minneapolis, Minn.
100-mi. Race
Tom Alley "Duesenberg" 1:31:30.0
65.6 mph

Nov. 10 7th Cactus Derby
Los Angeles to Phoenix
671-mi. Desert Road Race
Barney Oldfield "Stutz" 23:01:00.0
29.1 mph

Nov. 12 Indianapolis 2½-mi. Motor
Speedway
60-mi. Stock Car Speed Run
"Marmon" (41) :57:41.71 62.9 mph

Nov. 13 Cross-country Race
El Paso to Phoenix 533-mi. Desert Road
Race
H. B. Miller "Pope-Hartford" 14:35:48.00
36.7 mph

Nov. 26 2nd Corona Road Race
Los Angeles, Cal.
109 laps, 2.77-mi. course,
301-mi. Road Race
Ed Pullen "Mercer" 3:26:02.00
87.7 mph

Dec. 27 Ascot Park 1-mi. Dirt Track
Los Angeles, Cal.
50-mi. Oldfield-Burman Match Race
Bob Burman "Peugeot" :45:54.0
65.4 mph

Dec. 31 Cross-country Run
Los Angeles to Riverside, Cal.—58 miles
Billy Carlson "Maxwell" :56:25.8
60.6 mph

1915

Jan. 3 Bakersfield 1-mi. Dirt Track
Bakersfield, Cal.
50-mi. Race
Bob Burman "Peugeot" :40:58.0
73.0 mph

Jan. 9 Point Loma Road Race
San Diego, Cal.
51 laps, 5.982-mi. course,
305.082-mi. Road Race
Earl Cooper "Stutz" 4:40:10.20
65.35 mph

Feb. 3 Glendale Road Race
Glendale, Cal.
53 laps, 1.9-mi. course,
100.7-mi. Road Race
Eddie O'Donnell "Duesenberg"
2:07:07.00 47.81 mph

Feb. 7 Ascot Park 1-mi. Dirt Track
Los Angeles, Cal.
100-mi. Race
Eddie O'Donnell "Duesenberg" 1:41:31.0
59.1 mph

Feb. 27 American Grand Prize
Panama-Pacific Exposition
San Francisco, Cal.
3.8489-mi. course
400.28-mi. Road Race
Dario Resta "Peugeot" 7:07:57.00
56.13 mph

Mar. 6 Vanderbilt Cup Race
Panama-Pacific Exposition
San Francisco, Cal.
3.8489-mi. course
300.3-mi. Road Race
Dario Resta "Peugeot" 4:27:37.00
66.45 mph

Mar. 17 Venice Grand Prix
Venice, Cal.
300-mi. Road Race
Barney Oldfield "Maxwell" 4:24:09.40
68.50 mph

Mar. 20 Tucson Road Race
Tucson, Ariz.
49 laps, 2.1-mi. course, 103 miles
Barney Oldfield "Maxwell" 1:31:59.0
67.29 mph

Apr. 4 Ascot Park 1-mi. Dirt Track
Los Angeles, Cal.
50-mi. Match Race (Burman, Cooper,
Disbrow)
Bob Burman "Peugeot" :52:36.9
57.1 mph

May 1 Southwest Sweepstakes
Oklahoma City, Ok.
30 laps, 6.65-mi. course,
199.532-mi. Road Race
Bob Burman "Peugeot" 2:56:00.60
67.98 mph

May 7–18 Transcontinental Run
San Diego to New York, 3728.4 miles
Erwin G. "Cannonball" Baker "Stutz"
11 days, 7 hr., 15 min. 13.8 mph

May 30 Indianapolis 2½-mi. Motor
Speedway
Indianapolis, Indiana
500-mi. Race
Ralph DePalma "Mercedes" 5:35:55.51
89.84 mph

June 9 Galesburg 1-mi. Dirt Track
Galesburg, Ill.
100-mi. Race
Eddie O'Donnell "Duesenberg" 1:36:00.0
62.5 mph

June 13 Milwaukee 1-mi. Dirt Track
(Inaugural)
West Allis, Wis.
100-mi. Race
Louis Disbrow "Case"

June 24 Uniontown 3-mi. Hill Climb
Uniontown, Pa.
Charles Johnson "Packard Greyhound"
:03:27.2 52.1 mph

June 26 Maywood 2-mi. Board Speedway
(Inaugural)
Chicago, Ill.
500-mi. Race
Dario Resta "Peugeot" 5:07:26.00
97.58 mph

July 3 Sioux City 2-mi. Dirt Track
Sioux City, Iowa
300-mi. Race
E. V. Rickenbacker "Maxwell" 4:00:56.91
74.7 mph

July 5 4th Montamara Speed Carnival
Tacoma 2-mi. "Planked" Speedway
Tacoma, Wash.
250-mi. Montamarathon Trophy
Guy Ruckstall "Mercer" 2:57:03.00
84.8 mph
200-mi. Golden Potlatch Trophy
Ed Pullen "Mercer" 2:21:14.00 85.2 mph
100-mi. Intercity Trophy
Parsons "Parsons Spl." 1:15:27.00
79.5 mph

July 5 Omaha 1¼-mi. Board Speedway
(Inaugural)
Omaha, Nebraska
302-mi. Race
E. V. Rickenbacker "Maxwell" 3:17:32.20
91.74 mph

July 9 Burlington ½-mi. Dirt Track
Burlington, Iowa
100-mi. Race
Bob Burman "Peugeot" 2:07:29.66
47.0 mph

July 10 Maywood 2-mi. Board Speedway
Chicago, Ill.
10-mi. Stock Car Test
R. DePalma "Packard" (Twin Six)
:08:15.0 72.7 mph

Aug. 7 Maywood 2-mi. Board Speedway
Chicago, Ill.
100-mi. Chicago Challenge Race
Dario Resta "Peugeot" :58:54.20
101.86 mph
(First 100-mi. race in less than 60 minutes
in America)

Aug. 7 Des Moines 1-mi. Board Speedway
(Inaugural)
Des Moines, Iowa
300-mi. Race
R. Mulford "Duesenberg" 3:27:05.33
87.0 mph

Aug. 20 6th Elgin Road Races
Elgin, Illinois
Chicago Automobile Club Trophy
36 laps, 8.38-mi. course, 301-mi. Road Race
Earl Cooper "Stutz" 4:01:32.00
74.98 mph
Elgin National Trophy
36 laps, 8.38-mi. course, 301-mi. Road Race
Gil Anderson "Stutz" 3:54:25.87
77.26 mph

Aug. 28 Kalamazoo 1-mi. Dirt Track
Kalamazoo, Mich.
100-mi. Race
Ralph DePalma "Stutz" 1:33:31.4
65.32 mph

Sep. 4 Twin City 2-mi. Concrete Speedway
(Inaugural)
Fort Snelling, Minneapolis, Minnesota
500-mi. Race
Earl Cooper "Stutz" 5:47:29.30
86.35 mph

Sep. 18 Narragansett Park 1-mi. Asphalt
Speedway (Inaugural)
Providence, Rhode Island
100-mi. Race
E. V. Rickenbacker "Maxwell" 89:24.75
67.1 mph
25-mi. Race
Bob Burman "Peugeot" :21:29.96
69.76 mph

Sep. 27 Maywood 2-mi. Board Speedway
Chicago, Ill.
100-mi. Stock Car Trial
W. J. Davidson "Cadillac" (V-8) 82:46.00
72.49 mph

Oct. 9 Sheepshead Bay 2-mi. Board
Speedway (Inaugural)
Sheepshead Bay, Long Island, New York
350-mi. Vincent Astor Cup
Gil Anderson "Stutz" 3:24:42.00
102.6 mph

Nov. 2 Sheepshead Bay 2-mi. Board
Speedway
Sheepshead Bay, Long Island, New York
100-mi. Harkness Gold Cup
Dario Resta "Peugeot" :56:55.71
105.39 mph

Nov. 20 Phoenix Road Race
Phoenix, Ariz.
30 laps, 5-mi. course
150-mi. race, called at 109 miles (darkness)
Earl Cooper "Stutz" 1:42:30.0 63.8 mph

Nov. 25 San Francisco Road Race
San Francisco, Cal.
27 laps, 3.85-mi. course, 104 miles
Earl Cooper "Stutz" 1:48:37.6 57.4 mph

Nov. 25 Sheepshead Bay 2-mi. Board
Speedway
Sheepshead Bay, Long Island, N.Y.
Class B (231-300 cu. in.) Stock Car Records
Ralph Mulford "Hudson" (Super 6)
10 mi. :07:54.40 76.0 mph
20 mi. :15:45.80 76.4 mph
50 mi. :39:30.80 76.0 mph
100 mi. 1:20:21.40 74.9 mph

1916

Mar. 9 Ascot Park 1-mi. Dirt Track
Los Angeles, Cal.
100-mi. Race
"George Washington Sweepstakes"
Eddie Pullen "Mercer" 1:30:42.0
66.1 mph

Apr. 8 3rd Corona Grand Prize Road Race
Los Angeles, Cal.
2.76-mi. course
300-mi. Road Race
Ed O'Donnell "Duesenberg" 3:29:52.00
85.6 mph

Apr. 10 Daytona Beach, Fla.
1-mi. Straightaway Stock Car Record

R. Mulford "Hudson" (Super 6) :35.11
102.5 mph

Apr. 15 Ascot Park 1-mi. Dirt Track
Los Angeles, Cal.
150-mi. Ascot Motor Derby
Ed O'Donnell "Duesenberg" 2:17:09.00
65.4 mph

May 2 Sheepshead Bay 2-mi. Board
Speedway
Sheepshead Bay, Long Island, N.Y.
24-hr. Stock Car Run
R. Mulford "Hudson" (Super 6)
1819 miles 75.8 mph

May 8–15 Transcontinental Record
Los Angeles to New York—3380.7 mi.
Erwin G. "Cannonball" Baker
"Cadillac" (V-8) 7 days, 11 hr., 52 min.
18.8 mph

May 13 Sheepshead Bay 2-mi. Board
Speedway
Sheepshead Bay, Long Island, N.Y.
150-mi. Metropolitan Trophy
E. V. Rickenbacker "Maxwell" 1:33:31.00
96.53 mph
50-mi. Queens Cup
R. Mulford "Peugeot" :28:45.04
104.34 mph
20-mi. Coney Island Cup
John Aitken "Peugeot" :11:15.80
106.71 mph

May 30 Indianapolis 2½-mi. Motor
Speedway
Indianapolis, Indiana
300-mi. Race
Dario Resta "Peugeot" 3:34:17.00
83.26 mph

June 11 Maywood 2-mi. Board Speedway
Chicago, Ill.
300-mi. Race
Dario Resta "Peugeot" 3:02.31.64
98.61 mph

June 24 Des Moines 1-mi. Board
Speedway
Des Moines, Iowa
150-mi. Race
Ralph DePalma "Mercedes" 1:36:36.33
92.66 mph

June 29 Sheepshead Bay 2-mi. Board
Speedway
Sheepshead Bay, Long Island, N.Y.
Two Weeks' Non-stop Run
(Various Drivers) "King" 32.0 mph

July 4 Twin City 2-mi. Concrete Speedway
Minneapolis, Minn.
150-mi. Race
Ralph DePalma "Mercedes" 1:38:49.20
91.08 mph

July 8 Sioux City 2-mi. Dirt Track
Sioux City, Iowa
10-mi. Race
Wilbur D'Alene "Duesenberg" :07:31.96
79.6 mph
20-mi. Race
Howdy Wilcox "Premier" :15:18.78
78.4 mph
50-mi. Race
Howdy Wilcox "Premier" :40:59.0
72.57 mph

July 8 Comstock Park 1-mi. Dirt Track
Grand Rapids, Mich.

100-mi. Race
Ora Haibe "Ogren" 1:46:03.40 56.5 mph

July 15 Omaha 1¼-mi. Board Speedway
Omaha, Nebraska
150-mi. Race
Dario Resta "Peugeot" 1:30:43.88
99.02 mph
50-mi. Race
Ralph DePalma "Mercedes" :29:02.47
103.45 mph

July 22 Kansas City 1⅛-mi. Dirt Track
Kansas City, Mo.
100-mi. Race
Ralph DePalma "Mercedes" 1:42:54.00
58.4 mph

July 24–29 Transcontinental Record
New York to San Francisco—3476 mi.
S. B. Stevens & others "Marmon" (34)
5 days, 18 hr., 30 min. 25.1 mph

Aug. 5 5th Montamara Speed Carnival
Tacoma, Wash.
300-mi. Montamarathon Race
E. V. Rickenbacker "Maxwell" 3:21:40.10
89.3 mph

Aug. 12 Pikes Peak Hill Climb
Colorado Springs, Col.
12.6-mi. course
Rea Lentz "Romano" :20:55.6 36.0 mph

Aug. 19 Maywood 2-mi. Board Speedway
Chicago, Ill.
50-mi. Race, "Speedway Grand Prix"
Dario Resta "Peugeot" :25:52.49
100.42 mph

Sep. 4 Cincinnati 2-mi. Board Speedway
(Inaugural)
Cincinnati, Ohio
300-mi. Race
John Aitken "Peugeot" 3:05:27.22
97.06 mph

Sep. 9 Harvest Racing Classic
Indianapolis 2½-mi. Motor Speedway
Indianapolis, Indiana
20-mi. Race
J. Aitken "Peugeot" :12:37.35 95.08 mph
50-mi. Race
J. Aitken "Peugeot" :32:40.33 91.83 mph
100-mi. Race
J. Aitken "Peugeot" 1:07:05.04
89.44 mph

Sep. 19 Transcontinental Record
San Francisco to New York
3476 mi.
Vincent, Patterson & Mulford "Hudson"
(Super 6) 5 days, 3 hr., 31 min.
27.19 mph

Sep. 30 Sheepshead Bay 2-mi. Board
Speedway
Sheepshead Bay, Long Island, N.Y.
250-mi. Vincent Astor Cup
John Aitken "Peugeot" 2:23:04.03
104.83 mph

Oct. 14 Maywood 2-mi. Board Speedway
Chicago, Ill.
250-mi. Grand American Prize
Dario Resta "Peugeot" 2:24:16.68
103.99 mph

Oct. 30 Sheepshead Bay 2-mi. Board
Speedway
Sheepshead Bay, Long Island, N.Y.
100-mi. Harkness Trophy

John Aitken "Peugeot" :56:37.65
105.95 mph
50-mi. Race
J. LeCain "Delage" :28:49.59 104.2 mph

Nov. 13 Cross-country Race Douglas to
Phoenix, Ariz. 273-mi. Desert Road Race
E. L. Cord "Paige" 8:30:00.00 30.0 mph

Nov. 16 Vanderbilt Cup Race
Santa Monica 8.417-mi. Road Course
Santa Monica, Cal.
35-lap, 294.03-mi. Road Race
Dario Resta "Peugeot" 3:22:48.40
86.98 mph

Nov. 18 American Grand Prize
Santa Monica 8.417-mi. Road Course
Santa Monica, Cal.
48-lap, 403.24-mi. Road Race
Howard Wilcox "Peugeot" 4:42:47.00
85.59 mph

Nov. 30 Ascot Park 1-mi. Paved Speedway
Los Angeles, Cal.
150-mi. Race
E. V. Rickenbacker "Duesenberg"
2:13:15.50 67.54 mph

Nov. 30 Phoenix Fair 1-mi. Dirt Track
Phoenix, Ariz.
100-mi. Race
R. H. Delno "Stutz" 1:38:29.35 60.0 mph

Dec. 2 Uniontown 1⅛-mi. Board Speedway
(Inaugural)
Uniontown, Pa.
112.5-mi. Race
L. Chevrolet "Frontenac" 1:14:12.40
90.69 mph

1917

Mar. 4 Ascot Park 1-mi. Paved Speedway
Los Angeles, Cal.
100-mi. Race
Earl Cooper "Stutz" 1:27:46.0
68.4 mph

May 10 Uniontown 1⅛-mi. Board
Speedway
Uniontown, Pa.
112-mi. Universal Trophy
W. Taylor "Newman-Stutz" 1:15:38.00
89.25 mph
112-mi. Dealers' Race
I. P. Fetterman "Peerless" 1:21:38.4
82.74 mph

May 30 Cincinnati 2-mi. Board Speedway
Cincinnati, Ohio
250-mi. International Sweepstakes
L. Chevrolet "Frontenac" 2:26:47.90
102.18 mph

June 1 Sheepshead Bay 2-mi. Board
Speedway
Sheepshead Bay, Long Island, N.Y.
100-mi. Harkness Trophy
Ralph DePalma "Packard 299" :58:21.00
102.0 mph
10-mi. Race (1st heat)
Ralph Mulford "Frontenac" :06:10.4
97.4 mph
10-mi. Race (2nd heat)
Dario Resta "Resta" :06:07.0 98.0 mph
10-mi. Race (3rd heat)
Louis Chevrolet "Frontenac" :05:57.4
100.1 mph

June 16 Maywood 2-mi. Board Speedway
Chicago, Ill.
250-mi. Race
Earl Cooper "Stutz" 2:25:28.80
103.15 mph

July 4 Omaha 1¼-mi. Board Speedway
Omaha, Nebraska
150-mi. Race
Ralph Mulford "Hudson" 1:28:53.00
101.4 mph
50-mi. Race
Dave Lewis "Hoskins" :29:03.00
102.85 mph

July 4 Uniontown 1⅛-mi. Board Speedway
Uniontown, Pa.
112-mi. Race
I. P. Fetterman "Peerless" 1:13:40.56
90.9 mph

July 14 Sheepshead Bay 2-mi. Board
Speedway
Sheepshead Bay, Long Island, N.Y.
Speed Trials
Willard Rader "Packard 905"
1 mi. :00:29.5 121.8 mph
2 mi. :00:58.0 124.2 mph
4 mi. :01:57.5 122.3 mph
6 mi. :03:00.0 120.0 mph

July 14 Twin City 2-mi. Concrete Speedway
Minneapolis, Minn.
50-mi. Race
Earl Cooper "Stutz" :30:50.0 97.4 mph
100-mi. Race
Ira Vail "Hudson" 1:02:19.73 96.1 mph

July 28 Sheepshead Bay 2-mi. Board
Speedway
Sheepshead Bay, Long Island, N.Y.
Non-competitive Speed Trials
Willard Rader "Packard 905"
1 mi. :28.76 125.1 mph
5 mi. 2:24.66 124.5 mph
10 mi. 4:50.88 123.7 mph

Aug. 4 Sheepshead Bay 2-mi. Board
Speedway
Sheepshead Bay, Long Island, N.Y.
24-hr. Stock Car Endurance Run
Joe Dawson "Chalmers" 1898 mi.
79.08 mph

Aug. 9 St. Louis 1-mi. Dirt Track
St. Louis, Mo.
Non-competitive Speed Records
Barney Oldfield "Miller" (Golden
Submarine)
1-mi. :00:45.00 80.0 mph
2-mi. :01:30.40 79.5 mph
3-mi. :02:17.60 78.5 mph
4-mi. :03:05.60 77.5 mph
5-mi. :03:53.60 77.2 mph
10-mi. :07:56.20 75.5 mph
15-mi. :12:00.80 75.0 mph
20-mi. :15:52.20 75.5 mph
25-mi. :19:57.60 75.4 mph
50-mi. :40:47.60 73.5 mph

Sep. 3 Tacoma 2-mi. Plank Speedway
Tacoma, Wash.
100-mi. Race
Earl Cooper "Stutz" 1:08:51.0 87.1 mph

Sep. 3 Maywood 2-mi. Board Speedway
Chicago, Ill.
50-mi. Race
Ralph DePalma "Packard 299" :28:09.0
106.7 mph
100-mi. Race
Louis Chevrolet "Frontenac" :56:29.5
106.1 mph

Sep. 8 Uniontown 1⅛-mi. Board Speedway
Uniontown, Pa.
112.5-mi. Race
Frank Elliott "Delage" 1:14:26.0
90.5 mph

Sep. 15 Narragansett 1-mi. Paved Speedway
Providence, R.I.
100-mi. Race
Tommy Milton   "Duesenberg"   1:24:42.23
70.9 mph
25-mi. Race
Tommy Milton   "Duesenberg"   :19:46.0
75.7 mph
5-mi. Race
Ralph Mulford   "Frontenac"   :03:58.0
75.6 mph

Sep. 22 Sheepshead Bay 2-mi. Board Speedway
Sheepshead Bay, Long Island, N.Y.
100-mi. Harkness Gold Trophy
L. Chevrolet   "Frontenac"   :54:20.98
110.4 mph
10-mi. Futurity Handicap
J. LeCain   "Delage"   :06:07.60   97.8 mph

Oct. 13 Maywood 2-mi. Board Speedway
Chicago, Ill.
20-mi. Race
Tom Alley   "Pan-American"   :11:22.10
105.9 mph
50-mi. Race
Ralph Mulford   "Frontenac"   :28:18.75
106.0 mph
50-mi. Race
Pete Henderson   "Roamer"   :27:22.21
109.0 mph

Oct. 29 Uniontown 1⅛-mi. Board Speedway
Uniontown, Pa.
168.75-mi. Race
Eddie Hearne   "Duesenberg"   1:49:02.45
93.0 mph

Nov. 16 Sheepshead Bay 2-mi. Board Speedway
Sheepshead Bay, Long Island, N.Y.
Non-competitive Speed Trial
Ralph DePalma   "Packard 299"
1-hr. (110 miles)   110.0 mph
2-hr. (219 miles)   109.5 mph
3-hr. (320 miles)   106.9 mph
4-hr. (428 miles)   107.2 mph
5-hr. (522 miles)   104.4 mph
6-hr. (616 miles)   102.8 mph

Nov. 29 Ascot Park 1-mi. Paved Speedway
Los Angeles, Cal.
10-mi. Race
Louis Chevrolet   "Frontenac"   :07:51.0
76.4 mph
50-mi. Race
Eddie Hearne   "Duesenberg"   :41:54.80
71.6 mph

1918

May 16 Uniontown 1⅛-mi. Board Speedway
Uniontown, Pa.
5⅝-mi. Match Race
Barney Oldfield   "Golden Submarine"
:03:18.51   102.0 mph
27-mi. Race (1st heat)
Tommy Milton   "Duesenberg"   :15:59.52
101.1 mph
27-mi. Race (2nd heat)
Ralph Mulford   "Frontenac"   :16:37.09
95.3 mph
27-mi. Race (3rd heat)
Eddie Hearne   "Frontenac"   :16:49.64
94.85 mph
27-mi. Race (4th heat)
Louis Chevrolet   "Frontenac"   :17:03.68
93.4 mph

27-mi. Race (5th heat)
Ralph Mulford   "Frontenac"   :16:42.82
97.0 mph

June 1 Sheepshead Bay 2-mi. Board Track
Sheepshead Bay, Long Island, N.Y.
100-mi. Harkness Trophy
R. DePalma   "Packard" (299)   :58:21.00
102.0 mph

June 26 Maywood 2-mi. Board Speedway
Chicago, Ill.
100-mi. Chicago Automobile Derby
L. Chevrolet   "Frontenac"   :55:29.60
108.12 mph

July 4 Cincinnati 2-mi. Board Speedway
Cincinnati, Ohio
100-mi. AAA Championship Race
Ralph DePalma   "Packard" (299)   (no time)

July 4 Tacoma 2-mi. Plank Speedway
Tacoma, Wash.
25-mi. Race
Cliff Durant "Chevrolet"   :15:09.4
98.9 mph
50-mi. Race
Cliff Durant   "Chevrolet"   :30:37.6
97.6 mph
75-mi. Race
Eddie Hearne   "Duesenberg"   :47:43.5
94.2 mph

July 18 Uniontown 1⅛-mi. Board Speedway
Uniontown, Pa.
112.5-mi. Race
Louis Chevrolet   "Frontenac"   1:11:22.45
95.0 mph
5⅝-mi. Match Race (1st Heat)
Barney Oldfield   "Golden Submarine"
:03:20.0   101.0 mph
5⅝-mi. Match Race (2nd Heat)
Louis Chevrolet   "Frontenac"   :03:17.6
102.4 mph
5⅝-mi. Match Race (3rd Heat)
Eddie Hearne   "Duesenberg"   :03:35.56
94.0 mph
18-mi. Australian Pursuit Race
Denny Hickey   "Hudson"   :17:16.0
62.6 mph

July 28 Maywood 2-mi. Board Speedway
Chicago, Ill.
2-mi.
D. Resta   "Peugeot"   :01:18.0   92.3 mph
10-mi.
R. DePalma   "Packard" (299)   :05:24.80
110.8 mph
20-mi.
R. DePalma   "Packard" (299)   :10:50.20
110.7 mph
30-mi.
R. DePalma   "Packard" (299)   :16:54.80
106.24 mph

Aug. 17 Sheepshead Bay 2-mi. Board Speedway
Sheepshead Bay, Long Island, N.Y.
2-mi. Race
Ralph DePalma   "Packard" (299)
:01:05.60   110.0 mph
10-mi. Race
Ralph DePalma   "Packard" (299)
:05:23.80   111.0 mph
30-mi. Race
Ralph DePalma   "Packard" (299)
:16:31.20   109.0 mph
50-mi. Race
Ralph DePalma   "Packard" (299)
:27:29.20   109.1 mph

Sep. 2 Uniontown 1⅛-mi. Board Speedway

Uniontown, Pa.
112.5-mi. Race
Ralph Mulford   "Frontenac"   1:10:11.17
96.17 mph

Contest Board of AAA suspended racing for duration of war

1919

Feb. 18 Daytona Beach, Fla.
1-mi. Straightaway Record
Ralph DePalma   "Packard 905"   :24.02
149.9 mph

Mar. 15 Santa Monica 8.417-mi. Road Course
Santa Monica, Cal.
30-lap, 250.24-mi. Road Race
Cliff Durant   "Chevrolet"   3:04:45.00
81.28 mph

Mar. 23 Ascot 1-mi. Asphalt Speedway
Los Angeles, Cal.
150-mi. Race
Roscoe Sarles   "Roamer Spl."   2:07:02.00
71.0 mph

May 20 Uniontown 1⅛-mi. Board Speedway
Uniontown, Pa.
112.5-mi. Race
Tommy Milton   "Duesenberg"   1:10:09.32
96.2 mph

May 30 Indianapolis 2½-mi. Motor Speedway
Indianapolis, Indiana
500-mi. Race
Howard Wilcox   "Peugeot"   5:40:42.87
88.1 mph

June 14 Sheepshead Bay 2-mi. Board Speedway
Sheepshead Bay, Long Island, N.Y.
50-mi. Race
Ralph DePalma   "Packard" (299)   :26:23.40
113.8 mph
30-mi. Race
Ralph Mulford   "Frontenac"   :16:20.60
112.5 mph
10-mi. Race
Tommy Milton   "Duesenberg"   :05:20.20
112.1 mph
10-mi. Race—Special Event
Ralph Mulford   "Frontenac"   :05:24.20
111.0 mph

July 4 Tacoma 2-mi. Board Speedway
Tacoma, Wash.
80-mi. Race
Louis Chevrolet   "Frontenac"   :49:19.40
97.4 mph
60-mi. Race
Louis Chevrolet   "Frontenac"   :36:27.20
98.5 mph
40-mi. Race
Ralph Mulford   "Frontenac"   :24:02.80
99.5 mph

July 4 Sheepshead Bay 2-mi. Board Speedway
Sheepshead Bay, Long Island, N.Y.
100-mi. Race
Gaston Chevrolet   "Frontenac"   :54:17.13
110.5 mph

July 19 Uniontown 1⅛-mi. Board Speedway
Uniontown, Pa.
22½-mi. Race

Tommy Milton "Duesenberg" :13:22.85
101.17 mph

Aug. 23 7th Elgin Road Race
Elgin, Ill.
301-mi. Road Race
Tommy Milton "Duesenberg" 4:05:27.00
73.9 mph

Sep. 1 Uniontown 1⅛-mi. Board
Speedway
Uniontown, Pa.
225-mi. Race
Joe Boyer "Frontenac" 2:24:19.68
93.5 mph

Sep. 20 Sheepshead Bay 2-mi. Board
Speedway
Sheepshead Bay, Long Island, N.Y.
150-mi. Race
Gaston Chevrolet "Frontenac"
1:22:34.20 108.99 mph

Oct. 12 Cincinnati 2-mi. Board Speedway
Cincinnati, Ohio
250-mi. Race
Joe Boyer "Frontenac" 2:27:19.29
101.69 mph

Nov. 8 Phoenix 1-mi. Dirt Track
Phoenix, Ariz.
100-mi. Race
Eddie Hearne "Chevrolet" 1:29:09.0
67.4 mph

Nov. 10 Sheepshead Bay 2-mi. Board
Speedway
Sheepshead Bay, long Island, N.Y.
Non-competitive Speed Trials
125-mi. Class C (161-183 cu. in.)
E. O'Donnell "Duesenberg" 1:20:26.80
92.8 mph
25-mi. (231-300 cu. in.)
Tommy Milton "Duesenberg" :12:55.74
116.2 mph
25-mi. (301-450 cu. in.)
Dave Lewis "Duesenberg" :13:31.63
111.0 mph

Nov. 17 Sheepshead Bay 2-mi. Board
Speedway
Sheepshead Bay, Long Island, N.Y.
Stripped Model Stock Car Speed Trial
Ralph DePalma "Cunningham" 10-mi.
:06:35.40 91.0 mph

Nov. 21 Sheepshead Bay 2-mi. Board
Speedway
Sheepshead Bay, Long Island, N.Y.
Non-competitive Speed Trials
100 miles (303 cu. in.)
Dave Lewis "Duesenberg" :53:25.40
112.0 mph
300 miles (183 cu. in.)
Jimmy Murphy "Duesenberg" 3:15:44.0
92.0 mph

Dec. 12 Cincinnati 2-mi. Board Speedway
Cincinnati, Ohio
Endurance Run
"Essex" (Stock Chassis)
 1 hr. 69.3 mph
12 hr. 68.3 mph
24 hr. 64.1 mph
36 hr. 64.6 mph
48 hr. 60.7 mph

1920

Feb. 28 Beverly Hills 1¼-mi. Board
Speedway (Inaugural)
Los Angeles, Cal.
250-mi. Race
Jimmy Murphy "Duesenberg" 2:25:17.59
103.2 mph

Apr. 27 Daytona Beach, Fla.
1-mi. Straightaway Record
Tommy Milton "Duesenberg" :23.07
156.0 mph

May 25 Cross-country Speed Run
Indianapolis-Cincinnati round trip
203-mi.
E. G. "Cannonball" Baker "Cole"
4:22:00.0 50.9 mph

May 30 Indianapolis 2½-mi. Motor
Speedway
Indianapolis, Indiana
500-mi. Race
Gaston Chevrolet "Monroe" 5:38:32.0
88.5 mph

June 19 Uniontown 1⅛-mi. Board
Speedway
Uniontown, Pa.
225-mi. Universal Trophy
T. Milton "Duesenberg" 2:22:44.36
94.9 mph

July 5 Tacoma 2-mi. Board Speedway
Tacoma, Wash.
225-mi. Race
Tommy Milton "Duesenberg" 2:23:28.0
95.0 mph

Aug. 1 Driving Park 1-mi. Dirt Track
Columbus, Ohio
100-mi. Match Race
Gaston Chevrolet "Monroe" 1:29:23.0
67.0 mph

Aug. 28 8th Elgin Road Race
Elgin, Ill.
30 laps, 8.3-mi. course,
251-mi. Road Race
Ralph DePalma "Ballot" 3:09:54.00
79.0 mph

Sep. 7 Pikes Peak Hill Climb
Colorado Springs, Col.
12.6-mi. course
Otto Loesche "Lexington" :22:25.40
33.6 mph

Oct. 2 Fresno 1-mi. Board Speedway
(Inaugural)
Fresno, Cal.
200-mi. Race
Jimmy Murphy "Duesenberg" 97.3 mph

Nov. 25 Beverly Hills 1¼-mi. Board
Speedway
Los Angeles, Cal.
250-mi. Race
Roscoe Sarles "Duesenberg" 103.2 mph

1921

Jan. 21 Daytona Beach, Fla.
1-mi. Straightaway Stock Chassis Record
Ralph Mulford "Paige 6-66" :35.01
102.83 mph

Feb. 28 Beverly Hills 1¼-mi. Board
Speedway
Los Angeles, Cal.
50-mi. Race
Ralph DePalma "Ballot" 107.3 mph

Apr. 22 Daytona Beach, Fla.
1-mi. Straightaway Stock Chassis Record
L. F. Goodspeed "Roamer" :34.25
105.1 mph

Apr. 30 Fresno 1-mi. Board Speedway
Fresno, Cal.
150-mi. Race
Joe Thomas 100.4 mph

May 20 Uniontown 1⅛-mi. Board
Speedway
Uniontown, Pa.
100-mi. Speed Trial
R. Mulford "Paige" 1:06:53.26
89.6 mph

May 30 Indianapolis 2½-mi. Motor
Speedway
Indianapolis, Indiana
500-mi. Race
T. Milton "Frontenac" 5:34:44.65
89.6 mph

June 18 Uniontown 1⅛-mi. Board
Speedway
Uniontown, Pa.
225-mi. Race
Roscoe Sarles "Duesenberg" 97.75 mph

July 1 Nevada Highway Race
Reno, Elko, Tonopah, Reno
1015 miles
Bill Branlette "Lincoln" 29:49:49.0
35 mph

July 4 Tacoma 2-mi. Planked Speedway
Tacoma, Wash.
250-mi. Race
T. Milton "Durant" 2:34:00.0 98.0 mph

Aug. 5 Cross-country Speed Run
New York to Chicago
"Essex" 24:43:52.00

Aug. 9 Transcontinental Record
San Francisco to New York
"Essex" 4 days, 14 hr., 43 min.

Aug. 14 Cotati 1¼-mi. Board Speedway
(Inaugural)
Santa Rosa, Cal.
150-mi. Race
E. Hearne "Duesenberg-Distil"
1:21:19.20 110.6 mph

Sep. 1 Indianapolis 2½-mi. Motor
Speedway
Indianapolis, Indiana
50-mi. Race
Howard Wilcox "Peugeot" :30:50.64
97.5 mph

Sep. 5 Pikes Peak Hill Climb
Colorado Springs, Col.
12.6-mi. Course
King Rhiley "Hudson" :19:16.20
39.4 mph

Sep. 5 Uniontown 1⅛-mi. Board Speedway
Uniontown, Pa.
225-mi. Race
I. P. Fetterman "Duesenberg" 2:15:16.00
99.8 mph

Oct. 1 Fresno 1-mi. Board Speedway
Fresno, Cal.
150-mi. Race
Earl Cooper 100.9 mph

Oct. 23 Northbay (formerly Cotati) 1¼-mi.
Board Speedway
Santa Rosa, Cal.
150-mi. Race
Roscoe Sarles "Duesenberg" 110.32 mph

Oct. 30 Northbay 1¼-mi. Board Speedway
Santa Rosa, Cal.
1000-mi. Endurance Speed Run
W. L. Cooper "Oldsmobile" 14:59:00.0
66.7 mph

Nov. 30   Beverly Hills 1¼-mi. Board
Speedway
Los Angeles, Cal.
250-mi. Race
E. Hearne   "Duesenberg"   2:15:55.0
109.7 mph

Dec. 11   San Carlos 1¼-mi. Board
Speedway (Inaugural)
San Francisco, Cal.
250-mi. Race
Jimmy Murphy   "Duesenberg"   2:15:11.2
111.8 mph
25-mi. Stock Car Race
Crosby   "Essex"   :17:32.8   86.4 mph

1922

Jan. 14   Beverly Hills 1¼-mi. Board
Speedway
Los Angeles, Cal.
24-hr. Stock Car Record
Charles Basle & Douglas Phillips
"Apperson V-8"   1928.75 miles   80.3 mph

Mar. 5   Beverly Hills 1¼-mi. Board
Speedway
Los Angeles, Cal.
250-mi. Race
Tommy Milton   "Duesenberg"   2:15:20.0
110.8 mph

Apr. 2   Beverly Hills 1¼-mi. Board
Speedway
Los Angeles, Cal.
50-mi. Race
Tommy Milton   "Duesenberg"   :26:01.0
115.2 mph

Apr. 7   Daytona Beach, Fla.
1-mi. Straightaway Record
Sig Haugdahl   "Wisconsin Spl."   :19.97
180.3 mph

Apr. 16   San Carlos 1¼-mi. Board
Speedway
San Francisco, Cal.
150-mi. Race
Harry Hartz   "Duesenberg"   1:20:38.0
111.2 mph

Apr. 18   Mt. Wilson Hill Climb
Los Angeles, Cal.
9.5-mi. Course
Stock Car Record
Walter Lord   "Velie"   :27:52.00   20.4 mph

Apr. 27   Fresno 1-mi. Board Speedway
Fresno, Cal.
Raisin Day Classic
150-mi. Race
Jimmy Murphy   102.85 mph

May 7   Northbay 1¼-mi. Board Speedway
Santa Rosa, Cal.
50-mi. Race
Pietro Bordino   "Fiat"   :26:13.36
114.5 mph
100-mi. Race
J. Murphy   "Duesenberg"   :52:01.23
115.34 mph

May 30   Indianapolis 2½-mi. Motor
Speedway
Indianapolis, Indiana
500-mi. Race
J. Murphy   "Murphy Spl."   5:17:30.79
94.5 mph

June 14   San Carlos 1¼-mi. Board
Speedway

San Francisco, Cal.
250-mi. Race
Joe Thomas   109.2 mph

June 17   Uniontown 1⅛-mi. Board
Speedway
Uniontown, Pa.
225-mi. Race
Jimmy Murphy   "Murphy Special"
2:12:01.13   102.2 mph

Aug. 6   Northbay 1¼-mi. Board Speedway
Santa Rosa, Cal.
50-mi. Race
Frank Elliott   "Leach"   :25:49.70
107.5 mph
100-mi. Race
Frank Elliott   "Leach"   :53:00.00
113.7 mph

Sep. 4   Pikes Peak Hill Climb
Colorado Springs, Col.
12.6-mi. course
Noel Bullock   "Ford"   :19:50.80   37.8 mph

Sep. 17   Kansas City 1¼-mi. Board
Speedway (Inaugural)
Kansas City, Mo.
300-mi. Race
Tommy Milton   "Leach"   2:47:52.96
108.8 mph

Sep. 30   Fresno 1-mi. Board Speedway
Fresno, Cal.
150-mi. Race
Bennett Hill   "Miller"   1:27:46.20
103.8 mph

Oct. 29   Beverly Hills 1¼-mi. Board
Speedway
Los Angeles, Cal.
100-mi. Race
Bennett Hill   "Miller"   :52:38.40
114.5 mph

Nov. 12   St. Louis 1-mi. Dirt Track
St. Louis, Mo.
1-mi. Speed Trial
Sig Haugdahl   "Wisconsin Spl."   :40.09
90.0 mph

Dec. 3   Beverly Hills 1¼-mi. Dirt Track
Los Angeles, Cal.
250-mi. Race
Jimmy Murphy   "Duesenberg"   114.91 mph

1923

Feb. 25   Beverly Hills 1¼-mi. Board
Speedway
Los Angeles, Cal.
250-mi. Race
J. Murphy   "Durant Spl."   2:09:43.61
114.6 mph

Apr. 26   Fresno 1-mi. Board Speedway
Fresno, Cal.
150-mi. Raisin Day Classic
J. Murphy   "Durant"   1:26:54.00
103.55 mph

Apr. 27–29   Indianapolis 2½-mi. Motor
Speedway
Indianapolis, Ind.
Stock Car Endurance Run,
3155 miles
"Duesenberg Model A"   50:21:01.00
62.63 mph

May 30   Indianapolis 2½-mi. Motor
Speedway

Indianapolis, Ind.
500-mi. Race
Tommy Milton   "H.C.S. Special"
5:29:50.17   90.9 mph

July 4   Kansas City 1¼-mi. Board
Speedway
Kansas City, Mo.
250-mi. Race
Eddie Hearne   "Durant Spl."   2:21:21.15
105.8 mph

Aug. 12   Chicago 1-mi. Dirt Track
Chicago, Ill.
1 Lap Time Trial
Ralph DePalma   "Duesenberg"   :00:51.6
69.8 mph
25-mi. Race
Howdy Wilcox   "Frontenac"   :23:44.40
65.7 mph

Sep. 3   Pikes Peak Hill Climb
Colorado Springs, Col.
12.6-mi. course
Glen Shultz   "Essex"   :18:47.60   40.2 mph

Sep. 4   Altoona 1¼-mi. Board Speedway
(Inaugural)
Tipton, Pa.
200-mi. Race
Eddie Hearne   "Durant Spl."   1:47:37.35
111.5 mph

Sep. 10   Climb to the Clouds
Mt. Washington, Gorham, N.H.
8-mi. course
R. Mulford   "Chandler"   :17:00.00
25.3 mph

Sep. 12   Syracuse 1-mi. Dirt Track
Syracuse, N.Y.
100-mi. Race
Tommy Milton   "H.C.S. Special"
1:15:00.23   79.97 mph

Sep. 29   Fresno 1-mi. Board Speedway
Fresno, Cal.
150-mi. Race
Harry Hartz   "Durant Spl."   103.6 mph

Oct. 21   Kansas City 1¼-mi. Board
Speedway
Kansas City, Mo.
250-mi. Race
Harlan Fengler   "Wade Spl."   2:12:55.40
113.2 mph

Nov. 29   Beverly Hills 1¼-mi. Board
Speedway
Los Angeles, Cal.
250-mi. Race
Bennett Hill   "Miller"   2:13.25.00
112.44 mph

1924

Feb. 19   Transcontinental Record
New York to Los Angeles
3398 miles
"Cannonball" Baker   "Gardner"
4 days, 14 hr., 15 min.   30.9 mph

Feb. 24   Beverly Hills 1¼-mi. Board
Speedway
Los Angeles, Cal.
250-mi. Race
Harlan Fengler   "Wade Spl."   2:09:14.60
116.6 mph

Apr. 14 Muroc Dry Lake, Cal.
1-mi. Straightaway Records
183 cu. in. Class
Tommy Milton "Miller" 151.3 mph
122 cu. in. Class
Tommy Milton "Miller" 141.2 mph

May 30 Indianapolis 2½-mi. Motor
Speedway
Indianapolis, Ind.
500-mi. Race
L. L. Corum & Joseph Boyer "Duesenberg"
5:05:23.51 98.2 mph

June 14 Altoona 1¼-mi. Board Speedway
Tipton, Pa.
250-mi. Race
Jimmy Murphy "Miller" 2:10:57.00
114.22 mph

July 4 Kansas City 1¼-mi. Board
Speedway
Kansas City, Mo.
150-mi. Race
Jimmy Murphy "Miller" 1:18:39.40
114.4 mph

July 16 Mt. Wilson Hill Climb
Los Angeles, Cal.
9.5-mi. course
Ralph DePalma "Chrysler" :25:48.55
22.1 mph

Sep. 1 Altoona 1¼-mi. Board Speedway
Tipton, Pa.
250-mi. Race
Jimmy Murphy "Miller" 2:11:08.40
113.9 mph

Sep. 1 Pikes Peak Hill Climb
Colorado Springs, Col.
12.6-mi. course
Otto Loesche "Lexington" :18:15.00
41.5 mph

Sep. 15 Syracuse 1-mi. Dirt Track
Syracuse, N.Y.
150-mi. Race
Phil Shafer "Duesenberg" 1:54:25.20
70.1 mph

Sep. 17 Fresno 1-mi. Board Speedway
Fresno, Cal.
1000-mi. Stock Car Run
Ralph DePalma "Chrysler" 16:18:54.80
59.52 mph

Oct. 13 Fresno 1-mi. Board Speedway
Fresno, Cal.
150-mi. Race
Earl Cooper "Studebaker-Miller"
1:25:13.00 105.68 mph

Oct. 27 Charlotte 1¼-mi. Board
Speedway (Inaugural)
Charlotte, N.C.
250-mi. Race
Tommy Milton "Miller" 2:06:56.09
115.8 mph

Nov. 3 Mt. Diablo Hill Climb
Mt. Diablo, Cal.
11.6-mi. course
Ralph Mulford "Cleveland" :22:36.60
30.8 mph

Nov. 20 Mt. Wilson Hill Climb
Los Angeles, Cal.
9.5-mi. course
Ralph Mulford "Cleveland" :24:47.04
23.0 mph

Nov. 22 Tanforan 1-mi. Dirt Track
San Francisco, Cal.
100-mi. Race
Ralph DePalma "Miller" 1:42:06.0
58.7 mph

Nov. 26 Ascot Road Race
Los Angeles, Cal.
50 laps, 5-mi. course, 250-mi. Road Race
Frank Lockhart "Duesenberg"

Dec. 14 Culver City 1¼-mi. Board
Speedway (Inaugural)
Los Angeles, Cal.
250-mi. Race
Bennett Hill "Miller" 1:58:18.60
126.9 mph

Dec. 16 Culver City 1¼-mi. Board
Speedway
Los Angeles, Cal.
1000-mi. Stock Car Run
Ralph Mulford "Cleveland" 14:08:31.8
70.6 mph

1925

Jan. 13 Culver City 1¼-mi. Board
Speedway
Los Angeles, Cal.
1000-mi. Stock Car Speed Trial
R. DePalma "Chrysler" 13:07:12.00
76.3 mph

Jan. 27 Culver City 1¼-mi. Board
Speedway
Los Angeles, Cal.
1000-mi. Stock Car Run
Ralph Mulford "Cleveland" 12:25:22.6
80.6 mph

Feb. 4 Culver City 1¼-mi. Board
Speedway
Los Angeles, Cal.
1000-mi. Stock Car Speed Trial
Ralph Mulford "Chandler" 11:29:54.0
86.9 mph

Mar. 4 Culver City 1¼-mi. Board
Speedway
Los Angeles, Cal.
250-mi. Washington's Birthday Race
Tommy Milton "Miller" 1:58:13.00
126.9 mph

Mar. 22 Tanforan 1-mi. Dirt Track
San Francisco, Cal.
10-mi. Race
Ralph DePalma "Miller" :08:22.0
71.8 mph

Apr. 11 Fair Park 1-mi. Dirt Track
Dallas, Tex.
100-mi. Race
Ralph DePalma "Miller" 1:24:40.4
71.0 mph

Apr. 19 Culver City 1¼-mi. Board
Speedway
Los Angeles, Cal.
Sprint Races
25-mi. Leon Duray "Miller" 134.0 mph
25-mi. P. DePaolo "Duesenberg"
135.0 mph
25-mi. P. Bordino "Fiat" 133.0 mph
25-mi. R. McDonough "Miller"
130.0 mph
50-mi. H. Hartz "Miller" 135.2 mph

Apr. 30 Fresno 1-mi. Board Speedway
Fresno, Cal.
150-mi. Raisin Day Classic
Peter DePaolo "Duesenberg" 1:25:49.00
104.8 mph

May 10 Bakersfield 1-mi. Dirt Track
Bakersfield, Cal.
1-lap Record
Frank Lockhart "Miller" :39.8 90.45 mph

May 11 Charlotte 1¼-mi. Board Speedway
Charlotte, N.C.
250-mi. Race
Earl Cooper "Miller" 2:02:55.00
121.6 mph

May 30 Indianapolis 2½-mi. Motor
Speedway
Indianapolis, Ind.
500-mi. Race
Peter DePaolo "Duesenberg" 4:56:39.46
101.1 mph
(Note: First 500-mi. Race in America at 100
mph or better.)

June 13 Altoona 1¼-mi. Board Speedway
Tipton, Pa.
250-mi. Race
Peter DePaolo "Duesenberg" 2:09:45.10
115.09 mph

July 4 Rockingham Park 1¼-mi. Dirt Track
Salem, N.H.
100-mi. Race
Ralph DePalma "Miller" 1:18:07.6
76.9 mph

July 11 Laurel 1⅛-mi. Board Speedway
(Inaugural)
Laurel, Md.
250-mi. Race
Peter DePaolo "Duesenberg" 2:01:39.28
122.84 mph

July Transcontinental Speed Run
3423-mi. New York to San Francisco
L. B. Miller & J. E. Weiber "Wills Sainte
Clair" 102:45:00.00 33.3 mph

Sep. 7 Pikes Peak Hill Climb
Colorado Springs, Col.
12.6-mi. course
C. H. Meyers "Chandler Spl." :17:48.40
43.8 mph

Sep. 7 Altoona 1¼-mi. Board Speedway
Tipton, Pa.
250-mi. Race
Bob McDonough "Miller" 2:06:54.5
118.4 mph

Sep. 19 Syracuse 1-mi. Dirt Track
Syracuse, N.Y.
100-mi. Race
Ralph DePalma "Miller" 1:15:18.98
79.5 mph

Oct. 3 Fresno 1-mi. Board Speedway
Fresno, Cal.
150-mi. Race
Fred Comer "Miller" 1:28:05.0
102.2 mph

Oct. 24 Laurel 1⅛-mi. Board Speedway
Laurel, Md.
250-mi. Race
Bob McDonough "Miller" 1:59:02.71
126.3 mph

Oct. 31 Rockingham 1¼-mi. Board
Speedway (Inaugural)

Salem, N.H.
250-mi. Race
Peter DePaolo "Duesenberg" 1:59:02.5
126.85 mph

Nov. 11 Charlotte 1¼-mi. Board Speedway
Charlotte, N.C.
250-mi. Race
Tommy Milton "Duesenberg" 2:00:01.67
125.31 mph

Nov. 29 Culver City 1¼-mi. Board
Speedway
Los Angeles, Cal.
250-mi. Race
Frank Elliott "Miller" 1:57:18.2
127.87 mph

1926

Feb. 22 Fulford 1¼-mi. Board Speedway
(Inaugural)
Miami Beach, Fla.
300-mi. Race
Peter DePaolo "Duesenberg" 2:19:12.95
129.3 mph

Mar. 21 Culver City 1¼-mi. Board
Speedway
Los Angeles, Cal.
250-mi. Race
Bennett Hill "Miller" 1:54:14.8
131.295 mph

Apr. 15 Fresno 1-mi. Board Speedway
Fresno, Cal.
25-mi. Race
Earl Cooper "Junior 8" :14:25.4
104.0 mph
50-mi. Race
Peter DePaolo "Duesenberg" :29:40.0
103.2 mph

May 1 Atlantic City 1½-mi. Board
Speedway (Inaugural)
Amatol, N.J.
300-mi. Race
Harry Hartz "Miller" 2:14:14.18
134.191 mph

May 12 Charlotte 1¼-mi. Board Speedway
Charlotte, N.C.
250-mi. Race
Earl Devore "Miller" 2:04:54.5
120.08 mph

May 30 Indianapolis 2½-mi. Motor
Speedway
Indianapolis, Ind.
500-mi. Race stopped at 400 mi. due to rain
Frank Lockhart "Miller" 4:10:17.95
95.9 mph

June 17 Altoona 1¼-mi. Board Speedway
Tipton, Pa.
250-mi. Race
Dave Lewis "Miller" 2:13:24.61
112.4 mph

June 17 Transcontinental Speed Run
3471-mi. New York to San Francisco
Ab Jenkins & Ray Peck "Studebaker"
(Sheriff) 86:20:00.00 40.2 mph

June 17 Langhorne 1-mi. Dirt Track
(Inaugural)
Langhorne, Pa.
50-mi. Race
Fred Winnai "Duesenberg" :42:37.40
70.0 mph

June 19 Laurel 1⅛-mi. Board Speedway
Laurel, Md.

100-mi. Jimmy Gleason 105.0 mph
50-mi. Jimmy Gleason 110.7 mph

June 27 Detroit 1-mi. Dirt Track
Detroit, Mich.
100-mi. Race
Frank Lockhart "Miller" 1:25:56.82
69.6 mph

July 4 Langhorne 1-mi. Dirt Track
Langhorne, Pa.
50-mi. Race
Ray Keech "Miller" :42:38.80 69.8 mph

July 5 Rockingham 1¼-mi. Board
Speedway
Salem, N.H.
50-mi.
P. DePaolo "Duesenberg" :23:23.52
128.251 mph
200-mi.
E. Cooper "Miller" (Front Drive)
1:42:56.95 116.373 mph

July 17 Atlantic City 1½-mi. Board
Speedway
Amatol, N.J.
Sprint Races
60-mi.
N. Batten "Miller" :29:48.75 120.8 mph
60-mi.
F. Comer "Miller" :28:51.58 124.7 mph
60-mi.
H. Hartz "Miller" :27:58.85 128.7 mph
120-mi.
H. Hartz "Miller" :58:20.50 123.4 mph

Aug. 7 Langhorne 1-mi. Dirt Track
Langhorne, Pa.
25-mi. Race
F. Winnai "Duesenberg" :19:32.20
76.8 mph
1-mi. Lap Record
Fred Winnai "Duesenberg" :38.80
90.2 mph

Aug. 23 Transcontinental Speed Run
3368-mi. San Francisco to New York
L. B. Miller & J. E. Weiber "Wills Sainte
Clair" 83:12:00.00 40.5 mph

Aug. 26 Charlotte 1¼-mi. Board Speedway
Charlotte, N.C.
25-mi. Sprint
Earl Cooper "Miller" :11:38.50
128.9 mph
25-mi. Sprint
Dave Lewis "Miller" :11:58.16
125.2 mph
150-mi. Race
Frank Lockhart "Miller" 1:14:27.30
120.9 mph
50-mi. Race
Frank Lockhart "Miller" :24:28.80
122.549 mph

Aug. 29 Hawthorne 1-mi. Dirt Track
Chicago, Ill.
20-mi. Race
Ralph DePalma "Miller" :16:36.8
72.3 mph

Sep. 4 Syracuse 1-mi. Dirt Track
Syracuse, N.Y.
50-mi. Race
Ralph DePalma "Miller" :38:02.30
79.0 mph

Sep. 6 Pikes Peak Hill Climb
Colorado Springs, Col.
12.6-mi. course
Glen Shultz "Stutz" 18:19.20 41.4 mph

Sep. 11 Detroit 1-mi. Dirt Track
Detroit, Mich.
100-mi. Race
Frank Lockhart "Miller" 1:21:30.63
73.610 mph

Sep. 18 Altoona 1¼-mi. Board Speedway
Tipton, Pa.
250-mi. Race
Frank Lockhart "Miller" 2:08:53.33
116.379 mph

Sep. Laurel 1⅛-mi. Board Speedway
Laurel, Md.
100-mi. Race
Jimmy Gleason "Miller" 113.0 mph

Oct. 2 Fresno 1-mi. Board Speedway
Fresno, Cal.
25-mi. Race
Peter DePaolo "Duesenberg" :15:14.4
98.42 mph
25-mi. Race
Bennett Hill "Miller" :14:07.0
106.25 mph
50-mi. Race
Frank Lockhart "Miller" :29:46.8
100.75 mph

Oct. 12 Rockingham 1¼-mi. Board
Speedway
Salem, N.H.
200-mi. Race
Harry Hartz "Miller" 1:37:21.24
123.261 mph
25-mi. Race
Bennett Hill "Miller Front Drive"
:11:32.43 130.057 mph
25-mi. Race
Leon Duray "Miller Front Drive"
:11:30.22 130.393 mph

Oct. 31 Detroit 1-mi. Dirt Track
Detroit, Mich.
100-mi. Race
Ross "Ross Spl." 1:24:55.35 71.424 mph

Nov. 11 Charlotte 1¼-mi. Board Speedway
Charlotte, N.C.
25-mi. Race
Frank Lockhart "Miller" 132.4 mph
25-mi. Race
Dave Lewis "Miller" 127.0 mph
100-mi. Race
Leon Duray "Miller" :49:09.73
122.045 mph

1927

Mar. 6 Culver City 1¼-mi. Board
Speedway
Los Angeles, Cal.
250-mi. Race
Leon Duray "Miller" 2:00:16.60
124.7 mph

Mar. 18 Culver City 1¼-mi. Board
Speedway
Los Angeles, Cal.
1000-mi. Stock Car Speed Trial
Wade Morton "Auburn 8-88" 68.37 mph

Mar. 29 Daytona Beach, Fla.
1-mi. Straightaway Record
H. O. D. Segrave "Mystery S Sunbeam"
:17.67 203.79 mph

Apr. 5 Culver City 1¼-mi. Board
Speedway

Los Angeles, Cal.
Long Distance Stock Car Run
5000 miles
Harry Hartz & others "Studebaker"
81:48:22.0 61.12 mph

Apr. 11 Muroc Dry Lake, Cal.
1-mi. Straightaway 91 cu. in. Record
Frank Lockhart "Miller" 164.0 mph

Apr. 22 Indianapolis 2½-mi. Motor
Speedway
Indianapolis, Ind.
Stevens Challenge Trophy
24-hr. Stock Car Speed Run
Anderson, Rooney & Keene "Stutz"
1642.6 miles 68.4 mph

May 7 Atlantic City 1½-mi. Board
Speedway
Amatol, N.J.
200-mi. Race
Dave Lewis "Miller" 1:32:15.97
130.058 mph
75-mi. Stock Car Race
Tom Rooney "Stutz" :52:10.54
86.247 mph
1½-mi. (lap) Record
Frank Lockhart "Miller" :36.66
147.7 mph

May 21 Culver City 1¼-mi. Board
Speedway
Los Angeles, Cal.
1000-mi. Closed Body Stock Car Run
Barney Oldfield "Hudson" 13:05:00.0
76.4 mph

May 30 Indianapolis 2½-mi. Motor
Speedway
Indianapolis, Ind.
500-mi. Race
George Souders "Duesenberg" 5:07:33.8
97.5 mph

June 5 Detroit 1-mi. Dirt Track
Detroit, Mich.
100-mi. Race
Frank Lockhart "Miller"

June 11 Altoona 1¼-mi. Board Speedway
Tipton, Pa.
200-mi. Race
Peter DePaolo "Miller" 1:42:56.80
116.6 mph

June 20 Atlantic City 1½-mi. Board
Speedway
Amatol, N.J.
Speed Trial for 300 cu. in. Stock Car
Ralph DePalma "Chrysler"
1 hour 89.091 mph
5-mi. 88.8 mph
50-mi. 89.2 mph

June 24 General Motors Concrete
Speedway
General Motors Proving Grounds
Milford, Mich.
252 laps, 951.87-mi.
W. Rader & G. Bell "LaSalle" 9:59:39.40
95.3 mph

July 4 Rockingham 1¼-mi. Board
Speedway
Salem, N.H.
200-mi. Race
Peter DePaolo "Miller" 1:36:30.22
124.3 mph
100-mi. Stock Car Race
Wade Morton "Auburn" 89.9 mph

Aug. 7 Atlantic City 1½-mi. Board
Speedway

Amatol, N.J.
Long Distance Stock Car Run—
15,000 miles
Wade Morton & Ab Jenkins "Auburn 8-88"
61.377 mph

Sep. 2 Transcontinental Speed Run
New York to San Francisco
Ab Jenkins "Studebaker" 77:40:00.00

Sep. 5 Pikes Peak Hill Climb
Colorado Springs, Col.
12.6-mi. Course
Stock Car Class
Bill Bentrup "Stutz" :21:59.60 32.4 mph
Special Car Class
Glen Shultz "Stutz Spl." :18:25.20
41.0 mph

Sep. 5 Atlantic City 1½-mi. Board
Speedway
Amatol, N.J.
75-mi. Stock Car Race
Ralph Hepburn "Studebaker" :52:21.0
85.95 mph
150-mi. Stock Car Race
Tom Rooney "Stutz" 1:32:27.00
96.31 mph

Sep. 5 Altoona 1¼-mi. Board Speedway
Tipton, Pa.
200-mi. Race
Frank Lockhart "Miller" 1:42:49.40
116.7 mph

Sep. 19 Charlotte 1¼-mi. Board Speedway
Charlotte, N.C.
100-mi. Race
Babe Stapp "Miller" :50:02.13
119.914 mph
25-mi. Race
Frank Lockhart "Miller" :11:45.66
127.6 mph

Sep. 25 Cleveland 1-mi. Dirt Track
Cleveland, Ohio
1-mi. Track Record
(non-competitive)
Frank Lockhart "Miller" :39.95 92.5 mph
100-mi. Race
Frank Lockhart "Miller" 1:14:00.40
82.826 mph

Oct. 7 Atlantic City 1½-mi. Board
Speedway
Amatol, N.J.
24-hr. Stock Car Endurance Run
H. Hartz, R. Hepburn & J. Gleason
"Studebaker" 1814.96 miles 75.6 mph

Oct. 12 Rockingham 1¼-mi. Board
Speedway
Salem, N.H.
75-mi. Race
Frank Lockhart "Miller" 126.7 mph
10-mi. Race
Harry Hartz "Miller Front-Drive"
:05:12.45 115.2 mph
10-mi. Race
Cliff Woodbury "Miller" :05:14.00
114.5 mph
50-mi. Race
Harry Hartz "Miller Front-Drive"
:23:39.22 126.83 mph

Nov. 3 Atlantic City 1½-mi. Board
Speedway
Amatol, N.J.
25,000-mi. Stock Car Run
"Studebaker" 65.31 mph

1928

Feb. 19 Daytona Beach, Fla.
1-mi. Straightaway Record
Malcolm Campbell "Bluebird" :17.40
206.96 mph

Feb. 21 Daytona Beach, Fla.
1-mi. Straightaway Stock Car Record
Wade Morton "Auburn 115" 104.347 mph

Feb. 23 Daytona Beach, Fla.
1-mi. Straightaway Stock Car Record
Gil Anderson "Stutz Blackhawk"
106.53 mph

Apr. 22 Daytona Beach, Fla.
1-mi. Straightaway Record
Ray Keech "Triplex" :17.345
207.552 mph

Apr. 25 Daytona Beach, Fla.
1-mi. 183 cu. in. Straightaway Record
Frank Lockhart "Stutz Blackhawk Spl."
198.3 mph

May 30 Indianapolis 2½-mi. Motor
Speedway
Indianapolis, Ind.
500-mi. Race
Louis Meyer "Miller" 5:01:33.75
99.5 mph

June 9 Transcontinental Round-trip Speed
Run
Los Angeles, New York, Los Angeles
6692.8-mi.
"Cannonball" Baker "Franklin"
6 days, 13 hr., 23 min. 42.3 mph

June 10 Detroit 1-mi. Dirt Track
Detroit, Mich.
100-mi. Race
Ray Keech "Miller" 1:17:15.33
77.9 mph

June 14 Packard 2½-mi. Concrete
Speedway
Packard Proving Grounds
Utica, Mich.
2½-mi. (lap) Record
Leon Duray "Miller" (Front Drive)
:01:00.739 148.17 mph

July 4 Atlantic City 1½-mi. Board
Speedway
Amatol, N.J.
100-mi. Race
Fred Winnai "Duesenberg" :59:38.40
101.0 mph

July 4 Rockingham 1¼-mi. Board
Speedway
Salem, N.H.
185-mi. Race
Ray Keech "Simplex Spl." 121.8 mph

Aug. 8 Atlantic City 1½-mi. Board
Speedway
Amatol, N.J.
Long-distance Record
Stock Car, Unlimited Class
30,000-mi.
Tony Gulotta, Cliff Bergere & Johnny
Kreiger "Studebaker" 438:46:55.47
68.37 mph

Aug. 19 Altoona 1¼-mi. Board Speedway
Tipton, Pa.
200-mi. Race
Lou Meyer "Stutz" (Miller) 117.02 mph

Sep. Pikes Peak Hill Climb
Colorado Springs, Col.
12.6-mi. course
Stock Car Class
Wade Morton "Auburn" :21:45.40
34.6 mph
Special Car Class
Glen Shultz "Stutz Spl." :17:41.60
42.6 mph

Sep. 16 Atlantic City 1½-mi. Board
Speedway
Amatol, N.J.
100-mi. Race
Ray Keech "Simplex" :45:31.31
131.6 mph

Sep. 21 Climb to the Clouds
Mt. Washington, Gorham, N.H.
8-mi. course
"Cannonball" Baker "Franklin Spl."
:14:49.50

1929

Mar. 11 Daytona Beach, Fla.
1-km. Straightaway Record
H. O. D. Segrave "Golden-Arrow" :09.67
231.446 mph

May 26 Toledo 1-mi. Dirt Track
Toledo, Ohio
100-mi. Race
Wilbur Shaw "Miller" 1:18:28.40
76.46 mph

May 30 Indianapolis 2½-mi. Motor
Speedway
Indianapolis, Ind.
500-mi. Race
Ray Keech "Simplex" 5:07:25.42
97.59 mph

June 2 Cleveland 1-mi. Dirt Track
Cleveland, Ohio
85-mi. Race
Wilbur Shaw "Miller" 1:11:15.49
71.57 mph

June 9 Detroit 1-mi. Dirt Track
Detroit, Mich.
100-mi. Race
Cliff Woodbury "Boyle Spl." (Miller)
1:18:42.95 76.22 mph

June 15 Altoona 1¼-mi. Board Speedway
Tipton, Pa.
200-mi. Race stopped at 150-mi. due to
accident
Ray Keech (posthumously) "Simplex
Piston Ring Spl." (Miller) 1:13:34.8
118.4 mph

June 30 Indianapolis 2½-mi. Motor
Speedway
Indianapolis, Ind.
Non-stop Economy Run
"Roosevelt" 440 hr., 40 min.
13,457.5 miles 30.55 mph

Aug. 18 Toledo 1-mi. Dirt Track
Toledo, Ohio
100-mi. Race
Wilbur Shaw "Miller" 1:16:09.20
78.94 mph

Aug. 31 Syracuse 1-mi. Dirt Track
Syracuse, N.Y.
100-mi. Race

Wilbur Shaw "Miller" 1:14:00.80
81.07 mph

Sep. 2 Pikes Peak Hill Climb
Colorado Springs, Col.
12.6-mi. course
Stock Car Class
Glen Shultz "Studebaker" :21:43.60
35.0 mph
Special Car Class
Ed. Phillips "Shultz Spl." :18:22.80
41.1 mph

Sep. 2 Altoona 1¼-mi. Board Speedway
Tipton, Pa.
200-mi. Race
Louis Meyer "Miller" 1:49:36.80
110.0 mph

Sep. 28 Cleveland 1-mi. Dirt Track
Cleveland, Ohio
100-mi. Race
"Deacon" Litz "Miller" 1:17:50.5
77.07 mph

Nov. 21 Transcontinental Speed Run
3259 miles—New York, N.Y., to
Los Angeles, Cal.
E. G. "Cannonball" Baker "Franklin"
2 days, 21 hr., 31 min. 46.89 mph

1930

May 3 Langhorne 1-mi. Dirt Track
Langhorne, Pa.
100-mi. Race
Wm. Cummings "Century Tire" 1:17:36.00
77.3 mph

May 30 Indianapolis 2½-mi. Motor
Speedway
Indianapolis, Ind.
500-mi. Race
Billy Arnold "Miller" 4:58:39.72
100.5 mph

June 9 Detroit 1-mi. Dirt Track
Detroit, Mich.
100-mi. Race
Wilbur Shaw "Empire State" 1:27:54.30
68.3 mph

June 14 Altoona 1¼-mi. Board Speedway
Tipton, Pa.
200-mi. Race
Billy Arnold "Miller-Hartz" 1:47:56.40
111.0 mph

July 4 Langhorne 1-mi. Dirt Track
Langhorne, Pa.
1-mi. Track Record (91½ cu. in.)
Frank Farmer "Miller" :37.40 96.7 mph

Sep. 1 Altoona 1¼-mi. Board Speedway
Tipton, Pa.
116¼-mi. Race
Billy Arnold "Miller-Hartz" 1:01:35.00
113.0 mph

Sep. Pikes Peak Hill Climb
Colorado Springs, Col.
12.6-mi. course
Stock Car Class
W. F. Shepherd "Willys-Overland"
24:18.20 31.1 mph
Special Car Class
Glen Shultz "Stutz Spl." 18:08.70
41.5 mph

Sep. 6 Syracuse 1-mi. Dirt Track
Syracuse, N.Y.
100-mi. Race

Bill Cummings "Duesenberg" 1:11:52.18
83.5 mph

1931

Feb. 5 Daytona Beach, Fla.
1-km. Straightaway Record (Unlimited)
Malcolm Campbell "Bluebird II" :09.09
246.09 mph

Feb. 6 Daytona Beach, Fla.
1-mi. Straightaway Record
(45 cu. in. Class)
Malcolm Campbell "Austin Seven"
94.03 mph
1-mi. Straightaway Record
(Diesel)
C. L. Cummins "Cummins-Diesel"
97.91 mph

May 9 Langhorne 1-mi. Dirt Track
Langhorne, Pa.
100-mi. Race
Billy Arnold "Duesenberg" 1:17:10.00
77.75 mph

May 30 Indianapolis 2½-mi. Motor
Speedway
Indianapolis, Ind.
500-mi. Race
Louis Schneider "Bowes" 5:10:27.93
96.23 mph

June 30 Climb to the Clouds
Mt. Washington, Gorham, N.H.
8-mi. course
Ab Jenkins "Studebaker" :14:49.60
32.35 mph

July 4 Altoona 1¼-mi. Board Speedway
Tipton, Pa.
100-mi. Race
Lou Moore "Boyle Valve Spl." :53:10.0
112.8 mph

Sep. 7 Altoona 1¼-mi. Board Speedway
Tipton, Pa.
100-mi. Race
Shorty Cantlon "Miller" :54:43.00
109.0 mph

Sep. 11 Syracuse 1-mi. Dirt Track
Syracuse, N.Y.
100-mi. Race
Lou Moore "Boyle Valve Spl." 1:20:59.83
75.0 mph

Sep. Pikes Peak Hill Climb
Colorado Springs, Col.
12.6-mi. course
Stock Car Class
W. F. Shepherd "Willys-Overland"
:25:09.50 30.0 mph
Special Car Class
C. H. Myers "Hunt Spl." :17:10.30
44.0 mph

Oct. 24 Indianapolis 2½-mi. Motor
Speedway
Stevens Challenge Trophy
24-hr. Stock Car Record
"Marmon" (V-16) 1834.215 miles
76.43 mph

Nov. 3 Muroc Dry Lake
Mojave Desert, Cal.
1-mi. Straightaway &
5-mi. Circular Courses
1-mi. Straightaway Stock Car Run

George Hunt "Studebaker" 91.79 mph
1-hr. Stock Car Run
George Hunt "Studebaker" 90.35 miles
90.35 mph

Nov. 11 Oakland 1-mi. Banked Dirt Track
Oakland, Cal.
100-mi. Race
Ernie Triplett "Tucker Tappet" (Ford)
1:19:36.0 75.37 mph

1932

Jan. 1 Oakland 1-mi. Dirt Track
Oakland, Cal.
1-mi. (lap) Record
Bryan Saulpaugh :35.31 101.95 mph

Feb. 24 Daytona Beach, Fla.
1-mi. Straightaway Record (Unlimited)
Malcolm Campbell "Napier-Campbell"
:14.175 253.97 mph

Mar. 30 Daytona Beach, Fla.
1-mi. Straightaway Record
(4 cyl. Racing Class)
Wilbur Shaw "Whippet" (Frontenac)
137.25 mph

May 16 Muroc Dry Lake, Cal.
1-mi. Straightaway Record
(4 cyl. Racing Class)
W.H. Stubblefield "Gilmore Spl." :24.43
147.36 mph

May 30 Indianapolis 2½-mi. Motor
Speedway
Indianapolis, Ind.
500-mi. Race
Fred Frame "Miller-Hartz" 4:48:03.79
104.14 mph

June 6 Detroit 1-mi. Dirt Track
Detroit, Mich.
84-mi. Race
Bob Carey "Meyer Spl." 71.57 mph

July Muroc Dry Lake
Mojave Desert, Cal.
Stock Car (305-488 cu. in.)
Speed Runs
1-mi. Straightaway
Ab Jenkins "Auburn Twelve" 100.77 mph
500 miles
Ab Jenkins "Auburn Twelve" 88.95 mph

Sep. 5 Pikes Peak Hill Climb
Colorado Springs, Col.
12.6-mi. course
Stock Car Class
Chet Miller "Essex-Terraplane" :21:20.90
35.4 mph
Special Car Class
Glen Shultz "Shultz-Stutz" :16:47.20
45.0 mph

Sep. 19 Bonneville Salt Flats, Utah
24-hr. Speed Record (Unlimited)
Ab Jenkins "Pierce-Arrow" 2710 miles
112.94 mph
(Note: First 24-hr. Speed Run on the
Bonneville Salt Flats)

Sep. 24 Langhorne 1-mi. Dirt Track
Langhorne, Pa.
50-mi. Race
Bill Cummings "Boyle Spl." :32:45.40
91.2 mph

Oct. Muroc Dry Lake
Mojave Desert, Cal.
800-mi. Speed Run
Ralph DePalma "Miller" 112.5 mph.

Nov. 27 Oakland 1-mi. Banked Dirt Track
Oakland, Cal.
1-lap Time Trial
Wilbur Shaw :35.26 102.098 mph

Climb to the Clouds
Mt. Washington, Gorham, N.H.
8-mi. Course
E. G. "Cannonball" Baker "Graham"
:13:26.0 35.9 mph

1933

Feb. 22 Daytona Beach, Fla.
1-km. Straightaway Record (Unlimited)
Malcolm Campbell "Bluebird II" :08.21
272.46 mph
1-mi. Straightaway Stock Car Run
Chet Miller "Essex Terraplane 8" :49.94
85.836 mph

Apr. 24 Oakland 1-mi. Dirt Track
Oakland, Cal.
150-mi. Race
Chet Gardner 1:38:41.5 91.0 mph

May 30 Indianapolis 2½-mi. Motor
Speedway
Indianapolis, Ind.
500-mi. Race
Louis Meyer "Tydol Spl." 4:48:00.75
104.16 mph

Aug. 7 Bonneville Salt Flats, Utah
24-hr. Speed Record (Unlimited)
Ab Jenkins "Pierce-Arrow" 117.77 mph

Aug. 11 Langhorne 1-mi. Dirt Track
Langhorne, Pa.
25-mi. Race
Al Gordon "Miller" :16:14.00 92.10 mph
1-mi. (lap) Record
Doc Mackenzie "Miller" :36.00
100.0 mph

Aug. 26 9th Elgin Road Races
Elgin, Ill.
24-lap, 8.5-mi. course,
203-mi. Stock Car Race
Fred Frame "Ford" (V-8) 2:32:06.10
80.2 mph
24-lap, 8.5-mi. course,
203-mi. Special Car Race
Phil Shafer "Buick" 88.3 mph

Sep. Pikes Peak Hill Climb
Colorado Springs, Col.
12.6-mi. course
Stock Car Class
Chet Miller "Essex-Terraplane" :21:20.40
35.4 mph
Special Car Class
Glen Shultz "Shultz Spl." :17:27.50
41.6 mph

Sep. 9 Langhorne 1-mi. Dirt Track
Langhorne, Pa.
50-mi. Race
Johnny Hannon "Miller" :34:22.00
87.0 mph

Nov. 12 Oakland 1-mi. Dirt Track
Oakland, Cal.
100-mi. Race
Al Gordon "Gilmore-Lion Spl." 1:28:08.0
82.58 mph

1934

Feb. 18 Los Angeles Municipal Airport—
"Mines Field"
Los Angeles, Cal.
131 laps, 1.9-mi. course,
250.64-mi. Road Race
W. H. Stubblefield "Ford" (V-8)
62.37 mph

Apr. 23 Ascot 1.385-mi. Road Course
Los Angeles, Cal.
109-lap, 151.05-mi. Stock Car Road Race
Louis Meyer "Ford" (V-8) 51.33 mph

May 30 Indianapolis 2½-mi. Motor
Speedway
Indianapolis, Ind.
500-mi. Race
Bill Cummings "Boyle Spl." 4:46:05.20
104.86 mph

July 7 Climb to the Clouds
Mt. Washington, Gorham, N.H.
8-mi. course
Al Miller "Hudson" :13:20.60 36.0 mph

Aug. 16 Bonneville Salt Flats, Utah
24-hr. Speed Record (Unlimited)
3053.3 miles
Ab Jenkins "Ab Jenkins Spl." 127.23 mph

Aug. Bonneville Salt Flats, Utah
24-hr. Speed Record (Stock Car)
2026.4 miles
H. Hartz & W. Shaw "Chrysler Airflow"
84.43 mph

Aug. Transcontinental Speed Run
Halifax, N.S. to Vancouver, B.C.
4284 miles
Bob McKenzie "Studebaker" 84:22:00.0
50.78 mph

Sep. 3 Pikes Peak Hill Climb
Colorado Springs, Col.
12.6-mi. course
Stock Car Class
Bus Hammond "Ford" (V-8) :19:25.70
38.7 mph
Special Car Class
Louis Unser "Stutz Spl:" :16:01.80
47.4 mph

Dec. 23 Los Angeles Airport 1.56-mi. Dirt
Track
Los Angeles, Cal.
200-mi. Race—halted at
196.87 mi. due to fog
Kelly Petillo "Gilmore Spl." 81.62 mph

1935

Mar. 2 Daytona Beach, Fla.
1-mi. Straightaway Run
Bill Cummings "Cummings Diesel"
137.195 mph

Mar. 7 Daytona Beach, Fla.
1-mi. Straightaway Record (Unlimited)
Malcolm Campbell "Bluebird II" :13.01
276.82 mph

Apr. Muroc Dry Lake
Mojave Desert, Cal.
Stock Car Distance Records
W. Shaw, Babe Stapp, Al Gordon
"Hudson"
1-mi. 92.7 mph
1000-mi. 86.2 mph
12-hr. 86.3 mph

May 30 Indianapolis 2½-mi. Motor
Speedway
Indianapolis, Ind.
500-mi. Race
Kelly Petillo "Gilmore Spl." 4:42:22.71
106.24 mph

Aug. 6 Bonneville Salt Flats, Utah
24-hr. Record (419 cu. in. Stock Car Class)
Ab Jenkins & Tony Gullotta "Duesenberg"
134.58 mph

Sep. 3 Bonneville Salt Flats, Utah
1-mi. Straightaway Record (Unlimited)
Malcolm Campbell "Bluebird II" :11.96
301.13 mph

Oct. 13 Langhorne 1-mi. Dirt Track
Langhorne, Pa.
100-mi. Race
K. Petillo "Gilmore Spl." 1:05:17.30
91.8 mph

Bonneville Salt Flats, Utah
24-hr. Record (Unlimited)
George Eyston "Speed of the Wind"
140.52 mph

1936

Jan. 12 Oakland 1-mi. Dirt Track
Oakland, Cal.
150-mi. Race
Al Gordon "Miller" 1:50:33.25 81.4 mph

Mar. 8 Beach & Road Race Classic
Daytona Beach, Fla.
241-mi. Beach & Road Race
Milt Marion "Ford" (V-8) 4:54:42.0
48.94 mph

May 10 Lakewood 1-mi. Dirt Track
Atlanta, Ga.
50-mi. Race
Mauri Rose :40:11.3 74.6 mph

May 17 Langhorne 1-mi. Dirt Track
Langhorne, Pa.
50-mi. Race
Doc Mackenzie "Cragar Spl." :32:47.00
91.5 mph

May 30 Indianapolis 2½-mi. Motor
Speedway
Indianapolis, Ind.
500-mi. Race
Louis Meyer "Ring Free Spl." 4:35:03.39
109.1 mph

June 7 Roby 1-mi. Dirt Track
Hammond, Ind.
50-mi. Race
Rex Mays :37:36.0 79.8 mph

June 20 Goshen "Good Time" 1-mi. Dirt
Track
Goshen, N.Y.
100-mi. AAA Championship Race
Rex Mays 1:18:31.41 76.4 mph

June 21 Milwaukee 1-mi. Dirt Track
West Allis, Wis.
40-mi. Race
Frank McGurr :29:38.11 81.2 mph

June 21 Langhorne 1-mi. Dirt Track
Langhorne, Pa.
100-mi. Race
Floyd Davis "Miller" 1:04:33.4 93.0 mph

July 4 Roby 1-mi. Dirt Track
Hammond, Ind.
50-mi. Race
Rex Mays "Miller" :37:33.72 79.74 mph

July 14 Bonneville Salt Flats, Utah
Distance Speed Records (Unlimited)
George Eyston "Speed of the Wind"
24-hr. 149.1 mph
48-hr. 6545 miles 136.4 mph

Sep. 7 Altoona 1⅛-mi. Dirt Track
Tipton, Pa.
100.125-mi. AAA Championship Race
Louis Meyer 1:09:20.00 86.54 mph

Sep. 7 Pikes Peak Hill Climb
Colorado Springs, Col.
12.6-mi. course
Louis Unser "Perry Spl." :16:28.20
45.8 mph

Sep. 15 Syracuse 1-mi. Dirt Track
Syracuse, N.Y.
100-mi. Race
Mauri Rose "F.W.D." 1:12:50.11
82.4 mph

Oct. 4 Goshen "Good Time" 1-mi. Dirt
Track
Goshen, N.Y.
35-mi. Race
Rex Mays :26:12.78 80.0 mph

Oct. 12 Vanderbilt Trophy Race
Roosevelt 4-mi. Raceway
Old Westbury, Long Island, N.Y.
300-mi. Race
Tazio Nuvolari "Alfa-Romeo" 4:32:44.04
65.9 mph

Nov. 8 Oakland 1-mi. Dirt Track
Oakland, Cal.
100-mi. Race
Pat Cunningham "Offy Midget"
83.74 mph

Bonneville Salt Flats, Utah
Distance Speed Runs (Unlimited)
A. Jenkins & Stapp "Mormon Meteor I"
24-hr. 153.8 mph
48-hr. 148.6 mph

1937

Mar. 14 Ormond Beach 1-mi. Beach Course
Ormond Beach, Fla.
100-mi. Race
Tommy Elmore "Ford V-8 Spl." 1:44:06.0
57.6 mph

May 30 Indianapolis 2½-mi. Motor
Speedway
Indianapolis, Ind.
500-mi. Race
W. Shaw "Shaw-Gilmore Spl."
4:24:07.80 113.58 mph

June 19 Langhorne 1-mi. Dirt Track
Langhorne, Pa.
50-mi. Race
Mauri Rose :33:06.42 90.4 mph

June 22 Indianapolis 2½-mi. Motor
Speedway
Indianapolis, Ind.
24-hr. Stock Car Run for Stevens
Challenge Trophy
Ab Jenkins "Cord" (Supercharged)
1909.851 miles 79.577 mph

July 5 Vanderbilt Trophy Race
Roosevelt 3⅓-mi. Raceway
Old Westbury, Long Island, N.Y.
300-mi. Race
Bernd Rosemeyer "Auto-Union"
3:38:00.75 82.56 mph

July 11 Climb to the Clouds
Mt. Washington, Gorham, N.H.
8-mi. course
B. Collier, Jr. "Alfa-Romeo" :14:50.50
32.4 mph

Aug. 21 Springfield 1-mi. Dirt Track
Springfield, Ill.
100-mi. Race—Halted at
95 mi. due to darkness
Mauri Rose 1:09:45.00 86.0 mph

Aug. 22 Milwaukee 1-mi. Dirt Track
West Allis, Wis.
25-mi. Race
Billy Winn :17:27.12 86.0 mph

Aug. 26 Milwaukee 1-mi. Dirt Track
West Allis, Wis.
25-mi. Race
Billy Winn :16:52.40 88.6 mph

Aug. 29 Milwaukee 1-mi. Dirt Track
West Allis, Wis.
100-mi. Race—Halted at 96 mi.
Rex Mays 1:07:59.4 84.5 mph

Sep. 6 Pikes Peak Hill Climb
Colorado Springs, Col.
12.6-mi. course
Louis Unser "Perry Spl." :16:27.40
45.9 mph

Sep. 12 Syracuse 1-mi. Dirt Track
Syracuse, N.Y.
100-mi. Race
Billy Winn 1:08:34.71 87.4 mph

Sep. 17 Bonneville 11-mi. Circular Course
Wendover, Utah
24-hr. Stock Car Run
Ab Jenkins/Updike/Oliver "Cord"
(Supercharged) 2441.33 miles 101.72 mph

Sep. 21 Bonneville Salt Flats, Utah
24-hr. Record (unlimited)
Ab Jenkins & Louis Meyer "Mormon
Meteor II" 157.27 mph

Nov. 19 Bonneville Salt Flats, Utah
1-km. Straightaway Record (Unlimited)
George Eyston "Thunderbolt" :07.17
312.0 mph

1938

May 30 Indianapolis 2½-mi. Motor
Speedway
Indianapolis, Ind.
500-mi. Race
Floyd Roberts "Burd Spl." 4:15:58.40
117.2 mph

Aug. 6 Round-the-houses Road Race
Alexandria Bay, N.Y.
79.8-mi. Road Race
Miles Collier "MG" 1:36:11.00 49.8 mph

Aug. 27 Bonneville Salt Flats, Utah
1-mi. Straightaway Record (Unlimited)
George Eyston "Thunderbolt" :10.42
345.5 mph

Sep. Pikes Peak Hill Climb
Colorado Springs, Col.
12.6-mi. course
Louis Unser "Loop Spl." :15:49.90
47.5 mph

Sep. 15 Bonneville Salt Flats, Utah
1-mi. Straightaway Record (Unlimited)
John Cobb "Railton Red-Lion" :10.28
350.2 mph

Sep. 16 Bonneville Salt Flats, Utah
1-mi. Straightaway Record (Unlimited)
George Eyston "Thunderbolt" :10.07
357.5 mph

1939

May 30 Indianapolis 2½-mi. Motor
Speedway
Indianapolis, Ind.
500-mi. Race
Wilbur Shaw "Boyle Spl." 4:20:47.39
115.04 mph

June 17 Indianapolis 2½-mi. Motor
Speedway
Indianapolis, Ind.
15,000-mi. Stock Car Run
"Studebaker Champion"
10 days, 1 hr., 51 min. 62.02 mph

Aug. 23 Bonneville Salt Flats, Utah
1-km. Straightaway Record (Unlimited)
John Cobb "Railton Red-Lion"
369.74 mph

Sep. 11 Bonneville Salt Flats, Utah
20,000-mi. Stock Car Run
Chet Miller & others "Hudson"
283:22:07.09 70.58 mph

Sep. Pikes Peak Hill Climb
Colorado Springs, Col.
12.6-mi. course
Louis Unser "Snowberger Spl." :15:39.40
48.1 mph

1940

May 30 Indianapolis 2½-mi. Motor
Speedway
Indianapolis, Ind.
500-mi. Race
Wilbur Shaw "Boyle Spl." 4:22:31.17
114.28 mph

July 6 Montauk 2.85-mi. Road Race
Montauk Point, L.I., N.Y.
62.7-mi. Road Race (22 laps)
George Rand "Maserati" 61.19 mph

July 23 Bonneville Salt Flats, Utah
24-hr. Speed Run (Unlimited)
Ab Jenkins/Cliff Bergere "Mormon
Meteor III" 3868.41 miles 161.18 mph

Sep. Pikes Peak Hill Climb
Colorado Springs, Col.
12.6-mi. course
Al Rogers "Ford Spl." :15:59.9 47.4 mph

Oct. 6 New York World's Fair Road Race
"World of Tomorrow," Flushing, L.I., N.Y.
1¼-hr. Road Race
Frank Griswold "Alfa-Romeo"

Langhorne 1-mi. Dirt Track
Langhorne, Pa.
100-mi. Race

Duke Nalon "Dreyer" 1:04:47.47
97.07 mph

1941

May 30 Indianapolis 2½-mi. Motor
Speedway
Indianapolis, Ind.
500-mi. Race
Floyd Davis & Mauri Rose "Noc-out Spl."
4:20:36.24 115.12 mph

June 22 Langhorne 1-mi. Dirt Track
Langhorne, Pa.
100-mi. Race
Duke Nalon 1:04:39.88 92.9 mph

July 4 Land's End 14½-mi. Hill Climb
Grand Junction, Col.
Louis Unser "Offenhauser" :17:11.5
50.6 mph

Sep. Pikes Peak Hill Climb
Colorado Springs, Col.
12.6-mi. course
Louis Unser "Bowes Seal Fast Spl."
(Maserati) :15:35.5 48.1 mph

All recognized racing curtailed during
1942, 1943, 1944 & 1945

1946

Apr. 14 Daytona 3.2-mi. Beach & Road
Course
Daytona Beach, Fla.
160-mi. Modified Stock Car Race
Red Byron "Ford" 80.2 mph

May 30 Indianapolis 2½-mi. Motor
Speedway
Speedway, Ind.
500-mi. AAA Championship Race
George Robson "Thorne Spl." 4:21:16.71
114.82 mph

June 30 Langhorne 1-mi. Dirt Track
Langhorne, Pa.
100-mi. AAA Championship Race
Rex Mays "Bowes Seal Fast Spl."
1:10:28.14 85.2 mph

July 4 Lakewood Park 1-mi. Dirt Track
Atlanta, Ga.
50-mi. AAA Championship Race
Ted Horn "Peter's Offy" :42:22.0
70.6 mph

July 14 Trenton 1-mi. Dirt Track
Trenton, N.J.
100-mi. Midget Car Race
Len Duncan 1:31:39.82 65.4 mph

Sept. 1 Lakewood Park 1-mi. Dirt Track
Atlanta, Ga.
200-mi. AAA Championship Race
Halted at 98 miles due to accident.
Ted Horn (No Time)

Sept. 2 Pikes Peak 12.6-mi. Hill Climb
Course
Colorado Springs, Colo.
Louis Unser "Maserati" :15:28.70
48.70 mph

Sept. Indiana Fairgrounds 1-mi. Dirt Track
Indianapolis Ind.
100-mi. AAA Championship Race
Rex Mays "Bowes Seal Fast Spl."
1:16:03.43 78.8 mph

Sept. 22 Milwaukee 1-mi. Dirt Track
West Allis, Wis.
100-mi. AAA Championship Race
Rex Mays "Bowes Seal Fast Spl."
1:10:44.57 84.815 mph

Oct. 6 Goshen 1-mi. Dirt Track
Goshen, N.Y.
100-mi. AAA Championship Race
Tony Bettenhausen 1:17:16.52 77.75 mph

1947

May 30 Indianapolis 2½-mi. Motor
Speedway
Speedway, Ind.
500-mi. AAA Championship Race
Mauri Rose "Blue Crown Spl."
4:17:52.17 116.338 mph

June 8 Milwaukee 1-mi. Dirt Track
West Allis, Wis.
100-mi. AAA Championship Race
Bill Holland "Peter's Offy" 1:08:44.64
87.281 mph

June 22 Langhorne 1-mi. Dirt Track
Langhorne, Pa.
100-mi. AAA Championship Race
Bill Holland "Peter's Offy" 1:08:23.59
90.23 mph

July 13 Bainbridge 1-mi. Dirt Track
Bainbridge, Ohio
100-mi. AAA Championship Race—
Stopped at 90 miles due to cloudburst.
Ted Horn "T.H.E. Spl." 1:03:14.89
85.7 mph

Aug. 10 Langhorne 1-mi. Dirt Track
Langhorne, Pa.
200-mi. National Stock Car Race
Bob Flock 2:54:10.48 68.0 mph

Aug. 17 Goshen 1-mi. Dirt Track
Goshen, N.Y.
100-mi. AAA Championship Race
Tony Bettenhausen "Belanger Spl."
1:14:56.54 80.0 mph

Aug. 24 Milwaukee 1-mi. Dirt Track
West Allis, Wis.
100-mi. AAA Championship Race
Ted Horn "T.H.E. Spl." 1:11:08.64
84.33 mph

Sept. 1 Pikes Peak 12.6-mi. Hill Climb
Course
Colorado Springs, Colo.
Louis Unser "Maserati" :16:34.77
45.5 mph

Sept. 16 Bonneville Salt Flats
Wendover, Utah
1-mi. Straightaway Record (Unlimited)
John Cobb "Railton Mobil Spl." :09.13
394.196 mph

Sept. 28 Springfield 1-mi. Dirt Track
Springfield, Ill.
100-mi. AAA Championship Race
Tony Bettenhausen "Belanger Spl."
1:04:51.08 92.5 mph

Nov. 2 Arlington Downs 1 1/16-mi. Dirt
Track
Dallas, Texas
100-mi. AAA Championship Race
Ted Horn "T.H.E. Spl." 1:10:25.20
85.0 mph

1948

Apr. 25 Arlington Downs 1 1/16-mi. Dirt
Track
Dallas, Texas
100-mi. AAA Championship Race
Ted Horn "T.H.E. Spl."

May 31 Indianapolis 2½-mi. Motor
Speedway
Speedway, Ind.
500-mi. AAA Championship Race
Mauri Rose "Blue Crown Spl." 4:10:23.33
119.814 mph

June 6 Milwaukee 1-mi. Dirt Track
West Allis, Wis.
100-mi. AAA Championship Race
Emil Andres "Tuffanelli Offy" 1:10:19.43
85.319 mph

June 20 Langhorne 1-mi. Dirt Track
Langhorne, Pa.
100-mi. AAA Championship Race
Walt Brown "Offy" 1:06:55.65 89.6 mph

Aug. 14 Milwaukee 1-mi. Dirt Track
West Allis, Wis.
100-mi. AAA Championship Race
Johnny Mantz "Agajanian Spl."
1:10:19.080 85.326 mph

Aug. 21 Springfield 1-mi. Dirt Track
Springfield, Ill.
100-mi. AAA Championship Race
Ted Horn "T.H.E. Spl." 1:06:17.00
90.6 mph

Aug. 29 Milwaukee 1-mi. Dirt Track
West Allis, Wis.
200-mi. AAA Championship Race
Myron Fohr/Tony Bettenhausen
"Marchese Bros. Spl." 2:18:21.21
86.734 mph

Sept. 6 Lakewood Park 1-mi. Dirt Track
Atlanta, Ga.
100-mi. AAA Championship Race
Mel Hansen "Carter Spl."
1:15:41.00 79.27 mph

Oct. 2 Watkins Glen 6.6-mi. Road Course
Watkins Glen, N.Y.
8-lap (52.8 miles) SCCA Sports Car Race
Frank Griswold "Alfa Romeo" :49:40.60
63.6 mph

Oct. 10 DuQuoin 1-mi. Dirt Track
DuQuoin, Ill.
100-mi. AAA Championship Race
Johnny Parsons "Kurtis-Kraft Spl."
1:11:47.70 83.4 mph

1949

Apr. 19 Indianapolis 2½-mi. Motor
Speedway
Speedway, Ind.
Class D (122-183 cu. in.) Stock Car Records
Alan Hess, Charles Goodacre, Dennis
Buckley, Gordon Coates "Austin Atlantic"
24 hr. 1860.26 miles 77.51 mph
7 days 11,850 miles 70.54 mph

May 30 Great Bend 3-mi. Airport Course
Great Bend, Kansas
150-mi. Stock Car Race
Bill Robinson "Packard" 1:58:00.0
76.4 mph

May 30 Indianapolis 2½-mi. Motor

Speedway
Speedway, Ind.
500-mi. AAA Championship Race
Bill Holland "Blue Crown Spl." 4:07:15.97
121.327 mph

June 5 Milwaukee 1-mi. Dirt Track
West Allis, Wis.
100-mi. AAA Championship Race
Myron Fohr "Marchese Bros. Spl."
1:11:45.44 83.615 mph

June 11 Bridgehampton 4-mi. Road Course
Bridgehampton, Long Island, N.Y.
100-mi. SCCA Sports Car Race
George Huntoon "Alfa Romeo" 1:20:37.9
74.42 mph

June 12 Langhorne 1-mi. Dirt Track
Langhorne, Pa.
150-mi. ARDC Midget Auto Race
Bill Schindler 1:58:45.18 75.8 mph

June 19 Trenton 1-mi. Dirt Track
Trenton, N.J.
100-mi. AAA Championship Race
Myron Fohr "Marchese Bros. Spl."
1:19:11.56 75.79 mph

Aug. 20 Springfield 1-mi. Dirt Track
Springfield, Ill.
100-mi. AAA Championship Race
Mel Hansen "Bowes Seal Fast Spl."
1:08:15.0 88.0 mph

Aug. 26 Milwaukee 1-mi. Dirt Track
West Allis, Wis.
100-mi. Stock Car Race
Paul Russo "Cadillac" 1:23:33.66
67.0 mph

Aug. 28 Milwaukee 1-mi. Dirt Track
West Allis, Wis.
200-mi. AAA Championship Race
Johnny Parsons "Walsh Kurtis-Kraft"
2:19:49.95 85.818 mph

Sept. 10 Syracuse 1-mi. Dirt Track
Syracuse, N.Y.
100-mi. AAA Championship Race
Johnny Parsons "Offy" 1:09:36.52
85 mph

Sept. 11 Detroit 1-mi. Dirt Track
Detroit, Mich.
100-mi. AAA Championship Race
Tony Bettenhausen "Belanger Spl."
1:13:50.00 81.25 mph

Oct. 16 Langhorne 1-mi. Dirt Track
Langhorne, Pa.
100-mi. AAA Championship Race
Johnny Parsons "Offy" 1:04:05.22
93.5 mph

Watkins Glen 6.6-mi. Road Course
Watkins Glen, N.Y.
99-mi. AAA/SCCA Road Race
Miles Collier "Ford-Riley" 68.5 mph

Oct. 30 Sacramento 1-mi. Dirt Track
Sacramento, Calif.
100-mi. AAA Championship Race
Fred Agabashian "Offenhauser"
1:11:01.05 85 mph

Nov. 6 Del Mar 1-mi. Dirt Track
Del Mar, Calif.
100-mi. AAA Championship Race
Jimmy Davies "Clancy Spl." 1:10:17.47
85.5 mph

1950

Feb. 5 Daytona 4.16-mi. Beach & Road
Course
Daytona Beach, Fla.
200-mi. NASCAR Stock Car Race
Harold Kite "Lincoln" 2:26:30.0
81.75 mph

Apr. 2 Oakland ⅝-mi. Paved Oval
Oakland, Calif.
1-lap AAA Record
Troy Ruttman "Offenhauser" :19.24
116.89 mph

Apr. 16 Langhorne 1-mi. Dirt Track
Langhorne, Pa.
150-mi. NASCAR Stock Car Race
Curtis Turner "Oldsmobile" 2:09:40.98
69.4 mph

May 9 Pan American Road Race
Juarez to Oaxaca, Mexico
2178-mi. Stock Car Race
William Sterling "Cadillac" 19:30:03.00

May 30 Indianapolis 2½-mi. Motor
Speedway
Speedway, Ind.
500-mi. AAA Championship Race
Stopped at 345 miles due to rain.
Johnny Parsons "Offy" 2:46:55.97
124.002 mph

June 11 Milwaukee 1-mi. Dirt Track
West Allis, Wis.
100-mi. AAA Championship Race
Tony Bettenhausen "Belanger Spl."
1:10:33.93 85.028 mph

June 25 Langhorne 1-mi. Dirt Track
Langhorne, Pa.
100-mi. AAA Championship Race
Jack McGrath "Hinkle Spl." 1:07:47.01
89 mph

July 5 Milwaukee 1-mi. Dirt Track
West Allis, Wis.
150-mi. AAA Stock Car Race
Myron Fohr "Lincoln" 2:16:58.57
65.6 mph

Aug. 19 Springfield 1-mi. Dirt Track
Springfield, Ill.
100-mi. AAA Championship Race
Paul Russo "Russo-Nichels" 1:05:44.0
91.5 mph

Aug. 20 Milwaukee 1-mi. Dirt Track
West Allis, Wis.
100-mi. AAA Midget Car Race
Tony Bettenhausen "Eric Lund Spl."
1:10:41.33 85.0 mph

Aug. 24 Milwaukee 1-mi. Dirt Track
West Allis, Wis.
100-mi. AAA Stock Car Race
Norm Nelson "Oldsmobile" 1:25:58.37
69.9 mph

Aug. 27 Milwaukee 1-mi. Dirt Track
West Allis, Wis.
200-mi. AAA Championship Race
Walt Faulkner "Grant Piston Ring Spl."
2:12:26.05 90.611 mph

Sept. 4 Darlington 1⅜-mi. Paved
Speedway (Inaugural)
Darlington, S.C.
500-mi. NASCAR Stock Car Race
Johnny Mantz "Plymouth" 6:38:40.26
76.26 mph

Sept. 4 Bonneville Salt Flats 12-mi. Course
Wendover, Utah
1 Hour American Class A Record
Ab Jenkins "Mormon Meteor"
195.95 mph

Sept. 4 DuQuoin 1-mi. Dirt Track
DuQuoin, Ill.
100-mi. AAA Stock Car Race
J. Frank "Oldsmobile" 1:39:26.57
60.4 mph

Sept. 9 Syracuse 1-mi. Dirt Track
Syracuse, N.Y.
100-mi. AAA Championship Race
Jack McGrath "Hinkle Spl." 1:08:41.33
87.5 mph

Sept. 10 Detroit 1-mi. Dirt Track
Detroit, Mich.
100-mi. AAA Championship Race
Henry Banks "Hopkins Spl." 1:12:25.04
82.85 mph

Sept. 10 Lakewood Park 1-mi. Dirt Track
Atlanta, Ga.
200-mi. AAA Stock Car Race
Billy Carden "Mercury" 3:13:52.63
61.8 mph

Sept. 11 Bonneville Salt Flats
Wendover, Utah
1-mi. Diesel Record
Jimmy Jackson "Cummins" 165.23 mph

Sept. 19 Langhorne 1-mi. Dirt Track
Langhorne, Pa.
200-mi. NASCAR Stock Car Race
Fonty Flock "Oldsmobile" 2:44:49.95
75 mph

Sept. 23 Watkins Glen 6.6-mi. Road
Course
Watkins Glen, N.Y.
99-mi. SCCA-AAA Sports Car Race
A. E. Goldschmidt "Cadillac-Allard"
1:22:24.6 72.2 mph

Oct. 1 Springfield 1-mi. Dirt Track
Springfield, Ill.
100-mi. AAA Championship Race
Tony Bettenhausen "Belanger Spl."
1:08:27.84 87.5 mph

Oct. 8 Bainbridge 1-mi. Dirt Track
Bainbridge, Ohio
100-mi. NASCAR Stock Car Race
Mike Little 1:38:41.0 60.8 mph

Oct. 29 Occoneechee 1-mi. Dirt Track
Hillsboro, N.C.
200-mi. NASCAR Stock Car Race
Halted at 175 miles due to darkness.
Lee Petty "Plymouth" 2:07:10.20
82.7 mph

Nov. 12 Phoenix 1-mi. Dirt Track
Phoenix, Ariz.
100-mi. AAA Championship Race
Jimmy Davies "Clancy Spl." 1:16:54.21
78.01 mph

Nov. 26 Bay Meadows 1-mi. Dirt Track
San Mateo, Calif.
150-mi. AAA Championship Race
Note: Referee flagged winner at 149 miles
by mistake.
Tony Bettenhausen "Belanger Spl."
1:43:45.40 86.41 mph

Dec. 10 Darlington 1⅜-mi. Paved
Speedway
Darlington, S.C.

200-mi. AAA Championship Race
Johnny Parsons "Russo-Nichels Spl."
1:54:47.24 104.651 mph

Dec. 31 Sebring 5.2-mi. Airport Circuit
Sebring, Fla.
6-hr. Sports Car Race (Inaugural)
Fritz Koster/Ralph Deshon "Crosley"
288.3 miles 48.05 mph

1951

Feb. 12 Daytona 4.1-mi. Beach & Road
Course
Daytona Beach, Florida
160-mi. NASCAR Stock Car Race
Marshall Teague "Hudson Hornet"
1:56:32.0 82.39 mph

Apr. 22 Phoenix 1-mi. Dirt Track
Phoenix, Ariz.
150-mi. NASCAR Stock Car Race
Marshall Teague "Hudson Hornet"
2:21:16.0 63.8 mph

May 30 Indianapolis 2½-mi. Motor
Speedway
Speedway, Ind.
500-mi. AAA Championship Race
Lee Wallard "Belanger Spl." 3:57:38.05
126.244 mph

June 9 Bridgehampton 4-mi. Road Course
Bridgehampton, Long Island, N.Y.
100-mi. SCCA Sports Car Race
Tommy Cole "Chrysler-Allard" 1:12:50.2
86.9 mph

June 10 Milwaukee 1-mi. Dirt Track
West Allis, Wis.
100-mi. AAA Championship Race
Tony Bettenhausen "Belanger Spl."
1:06:33.19 90.154 mph

June 24 Langhorne 1-mi. Dirt Track
Langhorne, Pa.
100-mi. AAA Championship Race
Tony Bettenhausen "Belanger Spl."
1:04:54.18 92.37 mph

July 4 Darlington 1⅜-mi. Paved Speedway
Darlington, S.C.
250-mi. AAA Championship Race
Walt Faulkner "Grant Piston Ring Spl."
2:23:14.4 104.239 mph

July 15 Milwaukee 1-mi. Dirt Track
West Allis, Wis.
150-mi. AAA Stock Car Race
Rodger Ward "Oldsmobile" 2:12:39.71
68.2 mph

Aug. 13 Detroit 1-mi. Dirt Track
Detroit, Mich.
250-mi. NASCAR Stock Car Race
Tommy Thompson "Chrysler" 4:21:28.0
62.45 mph

Aug. 18 Springfield 1-mi. Dirt Track
Springfield, Ill.
100-mi. AAA Championship Race
Tony Bettenhausen "Belanger Spl."
1:06:37.59 90.04 mph

Aug. 26 Milwaukee 1-mi. Dirt Track
West Allis, Wis.
200-mi. AAA Championship Race
Walt Faulkner "Grant Piston Ring Spl."
2:11:22.04 91.348 mph

Aug. 26 Bay Meadows 1-mi. Dirt Track
San Mateo, Calif.

250-mi. Stock Car Race
Johnny Soares "Oldsmobile" 3:53:00.0
65.0 mph

Sept. 1 DuQuoin 1-mi. Dirt Track
DuQuoin, Ill.
100-mi. AAA Championship Race
Tony Bettenhausen "Belanger Spl."
1:07:56.48 88.1 mph

Sept. 3 DuQuoin 1-mi. Dirt Track
DuQuoin, Ill.
200-mi. AAA Championship Race—
Stopped at 101 miles due to rain.
Tony Bettenhausen "Belanger Spl."
1:09:19.0 87.4 mph

Sept. 3 Darlington 1⅜-mi. Paved Speedway
Darlington, S.C.
500-mi. NASCAR Stock Car Race
Herb Thomas "Hudson Hornet"
6:30:05.00 75.6 mph

Sept. 8 Syracuse 1-mi. Dirt Track
Syracuse, N.Y.
100-mi. AAA Championship Race—
Halted at 67 miles due to accident.
Tony Bettenhausen "Belanger Spl."
(No Time)

Sept. 9 Detroit 1-mi. Dirt Track
Detroit, Mich.
100-mi. AAA Championship Race
Paul Russo "Russo-Nichols Spl."
1:11:44.21 83.5 mph

Sept. 17 Langhorne 1-mi. Dirt Track
Langhorne, Pa.
150-mi. NASCAR Stock Car Race
Herb Thomas "Hudson Hornet"
2:09:40.98 69.4 mph

Sept. 23 Centennial Park 1-mi. Dirt Track
Denver, Colo.
100-mi. AAA Championship Race
Tony Bettenhausen "Belanger Spl."
1:09:15.00 86.6 mph

Oct. 8 Occoneechee 1-mi. Dirt Track
Hillsboro, N.C.
150-mi. NASCAR Stock Car Race
Herb Thomas "Hudson Hornet"
2:04:13.00 73.04 mph

Oct. 21 San Jose 1-mi. Dirt Track
San Jose, Calif.
100-mi. AAA Championship Race
Tony Bettenhausen "Belanger Spl."
1:14:24.0 80.6 mph

Nov. 4 Phoenix 1-mi. Dirt Track
Phoenix, Ariz.
100-mi. AAA Championship Race
Johnny Parsons "Ed Walsh Spl."
1:10:54.0 84.4 mph

Nov. 11 Lakewood Park 1-mi. Dirt Track
Atlanta, Ga.
100-mi. NASCAR Stock Car Race
Tim Flock "Hudson Hornet" 1:40:04.0
60.0 mph

Nov. 11 Bay Meadows 1-mi. Dirt Track
San Mateo, Calif.
150-mi. AAA Championship Race
Johnny Parsons "Wynn Oil Spl."
1:42:36.80 88.75 mph

Nov. 25 Pan-American Road Race
Tuxtla to Ciudad Juarez, Mexico

1933-mi. Road Race
Piero Taruffi "Ferrari" 21:27:52.0
88.0 mph

1952

Feb. 10 Daytona 4-mi. Beach & Road
Course
Daytona Beach, Fla.
150-mi. NASCAR Stock Car Race
Marshall Teague "Hudson Hornet"
1:46:19.0 84.65 mph

Mar. 2 Bay Meadows 1-mi. Dirt Track
San Mateo, Calif.
100-mi. AAA Championship Race
Bobby Ball 1:14:34.00 80.46 mph

Mar. 15 Sebring 5.2-mi. Airport Course
Sebring, Fla.
12-hr. Sports Car Race
Harry Gray/Larry Kulok "Frazer Nash"
754 miles 62.83 mph

Apr. 20 Lakewood Park 1-mi. Dirt Track
Atlanta, Ga.
100-mi. NASCAR Stock Car Race
Bill Blair "Oldsmobile" 1:29:43.0
66.88 mph

May 4 Langhorne 1-mi. Dirt Track
Langhorne, Pa.
150-mi. NASCAR Stock Car Race
Dick Rathman "Hudson Hornet"
2:13:00.0 65.91 mph

May 10 Darlington 1⅜-mi. Paved
Speedway
Darlington, S.C.
100-mi. NASCAR Stock Car Race
Dick Rathman "Hudson Hornet"
1:11:35.0 83.82 mph

May 30 Indianapolis 2½-mi. Motor
Speedway
Speedway, Ind.
500-mi. AAA Championship Race
Troy Ruttman "Agajanian Spl." 3:52:41.88
128.922 mph

June 8 Milwaukee 1-mi. Dirt Track
West Allis, Wis.
100-mi. AAA Championship Race
Mike Nazaruk "McNamara Spl."
1:05:02.22 92.256 mph

July 4 Southland (later known as
"Raleigh") 1-mi. Paved Speedway
(Inaugural)
Raleigh, N.C.
200-mi. AAA Championship Race
Troy Ruttman "Agajanian Spl." 2:14:40.0
89.108 mph

Aug. 16 Springfield 1-mi. Dirt Track
Springfield, Ill.
100-mi. AAA Championship Race
Bill Schindler "Chapman Spl." 1:03:36.14
94.34 mph

Aug. 21 Milwaukee 1-mi. Dirt Track
West Allis, Wis.
100-mi. AAA Stock Car Race
Frank Luptow "Hudson Hornet" 1:24:33.0
70.96 mph

Aug. 24 Milwaukee 1-mi. Dirt Track
West Allis, Wis.
200-mi. AAA Championship Race
Chuck Stevenson "Springfield Welding
Spl." 2:27:26.115 81.152 mph

Aug. 30 Detroit 1-mi. Dirt Track
Detroit, Mich.

100-mi. AAA Championship Race
Bill Vukovich "Agajanian Spl." 1:13:34.0
81.56 mph

Sept. 1 DuQuoin 1-mi. Dirt Track
DuQuoin, Ill.
100-mi. AAA Championship Race
Chuck Stevenson "Springfield Welding
Spl." 1:07:52.0 88.40 mph

Sept. 1 Darlington 1⅜-mi. Paved
Speedway
Darlington, S.C.
500-mi. NASCAR Stock Car Race
Fonty Flock "Oldsmobile" 6:42:37.0
74.57 mph

Sept. 6 Syracuse 1-mi. Dirt Track
Syracuse, N.Y.
100-mi. AAA Championship Race
Jack McGrath "Hinkle Spl." 1:07:01.0
89.53 mph

Sept. 7 Milwaukee 1-mi. Dirt Track
West Allis, Wis.
200-mi. AAA Stock Car Race
Marshall Teague "Hudson Hornet"
2:51:28.0 69.98 mph

Sept. 28 Centennial Park 1-mi. Dirt Track
Denver, Colo.
100-mi. AAA Championship Race
Bill Vukovich "Agajanian Spl." 1:08:09.1
88.0 mph

Road America 6.5-mi. Road Course
Elkhart Lake, Wis.
31-lap, 201.5-mi. Sports Car Race
John Fitch "Cunningham" 2:16:13.4
87.5 mph

Nov. 11 Phoenix 1-mi. Dirt Track
Phoenix, Ariz.
100-mi. Championship Race
Johnny Parsons "Ricketts Spl." 1:09:52.0
85.87 mph

Nov. 23 Pan-American Road Race
Juarez, Mexico
1934-mi. Road Race
Sports Car Division
Karl Kling "Mercedes-Benz" 18:51:19.0
103.07 mph
Stock Car Division
Chuck Stevenson "Lincoln" 21:15:38.0
91.41 mph

1953

Feb. 15 Daytona 4.1-mi. Beach & Road
Course
Daytona Beach, Fla.
39-lap, 160-mi. NASCAR Stock Car Race
Bill Blair "Oldsmobile" 1:46:51.0
89.50 mph

Mar. 9 Sebring 5.2-mi. Airport Course
Sebring, Fla.
12-hr. Sports Car Race
John Fitch/Phil Walters "Cunningham"
899.6 mi. 74.96 mph

May 30 Indianapolis 2½-mi. Motor
Speedway
Speedway, Ind.
500-mi. AAA Championship Race
Bill Vukovich "Fuel Injection Spl."
3:53:01.69 128.740 mph

May 30 Raleigh 1-mi. Paved Speedway
Raleigh, N.C.

300-mi. NASCAR Stock Car Race
Fonty Flock "Hudson Hornet" 4:14:51.0
70.61 mph

June 7 Milwaukee 1-mi. Dirt Track
West Allis, Wis.
100-mi. AAA Championship Race
Jack McGrath "Hinkle Spl." 1:04:00.700
93.733 mph

June 21 Langhorne 1-mi. Dirt Track
Langhorne, Pa.
200-mi. NASCAR International Stock Car
Race
Dick Rathman "Hudson Hornet"
3:06:14.18 64.5 mph

June 21 Springfield 1-mi. Dirt Track
Springfield, Ill.
100-mi. AAA Championship Race
Rodger Ward "Walker Electric Spl."
1:07:03.09 89.5 mph

Aug. 22 Springfield 1-mi. Dirt Track
Springfield, Ill.
100-mi. AAA Championship Race
Sam Hanks "Bardahl Spl." 1:05:59.04
90.80 mph

Aug. 24 Milwaukee 1-mi. Dirt Track
West Allis, Wis.
100-mi. AAA Stock Car Race
Sam Hanks "Hudson Hornet" 1:28:54.528
67.491 mph

Aug. 27 Milwaukee 1-mi. Dirt Track
West Allis, Wis.
150-mi. AAA Stock Car Race
Don O'Dell "Packard" 2:04:13.502
72.4 mph

Aug. 29 Floyd Bennett 2.4-mi. Airport
Course
Floyd Bennett Field, Brooklyn, N.Y.
240-mi. Sports Car Race
Phil Walters "Cunningham" 2:54:09.36
82.5 mph

Aug. 30 Milwaukee 1-mi. Dirt Track
West Allis, Wis.
200-mi. AAA Championship Race
Chuck Stevenson "Agajanian Spl."
2:13:57.470 88.945 mph

Sept. 7 DuQuoin 1-mi. Dirt Track
DuQuoin, Ill.
100-mi. AAA Championship Race
Sam Hanks "Bardahl Spl." 1:06:40.71
90.0 mph

Sept. 7 Darlington 1⅜-mi. Paved
Speedway
Darlington, S.C.
500-mi. NASCAR Stock Car Race
Buck Baker "Oldsmobile" 5:23:19.0
92.78 mph

Sept. 12 Syracuse 1-mi. Dirt Track
Syracuse, N.Y.
100-mi. AAA Championship Race
Tony Bettenhausen "Belanger Spl."
1:20:59.0 74.0 mph

Sept. 19 Watkins Glen 4.6-mi. Road Course
Watkins Glen, N.Y.
101.2-mi. Sports Car Race
Walter Hansgen "Jaguar" 76.1 mph

Sept. 20 Langhorne 1-mi. Dirt Track
Langhorne, Pa.
250-mi. NASCAR Stock Car Race
Dick Rathman "Hudson Hornet"
3:43:43.52 67 mph

Sept. 26   Indiana Fairgrounds 1-mi. Dirt Track
Indianapolis, Ind.
100-mi. AAA Championship Race
Bob Sweikert   "Dean Van Lines Spl."
1:08:48.82   87.2 mph

Oct. 30   Indianapolis 2½-mi. Motor Speedway
Speedway, Ind.
24-hr. Stock Car Run for Stevens Challenge Trophy
Tony Bettenhausen/Bill Taylor/Pat O'Connor   "Chrysler"   2157.5 miles
89.89 mph

Nov. 11   Phoenix 1-mi. Dirt Track
Phoenix, Ariz.
100-mi. AAA Championship Race
Tony Bettenhausen   "Belanger Spl."
1:11:33.0   83.8 mph

Nov. 23   Pan American Road Race
1912-mi. Tuxtla Gutierrez to Juarez, Mexico
Sports Car Division
Juan Manuel Fangio   "Lancia"   18:11:00.0
105.73 mph
Stock Car Division
Chuck Stevenson   "Lincoln"   20:31:32.0
93.02 mph

1954

Jan. 31   MacDill Air Force Base 3.4-mi. Circuit
Tampa, Fla.
200-mi. Sports Car Race
Jim Kimberly   "Ferrari"   75.88 mph

Feb. 21   Daytona 4.1-mi. Beach & Road Course
Daytona Beach, Fla.
160-mi. NASCAR Stock Car Race
Lee Petty   "Chrysler"   1:47:40.0
89.14 mph

Mar. 7   Sebring 5.2-mi. Airport Course
Sebring, Fla.
12-hr. Sports Car Race
Stirling Moss/Bill Lloyd   "Osca"
883.6 miles   73.63 mph

Mar. 14   Hunter Air Force Base 5-mi. Course
Savannah, Ga.
150-mi. Sports Car Race
Jim Kimberly   "Ferrari"   97.2 mph

May 2   Langhorne 1-mi. Dirt Track
Langhorne, Pa.
100-mi. NASCAR Stock Car Race
Herb Thomas   "Hudson Hornet"
2:00:22.19   49.18 mph

May 2   Andrews Air Force Base 4.25-mi. Course
Washington, D.C.
200-mi. Sports Car Race
Bill Spear   "Ferrari"   81.85 mph

May 30   Raleigh 1-mi. Paved Speedway
Raleigh, N.C.
250-mi. NASCAR Stock Car Race
Herb Thomas   "Hudson Hornet"
3:22:51.0   73.91 mph

May 30   Indianapolis 2½-mi. Motor Speedway
Speedway, Ind.
500-mi. AAA Championship Race
Bill Vukovich   "Fuel Injection Spl."
3:49:17.27   130.840 mph

June 6   Milwaukee 1-mi. Paved Speedway
West Allis, Wis.
100-mi. AAA Championship Race
Chuck Stevenson   "Agajanian Spl."
1:01:31.297   97.526 mph

June 13   Linden 2-mi. Airport Course
Linden, N.J.
100-mi. NASCAR Stock Car Race
Al Keller   "Jaguar"   1:17:20.40   77.58 mph

June 20   Langhorne 1-mi. Dirt Track
Langhorne, Pa.
100-mi. AAA Championship Race
Jimmy Bryan   "Dean Van Lines Spl."
1:01:30.60   97.54 mph

July 5   Darlington 1⅜-mi. Paved Speedway
Darlington, S.C.
200-mi. AAA Championship Race
Manuel Ayulo   "Peter Schmidt Spl."
1:37:55.92   123.012 mph

July 10   Milwaukee 1-mi. Paved Speedway
West Allis, Wis.
150-mi. AAA Stock Car Race
Tony Bettenhausen   "Chrysler"
2:06:47.241   70.8 mph

Aug. 21   Springfield 1-mi. Dirt Track
Springfield, Ill.
100-mi. AAA Championship Race
Jimmy Davies   "Pat Clancy Spl."
1:04:49.96   92.57 mph

Aug. 22   Bay Meadows 1-mi. Dirt Track
San Mateo, Calif.
250-mi. NASCAR Stock Car Race
Hershel McGriff   "Oldsmobile"   3:50:48.0
64.99 mph

Aug. 24   Bonneville Salt Flats 10-mi. Course
Wendover, Utah
24-hr. Sports Car Run
Donald Healey/Geo. Eyston/Carroll Shelby
"Austin-Healey"   3174.96 miles   132.29 mph

Aug. 29   Milwaukee 1-mi. Paved Speedway
West Allis, Wis.
200-mi. AAA Championship Race
Manuel Ayulo   "Peter Schmidt Spl."
2:04:39.660   95.728 mph

Sept. 6   DuQuoin 1-mi. Dirt Track
DuQuoin, Ill.
100-mi. AAA Championship Race—
Halted at 83 miles due to accident.
Sam Hanks   "Belanger Spl."   (No Time)

Sept. 6   Darlington 1⅜-mi. Paved Speedway
Darlington, S.C.
500-mi. NASCAR Stock Car Race
Herb Thomas   "Hudson Hornet"
5:15:01.0   94.93 mph

Sept. 11   Syracuse 1-mi. Dirt Track
Syracuse, N.Y.
100-mi. AAA Championship Race
Bob Sweikert   "Lutes Spl."   1:06:25.82
90.03 mph

Sept. 12   Milwaukee 1-mi. Paved Speedway
West Allis, Wis.
200-mi. AAA Stock Car Race
Marshall Teague   "Hudson Hornet"
2:39:56.903   75.025 mph

Sept. 18   Indiana Fairgrounds 1-mi. Dirt Track
Indianapolis, Ind.
100-mi. AAA Championship Race

Bob Sweikert   "Lutes Spl."   1:10:15.70
84.65 mph

Sept. 18   Watkins Glen 4.6-mi. Road Course
Watkins Glen, N.Y.
101.2-mi. Sports Car Race
Jim Kimberly   "Ferrari"   1:12:34.6
83.3 mph

Sept. 27   Langhorne 1-mi. Dirt Track
Langhorne, Pa.
250-mi. NASCAR Stock Car Race
Herb Thomas   "Hudson Hornet"
3:30:42.89   71.4 mph

Oct. 17   Sacramento 1-mi. Dirt Track
Sacramento, Calif.
100-mi. AAA Championship Race
Jimmy Bryan   "Dean Van Lines Spl."
1:09:00.80   87.0 mph

Nov. 7   March Air Force Base 3.5-mi. Circuit
Riverside, Calif.
121½-mi. Sports Car Race
Bill Spear   "Ferrari"   1:30:30.0   81.2 mph

Nov. 8   Phoenix 1-mi. Dirt Track
Phoenix, Ariz.
100-mi. AAA Championship Race
Jimmy Bryan   "Dean Van Lines Spl."
1:10:59.15   84.4 mph

Nov. 14   Las Vegas Park 1-mi. Dirt Track
Las Vegas, Nev.
100-mi. AAA Championship Race
Jimmy Bryan   "Dean Van Lines Spl."
1:10:44.37   85.1 mph

Nov. 23   Pan-American 1908-mi. Road Race
Tuxtla to Juarez, Mexico
Sports Cars
Umberto Maglioli   "Ferrari"   17:40:26.0
106.1 mph
Stock Cars
Ray Crawford   "Lincoln"   20:40:19.0
89.8 mph

1955

Feb. 27   Daytona 4.1-mi. Beach & Road Course
Daytona Beach, Fla.
160-mi. NASCAR Stock Car Race
Tim Flock   "Chrysler"   1:44:17.0
92.056 mph

Mar. 13   Sebring 5.2-mi. Airport Course
Sebring, Fla.
12-hr. Sports Car Race
Mike Hawthorn/Phil Walters   "Jaguar"
946.9 miles   78.86 mph

May 30   Indianapolis 2½-mi. Motor Speedway
Speedway, Ind.
500-mi. AAA Championship Race
Bob Sweikert   "John Zink Spl."   3:53:59.13
128.209 mph

June 5   Milwaukee 1-mi. Paved Speedway
West Allis, Wis.
100-mi. AAA Championship Race
Johnny Thompson   "Schmidt Spl."
1:00:42.108   98.844 mph

June 26   Langhorne 1-mi. Dirt Track
Langhorne, Pa.
100-mi. AAA Championship Race
Jimmy Bryan   "Dean Van Lines Spl."
1:02:40.71   95.72 mph

July 17 Milwaukee 1-mi. Paved Speedway
West Allis, Wis.
150-mi. AAA Stock Car Race
Norm Nelson "Chrysler" 1:58:28.88
76.2 mph

Aug. 20 Springfield 1-mi. Dirt Track
Springfield, Ill.
100-mi. AAA Championship Race
Jimmy Bryan "Dean Van Lines Spl."
1:06:16.848 90.523 mph

Aug. 28 Milwaukee 1-mi. Paved Speedway
West Allis, Wis.
250-mi. AAA Championship Race
Pat Flaherty "Dunn Eng'g. Spl."
2:37:50.418 95.033 mph

Sept. 1 Syracuse 1-mi. Dirt Track
Syracuse, N.Y.
100-mi. AAA Championship Race
Bob Sweikert "John Zink Spl." 1:06:43.0
92.998 mph

Sept. 15 DuQuoin 1-mi. Dirt Track
DuQuoin, Ill.
100-mi. AAA Championship Race
Jimmy Bryan "Dean Van Lines Spl."
1:04:09.0 93.58 mph

Sept. 17 Indiana Fairgrounds 1-mi. Dirt
Track
Indianapolis, Ind.
100-mi. AAA Championship Race
Jimmy Bryan "Dean Van Lines Spl."
1:11:26.85 83.98 mph

Sept. 18 Langhorne 1-mi. Dirt Track
Langhorne, Pa.
250-mi. NASCAR Stock Car Race
Tim Flock "Chrysler" 3:12:35.0
77.89 mph

Sept. 30 Raleigh 1-mi. Paved Speedway
Raleigh, N.C.
100-mi. NASCAR Stock Car Race
Tim Flock "Chrysler" 1:21:52.0
73.29 mph

Oct. 9 Memphis 1½-mi. Paved Speedway
Memphis, Tenn.
300-mi. NASCAR Stock Car Race
Speedy Thompson "Ford" 3:34:25.0
84.72 mph

Oct. 16 Sacramento 1-mi. Dirt Track
Sacramento, Calif.
100-mi. AAA Championship Race
Jimmy Bryan "Dean Van Lines Spl."
1:09:36.0 87.2 mph

Nov. 5 Phoenix 1-mi. Dirt Track
Phoenix, Ariz.
100-mi. AAA Champion Race*
Halted at 97 miles due to spin out.
Jimmy Bryan "Dean Van Lines Spl."
1:09:24.0 83.6 mph
* Final Championship Race sanctioned by
the Contest Board of the AAA.

1956

Jan. 15 Torrey Pines 2.7-mi. Road Course
Torrey Pines, Calif.
1-hr. Sports Car Race
Masten Gregory "Maserati" 72.9 miles
72.9 mph

Jan. 22 Phoenix 1-mi. Dirt Track
Phoenix, Ariz.
150-mi. NASCAR Stock Car Race
Buck Baker "Chrysler" 2:19:44.0
84.4 mph

Feb. 26 Ford 5-mi. Test Track
Kingman, Ariz.
100-mi. NASCAR Stock Car Speed Trial
Johnny Mantz "Mercury" :46:28.70
129.645 mph

Feb. 26 Daytona 4.1-mi. Beach & Road
Course
Daytona Beach, Fla.
152-mi. NASCAR Stock Car Race
Tim Flock "Chrysler" 1:40:24.0
90.836 mph

Mar. 24 Sebring 5.2-mi. Airport Course
Sebring, Fla.
12-hr. Sports Car Race
Juan Manuel Fangio/Eugenio Castellotti
"Ferrari" 1008.8 miles 84.07 mph

Apr. 22 Pebble Beach 2.1-mi. Road Course
Pebble Beach, Calif.
100-mi. Sports Car Race
Carroll Shelby "Ferrari" 1:24:18.0
71.74 mph

Apr. 23 Langhorne 1-mi. Dirt Track
Langhorne, Pa.
150-mi. NASCAR Stock Car Race
Buck Baker "Chrysler" 1:58:32.0
75.8 mph

Apr. 26 Darlington 1⅜-mi. Paved Speedway
Darlington, S.C.
24-hr. NASCAR Stock Car Run
Jim Reed/Paul Goldsmith "Chevrolet"
2438 miles 101.58 mph

May 20 Langhorne 1-mi. Dirt Track
Langhorne, Pa.
150-mi. NASCAR Stock Car Race
Dan Letner "Dodge" 2:05:36.21
71.7 mph

May 27 Charlotte 1½-mi. Paved Speedway
Charlotte, N.C.
150-mi. NASCAR Stock Car Race
Speedy Thompson "Chrysler" 1:32:16.0
97.7 mph

May 30 Indianapolis 2½-mi. Motor
Speedway
Speedway, Ind.
500-mi. USAC Championship Race*
Pat Flaherty "John Zink Spl." 3:53:28.24
128.490 mph
* First race to be sanctioned by USAC.

June 10 Milwaukee 1-mi. Paved Speedway
West Allis, Wis.
100-mi. USAC Championship Race
Pat Flaherty "John Zink Spl." 1:00:37.880
98.959 mph

June 24 Langhorne 1-mi. Dirt Track
Langhorne, Pa.
100-mi. USAC Championship Race
George Amick "Central Excavating Spl."
1:03:00.104 95.4 mph

June 24 Road America 4-mi. Road Course
Elkhart Lake, Wis.
152-mi. SCCA Sports Car Race
Carroll Shelby "Ferrari" 1:53:22.74
80.04 mph

June Indianapolis 2½-mi. Motor Speedway
Speedway, Ind.
500-mi. USAC Stock Car Trial
Chuck Stevenson/Johnny Mantz "Ford"
107.126 mph

July 4 Darlington 1⅜-mi. Paved Speedway
Darlington, S.C.
200-mi. USAC Championship Race
Pat O'Connor "Sumar Spl." 124.883 mph

July 4 Pikes Peak 12.6-mi. Hill Climb
Colorado Springs, Colo.
Championship Car Div.
Bobby Unser "Jaguar Spl." :14:27.0
52.2 mph

July 14 Lakewood Park 1-mi. Dirt Track
Atlanta, Ga.
100-mi. USAC Championship Race
Eddie Sachs "Glessner Spl." (No Time)

July 15 Milwaukee 1-mi. Paved Speedway
West Allis, Wis.
150-mi. USAC Stock Car Race
Troy Ruttman "Mercury" 1:48:18.933
83.10 mph

Aug. 12 Road America 4-mi. Road Course
Elkhart Lake, Wis.
250-mi. NASCAR Stock Car Race
Tim Flock "Mercury" 3:29:50.0
71.49 mph

Aug. 18 Springfield 1-mi. Dirt Track
Springfield, Ill.
100-mi. USAC Championship Race
Jimmy Bryan "Dean Van Lines Spl."
1:07:49.12 87.3 mph

Aug. 26 Milwaukee 1-mi. Paved Speedway
West Allis, Wis.
250-mi. USAC Championship Race
Jimmy Bryan "Dean Van Lines Spl."
2:41:45.310 92.733 mph

Sept. 3 Darlington 1⅜-mi. Paved Speedway
Darlington, S.C.
500-mi. NASCAR Stock Car Race
Curtis Turner "Ford" 5:15:33.0
95.57 mph

Sept. 3 DuQuoin 1-mi. Dirt Track
DuQuoin, Ill.
100-mi. USAC Championship Race
Jimmy Bryan "Dean Van Lines Spl."
1:05:25.57 91.2 mph

Sept. 8 Syracuse 1-mi. Dirt Track
Syracuse, N.Y.
100-mi. USAC Championship Race
Tony Bettenhausen "Schmidt Spl."
1:06:04.6 90.9 mph

Sept. 9 Road America 4-mi. Road Course
Elkhart Lake, Wis.
6-hr. SCCA Sports Car Race
John Kilborn/Howard Hively "Ferrari"
480 miles 73.738 mph

Sept. 14 Watkins Glen 2.3-mi. Road Course
Watkins Glen, N.Y.
50-mi. SCCA Sports Car Race
George Constantine "Jaguar" 71.4 mph

Sept. 14 Indiana Fairgrounds 1-mi. Dirt
Track
Indianapolis, Ind.
100-mi. USAC Championship Race
Jimmy Bryan "Dean Van Lines Spl."
1:14:19.48 80.8 mph

Sept. 15 Milwaukee 1-mi. Paved Speedway
West Allis, Wis.
250-mi. USAC Stock Car Race
Jimmy Bryan "Mercury" 2:55:03.837
85.67 mph

Sept. 24   Langhorne 1-mi. Dirt Track
Langhorne, Pa.
300-mi. NASCAR Stock Car Race
Paul Goldsmith   "Chevrolet"   4:06:33.97
73.1 mph

Oct. 21   Sacramento 1-mi. Dirt Track
Sacramento, Calif.
100-mi. USAC Championship Race
Jud Larson   "John Zink Spl."   1:09:07.06
87.0 mph

Nov. 4   Paramount Ranch 2-mi. Paved Road
Course
Agoura, Calif.
250-mi. USAC Stock Car Race
Sam Hanks   "Mercury"   3:36:44.0
69.2 mph

Nov. 12   Phoenix 1-mi. Dirt Track
Phoenix, Ariz.
100-mi. USAC Championship Race
George Amick   "Hopkins Spl."   1:05:20.44
91.8 mph

1957

Feb. 17   Daytona 4.1-mi. Beach & Road
Course
Daytona Beach, Fla.
100-mi. NASCAR Stock Car Race
Cotton Owens   "Pontiac"   1:34:29.0
101.60 mph

Mar. 23   Sebring 5.2-mi. Airport Course
Sebring, Fla.
12-hr. Sports Car Race
Juan Manuel Fangio/Jean Behra
"Maserati"   1024.4 miles   85.36 mph

Apr. 14   Langhorne 1-mi. Dirt Track
Langhorne, Pa.
150-mi. NASCAR Stock Car Race
"Fireball" Roberts   "Ford"   1:44:50.0
85.85 mph

May 30   Indianapolis 2½-mi. Motor
Speedway
Speedway, Ind.
500-mi. USAC Championship Race
Sam Hanks   "Belond Exhaust Spl."
3:41:14.25   135.601 mph

June 2   Langhorne 1-mi. Dirt Track
Langhorne, Pa.
100-mi. USAC Championship Race
Johnny Thompson   "D-A Lubricant Spl."
:59:53.74   100.194 mph

June 9   Lime Rock Park 1½-mi. Road
Course
Lime Rock, Conn.
60-mi. SCCA Sports Car Race
Carroll Shelby   "Maserati"   80 mph

June 9   Milwaukee 1-mi. Paved Speedway
West Allis, Wis.
100-mi. USAC Championship Race
Rodger Ward   "Wolcott Fuel Injection Spl."
1:01:21.397   97.789 mph

June 23   Trenton 1-mi. Paved Speedway
(Inaugural)
Trenton, N.J.
300-mi. NASCAR Stock Car Race
Sam Hanks   "Mercury"   3:35:00.0
88.366 mph

June 23   Detroit 1-mi. Dirt Track
Detroit, Mich.
100-mi. USAC Championship Race
Jimmy Bryan   "Dean Van Lines Spl."
1:09:00.0   86.9 mph

July 4   Lakewood Park 1-mi. Dirt Track
Atlanta, Ga.
100-mi. USAC Championship Race
George Amick   "Hopkins Spl."   1:06:40.0
90.0 mph

Aug. 4   Watkins Glen 2.3-mi. Road Course
Watkins Glen, N.Y.
101.2-mi. NASCAR Stock Car Race
Buck Baker   "Chevrolet"   1:15:06.0
82 mph

Aug. 4   Virginia 3.2-mi. International
Raceway
Danville, Va.
64-mi. SCCA Sports Car Race
Carroll Shelby   "Maserati"   78.4 mph

Aug. 17   Springfield 1-mi. Dirt Track
Springfield, Ill.
100-mi. USAC Championship Race
Rodger Ward   "Wolcott Spl."   1:02:29.41
96.0 mph

Aug. 18   Montgomery 1.86-mi. Airport
Course
Montgomery, N.Y.
93-mi. SCCA Sports Car Race
Walt Hansgen   "Jaguar"   1:15:31.0
73.49 mph

Aug. 25   Milwaukee 1-mi. Paved Speedway
West Allis, Wis.
200-mi. USAC Championship Race
Jim Rathmann   "Chiropractic Spl."
2:02:16.926   98.133 mph

Sept. 1   DuQuoin 1-mi. Dirt Track
DuQuoin, Ill.
100-mi. USAC Championship Race
Jud Larson   "John Zink Spl."   1:05:58.29
90.7 mph

Sept. 2   Darlington 1⅜-mi. Paved Speedway
Darlington, S.C.
500-mi. NASCAR Stock Car Race
Al "Speedy" Thompson   "Chevrolet"
5:00:00.0   100.00 mph

Sept. 7   Syracuse 1-mi. Dirt Track
Syracuse, N.Y.
100-mi. USAC Championship Race
Elmer George   "HOW Spl."   1:03:03.0
95.2 mph

Sept. 8   Road America 4-mi. Road Course
Elkhart Lake, Wis.
500-mi. SCCA Sports Car Race
Phil Hill   "Ferrari"   6:08:30.0   81.4 mph

Sept. 14   Indiana Fairgrounds 1-mi. Dirt
Track
Indianapolis, Ind.
100-mi. USAC Championship Race
Jud Larson   "John Zink Spl."   1:05:23.65
91.7 mph

Sept. 15   Langhorne 1-mi. Dirt Track
Langhorne, Pa.
300-mi. NASCAR Stock Car Race
Gwyn Staley   "Chevrolet"   4:04:02.21
73.7 mph

Sept. 21   Watkins Glen 2.3-mi. Road
Course

Watkins Glen, N.Y.
101.2-mi. SCCA Sports Car Race
Walter Hansgen   "Jaguar"   84.7 mph

Sept. 22   Riverside 3.3-mi. Road Course
(Inaugural)
Riverside, Calif.
1-hr. Sports Car Race
Richie Ginther   "Ferrari"   85.8 mi.
85.8 mph

Sept. 29   Trenton 1-mi. Paved Speedway
Trenton, N.J.
100-mi. USAC Championship Race
Pat O'Connor   "Sumar Spl."   :59:50.0
100.279 mph

Sept. 30   Bridgehampton 2.96-mi. Road
Course (Inaugural)
Bridgehampton, Long Island, N.Y.
75-mi. SCCA Sports Car Race
Walter Hansgen   "Jaguar"   85.83 mph

Oct. 20   Sacramento 1-mi. Dirt Track
Sacramento, Calif.
100-mi. USAC Championship Race
Rodger Ward   "Wolcott Spl."   1:05:57.58
91.0 mph

Nov. 11   Phoenix 1-mi. Dirt Track
Phoenix, Ariz.
100-mi. USAC Championship Race
Jimmy Bryan   "Dean Van Lines Spl."
1:09:46.01   86.0 mph

Nov. 17   Riverside 3.7-mi. Road Course
Riverside, Calif.
92.5-mi. SCCA Sports Car Race
Carroll Shelby   "Maserati"   87.8 mph

1958

Feb. 9   Phoenix 1-mi. Dirt Track
Phoenix, Ariz.
100-mi. USAC Stock Car Race
Jimmy Bryan   "Mercury"   1:27:55.0
68.1 mph

Feb. 23   Daytona 4.1-mi. Beach & Road
Course
Daytona Beach, Fla.
160-mi. NASCAR Stock Car Race
Paul Goldsmith   "Pontiac"   1:34:53.0
101.18 mph

Mar. 8   Trenton 1-mi. Paved Speedway
Trenton, N.J.
1-lap Time Trial
Juan Manuel Fangio   "D-A Lubricant Spl."
:37.1   97.0 mph

Mar. 22   Sebring 5.2-mi. Airport Course
Sebring, Fla.
12-hr. Sports Car Race
Peter Collins/Phil Hill   "Ferrari"
1040 miles   86.67 mph

Mar. 30   Trenton 1-mi. Paved Speedway
Trenton, N.J.
100-mi. USAC Championship Race
Len Sutton   "Central Excavating Spl."
1:02:48.56   95.527 mph

Apr. 13   Lakewood Park 1-mi. Dirt Track
Atlanta, Ga.
100-mi. NASCAR Stock Car Race
Curtis Turner   "Ford"   1:15:56.0
79.0 mph

Apr. 13 Palm Springs 2.9-mi. Airport
Course
Palm Springs, Calif.
72.5-mi. Sports Car Race
Dan Gurney "Ferrari" :54:48.8   76.6 mph

May 10 Darlington 1⅜-mi. Paved Speedway
Darlington, S.C.
300-mi. NASCAR Stock Car Race
Curtis Turner "Ford" 2:44:48.0
109.624 mph

May 18 Langhorne 1-mi. Dirt Track
Langhorne, Pa.
250-mi. NASCAR Stock Car Race
Mike Klapak "Ford" 3:30:54.586
71.112 mph

May 30 Trenton 1-mi. Paved Speedway
Trenton, N.J.
500-mi. NASCAR Stock Car Race
Glenn "Fireball" Roberts "Chevrolet"
5:55:15.0   84.522 mph

May 30 Indianapolis 2½-mi. Motor
Speedway
Speedway, Ind.
500-mi. USAC Championship Race
Jimmy Bryan "Belond AP Spl." 3:44:13.80
133.791 mph

June 1 Bridgehampton 2.96-mi. Road
Course
Bridgehampton, Long Island, N.Y.
75-mi. Sports Car Race
Walt Hansgen "Jaguar" 84.9 mph

June 8 Milwaukee 1-mi. Paved Speedway
West Allis, Wis.
100-mi. USAC Championship Race
Art Bisch "Central Excavating Spl."
1:03:49.27   94.013 mph

June 15 Langhorne 1-mi. Dirt Track
Langhorne, Pa.
100-mi. USAC Championship Race
Eddie Sachs "Schmidt Spl." 1:05:14.062
91.977 mph

July 4 Raleigh 1-mi. Dirt Track
Raleigh, N.C.
250-mi. NASCAR Stock Car Race
Glenn "Fireball" Roberts "Chevrolet"
3:23:33.0   76.693 mph

July 6 Lakewood Park 1-mi. Dirt Track
Atlanta, Ga.
100-mi. USAC Championship Race
Jud Larson "John Zink Spl." 1:08:51.0
87.146 mph

July 13 Milwaukee 1-mi. Paved Speedway
West Allis, Wis.
150-mi. NASCAR Stock Car Race
Fred Lorenzen "Ford" 81 mph

Aug. 16 Springfield 1-mi. Dirt Track
Springfield, Ill.
100-mi. USAC Championship Race
Johnny Thompson "D-A Lubricant Spl."
1:01:08.33   98.13 mph

Aug. 17 Montgomery 1.86-mi. Airport
Course
Montgomery, N.Y.
92.5-mi. SCCA Sports Car Race
Chuck Daigh "Scarab" 77.1 mph

Aug. 21 Milwaukee 1-mi. Paved Speedway
West Allis, Wis.
200-mi. Stock Car Race
Pat Flaherty "Chevrolet" 85.06 mph

Aug. 24 Milwaukee 1-mi. Paved Speedway
West Allis, Wis.
200-mi. USAC Championship Race
Rodger Ward "Wolcott Spl." 2:02:41.263
94.864 mph

Aug. 28 Watkins Glen 2.3-mi. Road Course
Watkins Glen, N.Y.
186.3-mi. USAC Formula Libre Race
Joakim Bonnier "Maserati" 97.75 mph

Sept. 1 Darlington 1⅜-mi. Paved Speedway
Darlington, S.C.
500-mi. NASCAR Stock Car Race
Glenn "Fireball" Roberts "Chevrolet"
102.590 mph

Sept. 1 Trenton 1-mi. Paved Speedway
Trenton, N.J.
300-mi. NASCAR Stock Car Race
Fred Lorenzen "Ford" 3:21:09.0
89.24 mph

Sept. 1 DuQuoin 1-mi. Dirt Track
DuQuoin, Ill.
100-mi. NSAC Championship Race
Johnny Thompson "D-A Lubricant Spl."
1:03:19.36   94.9 mph

Sept. 6 Syracuse 1-mi. Dirt Track
Syracuse, N.Y.
100-mi. USAC Championship Race
Johnny Thompson "D-A Lubricant Spl."
1:03:11.35   94.95 mph

Sept. 7 Road America 4-mi. Road Course
Elkhart Lake, Wis.
500-mi. SCCA Sports Car Race
Lance Reventlow/Gaston Andrey "Ferrari"
6:18:35.96   79.1 mph

Sept. 7 Lime Rock 1½-mi. Road Course
Lime Rock, Conn.
150-mi. USAC Sports Car Race
George Constantine "Aston-Martin"
78.838 mph

Sept. 13 Indiana Fairgrounds 1-mi. Dirt
Track
Indianapolis, Ind.
100-mi. USAC Championship Race
Eddie Sachs "Schmidt Spl." 1:05:07.0
92.142 mph

Sept. 20 Watkins Glen 2.3-mi. Road Course
Watkins Glen, N.Y.
101.2-mi. Sports Car Race
Ed Crawford "Jaguar" 88.8 mph

Sept. 28 Trenton 1-mi. Paved Speedway
Trenton, N.J.
100-mi. USAC Championship Race
Rodger Ward "Wolcott Spl." 1:00:22.91
99.368 mph

Oct. 12 Riverside 3.275-mi. Road Course
Riverside, Calif.
203.05-mi. SCCA Sports Car Race
Chuck Daigh "Scarab" 88.76 mph

Oct. 26 Sacramento 1-mi. Dirt Track
Sacramento, Calif.
100-mi. USAC Championship Race
Johnny Thompson "D-A Lubricant Spl."
1:07:17.02   89.175 mph

Nov. 9 Laguna Seca 1.9-mi. Road Course
Monterey, Calif.
34.2-mi. Sports Car Race
Lance Reventlow "Scarab" :24:14.0
83.22 mph

Nov. 11 Phoenix 1-mi. Dirt Track
Phoenix, Ariz.
100-mi. USAC Championship Race
Jud Larson "Bowes Seal Fast Spl."
1:05:20.44   92.738 mph

1959

Feb. 22 Daytona 2.5-mi. Paved Tri-oval
Speedway
Daytona Beach, Fla.
500-mi. NASCAR Stock Car Race
Lee Petty "Oldsmobile" 3:41:22.0
135.521 mph

Mar. 8 Pomona 2-mi. Road Course
Pomona, Calif.
150-mi. USAC-FIA Sports Car Race
Ken Miles "Porsche" 1:44:58.0
85.8 mph

Mar. 21 Sebring 5.2-mi. Airport Course
Sebring, Fla.
12-hr. SCCA Sports Car Race
Phil Hill/Oliver Gendebien/Dan Gurney/
Chuck Daigh "Ferrari" 977.6 mi.
81.466 mph

Apr. 4 Daytona 2.5-mi. Paved Tri-oval
Speedway
Daytona Beach, Fla.
100-mi. USAC Championship Race
Jim Rathmann "Simoniz Spl." :35:24.0
170.261 mph

Apr. 5 Daytona 3.81-mi. Road & Speedway
Course
Daytona Beach, Fla.
6-hr. USAC-FIA Sports Car Race
Antonio Von Dory/Roberto Mieres
"Porsche" 560.07 mi.   93.34 mph.

Apr. 12 Trenton 1-mi. Paved Speedway
Trenton N.J.
100-mi. USAC Championship Race
Halted at 87 miles due to rain.
Tony Bettenhausen "Central Excavating
Spl." :57:15.69 91.161 mph

May 9 Darlington 1⅜-mi. Paved Speedway
Darlington S.C.
300-mi. NASCAR Stock Car Race
Glenn "Fireball" Roberts "Chevrolet"
2:35:58.0   115.903 mph

May 17 Trenton 1-mi. Paved Speedway
Trenton, N.J.
150-mi. NASCAR Stock Car Race
Tom Pistone "Ford" 1:43:02.0   88.66 mph

May 30 Indianapolis 2½-mi. Motor
Speedway
Speedway, Ind.
500-mi. USAC Championship Race
Rodger Ward "Leader Card Spl."
3:40:49.20   135.857 mph

May 31 Bridgehampton 2.86-mi. Road
Course
Bridgehampton, Long Island, N.Y.
71.5-mi. Sports Car Race
Walter Hansgen "Lister Jaguar" :48:06.2
88.5 mph

June 7 Milwaukee 1-mi. Paved Speedway
West Allis, Wis.

100-mi. USAC Championship Race
Johnny Thompson   "Racing Associates
Spl."   1:00:50.689   98.612 mph

June 14   Langhorne 1-mi. Dirt Track
Langhorne, Pa.
100-mi. USAC Championship Race
Van Johnson   "Vargo Spl."   1:00:16.176
99.005 mph

July 4   Daytona 2.5-mi. Paved Tri-Oval
Speedway
Daytona Beach, Fla.
250-mi. NASCAR Stock Car Race
Glenn "Fireball" Roberts   "Pontiac"
140.581 mph

July 19   Riverside 3.275-mi. Road Course
Riverside, Calif.
150-mi. Sports Car Race
Richie Ginther   "Ferrari"   1:44:06.0
88.75 mph

Aug. 22   Springfield 1-mi. Dirt Track
Springfield, Ill.
100-mi. USAC Championship Race
Len Sutton   "Central Excavating Spl."
1:03:02.0   97.087 mph

Aug. 29   Bonneville Salt Flats
Wendover, Utah
1-mi. Straightaway Record for Class A
Streamliner (489 cu. in. or more)
Mickey Thompson   "Challenger I"
330.512 mph

Aug. 30   Milwaukee 1-mi. Paved Speedway
West Allis, Wis.
200-mi. USAC Championship Race
Rodger Ward   "Leader Card Spl."
2:04:25.390   96.445 mph

Sept. 7   DuQuoin 1-mi. Dirt Track
DuQuoin, Ill.
100-mi. USAC Championship Race
Rodger Ward   "Leader Card Spl."
1:04:19.86   93.2 mph

Sept. 7   Darlington 1⅜-mi. Paved Speedway
Darlington, S.C.
500-mi. NASCAR Stock Car Race
Jim Reed   "Chevrolet"   4:28:30.0
111.836 mph

Sept. 12   Syracuse 1-mi. Dirt Track
Syracuse, N.Y.
100-mi. USAC Championship Race
Eddie Sachs   "Competition Eng'g. Spl."
1:03:44.85   94.12 mph

Sept. 13   Langhorne 1-mi. Dirt Track
Langhorne, Pa.
250-mi. Stock Car Race
Mike Klapak   "Ford"   81.440 mph

Sept. 13   Road America 4.0-mi. Road
Course
Elkhart Lake, Wis.
500-mi. Sports Car Race
Walt Hansgen/Ed Crawford   "Lister-Jaguar"
6:05:15.0   82.18 mph

Sept. 19   Indiana Fairgrounds 1-mi. Dirt
Track
Indianapolis, Ind.
100-mi. USAC Championship Race
Rodger Ward   "Leader Card Spl."
1:05:54.62   91.1 mph

Sept. 26   Watkins Glen 2.3-mi. Road Course
Watkins Glen, N.Y.

101.2-mi. Sports Car Race
Walt Hansgen   "Lister-Jaguar"   1:09:02.5
87.5 mph

Sept. 27   Trenton 1-mi. Paved Speedway
Trenton, N.J.
100-mi. USAC Championship Race
Eddie Sachs   "Competition Eng'g. Spl."
1:01:36.18   97.398 mph

Oct. 10   Riverside 3.275-mi. Road Course
Riverside, Calif.
203.05-mi. Sports Car Race
Phil Hill   "Ferrari"   2:16:45.0   89.09 mph

Oct. 18   Phoenix 1-mi. Dirt Track
Phoenix, Ariz.
100-mi. USAC Championship Race
Tony Bettenhausen   "Hopkins Spl."
1:07:49.71   88.3 mph

Oct. 25   Sacramento 1-mi. Dirt Track
Sacramento, Calif.
100-mi. USAC Championship Race
Jim Hurtubise   "Racing Associates Spl."
1:09:23.57   86.6 mph

Dec. 12   Sebring 5.2-mi. Airport Course
Sebring, Fla.
218.4-mi. FIA Grand Prix of U.S.
Bruce McLaren   "Cooper-Climax"
2:12:35.7   98.83 mph

1960

Feb. 14   Daytona 2½-mi. Paved Tri-oval
Speedway
Daytona Beach, Fla.
500-mi. NASCAR Stock Car Race
Robert "Junior" Johnson   "Chevrolet"
4:00:30.0   124.740 mph

Mar. 26   Sebring 5.2-mi. Airport Course
Sebring, Fla.
12-hr. Sports Car Race
Olivier Gendebien/Hans Herrmann
"Porsche"   1019.2 miles   84.927 mph

Apr. 3   Riverside 3.2-mi. Road Course
Riverside, Calif.
204-mi. Sports Car Race
Carroll Shelby   "Maserati"   87.5 mph

Apr. 10   Trenton 1-mi. Paved Speedway
Trenton, N.J.
100-mi. USAC Championship Race
Rodger Ward   "Leader Card Spl."
1:02:50.18   95.486 mph

May 30   Indianapolis 2½-mi. Motor
Speedway
Speedway, Ind.
500-mi. USAC Championship Race
Jim Rathmann   "Ken-Paul Spl."   3:36:11.36
138.767 mph

June 5   Milwaukee 1-mi. Paved Speedway
West Allis, Wis.
100-mi. USAC Championship Race
Rodger Ward   "Leader Card Spl."
1:00:19.38   99.465 mph

June 12   Hanford 1½-mi. Paved Speedway
Hanford, Calif.
250-mi. NASCAR Stock Car Race
Marv Porter   "Ford"   2:50:28.0   88.03 mph

June 19   Langhorne 1-mi. Dirt Track
Langhorne, Pa.
100-mi. USAC Championship Race
Jim Hurtubise   "Schmidt Spl."   :59:31.02
100.736 mph

June 19   Charlotte 1½-mi. Paved Speedway
(Inaugural)
Charlotte, N.C.
600-mi. NASCAR Stock Car Race
JoeLee Johnson   "Chevrolet"   5:34:06.0
107.750 mph

June 19   Road America 4-mi. Road Course
Elkhart Lake, Wis.
140-mi. Sports Car Race
Augie Pabst   "Scarab"   85.54 mph

July 3   Daytona 2½-mi. Paved Tri-oval
Speedway
Daytona Beach, Fla.
250-mi. NASCAR Stock Car Race
Jack Smith   "Pontiac"   1:42:09.0
146.842 mph

July 17   Montgomery 1.9-mi. Airport Course
Montgomery, N.Y.
190-mi. NASCAR Stock Car Race
Rex White   "Chevrolet"   2:15:24.0
88.48 mph

July 17   Continental Divide 2.8-mi. Road
Course
Castle Rock, Colo.
112-mi. SCCA Sports Car Race
Bob Holbert   "Porsche"   1:29:37.9
74.99 mph

July 31   Atlanta 1½-mi. Paved Speedway
Hampton, Ga.
300-mi. NASCAR Stock Car Race
Glenn "Fireball" Roberts   "Pontiac"
2:29:47.0   112.734 mph

July 31   Road America 4-mi. Road Course
Elkhart Lake, Wis.
200-mi. Sports Car Race
Jim Jeffords   "Maserati"   85.495 mph

Aug. 20   Springfield 1-mi. Dirt Track
Springfield, Ill.
100-mi. USAC Championship Race
Jim Packard   "Stearly Motor Spl."
1:06:00.0   90.6 mph

Aug. 28   Milwaukee 1-mi. Paved Speedway
West Allis, Wis.
200-mi. USAC Championship Race
Len Sutton   "Central Excavating Spl."
1:59:50.56   100.131 mph

Sept. 5   Darlington 1⅜-mi. Paved Speedway
Darlington, S.C.
500-mi. NASCAR Stock Car Race
Buck Baker   "Pontiac"   4:43:34.0
105.901 mph

Sept. 5   DuQuoin 1-mi. Dirt Track
DuQuoin, Ill.
100-mi. USAC Championship Race
A. J. Foyt   "Bowes Seal Fast Spl."
1:04:16.41   93.36 mph

Sept. 11   Road America 4-mi. Road Course
Elkhart Lake, Wis.
500-mi. Sports Car Race
Dave Causey/Luke Stear   "Maserati"
6:15:56.0   79.81 mph

Sept. 11   Syracuse 1-mi. Dirt Track
Syracuse, N.Y.
100-mi. USAC Championship Race
Bobby Grim   "Bill Forbes Spl."   1:04:20.29
93.257 mph

Sept. 17 Indiana Fairgrounds 1-mi. Dirt Track
Indianapolis, Ind.
100-mi. USAC Championship Race
A. J. Foyt "Bowes Seal Fast Spl."
1:07:12.0 89.286 mph

Sept. 24 Watkins Glen 2.3-mi. Paved Course
Watkins Glen, N.Y.
101-mi. Sports Car Race
Augie Pabst "Scarab" 88.4 mph

Sept. 25 Trenton 1-mi. Paved Speedway
Trenton, N.J.
100-mi. USAC Championship Race
Eddie Sachs "Dean Van Lines Spl."
1:00:28.19 99.223 mph

Oct. 9 Watkins Glen 2.3-mi. Road Course
Watkins Glen, N.Y.
230-mi. Formula Libre Race
Stirling Moss "Lotus-Climax" 2:10:02.2
105.8 mph

Oct. 16 Charlotte 1½-mi. Paved Speedway
Charlotte, N.C.
400-mi. NASCAR Stock Car Race
Alfred "Speedy" Thompson "Ford"
112.906 mph

Oct. 16 Riverside 3.275-mi. Road Course
Riverside, Calif.
203.05-mi. Sports Car Race
Bill Krause "Maserati" 2:13:10.0
91.48 mph

Oct. 23 Laguna Seca 1.9-mi. Road Course
Monterey, Calif.
2—100-mi. USAC Sports Car Races
1st Race
Stirling Moss "Lotus" 86.4 mph
2nd Race
Stirling Moss "Lotus" 87.3 mph

Oct. 30 Atlanta 1½-mi. Paved Speedway
Hampton, Ga.
500-mi. NASCAR Stock Car Race
Bobby Johns "Pontiac" 108.624 mph

Oct. 30 Sacramento 1-mi. Dirt Track
Sacramento, Calif.
100-mi. USAC Championship Race
A. J. Foyt "Bowes Seal Fast Spl."
1:10:45.49 85.0 mph

Nov. 13 Daytona 3.81-mi. Road Course
Daytona Beach, Fla.
114.3-mi. SCCA Sports Car Race
Augie Pabst "Scarab" 102.61 mph

Nov. 20 Phoenix 1-mi. Dirt Track
Phoenix, Ariz.
100-mi. USAC Championship Race
A. J. Foyt "Bowes Seal Fast Spl."
1:07:21.4 89.4 mph

Nov. 20 Riverside 3.275-mi. Road Course
Riverside, Calif.
245.63-mi. Grand Prix of U.S.
Stirling Moss "Lotus-Climax" 2:28:52.2
98.98 mph

1961

Mar. 25 Sebring 5.2-mi. Airport Course
Sebring, Fla.
12-hr. Sports Car Race
Olivier Gendebien/Phil Hill "Ferrari"
1092 mi. 90.7 mph

Apr. 9 Trenton 1-mi. Paved Speedway
Trenton, N.J.

100-mi. USAC Championship Race
Eddie Sachs "Dean Van Lines Spl."
1:00:48.17 98.679 mph

May 21 Charlotte 1½-mi. Paved Speedway
Charlotte, N.C.
2—100-mi. NASCAR Stock Car Races
1st Race
Richard Petty "Plymouth" :45:09.0
133.554 mph
2nd Race
Joe Weatherly "Pontiac" 115.591 mph

May 28 Charlotte 1½-mi. Paved Speedway
Charlotte, N.C.
600-mi. NASCAR Stock Car Race
David Pearson "Pontiac" 111.633 mph

May 30 Indianapolis 2½-mi. Motor Speedway
Speedway, Ind.
500-mi. USAC Championship Race
A. J. Foyt "Bowes Seal Fast Spl."
3:35:37.49 139.130 mph

June 4 Milwaukee 1-mi. Paved Speedway
West Allis, Wis.
100-mi. USAC Championship Race
Rodger Ward "Sun City Spl." :57:46.21
103.860 mph

June 18 Langhorne 1-mi. Dirt Track
Langhorne, Pa.
100-mi. USAC Championship Race
A. J. Foyt "Bowes Seal Fast Spl."
1:00:14.42 99.601 mph

July 4 Daytona 2½-mi. Paved Tri-oval Speedway
Daytona Beach, Fla.
250-mi. NASCAR Stock Car Race
David Pearson "Pontiac" 1:37:15.0
154.294 mph

July 9 Atlanta 1½-mi. Paved Speedway
Hampton, Ga.
250-mi. NASCAR Stock Car Race
Fred Lorenzen "Ford" 118.098 mph

Aug. 20 Milwaukee 1-mi. Paved Speedway
West Allis, Wis.
200-mi. USAC Championship Race
Lloyd Ruby "John Zink Spl." 1:58:03.990
101.638 mph

Aug. 21 Springfield 1-mi. Dirt Track
Springfield, Ill.
100-mi. USAC Championship Race
Jim Hurtubise "Sterling Plumbing Spl."
1:00:56.93 98.04 mph

Sept. 4 DuQuoin 1-mi. Dirt Track
DuQuoin, Ill.
100-mi. USAC Championship Race
A. J. Foyt "Bowes Seal Fast Spl."
1:04:41.49 92.8 mph

Sept. 4 Darlington 1⅜-mi. Paved Speedway
Darlington, S.C.
500-mi. NASCAR Stock Car Race
Nelson Stacy "Ford" 4:14:45.0
117.802 mph

Sept. 9 Syracuse 1-mi. Dirt Track
Syracuse, N.Y.
100-mi. USAC Championship Race
Rodger Ward "Leader Card Spl."
1:03:05.09 95.2 mph

Sept. 10 Road America 4-mi. Road Course
Elkhart Lake, Wis.
500-mi. Sports Car Race
Walter Hansgen/Augie Pabst "Maserati"
6:04:55.0 82.29 mph

Sept. 16 Indiana Fairgrounds 1-mi. Dirt Track
Indianapolis, Ind.
100-mi. USAC Championship Race
A. J. Foyt "Bowes Seal Fast Spl."
1:04:57.38 92.369 mph

Sept. 17 Atlanta 1½-mi. Paved Speedway
Hampton, Ga.
400-mi. NASCAR Stock Car Race
David Pearson "Pontiac" 125.494 mph

Sept. 23 Watkins Glen 2.3-mi. Road Course
Watkins Glen, N.Y.
92-mi. Sports Car Race
George Constantine "Ferrari" 1:01:27.0
89.51 mph

Sept. 24 Trenton 1-mi. Paved Speedway
Trenton, N.J.
100-mi. USCA Championship Race
Eddie Sachs "Dean Van Lines Spl."
:59:23.89 101.013 mph

Oct. 8 Watkins Glen 2.3-mi. Road Course
Watkins Glen, N.Y.
230-mi. Formula I Grand Prix of U.S.
Innes Ireland "Lotus-Climax" 2:13:45.8
103.22 mph

Oct. 15 Charlotte 1½-mi. Paved Speedway
Charlotte, N.C.
400-mi. NASCAR Stock Car Race
Joe Weatherly "Pontiac" 3:20:20.0
119.950 mph

Oct. 15 Riverside 3.275-mi. Road Course
Riverside, Calif.
203.05-mi. Sports Car Race
Jack Brabham "Cooper-Monaco"
2:09:33.8 94.06 mph

Oct. 22 Laguna Seca 1.9-mi. Road Course
Monterey, Calif.
2—100-mi. SCCA Sports Car Races
First Race
Stirling Moss "Lotus" 1:09:15.8
90.3 mph
Second Race
Stirling Moss "Lotus" 1:08:15.3
91.9 mph

Oct. 29 Sacramento 1-mi. Dirt Track
Sacramento, Calif.
100-mi. USAC Championship Race
Rodger Ward "Leader Card Spl."
1:07:35.0 88.5 mph

Nov. 19 Phoenix 1-mi. Dirt Track
Phoenix, Ariz.
100-mi. USAC Championship Race—
Halted after 89 laps due to darkness.
Parnelli Jones "Agajanian Spl."
(No Time)

1962

Feb. 11 Daytona 3.81-mi. Road Course
Daytona Beach, Fla.
3-hr. Race for GT & Sports Cars
Dan Gurney "Lotus" 312.42 miles
3:04:00.0 104.101 mph

Feb. 18 Daytona 2½-mi. Paved Tri-oval Speedway
Daytona Beach Fla.
500-mi. NASCAR Stock Car Race
Glenn "Fireball" Roberts "Pontiac"
3:10:41.0 152.529 mph

Mar. 24 Sebring 5.2-mi. Airport Course
Sebring, Fla.
12-hr. Sports Car Race
Jo Bonnier/Lucien Bianchi "Ferrari"
1071.2 miles 89.14 mph

Apr. 22 Trenton 1-mi. Paved Speedway
Trenton, N.J.
100-mi. USAC Championship Race
A. J. Foyt "Bowes Seal Fast Spl."
:59:20.7 101.101 mph

May 30 Indianapolis 2½-mi. Motor
Speedway
Speedway, Ind.
500-mi. USAC Championship Race
Rodger Ward "Leader Card Spl."
140.293 mph

June 10 Milwaukee 1-mi. Paved Speedway
West Allis, Wis.
100-mi. USAC Championship Race
A. J. Foyt "Bowes Seal Fast Spl."
:59:29.300 100.700 mph

June 17 Road America 4-mi. Road Course
Elkhart Lake, Wis.
152-mi. Sports Car Race
Jim Hall "Chaparral" 1:43:46.0
87.887 mph

July 1 Langhorne 1-mi. Dirt Track
Langhorne, Pa.
100-mi. USAC Championship Race
A. J. Foyt "Bowes Seal Fast Spl."
1:04:23.22 93.186 mph

July 4 Daytona 2½-mi. Paved Tri-oval
Speedway
Daytona Beach, Fla.
250-mi. NASCAR Stock Car Race
Glenn "Fireball" Roberts "Pontiac"
153.294 mph

July 22 Trenton 1-mi. Paved Speedway
Trenton, N.J.
200-mi. USAC Championship Race
Halted at 142 miles due to rain.
Rodger Ward "Leader Card Spl."
1:24:22.54 100.976 mph

Aug. 18 Springfield 1-mi. Dirt Track
Springfield, Ill.
100-mi. USAC Championship Race
Jim Hurtubise "Barnett Bros. Spl."
1:04:46.63 92.6 mph

Aug. 19 Milwaukee 1-mi. Paved Speedway
West Allis, Wis.
200-mi. USAC Championship Race
Rodger Ward "Leader Card Spl."
1:59:58.880 100.017 mph

Aug. 26 Langhorne 1-mi. Dirt Track
Langhorne, Pa.
100-mi. USAC Championship Race
Don Branson "Leader Card Spl."
:57:15.13 104.799 mph

Sept. 2 Darlington 1⅜-mi. Paved Speedway
Darlington, S.C.
500-mi. NASCAR Stock Car Race
Larry Frank "Ford" 118 mph

Sept. 8 Syracuse 1-mi. Dirt Track
Syracuse, N.Y.
100-mi. USAC Championship Race
Rodger Ward "Leader Card Spl."
1:02:46.81 95.571 mph

Sept. 9 Road America 4.0-mi. Road Course
Elkhart Lake, Wis.
500-mi. Sports Car Race
Jim Hall/Hap Sharp "Chaparral"
5:53:01.8 84.978 mph

Sept. 15 Indiana Fairgrounds 1-mi. Dirt
Track
Indianapolis, Ind.
100-mi. USAC Championship Race
Parnelli Jones "Willard Battery Spl."
90.604 mph

Sept. 15 Bridgehampton 2.86-mi. Road
Course
Bridgehampton, Long Island, N.Y.
245-mi. Sports Car Race
Bob Holbert "Porsche" 3:01:06.0
79.4 mph

Sept. 16 Bridgehampton 2.86-mi. Road
Course
Bridgehampton, Long Island, N.Y.
248.5-mi. Sports Car Race
Pedro Rodriguez "Ferrari" 2:47:48.2
88.66 mph

Sept. 22 Watkins Glen 2.3-mi. Road Course
Watkins Glen, N.Y.
101-mi. Sports Car Race
Walter Hansgen "Porsche" 90.29 mph

Sept. 23 Trenton 1-mi. Paved Speedway
Trenton, N.J.
200-mi. USAC Championship Race
Don Branson "Leader Card Spl."
1:57:02.38 102.529 mph

Oct. 7 Watkins Glen 2.3-mi. Road Course
Watkins Glen, N.Y.
230-mi. F.I.A. Grand Prix of U.S.
Jim Clark "Lotus" 2:07:13.0 108.61 mph

Oct. 14 Charlotte 1½-mi. Paved Speedway
Charlotte, N.C.
400-mi. NASCAR Stock Car Race
Junior Johnson "Pontiac" 3:04:52.0
132.250 mph

Oct. 14 Riverside 2.6-mi. Road Course
Riverside, Calif.
200.2-mi. Sports Car Race
Roger Penske "Zerex Spl." 95.57 mph

Oct. 28 Sacramento 1-mi. Dirt Track
Sacramento, Calif.
100-mi. USAC Championship Race
A. J. Foyt "Thompson Rotary" 1:02:59.0
95.26 mph

Oct. 28 Atlanta 1½-mi. Paved Speedway
Hampton, Ga.
400-mi. NASCAR Stock Car Race
Rex White "Chevrolet" 124.787 mph

Nov. 4 Mexico City 3.1-mi. Road Course
Mexico City, Mexico
186-mi. Formula I Grand Prix
Jim Clark/T. Taylor "Lotus" 2:03:50.9
87.4 mph

Nov. 11 Puerto Rico 1.7-mi. Road Course
Cavas, Puerto Rico
153-mi. Sports Car Race
Roger Penske "Zerex Spl." 76.5 mph

Nov. 18 Phoenix 1-mi. Dirt Track
Phoenix, Ariz.
100-mi. USAC Championship Race—
Halted at 51 miles due to accident.
Bobby Marshman "Hopkins Spl."
(No Time)

1963

Jan. 20 Riverside 2.7-mi. Road Course
Riverside, Calif.
500-mi. NASCAR Stock Car Race
Dan Gurney "Ford" 5:53:20.0 84.96 mph

Feb. 17 Daytona 3.81-mi. Road Course
Daytona Beach, Fla.
3-hr. Sports Car Race
Pedro Rodriguez "Ferrari" 308.61 miles
102.07 mph

Feb. 24 Daytona 2½-mi. Paved Tri-oval
Speedway
Daytona Beach, Fla.
500-mi. NASCAR Stock Car Race
Tiny Lund "Ford" 3:17:56.0 151.566 mph

Mar. 17 Atlanta 1½-mi. Paved Speedway
Hampton, Ga.
500-mi. NASCAR Stock Car Race
Fred Lorenzen "Ford" 130.592 mph

Mar. 23 Sebring 5.2-mi. Airport Course
Sebring, Fla.
12-hr. Sports Car Race
John Surtees/Lodovico Scarfiotti "Ferrari"
1086.8 miles 90.39 mph

Apr. 21 Trenton 1-mi. Paved Speedway
Trenton, N.J.
100-mi. USAC Championship Race
A. J. Foyt "Sheraton-Thompson Spl."
:58:32.48 102.491 mph

May 30 Indianapolis 2½-mi. Motor
Speedway
Speedway, Ind.
500-mi. USAC Championship Race
Parnelli Jones "Agajanian Willard Battery
Spl." 3:29:35.40 143.137 mph

June 2 Charlotte 1½-mi. Paved Speedway
Charlotte, N.C.
600-mi. NASCAR Stock Car Race
Fred Lorenzen "Ford" 4:31:52.0
132.417 mph

June 9 Milwaukee 1-mi. Paved Speedway
West Allis, Wis.
100-mi. USAC Championship Race
Rodger Ward "Kaiser Aluminum Spl."
:59:39.070 100.561 mph

June 23 Langhorne 1-mi. Dirt Track
Langhorne, Pa.
100-mi. USAC Championship Race
A. J. Foyt "Sheraton-Thompson Spl."
:57:37.05 104.136 mph

June 23 Road America 4-mi. Road Course
Elkhart Lake, Wis.
100-mi. Sports Car Race
Harry Hever "Chaparral" 86.846 mph

June 30 Atlanta 1½-mi. Paved Speedway
Hampton, Ga.
400-mi. NASCAR Stock Car Race
Junior Johnson "Chevrolet" 121.139 mph

July 4 Daytona 2½-mi. Paved Tri-oval
Speedway
Daytona Beach, Fla.
400-mi. NASCAR Stock Car Race
Glenn "Fireball" Roberts "Ford"
2:39:01.0 150.927 mph

July 21   Trenton 1-mi. Paved Speedway
Trenton, N.J.
150-mi. USAC Championship Race
A. J. Foyt   "Sheraton-Thompson Spl."
1:29:38.31   100.403 mph

July 21   Bridgehampton 2:85-mi. Road
Course
Bridgehampton, Long Island, N.Y.
100-mi. NASCAR Stock Car Race
Richard Petty   "Plymouth"   1:09:06.0
86.4 mph

Aug. 5   Bonneville Salt Flats
Wendover, Utah
1-mi. Straightaway Record
Craig Breedlove   "Spirit of America"
407.45 mph

Aug. 17   Springfield 1-mi. Dirt Track
Springfield, Ill.
100-mi. USAC Championship Race
Rodger Ward   "Kaiser Aluminum Spl."
1:02:47.77   95.5 mph

Aug. 18   Milwaukee 1-mi. Paved Speedway
West Allis, Wis.
200-mi. USAC Championship Race
Jim Clark   "Lotus-Ford"   1:54:53.098
104.452 mph
(First major U.S. race won by a rear-engined
race car)

Aug. 25   Springfield 1-mi. Dirt Track
Springfield, Ill.
100-mi. USAC Stock Car Race
Curtis Turner   "Ford"   1:07:14.77
89.5 mph

Sept. 2   DuQuoin 1-mi. Dirt Track
DuQuoin, Ill.
100-mi. USAC Championship Race
A. J. Foyt   "Sheraton-Thompson Spl."
1:03:00.18   97.8 mph

Sept. 2   Darlington 1⅜-mi. Paved Speedway
Darlington, S.C.
500-mi. NASCAR Stock Car Race
Glenn "Fireball" Roberts   "Ford"
3:54:23.0   129.784 mph

Sept. 8   Road America 4-mi. Road Course
Elkhart Lake, Wis.
500-mi. Sports Car Race
Bill Wuesthoff/Augie Pabst   "Elva-Porsche"
3:56:00.049   84.448 mph

Sept. 14   Indiana Fairgrounds 1-mi. Dirt
Track
Indianapolis, Ind.
100-mi. USAC Championship Race
Rodger Ward   "Kaiser Aluminum Spl."
93.545 mph

Sept. 15   Bridgehampton 2.86-mi. Road
Course
Bridgehampton, Long Island, N.Y.
315-mi. Sports Car Race
Walter Hansgen   "Cooper-Buick"
91.52 mph

Sept. 22   Trenton 1-mi. Paved Speedway
Trenton, N.J.
200-mi. USAC Championship Race
A. J. Foyt   "Sheraton-Thompson Spl."
1:58:23.51   100.358 mph

Oct. 6   Watkins Glen 2.3-mi. Road Course
Watkins Glen, N.Y.
253-mi. Grand Prix of U.S.
Graham Hill   "BRM"   2:19:22.1
109.91 mph

Oct. 13   Charlotte 1½-mi. Paved Speedway
Charlotte, N.C.
400-mi. NASCAR Stock Car Race
Junior Johnson   "Ford"   132.105 mph

Oct. 13   Riverside 2.6-mi. Road Course
Riverside, Calif.
200-mi. Sports Car Race
Dave MacDonald   "Cobra"   96.273 mph

Oct. 20   Laguna Seca 1.9-mi. Road Course
Monterey, Calif.
200-mi. Sports Car Race
Dave MacDonald   "Cobra"   83.2 mph

Oct. 27   Sacramento 1-mi. Dirt Track
Sacramento, Calif.
100-mi. USAC Championship Race
Rodger Ward   "Kaiser Aluminum Spl."
1:05:05.64   92.17 mph

Nov. 17   Phoenix 1-mi. Dirt Track
Phoenix, Ariz.
100-mi. USAC Championship Race
Rodger Ward   "Kaiser Aluminum Spl."
1:10:34.0   85.3 mph

1964

Jan. 19   Riverside 2.7-mi. Road Course
Riverside, Calif.
500-mi. Stock Car Race
Dan Gurney   "Ford"   5:28:47.0
91.154 mph

Feb. 16   Daytona 3.81-mi. Road Course
Daytona Beach, Fla.
2000km. (1243 mi.) Sports Car Race
Pedro Rodriguez/Phil Hill   "Ferrari"
98.23 mph

Feb. 23   Daytona 2½-mi. Paved Tri-oval
Speedway
Daytona Beach, Fla.
500-mi. NASCAR Stock Car Race
Richard Petty   "Plymouth"   3:14:23.0
154.334 mph

Mar. 21   Sebring 5.2-mi. Airport Course
Sebring, Fla.
12-hr. Sports Car Race
Mike Parkes/Umberto Maglioli   "Ferrari"
1112.8 miles   92.36 mph

Mar. 22   Phoenix 1-mi. Paved Speedway
Phoenix, Ariz.
100-mi. USAC Championship Race
A. J. Foyt   "Sheraton-Thompson Spl."
:55:47.71   107.536 mph

Apr. 5   Atlanta 1½-mi. Paved Speedway
Hampton, Ga.
500-mi. NASCAR Stock Car Race
Fred Lorenzen   "Ford"   133.879 mph

Apr. 19   Trenton 1-mi. Paved Speedway
Trenton, N.J.
100-mi. USAC Championship Race
A. J. Foyt   "Sheraton-Thompson Spl."
:57:24.0   104.530 mph

Apr. 26   Riverside 2.8-mi. Road Course
Riverside, Calif.
210-mi. USRRC Sports Car Race
Spi Hudson   "Nickey-Cooper"   95.8 mph

May 3   Indianapolis Raceway Park 2½-mi.
Road Course
Clermont, Ind.
300-mi. NASCAR Stock Car Race
Fred Lorenzen   "Ford"   79.127 mph

May 10   Darlington 1⅜-mi. Paved Speedway
Darlington, S.C.
300-mi. NASCAR Stock Car Race
Fred Lorenzen   "Ford"   130.013 mph

May 10   Pacific Raceway 2.25-mi. Road
Course
Kent, Wash.
153-mi. USRRC Sports Car Race
Dave MacDonald   "Cooper-Cobra"
91.5 mph

May 24   Charlotte 1½-mi. Paved Speedway
Charlotte, N.C.
600-mi. NASCAR Stock Car Race
Jim Paschal   "Plymouth"   4:46:15.0
125.764 mph

May 30   Indianapolis 2½-mi. Motor
Speedway
Indianapolis, Ind.
500-mi. USAC Championship Race
A. J. Foyt   "Sheraton-Thompson Spl."
3:23:35.83   147.35 mph

June 3   Atlanta 1½-mi. Paved Speedway
Hampton, Ga.
400-mi. NASCAR Stock Car Race
Ned Jarrett   "Ford"   112.500 mph

June 7   Milwaukee 1-mi. Paved Speedway
West Allis, Wis.
100-mi. USAC Championship Race
A. J. Foyt   "Sheraton-Thompson Spl."
:59:47.581   100.346 mph

June 21   Langhorne 1-mi. Dirt Track
Langhorne, Pa.
100-mi. USAC Championship Race
A. J. Foyt   "Sheraton-Thompson Spl."
:58:30.41   102.4 mph

July 4   Daytona 2½-mi. Paved Tri-oval
Speedway
Daytona Beach, Fla.
400-mi. NASCAR Stock Car Race
A. J. Foyt   "Dodge"   2:38:28.0
151.451 mph

July 12   Bridgehampton 2.85-mi. Road
Course
Bridgehampton, Long Island, N.Y.
142.5-mi. NASCAR Stock Car Race
Billy Wade   "Mercury"   1:37:29.0
86.10 mph

July 19   Trenton 1-mi. Paved Speedway
Trenton, N.J.
150-mi. USAC Championship Race
A. J. Foyt   "Sheraton-Thompson Spl."
1:25:14.11   105.590 mph

July 19   Greenwood Raceway 3-mi. Road
Course
Indianola, Iowa
165-mi. USRRC Sports Car Race
Ed Leslie   "Cooper-Ford"   87.24 mph

Aug. 9   Meadowdale Raceway 3.25-mi.
Road Course
Carpentersville, Ill.
170-mi. USRRC Sports Car Race
Jim Hall   "Chaparral"   95.40 mph

Aug. 23   Milwaukee 1-mi. Paved Speedway
West Allis, Wis.
200-mi. USAC Championship Race
Parnelli Jones   "Lotus-Ford"   1:54:33.473
104.751 mph

Aug. 30   Springfield 1-mi. Dirt Track
Springfield, Ill.
100-mi. USAC Stock Car Race

Bobby Marshman "Ford" 1:08:00.0
88.2 mph

Aug. 30 Mid-Ohio 2.4-mi. Road Course
Lexington, Ohio
168-mi. USRRC Sports Car Race
Hap Sharp "Chaparral" 80.33 mph

Sept. 7 DuQuoin 1-mi. Dirt Track
DuQuoin, Ill.
100-mi. USAC Championship Race
A. J. Foyt "Sheraton-Thompson Spl."
1:01:22.0 97.8 mph

Sept. 7 Darlington 1⅜-mi. Paved Speedway
Darlington, S.C.
500-mi. NASCAR Stock Car Race
Buck Baker "Dodge" 117.757 mph

Sept. 13 Road America 4-mi. Road Course
Elkhart Lake, Wis.
500-mi. USRRC Sports Car Race
Walter Hansgen/Augie Pabst "Ferrari"
87.660 mph

Sept. 20 Bridgehampton 2.85-mi. Road
Course
Bridgehampton, Long Island, N.Y.
500-km. Sports Car Race
Walter Hansgen "Zerex Spl." 92.9 mph

Sept. 26 Indiana Fairgrounds 1-mi. Dirt
Track
Indianapolis, Ind.
100-mi. USAC Championship Race
A. J. Foyt "Sheraton-Thompson Spl."
1:04:08.40 93.54 mph

Sept. 27 Trenton 1-mi. Paved Speedway
Trenton, N.J.
200-mi. USAC Championship Race
Parnelli Jones "Lotus-Ford" 2:04:27.70
96.415 mph

Oct. 2 Bonneville Salt Flats
Wendover, Utah
1-mi. Straightaway World's Record Run
Tom Green "Wingfoot Express"
413.2 mph

Oct. 4 Watkins Glen 2.3-mi. Road Course
Watkins Glen, N.Y.
253-mi. F.I.A. Grand Prix of U.S.
Graham Hill "BRM" 2:16:38.0
111.10 mph

Oct. 5 Bonneville Salt Flats
Wendover, Utah
1-mi. Straightaway World's Record Run
Art Arfons "Green Monster" 434.02 mph

Oct. 11 Riverside 2.6-mi. Road Course
Riverside, Calif.
200.2-mi. Sports Car Race
Parnelli Jones "Cobra-Cooper-Ford"
2:01:20.0 99.24 mph

Oct. 13 Bonneville Salt Flats
Wendover, Utah
1-mi. Straightaway World's Record Run
Craig Breedlove "Spirit of America"
468.72 mph

Oct. 18 Laguna Seca 1.9-mi. Road Course
Monterey, Calif.
2—100-mi. Sports Car Races
1st Race
Roger Penske "Chaparral" 94.5 mph
2nd Race
Roger Penske "Chaparral" 93.2 mph

Oct. 18 Charlotte 1½-mi. Paved Speedway
Charlotte, N.C.
400-mi. NASCAR Stock Car Race
Fred Lorenzen "Ford" 2:53:34.0
134.404 mph

Oct. 25 Sacramento 1-mi. Dirt Track
Sacramento, Calif.
100-mi. USAC Championship Race
A. J. Foyt "Sheraton-Thompson Spl."
1:05:36.0 91.4 mph

Oct. 27 Bonneville Salt Flats
Wendover, Utah
1-mi. Straightaway World's Record Run
Art Arfons "Green Monster" 536.71 mph

Nov. 1 Augusta 1-mi. Paved Speedway
Augusta, Ga.
300-mi. NASCAR Stock Car Race
Darel Dieringer "Mercury" 2:11:07.0
68.641 mph

Nov. 22 Phoenix 1-mi. Paved Speedway
Phoenix, Ariz.
200-mi. USAC Championship Race
Lloyd Ruby "Forbes Spl." 1:51:23.00
107.736 mph

1965

Jan. 17 Riverside 2.7-mi. Road Course
Riverside, Calif.
500-mi. NASCAR Stock Car Race
Dan Gurney "Ford" 5:41:42.0
87.708 mph

Feb. 14 Daytona 2½-mi. Paved Tri-oval
Speedway
Daytona Beach, Fla.
500-mi. NASCAR Stock Car Race—
Halted at 332.5 mi. due to rain.
Fred Lorenzen "Ford" 2:20:56.0
141.539 mph

Feb. 28 Daytona 3.81-mi. Road Course
Daytona Beach, Fla.
2000 kms (1243-mi.) Sports Car Race
Ken Miles/Lloyd Ruby "Ford GT 40"
12:27:09.0 99.94 mph

Mar. 27 Sebring 5.2-mi. Airport Course
Sebring, Fla.
12-hr. Sports Car Race
Jim Hall/Hal Sharp "Chaparral"
1019.2 mi. 84.72 mph

Mar. 28 Phoenix 1-mi. Paved Speedway
Phoenix, Ariz.
150-mi. USAC Championship Race
Don Branson "Wynn's Friction Proofing
Spl." 1:24:32.53 106.456 mph

Apr. 11 Atlanta 1½-mi. Paved Speedway
Hampton, Ga.
500-mi. NASCAR Stock Car Race
Marvin Panch/A. J. Foyt "Ford"
129.152 mph

Apr. 11 Pensacola 3-mi. Road Course
Pensacola, Fla.
201-mi. USRRC SCCA Sports Car Race
George Follmer "Lotus-Porsche"
92.073 mph

Apr. 25 Trenton 1-mi. Paved Speedway
Trenton, N.J.
100-mi. USAC Championship Race—
Halted at 87 miles due to rain.
Jim McElreath "Zink-Urschel Slick
Trackburner Spl." 97 mph

May 2 Riverside 2.6-mi. Road Course
Riverside, Calif.
182-mi. USRRC SCCA Sports Car Race
Jim Hall "Chaparral" 100.346 mph

May 9 Darlington 1⅜-mi. Paved Speedway
Darlington, S.C.
300-mi. NASCAR Stock Car Race
Junior Johnson "Ford" 2:41:38.0
111.775 mph

May 9 Laguna Seca 1.9-mi. Road Course
Monterey, Calif.
151.68-mi. USRRC SCCA Sports Car Race
Jim Hall "Chaparral" 94.622 mph

May 23 Charlotte 1½-mi. Paved Speedway
Charlotte, N.C.
600-mi. NASCAR Stock Car Race
Fred Lorenzen "Ford" 4:55:38.0
121.772 mph

May 23 Bridgehampton 2.85-mi. Road
Course
Bridgehampton, Long Island, N.Y.
213.75-mi. USRRC SCCA Sports Car Race
Jim Hall "Chaparral Chevy" 2:11:35.6
97.46 mph

May 31 Indianapolis 2½-mi. Motor
Speedway
Indianapolis, Ind.
500-mi. USAC Championship Race
Jimmy Clark "Lotus-Ford" 3:19:05.34
150.686 mph

June 6 Milwaukee 1-mi. Paved Speedway
West Allis, Wis.
100-mi. USAC Championship Race
Parnelli Jones :58:58.200 101.743 mph

June 13 Atlanta 1½-mi. Paved Speedway
Hampton, Ga.
400-mi. NASCAR Stock Car Race
Marvin Panch "Plymouth" 110.394 mph

June 20 Langhorne 1-mi. Paved Speedway
Langhorne, Pa.
100-mi. USAC Championship Race
Jim McElreath "Brabham-Offenhauser"
89.108 mph

June 27 Watkins Glen 2.3-mi. Road Course
Watkins Glen, N.Y.
200-mi. USRRC SCCA Sports Car Race
Jim Hall "Chaparral" 99.11 mph

July 4 Daytona 2½-mi. Paved Tri-oval
Speedway
Daytona Beach, Fla.
400-mi. NASCAR Stock Car Race
A. J. Foyt "Ford" 2:39:57.0 150.046 mph

July 11 Milwaukee 1-mi. Paved Speedway
West Allis, Wis.
200-mi. USAC Stock Car Race
Norm Nelson "Plymouth" 2:12:57.085
90.25 mph

July 18 Trenton 1-mi. Paved Speedway
Trenton, N.J.
150-mi. USAC Championship Race
A. J. Foyt "Sheraton-Thompson Spl."
1:31:20.77 98.526 mph

July 18 Watkins Glen 2.3-mi. Road Course
Watkins Glen, N.Y.
151.8-mi. NASCAR Stock Car Race
Marvin Panch "Ford" 98.43 mph

July 25 Indianapolis Raceway Park
1.875-mi. Road Course
Clermont, Ind.
150-mi. USAC Championship Race
Mario Andretti "Dean Van Lines Spl."
1:28:32.0 101.656 mph

Aug. 1 Atlanta 1½-mi. Paved Speedway
Hampton, Ga.
250-mi. USAC Championship Race
Johnny Rutherford "Moog St. Louis Spl."
1:46:28.7 141.728 mph

Aug. 1 Pacific Raceway 2.25-mi. Road
Course
Kent, Wash.
153-mi. USRRC SCCA Sports Car Race
Jim Hall "Chaparral II" 89.459 mph

Aug. 8 Langhorne 1-mi. Paved Speedway
Langhorne, Pa.
125-mi. USAC Championship Race
Jim McElreath "Zink-Urschel Spl."
1:11:31.53 104.857 mph

Aug. 14 Milwaukee 1-mi. Paved Speedway
West Allis, Wis.
150-mi. USAC Championship Race
Joe Leonard "All American Racers Spl."
97.276 mph

Aug. 14 Milwaukee 1-mi. Paved Speedway
West Allis, Wis.
150-mi. USAC Championship Race
Joe Leonard "All American Racers Spl."
1:32:31.150 97.276 mph

Aug. 21 Springfield 1-mi. Dirt Track
Springfield, Ill.
100-mi. USAC Championship Race
A. J. Foyt "Sheraton-Thompson Spl."
1:02:23.22 96.1 mph

Aug. 22 Milwaukee 1-mi. Paved Speedway
West Allis, Wis.
200-mi. USAC Championship Race
Gordon Johncock "Weinberger Homes
Spl." 1:59:27.520 100.470 mph

Sept. 6 DuQuoin 1-mi. Dirt Track
DuQuoin, Ill.
100-mi. USAC Championship Race
Don Branson "Wynn's Spl." 1:07:34.43
88.792 mph

Sept. 6 Darlington 1⅜-mi. Paved Speedway
Darlington, S.C.
500-mi. NASCAR Stock Car Race
Ned Jarrett "Ford" 4:19:09.0
115.878 mph

Sept. 5 Road America 4-mi. Road Course
Elkhart Lake, Wis.
500-mi. USRRC SCCA Sports Car Race
Hap Sharp/Jim Hall/Ron Hisson
"Chaparral II" 5:35:06.0 89.526 mph

Sept. 18 Indiana Fairgrounds 1-mi. Dirt
Track
Indianapolis, Ind.
100-mi. USAC Championship Race
A. J. Foyt "Sheraton-Thompson Spl."
1:10:42.85 84.907 mph

Sept. 19 Bridgehampton 2.85-mi. Road
Course
Bridgehampton, Long Island, N.Y.
310.2-mi. Sports Car Race
Hap Sharp "Chaparral II" 3:13:57.9
97.35 mph

Sept. 26 Trenton 1-mi. Paved Speedway
Trenton, N.J.

200-mi. USAC Championship Race
A. J. Foyt "Sheraton-Thompson Spl."
2:00:03.37 99.953 mph

Oct. 3 Watkins Glen 2.3-mi. Road Course
Watkins Glen, N.Y.
253-mi. Grand Prix of U.S.
Graham Hill "BRM" 2:20:36.1
107.98 mph

Oct. 10 Pacific Raceway 2.25-mi. Road
Course
Kent, Wash.
2—100-mi. Sports Car Races
1st Race
Jim Hall "Chaparral 2C" 1:02:31.4
97.3 mph
2nd Race
Jim Hall "Chaparral 2C" 1:03:29.8
93.3 mph

Oct. 17 Charlotte 1½-mi. Paved Speedway
Charlotte, N.C.
400-mi. NASCAR Stock Car Race
Fred Lorenzen "Ford" 3:21:44.0
119.117 mph

Oct. 17 Laguna Seca 1.9-mi. Road Course
Monterey, Calif.
2—100.7-mi. Sports Car Races
1st Race
Walter Hansgen "Lola Zerex Spl."
98.2 mph
2nd Race
Walter Hansgen "Lola Zerex Spl."
96.2 mph

Oct. 24 Sacramento 1-mi. Dirt Track
Sacramento, Calif.
100-mi. USAC Championship Race
Don Branson "Wynn's Spl." 1:09:30.0
86.355 mph

Oct. 26 Bonneville Salt Flats
Wendover, Utah
1-mi. Straightaway World's Record Run
Craig Breedlove "Spirit of America—
Sonic I" 555.127 mph

Oct. 31 Rockingham 1.017-mi. Paved
Speedway (Inaugural)
Rockingham, N.C.
500-mi. NASCAR Stock Car Race
Curtis Turner "Ford" 4:54:17.0
101.942 mph

Oct. 31 Riverside 2.6-mi. Road Course
Riverside, Calif.
200-mi. Sports Car Race
Hap Sharp "Chaparral" 1:56:28.0
102.989 mph

Nov. 7 Bonneville Salt Flats
Wendover, Utah
1-mi. Straightaway World's Record Run
Art Arfons "Green Monster" 576.55 mph

Nov. 12 Bonneville Salt Flats
Wendover, Utah
World's 1-mi. Land Speed Record Run
(For Piston-Engined Car)
Bob Summers "Golden Rod" 409.277 mph

Nov. 14 Stardust 3-mi. Road Course
(Inaugural)
Las Vegas, Nev.
195-mi. Sports Car Race
Hap Sharp "Chaparral" 106.68 mph

Nov. 15 Bonneville Salt Flats
Wendover, Utah
1-mi. Straightaway World's Record Run
Craig Breedlove "Spirit of America—
Sonic I" 600.601 mph

Nov. 21 Phoenix 1-mi. Paved Speedway
Phoenix, Ariz.
200-mi. USAC Championship Race
A. J. Foyt "Sheraton-Thompson Spl."
2:00:01.00 99.998 mph

1966

Jan. 23 Riverside 2.7-mi. Road Course
Riverside, Calif.
500-mi. Stock Car Race
Dan Gurney "Ford" 5:05:59.0
97.946 mph

Feb. 6 Daytona 3.81-mi. Road Course
Daytona Beach, Fla.
24-hr. Sports Car Race
Ken Miles/Lloyd Ruby "Ford GT"
2570.63 miles 107.952 mph

Feb. 27 Daytona 2½-mi. Paved Tri-oval
Speedway
Daytona Beach, Fla.
500-mi. NASCAR Stock Car Race—
Halted at 495 miles due to rain.
Richard Petty "Plymouth" 3:04:54.0
160.627 mph

Mar. 13 Rockingham 1.017-mi. Paved
Speedway
Rockingham, N.C.
500-mi. NASCAR Stock Car Race
Paul Goldsmith "Plymouth" 4:59:55.0
100.027 mph

Mar. 20 Phoenix 1-mi. Paved Speedway
Phoenix, Ariz.
150-mi. USAC Championship Race
Jim McElreath "Zink-Urschel-Slick
Trackburner Spl." 1:31:04.54 98.828 mph

Mar. 26 Sebring 5.2-mi. Airport Course
Sebring, Fla.
12-hr. Sports Car Race
Ken Miles/Lloyd Ruby "Ford"
1185.6 miles 98.572 mph

Mar. 27 Atlanta 1½-mi. Paved Speedway
Hampton, Ga.
500-mi. NASCAR Stock Car Race
Jim Hurtubise "Plymouth" 3:49.02.0
131.247 mph

Apr. 24 Stardust 3.0-mi. Road Course
Las Vegas, Nev.
180-mi. USRRC Sports Car Race
John Cannon "Vinegaroon-Chevy"
99.4 mph

Apr. 24 Trenton 1-mi. Paved Speedway
Trenton, N.J.
150-mi. USAC Championship Race—
Halted at 102 miles due to rain.
Rodger Ward "American Red Ball Spl."
1:01:15.51 99.904 mph

May 1 "Rebel 400"
Darlington 1⅜-mi. Paved Speedway
Darlington, S.C.
400-mi. NASCAR Stock Car Race
Richard Petty "Plymouth" 3:01:53.0
131.585 mph

May 1 Riverside 2.65-mi. Road Course
Riverside, Calif.
182-mi. USRRC Sports Car Race
Buck Fulp "Lola-Chevrolet" 1:49:26.0
99.78 mph

May 8 Laguna Seca 1.9-mi. Road Course
Monterey, Calif.
152-mi. USRRC Sports Car Race
Charlie Hayes "McLaren-Chevrolet"
95.50 mph

May 22 "Vanderbilt Cup"
Bridgehampton 2.85-mi. Road Course
Bridgehampton, Long Island, N.Y.
199.5-mi. USRRC Sports Car Race
Jerry Grant "Bardahl-Lola" 98.39 mph

May 22 "World 600"
Charlotte 1½-mi. Paved Speedway
Charlotte, N.C.
600-mi. NASCAR Stock Car Race
Marvin Panch "Plymouth" 4:26:35.0
135.04 mph

May 30 Indianapolis 2½-mi. Motor
Speedway
Speedway, Ind.
500-mi. USAC Championship Race
Graham Hill "American Red Ball Spl."
3:27:52.53 144.317 mph

June 5 Milwaukee 1-mi. Paved Speedway
West Allis, Wis.
100-mi. USAC Championship Race
Mario Andretti "Dean Van Lines Spl."
1:02:43.525 96.515 mph

June 12 Langhorne 1-mi. Paved Speedway
Langhorne, Pa.
100-mi. USAC Championship Race
Mario Andretti "Dean Van Lines Spl."
1:00:47.78 98.690 mph

June 12 Mid-America Raceway 2.8-mi.
Road Course
St. Louis, Mo.
300-mi. SCCA Trans-Am Race
Tom Yeager/Bob Johnson "Ford Mustang"
4:07:00.0 75.2 mph

June 26 Atlanta 1½-mi. Paved Speedway
Hampton, Ga.
300-mi. USAC Championship Race
Mario Andretti "Dean Van Lines Spl."
2:09:12.0 139.319 mph

June 26 Watkins Glen 2.3-mi. Road Course
Watkins Glen, N.Y.
200.1-mi. USRRC Sports Car Race
Buck Fulp "Lola-Chevrolet" 1:58:20.4
101.46 mph

July 4 "Firecracker 400"
Daytona 2½-mi. Paved Tri-oval Speedway
Daytona Beach, Fla.
400-mi. NASCAR Stock Car Race
Sam McQuagg "Dodge Charger"
2:31:02.0 153.818 mph

July 10 Bridgehampton 2.85-mi. Road
Course
Bridgehampton, Long Island, N.Y.
150-mi. NASCAR Stock Car Race
David Pearson "Dodge" 88.3 mph

July 10 Bryar Motorsport Park 1.6-mi. Road
Course
Louden, N.H.
250-mi. SCCA Trans-Am Race
Allan Moffatt "Lotus Cortina" 68.18 mph

July 24 Indianapolis Raceway Park
1.875-mi. Road Course
Clermont, Ind.
150-mi. USAC Championship Race
Mario Andretti "Dean Van Lines Spl."
1:34:22.0 95.373 mph

July 31 Pacific Raceway 2.25-mi. Road
Course
Kent, Wash.
157.5-mi. USRRC Sports Car Race
Mark Donohue "Lola-Chevrolet" 96.2 mph

July 31 Virginia International Raceway
3.2-mi. Road Course
Danville, Va.
400-mi. SCCA Trans-Am Race
Bob Johnson/Tom Yeager "Ford Mustang"
5:22:00:0 74.5 mph

Aug. 3 Atlanta 1½-mi. Paved Speedway
Hampton, Ga.
400-mi. NASCAR Stock Car Race
Richard Petty "Plymouth" 130.057 mph

Aug. 7 Langhorne 1-mi. Paved Speedway
Langhorne, Pa.
150-mi. USAC Championship Race
Roger McCluskey "G. C. Murphy Spl."
1:22:57.25 108.493 mph

Aug. 20 Springfield 1-mi. Dirt Track
Springfield, Ill.
100-mi. USAC Championship Race
Don Branson "Leader Card Spl."
1:02:59.79 95.243 mph

Aug. 27 Milwaukee 1-mi. Paved Speedway
West Allis, Wis.
200-mi. USAC Championship Race
Mario Andretti "Dean Van Lines Spl."
1:55:19.088 104.061 mph

Aug. 28 Mid-Ohio Raceway 2.4-mi. Road
Course
Lexington, Ohio
204-mi. USRRC SCCA Sports Car Race
Lothar Motschenbacher "McLaren-Olds"
2:55:22.2 84.13 mph

Sept. 4 Road America 4-mi. Road Course
Elkhart Lake, Wis.
500-mi. USRRC Sports Car Race
Chuck Parsons "McLaren-Chevrolet"
92.879 mph

Sept. 5 DuQuoin 1-mi. Dirt Track
DuQuoin, Ill.
100-mi. USAC Championship Race
Bud Tingelstad "Federal Engineering Spl."
1:03:05.42 95.102 mph

Sept. 5 "Southern 500"
Darlington 1⅜-mi. Paved Speedway
Darlington, S.C.
500-mi. NASCAR Stock Car Race
Darel Dieringer "Comet" 4:21:51.0
115.403 mph

Sept. 10 Indiana Fairgrounds 1-mi. Dirt
Track
Indianapolis, Ind.
100-mi. USAC Championship Race
Mario Andretti "Dean Van Lines Spl."
1:02:07.40 96.582 mph

Sept. 10 Green Valley Raceway 1.58-mi.
Road Course
Smithfield, Texas
6-hr. SCCA Trans-Am. Race
John McComb/Brad Brooker "Ford
Mustang" 248 laps-391.84 miles
65.306 mph

Sept. 18 Bridgehampton 2.85-mi. Road
Course
Bridgehampton, Long Island, N.Y.
199.5-mi. SCCA Can-Am Race
Dan Gurney "Lola-Ford" 1:53:48.5
105.58 mph

Sept. 18 Riverside 2.6-mi. Road Course
Riverside, Calif.
351-mi. SCCA Trans-Am Race
Jerry Titus "Ford Mustang" 4:01:00.0
87.297 mph

Sept. 25 Trenton 1-mi. Paved Speedway
Trenton, N.J.
200-mi. USAC Championship Race
Mario Andretti "Dean Van Lines Spl."
1:54:08.84 105.127 mph

Oct. 2 Watkins Glen 2.3-mi. Road Course
Watkins Glen, N.Y.
248.4-mi. F.I.A. Grand Prix of U.S.
Jim Clark "Lotus-BRM" 2:09:40.1
114.94 mph

Oct. 9 "Northwest GP"
Pacific Raceway 2.25-mi. Road Course
Kent, Wash.
2—101.25-mi. Sports Car Races
1st Race
Chuck Parsons "McLaren-Chevy" 98 mph
2nd Race
Chuck Parsons "McLaren-Chevy" 94 mph

Oct. 16 "National 500"
Charlotte 1½-mi. Paved Speedway
Charlotte, N.C.
500-mi. NASCAR Stock Car Race
Lee Roy Yarbrough "Dodge Charger"
3:49:45.0 130.576 mph

Oct. 16 Laguna Seca 1.9-mi. Road Course
Monterey, Calif.
2—53-lap, 100.7-mi. SCCA Can-Am Races
1st Race
Phil Hill "Chaparral-Chevy" 98.3 mph
2nd Race
Parnelli Jones "Lola-Chevrolet" 98.9 mph

Oct. 23 Sacramento 1-mi. Dirt Track
Sacramento, Calif.
100-mi. USAC Championship Race
Dick Atkins "Agajanian Rev 500 Spl."
1:07:44.69 88.568 mph

Oct. 30 "American 500"
Rockingham 1.017-mi. Paved Speedway
Rockingham, N.C.
500-mi. NASCAR Stock Car Race
Frod Lorenzen "Ford" 104.347 mph

Oct. 30 Riverside 3.275-mi. Road Course
Riverside, Calif.
203.5-mi. SCCA Can-Am Race
John Surtees "Lola-Chevrolet"
106.864 mph

Nov. 13 "Stardust GP"
Stardust 3.0-mi. Road Course
Las Vegas, Nev.
210-mi. SCCA Can-Am Race
John Surtees "Lola-Chevrolet" 1:55:27.5
109.25 mph

Nov. 20 Phoenix 1-mi. Paved Speedway
Phoenix, Ariz.
200-mi. USAC Championship Race
Mario Andretti "Dean Van Lines Spl."
1:54:37.68 104.697 mph

1967

Jan. 29 "Motor Trend 500"
Riverside 2.7-mi. Road Course
Riverside, Calif.

500-mi. NASCAR Stock Car Race
Parnelli Jones "Ford Fairlane" 5:29:03.0
91.080 mph

Feb. 3 Daytona Speedway 3.81-mi. Road Course
Daytona Beach, Fla.
300.99-mi. SCCA Trans-Am Race
Bob Tullius "Dodge Dart" 3:01:56.0
99.361 mph

Feb. 5 "Daytona Continental"
Daytona Speedway 3.81-mi. Road Course
Daytona Beach, Fla.
24-hr. Sports Car Race
Chris Amon/Lorenzo Bandini "Ferrari"
2537.46 miles 105.4 mph

Feb. 26 "Daytona 500"
Daytona 2½-mi. Paved Tri-oval Speedway
Daytona Beach, Fla.
500-mi. NASCAR Stock Car Race
Mario Andretti "Ford Fairlane" 3:24:11.0
146.926 mph

Mar. 31 Sebring 5.2-mi. Airport Course
Sebring, Fla.
4-hr. SCCA Trans-Am Race
Jerry Titus "Ford Mustang" 379.6 miles
94.824 mph

Apr. 1 Sebring 5.2-mi. Airport Course
Sebring, Fla.
12-hr. Sports Car Race
Mario Andretti/Bruce McLaren "Ford GT
Mk. IV" 1237.6 miles 103.0 mph

Apr. 2 "Atlanta 500"
Atlanta 1½-mi. Paved Speedway
Hampton, Ga.
500-mi. NASCAR Stock Car Race
Cale Yarborough "Ford" 3:49:06.0
148.996 mph

Apr. 9 "Jimmy Bryan 150"
Phoenix 1-mi. Paved Speedway
Phoenix, Ariz.
150-mi. USAC Championship Race
Lloyd Ruby "Gene White Brabham Spl."
1:44:17.60 86.296 mph

Apr. 16 Green Valley Raceway 1.6-mi.
Road Course
Smithfield, Texas
300.8-mi. SCCA Trans-Am Race
Dan Gurney "Mercury Cougar" 3:55:13.0
75.9 mph

Apr. 23 Trenton 1-mi. Paved Speedway
Trenton, N.J.
150-mi. USAC Championship Race
Mario Andretti "Dean Van Lines Spl."
1:21:56.35 109.837 mph

Apr. 23 Stardust Raceway 3-mi. Road
Course
Las Vegas, Nev.
183-mi. USRRC SCCA Sports Car Race
Mark Donohue "Lola-Chevrolet" 1:42:41.8
106.91 mph

Apr. 30 Riverside 2.6-mi. Road Course
Riverside, Calif.
182-mi. USRRC SCCA Sports Car Race
Mark Donohue "Lola-Chevrolet" 1:43:47.6
105.21 mph

May 7 Laguna Seca 1.9-mi. Road Course
Monterey, Calif.
159.6-mi. USRRC SCCA Sports Car Race
Lothar Motschenbacher "McLaren-
Chevrolet" 1:44:31.0 91.6 mph

May 13 "Rebel 400"
Darlington 1⅜-mi. Paved Speedway
Darlington, S.C.
400-mi. NASCAR Stock Car Race
Richard Petty "Plymouth" 3:11:02.0
125.671 mph

May 21 Bridgehampton 2.85-mi. Road
Course
Bridgehampton, Long Island, N.Y.
199.5-mi. USRRC SCCA Sports Car Race
Mark Donohue "Lola-Chevrolet" 1:56:07.4
103.6 mph

May 28 "World 600"
Charlotte 1½-mi. Paved Speedway
Charlotte, N.C.
600-mi. NASCAR Stock Car Race
Jim Paschal "Plymouth" 4:25:03.0
135.823 mph

May 30 Lime Rock 1.53-mi. Road Course
Lime Rock, Conn.
4-hr. SCCA Trans-Am Race
Peter Revson "Mercury Cougar"
328.5 miles 83.651 mph

May 31 Indianapolis 2½-mi. Motor
Speedway
Speedway, Ind.
500-mi USAC Championship Race—
Halted at 45 miles due to rain and run to
finish May 31.
A. J. Foyt "Sheraton-Thompson Spl."
3:18:24.22 151.207 mph

June 4 "Rex Mays Classic"
Milwaukee 1-mi. Paved Speedway
West Allis, Wis.
150-mi. USAC Championship Race
Gordon Johncock "Gilmore Broadcasting
Spl." 1:31:14.3 98.644 mph

June 11 Mid-Ohio 2.4-mi. Road Course
Lexington, Ohio
300-mi. SCCA Trans-Am Race
Jerry Titus "Ford Mustang" 3:54:51.2
76.664 mph

June 18 Langhorne 1-mi. Paved Speedway
Langhorne, Pa.
100-mi. USAC Championship Race
Lloyd Ruby "American Red Ball Spl."
:52:55.16 113.38 mph

June 18 "Carolina 500"
Rockingham 1.017-mi. Paved Speedway
Rockingham, N.C.
500-mi. NASCAR Stock Car Race
Richard Petty "Plymouth" 4:46:35.0
104.432 mph

June 25 Watkins Glen 2.3-mi. Road Course
Watkins Glen, N.Y.
200.1-mi. USRRC SCCA Sports Car Race
Mark Donohue "Lola-Chevrolet" 1:53:24.4
105.87 mph

July 4 "Firecracker 400"
Daytona 2½-mi. Paved Tri-oval Speedway
Daytona Beach, Fla.
400-mi. NASCAR Stock Car Race
Cale Yarborough "Ford Fairlane"
2:47:09.0 143.583 mph

July 4 "Paul Revere 250"
Daytona Speedway 3.81-mi. Road Course
Daytona Beach, Fla.
250-mi. SCCA Trans-Am Race
Parnelli Jones "Mercury Cougar"
106.075 mph

July 9 "Northern 300"
Trenton 1-mi. Paved Speedway
Trenton, N.J.
300-mi. NASCAR Stock Car Race
Richard Petty "Plymouth" 3:08:10.0
85.322 mph

July 16 Pacific Raceway 2.25-mi. Road
Course
Kent, Wash.
157.5-mi. USRRC SCCA Sports Car Race
Mark Donohue "Lola-Chevrolet" 1:37:07.1
97.27 mph

July 23 "Hoosier GP"
Indianapolis Raceway Park 1.875-mi. Road
Course
Clermont, Ind.
150-mi. USAC Championship Race
Mario Andretti "Dean Van Lines Spl."
1:19:13.06 113.612 mph

July 30 Langhorne 1-mi. Paved Speedway
Langhorne, Pa.
150-mi. USAC Championship Race
Mario Andretti "Dean Van Lines Spl."
1:19:31.0 113.183 mph

July 30 "Road America 500"
Road America 4-mi. Road Course
Elkhart Lake, Wis.
500-mi. USRRC SCCA Sports Car Race
Chuck Parsons/Skip Scott "McLaren-
Chevrolet" 5:23:42.8 92.67 mph

Aug. 6 Bryar Motorsport Park 1.6-mi. Road
Course
Loudon, N.H.
249.6-mi. SCCA Trans-Am Race
Peter Revson "Mercury Cougar" 3:22:03.0
74.12 mph

Aug. 6 "Dixie 500"
Atlanta 1½-mi. Paved Speedway
Hampton, Ga.
500-mi. NASCAR Stock Car Race
Dick Hutcherson "Ford" 3:47:18.0
132.248 mph

Aug. 13 Marlboro Park 1.7-mi. Road Course
Upper Marlboro, Md.
301-mi. SCCA Trans-Am Race
Mark Donohue/Craig Fisher "Chevrolet
Camaro" 4:45:30.0 63.23 mph

Aug. 19 Springfield 1-mi. Dirt Track
Springfield, Ill.
100-mi. USAC Championship Race
A. J. Foyt "Sheraton-Thompson Spl."
1:09:30.22 86.323 mph

Aug. 20 Milwaukee 1-mi. Paved Speedway
West Allis, Wis.
200-mi. USAC Championship Race
Mario Andretti "Dean Van Lines Spl."
1:53:52.03 105.386 mph

Aug. 20 "Buckeye Cup"
Mid-Ohio 2.4-mi. Road Course
Lexington, Ohio
204-mi. USRRC SCCA Sports Car Race
Mark Donohue "McLaren-Chevrolet"
2:17:11.0 87.11 mph

Aug. 27 Continental Divide 2.8-mi. Road
Course
Castle Rock, Colo.
263.2-mi. SCCA Trans-Am Race
Jerry Titus "Ford Mustang" 3:26:00.0
76.09 mph

Sept. 3 Road America 4-mi. Road Course
Elkhart Lake, Wis.
200-mi. SCCA Can-Am Race
Denis Hulme "McLaren-Chevrolet"
1:54:53.0 104.454 mph

Sept. 4 DuQuoin 1-mi. Dirt Track
DuQuoin, Ill.
100-mi. USAC Championship Race
A. J. Foyt "Sheraton-Thompson Spl."
1:04:07.05 93.579 mph

Sept. 4 "Southern 500"
Darlington 1⅜-mi. Paved Speedway
Darlington, S.C.
500-mi. NASCAR Stock Car Race
Richard Petty "Plymouth" 3:50:15.0
130.423 mph

Sept. 9 "Hoosier Hundred"
Indiana Fairgrounds 1-mi. Dirt Track
Indianapolis, Ind.
100-mi. USAC Championship Race
Mario Andretti "Dean Van Lines Spl."
1:02:47.80 95.546 mph

Sept. 10 Crow's Landing 3-mi. Road Course
Modesto, Calif.
3-hr. SCCA Trans-Am Race
Jerry Titus "Ford Mustang" 258 miles
85.2 mph

Sept. 17 Bridgehampton 2.85-mi. Road
Course
Bridgehampton, Long Island, N.Y.
199.5-mi. SCCA Can-Am Race
Denis Hulme "McLaren-Chevrolet"
1:50:07.6 109.13 mph

Sept. 17 Riverside 2.6-mi. Road Course
Riverside, Calif.
249.6-mi. SCCA Trans-Am Race
David Pearson "Mercury-Cougar"
2:39:41.6 94.719 mph

Sept. 24 Trenton 1-mi. Paved Speedway
Trenton, N.J.
200-mi. USAC Championship Race
A. J. Foyt "Sheraton-Thompson Spl."
2:10:07.15 92.223 mph

Oct. 1 Stardust Raceway 3-mi. Road Course
Las Vegas, Nev.
351-mi. SCCA Trans-Am Race
Mark Donohue "Chevrolet Camaro"
3:45:05.9 94.8 mph

Oct. 1 Sacramento 1-mi. Dirt Track
Sacramento, Calif.
100-mi. USAC Championship Race
A. J. Foyt "Sheraton-Thompson Spl."
1:08:25.32 87.69 mph

Oct. 1 Watkins Glen 2.3-mi. Road Course
Watkins Glen, N.Y.
248.4-mi. Formula I U.S. Grand Prix
Jim Clark "Lotus-Ford" 2:03:13.2
120.95 mph

Oct. 8 Pacific Raceway 2.25-mi. Road
Course
Kent, Wash.
303.75-mi. SCCA Trans-Am Race
Mark Donohue "Chevrolet Camaro"
3:28:05.8 87.6 mph

Oct. 15 Laguna Seca 1.9-mi. Road Course
Monterey, Calif.
201.4-mi. SCCA Can-Am Race
Bruce McLaren "McLaren-Chevrolet"
1:58:55.3 101.613 mph

Oct. 15 "National 500"
Charlotte 1½-mi. Paved Speedway
Charlotte, N.C.

500-mi. NASCAR Stock Car Race
Buddy Baker "Dodge Charger" 3:50:54.0
130.186 mph

Oct. 22 "California 200"
Hanford 1½-mi. Paved Speedway
Hanford, Calif.
200-mi. USAC Championship Race
Gordon Johncock "Gilmore Broadcasting
Spl." 1:34:34.29 127.523 mph

Oct. 29 "Times GP"
Riverside 3.275-mi. Road Course
Riverside, Calif.
203.05-mi. SCCA Can-Am Race
Bruce McLaren "McLaren-Chevrolet"
1:46:28.7 114.237 mph

Oct. 29 "American 500"
Rockingham 1.017-mi. Paved Speedway
Rockingham, N.C.
500-mi. NASCAR Stock Car Race
Bobby Allison "Ford" 98.42 mph

Nov. 12 Stardust Raceway 3-mi. Road
Course
Las Vegas, Nev.
210-mi. SCCA Can-Am Race
John Surtees "Lola Chevrolet" 1:52:05.5
113.41 mph

Nov. 19 Phoenix 1-mi. Paved Speedway
Phoenix, Ariz.
200-mi. USAC Championship Race
Mario Andretti "Dean Van Lines Spl."
1:49:13.07 109.872 mph

Nov. 26 "Rex Mays 300"
Riverside 2.6-mi. Road Course
Riverside, Calif.
301.6-mi. USAC Championship Race
Dan Gurney "Olsonite-Eagle Spl."
2:46:56.0 108.391 mph

1968

Jan. 21 "Motor Trend 500"
Riverside 2.7-mi. Road Course
Riverside, Calif.
500-mi. Stock Car Race
Dan Gurney "Ford Torino" 4:57:55.0
100.598 mph

Feb. 4 "24 Hours of Daytona"
Daytona Speedway 3.81-mi. Road Course
Daytona Beach, Fla.
24-hr. Sports Car Race
Vic Elford/Jochen Neerpasch "Porsche"
2526.69 miles 106.697 mph

Feb. 25 "Daytona 500"
Daytona 2½-mi. Paved Tri-oval Speedway
Daytona Beach, Fla.
500-mi. NASCAR Stock Car Race
Cale Yarborough "Mercury" 3:23:44.0
143.251 mph

Mar. 17 "California 200"
Hanford 1½-mi. Paved Speedway
Hanford, Calif.
200-mi. USAC Championship Race
Gordon Johncock "Johncock Racing Spl."
1:39:15.0 120.874 mph

Mar. 23 "12 Hours of Sebring"
Sebring 5.2-mi. Airport Course
Sebring, Fla.
12-hr. Sports Car Race
Hans Hermann/Jo Siffert "Porsche"
1232.4 miles 102.512 mph

Mar. 31 "Atlanta 500"
Atlanta 1½-mi. Paved Speedway
Hampton, Ga.
500-mi. NASCAR Stock Car Race
Cale Yarborough "Mercury" 3:59:24.0
125.564 mph

Mar. 31 "Stardust 150"
Stardust Raceway 3-mi. Road Course
Las Vegas, Nev.
150-mi. USAC Championship Race
Bobby Unser "Leader Card Rislone Spl."
1:19:27.40 113.1 mph

Apr. 7 Phoenix 1-mi. Paved Speedway
Phoenix, Ariz.
150-mi. USAC Championship Race
Bobby Unser "Rislone Eagle Spl."
1:29:24.53 100.003 mph

Apr. 21 Trenton 1-mi. Paved Speedway
Trenton, N.J.
150-mi. USAC Championship Race
Bobby Unser "Zecol Lubaid Spl."
1:27:02.57 103.397 mph

Apr. 28 Riverside 2.6-mi. Road Course
Riverside, Calif.
156-mi. USRRC SCCA Sport Car Race
Mark Donohue "McLaren-Chevrolet"
1:23:01.3 112.742 mph

May 5 Laguna Seca 1.9-mi. Road Course
Monterey, Calif.
152-mi. USRRC SCCA Sports Car Race
Mark Donohue "McLaren-Chevrolet"
1:26:17.99 105.68 mph

May 12 "Rebel 400"
Darlington 1⅜-mi. Paved Speedway
Darlington, S.C.
400-mi. NASCAR Stock Car Race
David Pearson "Ford" 3:00:55.0
132.699 mph

May 12 "War Bonnet 250"
War Bonnet Park 2.3-mi. Road Course
New Mannford, Okla.
253-mi. SCCA Trans-Am Race
Mark Donohue "Camaro" 3:03:53.4
82.549 mph

May 19 Bridgehampton 2.86-mi. Road
Course
Bridgehampton, Long Island, N.Y.
171-mi. USRRC SCCA Sports Car Race
Skip Scott "Simoniz Lola-Chevrolet"
1:35:29.8 107.868 mph

May 26 "World 600"
Charlotte 1½-mi. Paved Speedway
Charlotte, N.C.
600-mi. NASCAR Stock Car Race—
Halted at 382½ miles due to rain.
Buddy Baker "Dodge" 3:04:14.0
104.137 mph

May 30 Indianapolis 2½-mi. Motor
Speedway
Speedway, Ind.
500-mi. USAC Championship Race
Bobby Unser "Rislone Eagle Spl."
3:16:13.76 152.882 mph

May 30 Lime Rock Park 1.53-mi. Road
Course
Lime Rock, Conn.
261.63-mi. SCCA Trans-Am Race
Mark Donohue "Camaro" 3:48:49.0
87.21 mph

June 2 Mont Tremblant 1.53-mi. Road
Course

St. Jovite, Quebec, Can.
162-mi. USRRC SCCA Sports Car Race
Mark Donohue "McLaren-Chevrolet"
2:05:17.6   80.44 mph

June 9 "Rex Mays Memorial"
Milwaukee 1-mi. Paved Speedway
West Allis, Wis.
150-mi. USAC Championship Race
Lloyd Ruby "Gene White Spl." 1:29:20.38
100.739 mph

June 16 "Carolina 500"
Rockingham 1.017-mi. Paved Speedway
Rockingham, N.C.
500-mi. NASCAR Stock Car Race
Donnie Allison "Ford" 99.3 mph

June 23 Langhorne 1-mi. Paved Speedway
Langhorne, Pa.
150-mi. USAC Championship Race
Gordon Johncock "Gilmore Broadcasting
Spl." 1:26:59.21   103.464 mph

June 23 Bridgehampton 2.85-mi. Road
Course
Bridgehampton, Long Island, N.Y.
282.15-mi. SCCA Trans-Am Race
Mark Donohue "Camaro" 3:00:06.18
94.372 mph

June 30 Pacific Raceway 2.25-mi. Road
Course
Kent, Wash.
157.5-mi. USRRC SCCA Sports Car Race
Skip Scott "Lola-Chevrolet" 1:36:41.6
97.83 mph

July 4 "Firecracker 400"
Daytona 2½-mi. Paved Tri-oval Speedway
Daytona Beach, Fla.
400-mi. NASCAR Stock Car Race
Cale Yarborough "Mercury" 2:23:30.0
167.247 mph

July 7 "Rocky Mountain 150"
Continental Divide 2.66-mi. Road Course
Castle Rock, Colo.
150-mi. USAC Championship Race
A. J. Foyt "Sheraton-Thompson Spl."
1:49:23.0   83.17 mph

July 7 Meadowdale Raceway 3.2-mi. Road
Course
Carpentersville, Ill.
240-mi. SCCA Trans-Am Race
Mark Donohue "Camaro" 2:45:25.0
87.053 mph

July 13 Nazareth 1⅛-mi. Dirt Track
(Inaugural)
Nazareth, Pa.
100.125-mi. USAC Championship Race
Al Unser "Retzloff Chemical Spl."
1:00:01.05   100.095 mph

July 13 Watkins Glen 2.3-mi. Road Course
Watkins Glen, N.Y.
200.1-mi. USRRC SCCA Sports Car Race
Mark Donohue "McLaren-Chevrolet"
1:41:46.33   117.97 mph

July 14 "Northern 300"
Trenton 1-mi. Paved Speedway
Trenton, N.J.
300-mi. NASCAR Stock Car Race
Lee Roy Yarbrough "Ford Torino"
3:22:04.0   89.079 mph

July 14 Watkins Glen 2.3-mi. Road Course
Watkins Glen, N.Y.
6-hr. Sports Car Race

Jacky Ickx/Luzien Bianchi "Ford GT40"
657.8 miles   109.50 mph

July 21 "Indy 200"
Indianapolis Raceway Park 2.5-mi. Road
Course
Clermont, Ind.
2—100-mi. USAC Championship Races
1st Race:
Al Unser "Retzloff Chemical Spl."
1:01:59.2   96.795 mph
2nd Race:
Al Unser "Retzloff Chemical Spl."
86.768 mph

July 28 Langhorne 1-mi. Paved Speedway
Langhorne, Pa.
2—100-mi. USAC Championship Races
1st Race:
Al Unser "Retzloff Chemical Spl."
:55:44.15   107.650 mph
2nd Race:
Al Unser "Retzloff Chemical Spl."
:48:02.89   122.328 mph

July 28 "Road America 500"
Road America 4-mi. Road Course
Elkhart Lake, Wis.
500-mi. USRRC SCCA Sports Car Race
Chuck Parsons/Skip Scott "Lola-
Chevrolet" 94.73 mph

Aug. 4 "Dixie 500"
Atlanta 1½-mi. Paved Speedway
Hampton, Ga.
500-mi. NASCAR Stock Car Race
Lee Roy Yarbrough "Mercury Cyclone"
3:56:34.0   126.814 mph

Aug. 4 "Bryar 200"
Bryar Motorsports Park 1.6-mi. Road Course
Loudon, N.H.
200-mi. SCCA Trans-Am Race
Mark Donohue "Camaro" 73.71 mph

Aug. 11 Watkins Glen 2.3-mi. Road Course
Watkins Glen, N.Y.
2½-hr. SCCA Trans-Am Race
Jerry Titus "Ford Mustang" 262.2 miles
104.81 mph

Aug. 17 Springfield 1-mi. Dirt Track
Springfield, Ill.
100-mi. USAC Championship Race
Roger McCluskey "G. C. Murphy Spl."
1:06:37.96   102.9 mph

Aug. 18 "Tony Bettenhausen 200"
Milwaukee 1-mi. Paved Speedway
West Allis, Wis.
200-mi. USAC Championship Race
Lloyd Ruby "Gene White Spl." 1:50:21.579
108.735 mph

Aug. 18 "Buckeye 200"
Mid-Ohio 2.4-mi. Road Course
Lexington, Ohio
180-mi. USRRC SCCA Sports Car Race
Mark Donohue "McLaren-Chevrolet"
1:58:59.2   90.77 mph

Aug. 25 Continental Divide 2.8-mi. Road
Course
Castle Rock, Colo.
250-mi. SCCA Trans-Am Race
Mark Donohue "Camaro" 3:21:22.3
74.187 mph

Sept. 1 Road America 4-mi. Road Course
Elkhart Lake, Wis.
200-mi. SCCA Can-Am Sports Car Race
Denis Hulme "McLaren-Chevrolet"
2:06:55.8   94.541 mph

Sept. 2 "Southern 500"
Darlington 1⅜-mi. Paved Speedway
Darlington, S.C.
500-mi. NASCAR Stock Car Race
Cale Yarborough "Mercury" 3:58:05.0
126.132 mph

Sept. 2 DuQuoin 1-mi. Dirt Track
DuQuoin, Ill.
100-mi. USAC Championship Race
Mario Andretti "Overseas Nat'l. Airways Spl."
91.518 mph

Sept. 8 Riverside 2.6-mi. Road Course
Riverside, Calif.
250.6-mi. SCCA Trans-Am Race
Horst Kwech "Ford Mustang" 2:38:08.6
94.699 mph

Sept. 8 Indiana Fairgrounds 1-mi. Dirt
Track
Indianapolis, Ind.
100-mi. USAC Championship Race
A. J. Foyt "Sheraton-Thompson Spl."
1:04:18.76   93.296 mph

Sept. 15 Bridgehampton 2.85-mi. Road
Course
Bridgehampton, Long Island, N.Y.
200-mi. SCCA Can-Am Sports Car Race
Mark Donohue "McLaren-Chevrolet"
1:47:34.30   111.32 mph

Sept. 22 Trenton 1-mi. Paved Speedway
Trenton, N.J.
200-mi. USAC Championship Race
Mario Andretti "Overseas Airways Spl."
1:54:47.10   104.543 mph

Sept. 30 Sacramento 1-mi. Dirt Track
Sacramento, Calif.
100-mi. USAC Championship Race
A. J. Foyt "Sheraton-Thompson Spl."
1:08:52.33   84.94 mph

Oct. 6 Watkins Glen 2.3-mi. Road Course
Watkins Glen, N.Y.
248-mi. Formula I U.S. Grand Prix
Jackie Stewart "Matra-Ford" 1:59:20.29
124.46 mph

Oct. 6 Pacific Raceway 2.25-mi. Road Race
Kent, Wash.
303.75-mi. SCCA Trans-Am Race
Mark Donohue "Chevrolet Camaro"
3:26:20.2   88.34 mph

Oct. 13 Michigan 2-mi. Paved Speedway
(Inaugural)
Irish Hills, Mich.
250-mi. USAC Championship Race
Ronnie Bucknum "Weinberger Homes Spl."
163.043 mph

Oct. 13 Laguna Seca 1.9-mi. Road Course
Monterey, Calif.
152-mi. SCCA Can-Am Sports Car Race
John Cannon "McLaren-Chevrolet"
1:46:24.6   85.6 mph

Oct. 20 "National 500"
Charlotte 1½-mi. Paved Speedway
Charlotte, N.C.
500-mi. NASCAR Stock Car Race
Charlie Glotzbach "Dodge Charger"
3:42:58.0   135.324 mph

Oct. 27 "Times GP"
Riverside 3.275-mi. Road Course

Riverside, Calif.
203-mi. SCCA Can-Am Sports Car Race
Bruce McLaren "McLaren-Chevrolet"
1:46:36.1 114.353 mph

Oct. 27 "American 500"
Rockingham 1.017-mi. Paved Speedway
Rockingham, N.C.
500-mi. NASCAR Stock Car Race
Richard Petty "Plymouth" 4:45:30.0
105.060 mph

Nov. 3 Hanford 1½-mi. Paved Speedway
Hanford, Calif.
250-mi. USAC Championship Race
A. J. Foyt "Sheraton-Thompson Spl."
1:51:49.0 126.46 mph

Nov. 10 "Stardust GP"
Stardust 3.0-mi. Road Course
Las Vegas, Nev.
210-mi. SCCA Can-Am Sports Car Race
Denis Hulme "McLaren-Chevrolet"
1:52:15.38 113.1 mph

Nov. 17 "Bobby Ball 200"
Phoenix 1-mi. Paved Speedway
Phoenix, Ariz.
200-mi. USAC Championship Race
Gary Bettenhausen "Thermo King Spl."
1:54:19.0 105.263 mph

Dec. 1 "Rex Mays 300"
Riverside 2.6-mi. Road Course
Riverside, Calif.
300-mi. USAC Championship Race
Dan Gurney "Olsonite-Eagle Spl."
2:42:01.27 111.689 mph

1969

Feb. 1 "Trend 500"
Riverside 2.7-mi. Road Course
Riverside, Calif.
500-mi. NASCAR Stock Car Race
Richard Petty "Ford" 4:25:37.0
105.516 mph

Feb. 2 "24 Hours of Daytona"
Daytona 3.81-mi. Road Course
Daytona Beach, Fla.
24-hr. Sports Car Race
Mark Donohue/Chuck Parsons "Sunoco
Lola-Chevrolet" 2386.31 miles 99.26 mph

Feb. 23 "Daytona 500"
Daytona 2½-mi. Paved Tri-oval Speedway
Daytona Beach, Fla.
500-mi. NASCAR Stock Car Race
Lee Roy Yarbrough "Ford" 3:09:56.0
157.95 mph

Mar. 9 "Carolina 500"
Rockingham 1.017-mi. Paved Speedway
Rockingham, N.C.
500-mi. NASCAR Stock Car Race
David Pearson "Ford Torino" 4:55:22.0
102.569 mph

Mar. 22 Sebring 5.2-mi. Airport Course
Sebring, Fla.
12-hr. Sports Car Race
Jacky Ickx/Jack Oliver "Ford GT40"
1242.8 miles 103.363 mph

Mar. 30 "Atlanta 500"
Atlanta 1½-mi. Paved Speedway
Hampton, Ga.
500-mi. NASCAR Stock Car Race
Cale Yarborough "Mercury Cyclone"
3:46:12.0 132.759 mph

Mar. 30 "Jimmy Bryan 150"
Phoenix 1-mi. Paved Speedway
Phoenix, Ariz.
150-mi. USAC Championship Race
George Follmer "Follmer Spl." 1:21:55.07
109.853 mph

Apr. 13 "California 200"
Hanford 1½-mi. Paved Speedway
Hanford, Calif.
200-mi. USAC Championship Race
Mario Andretti "STP Oil Treatment Spl."
(No Time due to accident.)

May 10 "Rebel 400"
Darlington 1⅜-mi. Paved Speedway
Darlington, S.C.
400-mi. NASCAR Stock Car Race
Lee Roy Yarbrough "Mercury" 3:02:28.0
131.571 mph

May 11 Michigan Speedway 3.31-mi. Road
Course
Irish Hills, Mich.
4-hr. SCCA Trans-Am Race
Parnelli Jones "Ford Mustang"
344.24 miles 85.49 mph

May 25 "World 600"
Charlotte 1½-mi. Paved Speedway
Charlotte, S.C.
600-mi. NASCAR Stock Car Race
Lee Roy Yarbrough "Mercury" 4:27:56.0
134.36 mph

May 30 Lime Rock 1.53-mi. Road Course
Lime Rock, Conn.
2½-hr. SCCA Trans-Am Race
Sam Posey "Ford Mustang" 218.79 miles
87.27 mph

May 30 Indianapolis 2½-mi. Motor
Speedway
Speedway, Ind.
500-mi. USAC Championship Race
Mario Andretti "STP Oil Treatment Spl."
3:07:14.71 156.86 mph

June 1 Mosport Park 2.459-mi. Road
Course
Bowmanville, Ontario, Can.
196.72-mi. SCCA Can-Am Race
Bruce McLaren "McLaren-Chevrolet"
1:51:27.3 105.9 mph

June 8 Mid-Ohio 2.4-mi. Road Course
Lexington, Ohio
240-mi. SCCA Trans-Am Race
Ron Bucknum "Chevrolet Camaro"
2:56:23.0 83.53 mph

June 8 Milwaukee 1-mi. Paved Speedway
West Allis, Wis.
150-mi. USAC Championship Race
Art Pollard "STP Oil Treatment Spl."
1:20:14.720 112.157 mph

June 15 "Motor State 500"
Michigan 2-mi. Paved Speedway
Irish Hills, Mich.
500-mi. NASCAR Stock Car Race
Cale Yarborough "Mercury" 3:35:26.0
139.254 mph

June 22 Bridgehampton 2.85-mi. Road
Course
Bridgehampton, Long Island, N.Y.
250.8-mi. SCCA Trans-Am Race
George Follmer "Ford Mustang"
2:36:30.30 96.15 mph

June 29 Langhorne 1-mi. Paved Speedway
Langhorne, Pa.
150-mi. USAC Championship Race
Bobby Unser "Bardahl Spl." 1:20:03.22
112.42 mph

June 29 Pikes Peak 12.46-mi. Hill Climb
Colorado Springs, Colo.
Championship Class:
Mario Andretti "STP Oil Treatment Spl."
:12:44.07 58.18 mph

July 4 "Paul Revere 250"
Daytona Speedway 3.81-mi. Road Course
Daytona Beach, Fla.
251.46-mi. NASCAR Grand Touring Race
Pete Hamilton "Chevrolet Camaro"
100.975 mph

July 4 "Firecracker 400"
Daytona 2½-mi. Paved Tri-oval Speedway
Daytona Beach, Fla.
400-mi. NASCAR Stock Car Race
Lee Roy Yarbrough "Ford" 2:29:11.0
160.87 mph

July 6 Continental Divide 2.66-mi. Road
Course
Castle Rock, Colo.
150-mi. USAC Championship Race
Gordon Johncock "Gilmore Broadcasting
Spl." 1:47:52.0 88.44 mph

July 6 "Mason-Dixon 300"
Dover Downs 1-mi. Paved Speedway
(Inaugural)
Dover, Del.
300-mi. NASCAR Stock Car Race
Richard Petty "Ford" 2:35:28.0
115.77 mph

July 6 Donnybrooke 3-mi. Road Course
Brainerd, Minn.
252-mi. SCCA Trans-Am Race
Parnelli Jones "Ford Mustang" 2:32:42.0
98.94 mph

July 12 Watkins Glen 2.3-mi. Road Course
Watkins Glen, N.Y.
6-hr. Sports Car Race
Jo Siffert/Brian Redman "Porsche"
669.3 miles 111.19 mph

July 12 Nazareth 1⅛-mi. Dirt Track
Nazareth, Pa.
100.125-mi. USAC Championship Race
Mario Andretti "STP Oil Treatment Spl."
:56:45.25 105.851 mph

July 13 Watkins Glen 2.3-mi. Road Course
Watkins Glen, N.Y.
200.1-mi. SCCA Can-Am Sports Car Race
Bruce McLaren "McLaren-Chevrolet"
1:35:17.6 125.99 mph

July 13 "Northern 300"
Trenton 1½-mi. Paved Speedway (Inaugural)
Trenton, N.J.
300-mi. NASCAR Stock Car Race
David Pearson "Ford" 2:28:45.21
121.05 mph

July 19 Trenton 1½-mi. Paved Speedway
Trenton, N.J.
201-mi. USAC Championship Race
Mario Andretti "STP Oil Treatment Spl."
1:26:23.71 139.591 mph

July 20 Bryar Motorsport Park 1.6-mi. Road
Course
Loudon, N.H.
200-mi. SCCA Trans-Am Race
Mark Donohue "Chevrolet Camaro"
2:39:08.5 76.35 mph

July 27 Indianapolis Raceway Park 2½-mi.
Road Course
Clermont, Ind.
2—100-mi. USAC Championship Races
First Race:
Dan Gurney "Olsonite-Eagle" 1:05:01.40
92.053 mph
Second Race:
Peter Revson "Repco-Brabham"
1:03:10.80 94.967 mph

Aug. 10 Watkins Glen 2.3-mi. Road Course
Watkins Glen, N.Y.
2½-hr. SCCA Trans-Am Race
Mark Donohue "Chevrolet-Camaro"
269.1 miles 107.33 mph

Aug. 10 "Dixie 500"
Atlanta 1½-mi. Paved Speedway
Hampton, Ga.
500-mi. NASCAR Stock Car Race
Lee Roy Yarbrough "Ford" 3:45:35.0
133.001 mph

Aug. 17 Mid-Ohio 2.4-mi. Road Course
Lexington, Ohio
192-mi. SCCA Can-Am Sports Car Race
Denis Hulme "McLaren-Chevrolet"
2:02:16.6 94.21 mph

Aug. 17 "Yankee 600"
Michigan 2-mi. Paved Speedway
Irish Hills, Mich.
600-mi. NASCAR Stock Car Race
Halted at 330 miles due to rain.
David Pearson "Ford" 2:51:25.0
115.508 mph

Aug. 17 Milwaukee 1-mi. Paved Speedway
West Allis, Wis.
200-mi. USAC Championship Race
Al Unser "Vels-Parnelli Jones Ford Spl."
1:52:24.24 106.758 mph

Aug. 18 "Tony Bettenhausen 100"
Springfield 1-mi. Dirt Track
Springfield, Ill.
100-mi. USAC Championship Race
Mario Andretti "STP Oil Treatment Spl."
1:02:05.09 96.64 mph

Aug. 24 Laguna Seca 1.9-mi. Road Course
Monterey, Calif.
2½-hr. SCCA Trans-Am Race
Mark Donohue "Chevrolet Camaro"
226.1 miles 90.43 mph

Aug. 24 Dover Downs 1-mi. Paved
Speedway
Dover, Del.
200-mi. USAC Championship Race
Art Pollard "STP Oil Treatment Spl."
1:36:01.0 122.261 mph

Aug. 31 Road America 4-mi. Road Course
Elkhart Lake, Wis.
200-mi. SCCA Can-Am Sports Car Race
Bruce McLaren "McLaren-Chevrolet"
1:51:39.0 107.47 mph

Sept. 1 DuQuoin 1-mi. Dirt Track
DuQuoin, Ill.
100-mi. USAC Championship Race
Al Unser "Vels-Parnelli Jones Ford Spl."
1:03:20.52 94.724 mph

Sept 6 Indiana Fairgrounds 1-mi. Dirt
Track
Indianapolis, Ind.
100-mi. USAC Championship Race
A. J. Foyt "Sheraton-Thompson Spl."
1:04:05.80 93.609 mph

Sept. 7 Seattle Raceway 2.25-mi. Road
Course
Kent, Wash.
303.75-mi. SCCA Trans-Am Race
Ron Bucknum "Chevrolet Camaro"
3:24:26.1 89.15 mph

Sept. 13 Alabama 2.66-mi. Paved Tri-oval
Speedway (Inaugural)
Talladega, Ala.
401.66-mi. NASCAR GT Stock Car Race
Ken Rush "Chevrolet Camaro" 2:34:13.0
156.27 mph

Sept. 14 Bridgehampton 2.85-mi. Road
Course
Bridgehampton, Long Island, N.Y.
199.5-mi. SCCA Can-Am Sports Car Race
Denis Hulme "McLaren-Chevrolet"
1:45:40.58 113.72 mph

Sept. 14 "Talladega 500"
Alabama 2.66-mi. Paved Tri-oval Speedway
Talladega, Ala.
500.08-mi. NASCAR Stock Car Race
Richard Brickhouse "Dodge Daytona"
153.778 mph

Sept. 14 Donnybrooke 3-mi. Road Course
Brainerd, Minn.
2—102-mi. USAC Championship Races
1st Race:
Gordon Johncock "Gilmore Broadcasting
Spl." 110.436 mph
2nd Race:
Dan Gurney "Olsonite-Eagle Spl."
113.925 mph

Sept. 20 Nazareth 1⅛-mi. Dirt Track
Nazareth, Pa.
100.125-mi. USAC Championship Race
A. J. Foyt "Sheraton-Thompson Spl."
1:04:02.59 93.800 mph

Sept. 21 Sears Point Raceway 2.523-mi.
Road Course
Sonoma, Calif.
201.84-mi. SCCA Trans-Am Race
Mark Donohue "Chevrolet-Camaro"
2:29:49.0 80.83 mph

Sept. 21 Trenton 1½-mi. Paved Speedway
Trenton, N.J.
300-mi. USAC Championship Race
Mario Andretti "STP Oil Treatment Spl."
2:13:56.80 134.381 mph

Sept. 28 Michigan Speedway 3-mi. Road
Course
Irish Hills, Mich.
195-mi. SCCA Can-Am Sports Car Race
Bruce McLaren "McLaren-Chevrolet"
1:49:14.09 108.09 mph

Sept. 28 Sacramento 1-mi. Dirt Track
Sacramento, Calif.
100-mi. USAC Championship Race
Al Unser "Vel's-Parnelli Jones Ford Spl."
1:04:09.19 93.253 mph

Oct. 5 Watkins Glen 2.3-mi. Road Course
Watkins Glen, N.Y.
248.4-mi. Formula I Grand Prix of U.S.

Jochen Rindt "Lotus-Ford" 1:57:56.84
126.36 mph

Oct. 5 Riverside 2.54-mi. Road Course
Riverside, Calif.
254-mi. SCCA Trans-Am Race
Mark Donohue "Chevrolet-Camaro"
2:36:35.5 95.76 mph

Oct. 12 Laguna Seca 1.9-mi. Road Course
Monterey, Calif.
152-mi. SCCA Can-Am Sports Car Race
Bruce McLaren "McLaren-Chevrolet"
1:27:29.77 104.23 mph

Oct. 12 "National 500"
Charlotte 1½-mi. Paved Speedway
Charlotte, N.C.
500-mi. NASCAR Stock Car Race
Donnie Allison "Ford" 3:48:32.0
131.262 mph

Oct. 19 Seattle Raceway 2.25-mi. Road
Course
Kent, Wash.
2—101.25-mi. USAC Championship Races
1st Race:
Mario Andretti "STP Oil Treatment Spl."
85.55 mph
2nd Race:
Al Unser "Vel's-Parnelli Jones Ford Spl."
84.36 mph

Oct. 26 Riverside 3.3-mi. Road Course
Riverside, Calif.
201.3-mi. SCCA Can-Am Sports Car Race
Denis Hulme "McLaren-Chevrolet"
1:40:05.00 120.67 mph

Oct. 26 Rockingham 1.017-mi. Paved
Speedway
Rockingham, N.C.
500-mi. NASCAR Stock Car Race
Lee Roy Yarbrough "Ford" 111.93 mph

Oct. 26 "Vulcan 500"
Alabama 2.66-mi. Paved Tri-oval Speedway
Talladega, Ala.
500-mi. NASCAR Stock Car Race
Jimmy Vandiver "Dodge" 3:12:19.0
156.017 mph

Nov. 9 Texas 3-mi. Road Course
Bryan, Texas
210-mi. SCCA Can-Am Sports Car Race
Bruce McLaren "McLaren-Chevrolet"
1:54:24.4 109.84 mph

Nov. 16 Phoenix 1-mi. Paved Speedway
Phoenix, Ariz.
200-mi. USAC Championship Race
Al Unser "Vel's-Parnelli Jones Ford Spl."
1:48:59.0 110.109 mph

Dec. 7 Riverside 2.54-mi. Road Course
Riverside, Calif.
305.64-mi. USAC Championship Race
Mario Andretti "STP Oil Treatment Spl."
2:47:00.0 109.451 mph

Dec. 7 "Texas 500"
Texas 2-mi. Paved Speedway
Bryan, Texas
500-mi. NASCAR Stock Car Race
Bobby Isaac "Dodge" 3:27:57.0
144.265 mph

1970

Jan. 18 "Motor Trend 500"
Riverside 2.62-mi. Road Course
Riverside, Calif.
500-mi. NASCAR Stock Car Race
A. J. Foyt "Ford" 5:18:08.0 97.450 mph

Feb. 1 Daytona 2½-mi. Paved Tri-oval Speedway
Daytona Beach, Fla.
24-hr. Sports Car Race
Pedro Rodriguez/Leo Kinnunen "Porsche"
1810 miles 114.866 mph

Feb. 22 "Daytona 500"
Daytona 2½-mi. Paved Tri-oval Speedway
Daytona Beach, Fla.
500-mi. NASCAR Stock Car Race
Pete Hamilton "Plymouth" 3:20:32.0
149.601 mph

Mar. 8 "Carolina 500"
Rockingham 1.017-mi. Paved Speedway
Rockingham, N.C.
500-mi. NASCAR Stock Car Race
Richard Petty "Plymouth" 4:18:32.0
116.117 mph

Mar. 21 Sebring 5.2-mi. Airport Course
Sebring, Fla.
12-hr. SCCA Sports Car Race
S. Nino Vaccarella/Gnacio Giunti/
Mario Andretti "Ferrari" 1289.6 miles
107.290 mph

Mar. 28 Phoenix 1-mi. Paved Speedway
Phoenix, Ariz.
150-mi. USAC Championship Race
Al Unser "Johnny Lightning 500 Spl."
Red Flag (No Time)

Mar. 29 "Atlanta 500"
Atlanta 1½-mi. Paved Speedway
Hampton, Ga.
500-mi. NASCAR Stock Car Race
Bobby Allison "Dodge" 3:34:38.0
139.554 mph

Apr. 4 Sears Point 2.523-mi. Road Course
Sonoma, Calif.
150-mi. USAC Championship Race
Dan Gurney "Olsonite-Eagle" 1:44:26.0
86.179 mph

Apr. 12 "Alabama 500"
Alabama 2.66-mi. Paved Tri-oval Speedway
Talladega, Ala.
500-mi. NASCAR Stock Car Race
Pete Hamilton "Plymouth" 152.321 mph

Apr. 19 Laguna Seca 1.9-mi. Road Course
Monterey, Calif.
171-mi. SCCA Trans-Am Race
Parnelli Jones "Ford Mustang" 1:52:36.55
91.37 mph

Apr. 19 Riverside 2.54-mi. Road Course
Riverside, Calif.
101.6-mi. SCCA Cont'l. Champ. Race
John Cannon "Hogan-Starr-Chevrolet"
:53:40.36 114.04 mph

Apr. 26 Trenton 1½-mi. Paved Speedway
Trenton, N.J.
200-mi. USAC Championship Race
Lloyd Ruby "Daniels Cable Vision Spl."
1:28:41.87 135.967 mph

May 9 "Rebel 400"
Darlington 1⅜-mi. Paved Speedway
Darlington, S.C.
400-mi. NASCAR Stock Car Race
David Pearson "Ford" 129.688 mph

May 9 Lime Rock 1:53-mi. Road Course
Lime Rock, Conn.
2½-hr. SCCA Trans-Am Race
Parnelli Jones "Ford Mustang"
223.38 miles 88.91 mph

May 24 "World 600"
Charlotte 1½-mi. Paved Speedway
Charlotte, N.C.
600-mi. NASCAR Stock Car Race
Donnie Allison/Lee Roy Yarbrough "Ford"
4:37:36.0 129.680 mph

May 24 Edmonton 2.527-mi. Road Course
Edmonton, Alberta, Can.
102.09-mi. SCCA Cont'l. Champ. Race
Ron Grable "Lola-Chevrolet" :59:52.2
101.29 mph

May 30 Indianapolis 2½-mi. Motor Speedway
Speedway, Ind.
500-mi. USAC Championship Race
Al Unser "Johnny Lightning 500 Spl."
3:12:37.04 155.749 mph

May 31 Bryar Motorsport Park 1.6-mi.
Road Course
Loudon, N.H.
2-hr. SCCA Trans-Am Race
George Follmer "Ford Mustang"
148.8 miles 71.93 mph

June 7 "Motor State 400"
Michigan 2-mi. Paved Speedway
Cambridge Junction, Mich.
400-mi. NASCAR Stock Car Race
Cale Yarborough "Mercury" 138.302 mph

June 7 Seattle Raceway 2.25-mi. Road Course
Kent, Wash.
101.25-mi. SCCA Cont'l. Champ. Race
John Cannon "Hogan-Starr-Chevrolet"
:58:49.24 103.8 mph

June 7 Mid-Ohio 2.4-mi. Road Course
Lexington, Ohio
180-mi. SCCA Trans-Am Race
Parnelli Jones "Ford Mustang" 2:09:56.1
83.11 mph

June 7 "Rex Mays 150"
Milwaukee 1-mi. Paved Speedway
West Allis, Wis.
150-mi. USAC Championship Race
Joe Leonard "Johnny Lightning 500 Spl."
1:23:06.176 108.299 mph

June 14 "Falstaff 400"
Riverside 2.62-mi. Road Course
Riverside, Calif.
400-mi. NASCAR Stock Car Race
Richard Petty "Plymouth" 4:03:41.0
99.243 mph

June 14 Laguna Seca 1.9-mi. Road Course
Monterey, Calif.
95-mi. SCCA Cont'l. Champ. Race
Ron Grable "Lola-Chevrolet" :57:11.4
99.7 mph

June 16 Langhorne 1-mi. Paved Speedway
Langhorne, Pa.
150-mi. USAC Championship Race
Bobby Unser "Wagner Lockheed Brake
Fluid Spl." 1:24:39.85 106.302 mph

June 21 Bridgehampton 2.85-mi. Road
Course

Bridgehampton, Long Island, N.Y.
199.5-mi. SCCA Trans-Am Race
Mark Donohue "AMC Javelin" 2:12:43.3
90.55 mph

June 28 Sears Point 2.523-mi. Road Course
Sonoma, Calif.
100.92-mi. SCCA Cont'l. Champ. Race
Gus Hutchison "Brabham-Ford" 1:07:11.4
89.3 mph

June 28 "Rocky Mountain 150"
Continental Divide 2.66-mi. Road Course
Castle Rock, Colo.
150-mi. USAC Championship Race
Mario Andretti "STP Oil Treatment Spl."
1:48:17.0 84.013 mph

July 4 "Firecracker 400"
Daytona 2½-mi. Paved Tri-Oval Speedway
Daytona Beach, Fla.
400-mi. NASCAR Stock Car Race
Donnie Allison "Ford" 2:27:56.0
162.235 mph

July 4 Michigan 2-mi. Paved Speedway
Cambridge Junction, Mich.
200-mi. USAC Championship Race
Gary Bettenhausen "Thermo King Auto Air
Conditioning Spl." 1:25:20.0 140.625 mph

July 5 Dallas 2½-mi. Road Course
Lewisville, Texas
100-mi. SCCA Cont'l. Champ. Race
Gus Hutchison "Brabham-Ford" 1:02:44.0
98.03 mph

July 5 Donnybrooke 3-mi. Road Course
Brainerd, Minn.
210-mi. SCCA Trans-Am Race
Milt Minter "Chevrolet-Camaro" 2:10:20.2
96.67 mph

July 12 "Northern 300"
Trenton 1½-mi. Paved Speedway
Trenton, N.J.
300-mi. NASCAR Stock Car Race
Richard Petty "Plymouth" 2:29:07.12
120.709 mph

July 12 Watkins Glen 2.3-mi. Road Course
Watkins Glen, N.Y.
200.1-mi. SCCA Can-Am Sports Car Race
Denis Hulme "McLaren-Chevrolet"
2:42:26.0 118.56 mph

July 18 Road America 4-mi. Road Course
Elkhart Lake, Wis.
100-mi. SCCA Cont'l. Champ. Race
John Cannon "Hogan-Starr-Chevrolet"
:56:07.6 106.9 mph

July 19 Road America 4-mi. Road Course
Elkhart Lake, Wis.
200-mi. SCCA Trans-Am Race
Mark Donohue "AMC Javelin" 2:10:39.8
91.83 mph

July 28 Indianapolis Raceway Park 2½-mi.
Road Course
Clermont, Ind.
150-mi. USAC Championship Race
Al Unser "Johnny Lightning 500 Spl."
1:36:59.0 92.799 mph

Aug. 2 "Dixie 500"
Atlanta 1½-mi. Paved Speedway
Hampton, Ga.
500-mi. NASCAR Stock Car Race
Richard Petty "Plymouth" 3:39:53.0
142.712 mph

Aug. 16 "Yankee 400"
Michigan 2-mi. Paved Speedway
Cambridge Junction, Mich.
400-mi. NASCAR Stock Car Race
Charlie Glotzbach "Dodge" 2:42:38.0
148.264 mph

Aug. 16 Donnybrooke 3-mi. Road Course
Brainerd, Minn.
2—75-mi. SCCA Cont'l. Champ. Races
1st Race:
David Hobbs "Surtees-Chevrolet"
110.55 mph
2nd Race:
David Hobbs "Surtees-Chevrolet"
111.5 mph

Aug. 16 Watkins Glen 2.3-mi. Road Course
Watkins Glen, N.Y.
2-hr. SCCA Trans-Am Race
Vic Elford "Chevrolet-Camaro"
209.3 miles 103.8 mph

Aug. 22 Springfield 1-mi. Dirt Track
Springfield, Ill.
100-mi. USAC Championship Race
Al Unser "Johnny Lightning 500 Spl."
1:36:18.40 62.30 mph

Aug. 23 Milwaukee 1-mi. Paved Speedway
West Allis, Wis.
200-mi. USAC Championship Race
Al Unser "Johnny Lightning 500 Spl."
1:44:58.995 114.304 mph

Aug. 23 "Talladega 500"
Alabama 2.66-mi. Paved Speedway
Talladega, Ala.
500-mi. NASCAR Stock Car Race
Pete Hamilton "Plymouth" 3:09:17.0
158.517 mph

Aug. 23 Mid-Ohio 2.4-mi. Road Course
Lexington, Ohio
192-mi. SCCA Can-Am Sports Car Race
Denis Hulme "McLaren-Chevrolet"
2:01:03.3 95.16 mph

Aug. 30 Road America 4-mi. Road Course
Elkhart Lake, Wis.
200-mi. SCCA Can-Am Sports Car Race
Peter Gethin "McLaren-Chevrolet"
1:54:16.1 105.01 mph

Sept. 6 Ontario 2½-mi. Paved Speedway
Ontario, Calif.
500-mi. USAC Championship Race
Jim McElreath "Sheraton-Thompson ITT
Spl." 3:07:22.55 160.106 mph

Sept. 7 DuQuoin 1-mi. Dirt Track
DuQuoin, Ill.
100-mi. USAC Championship Race
Al Unser "Johnny Lightning 500 Spl."
1:01:07.66 98.155 mph

Sept. 7 "Southern 500"
Darlington 1⅜-mi. Paved Speedway
Darlington, S.C.
500-mi. NASCAR Stock Car Race
Buddy Baker "Dodge" 3:55:03.0
128.817 mph

Sept. 7 Lime Rock 1.53-mi. Road Course
Lime Rock, Conn.
107.1-mi. SCCA Cont'l. Champ. Race
David Hobbs "Surtees-Chevrolet"
1:01:58.8 103.62 mph

Sept. 12 "Hoosier 100"
Indiana Fairgrounds 1-mi. Dirt Track

Indianapolis, Ind.
100-mi. USAC Championship Race
Al Unser "Johnny Lightning 500 Spl."
1:01:13.70 97.887 mph

Sept. 13 Road Atlanta 2:52-mi. Road
Course
Gainesville, Ga.
190-mi. SCCA Can-Am Sports Car Race
Tony Dean "Porsche" 1:49:45.88
103.45 mph

Sept. 19 Sedalia 1-mi. Dirt Track
Sedalia, Mo.
100-mi. USAC Championship Race
Al Unser "Johnny Lightning 500 Spl."
1:01:12.01 98.039 mph

Sept. 20 "Mason-Dixon 300"
Dover Downs 1-mi. Paved Speedway
Dover, Del.
300-mi. NASCAR Stock Car Race
Richard Petty "Plymouth" 112.098 mph

Sept. 20 Seattle Raceway 2.25-mi. Road
Course
Kent, Wash.
202.5-mi. SCCA Trans-Am Race
Parnelli Jones "Ford Mustang" 2:13:28.5
90.93 mph

Sept. 27 Mid-Ohio 2.4-mi. Road Course
Lexington, Ohio
100.8-mi. SCCA Cont'l. Champ. Race
George Follmer "Lotus-Ford" 1:03:21.2
95.45 mph

Sept. 27 Donnybrooke 3-mi. Road Course
Brainerd, Minn.
210-mi. SCCA Can-Am Sports Car Race
Denis Hulme "McLaren-Chevrolet"
1:47:10.2 117.57 mph

Oct. 3 Trenton 1½-mi. Paved Speedway
Trenton, N.J.
300-mi. USAC Championship Race—
Halted at 264 miles due to rain.
Al Unser "Johnny Lightning 500 Spl."
1:55:05.00 137.630 mph

Oct. 4 Sacramento 1-mi. Dirt Track
Sacramento, Calif.
100-mi. USAC Championship Race
Al Unser "Johnny Lightning 500 Spl."
1:04:15.37 93.384 mph

Oct. 4 Riverside 2.54-mi. Road Course
Riverside, Calif.
200.66-mi. SCCA Trans-Am Race
Parnelli Jones "Ford Mustang" 2:01:48.0
99.22 mph

Oct. 11 "National 500"
Charlotte 1½-mi. Paved Speedway
Charlotte, N.C.
500-mi. NASCAR Stock Car Race
Lee Roy Yarbrough "Mercury" 4:03:28.0
123.246 mph

Oct. 18 Laguna Seca 1.9-mi. Road Course
Monterey, Calif.
152-mi. SCCA Can-Am Race for Sports Cars
Denis Hulme "McLaren-Chevrolet"
1:25:58.8 105.06 mph

Oct. 23 Bonneville Salt Flats
Wendover, Utah
1-mi. Straightaway World's Land Speed
Record
Gary Gabelich "Blue Flame" 622.407 mph

Oct. 25 Sebring 2.2-mi. Airport Course
Sebring, Fla.
99-mi. SCCA Continental Champ. Race
Mark Donohue "Lola-Chevrolet" :48:35.24
122.255 mph

Nov. 1 Riverside 3.3-mi. Road Course
Riverside, Calif.
201.3-mi. SCCA Can-Am Sports Car Race
Denis Hulme "McLaren-Chevrolet"
1:40:27.4 120.28 mph

Nov. 15 "American 500"
Rockingham 1.017-mi. Paved Speedway
Rockingham, N.C.
500-mi. NASCAR Stock Car Race
Cale Yarborough "Mercury" 4:14:24.0
117.811 mph

Nov. 21 Phoenix 1-mi. Paved Speedway
Phoenix, Ariz.
150-mi. USAC Championship Race
Swede Savage "Olsonite-Eagle Spl."
1:17:03.00 116.807 mph

1971

Jan. 10 "Motor Trend 500"
Riverside 2.6-mi. Road Course
Riverside, Calif.
500-mi. NASCAR Stock Car Race
Ray Elder "Dodge" 4:58:00.0
100.786 mph

Jan. 31 "24 Hours of Daytona"
Daytona Speedway 3.81-mi. Road Course
Daytona Beach, Fla.
24-hr. SCCA Sports Car Race
Pedro Rodriguez/Jackie Oliver "Porsche"
2621.28 miles 109.203 mph

Feb. 14 "Daytona 500"
Daytona 2½-mi. Paved Tri-oval Speedway
Daytona Beach, Fla.
500-mi. NASCAR Stock Car Race
Richard Petty "Plymouth" 3:24:41.0
144.456 mph

Feb. 28 "Miller 500"
Ontario 2½-mi. Paved Speedway
Ontario, Calif.
500-mi. NASCAR Stock Car Race
A. J. Foyt "Mercury 3:43:36.0
134.168 mph

Mar. 14 "Carolina 500"
Rockingham 1.017-mi. Paved Speedway
Rockingham, N.C.
500-mi. NASCAR Stock Car Race
Richard Petty "Plymouth" 4:12:55.0
118.696 mph

Mar. 20 "Florida Grand Prix of Endurance"
Sebring 5.2-mi. Airport Course
Sebring, Fla.
12-hr. Sports Car Race
Vic Elford/Gerard Larrousse "Porsche"
1352 miles 112.500 mph

Mar. 27 Phoenix 1-mi. Paved Speedway
Phoenix, Ariz.
150-mi. USAC Championship Race
Al Unser "Johnny Lightning 500 Spl."
1:20:40.22 111.565 mph

Mar. 28 "Questor Grand Prix"
Ontario Speedway 3.194-mi. Road Course
Ontario, Calif.
2—102.208-mi. Formula I Races
1st Race:
Mario Andretti "Ferrari" 109.400 mph

2nd Race:
Mario Andretti "Ferrari" 109.980 mph

Apr. 3 "Atlanta 500"
Atlanta 1.58-mi. Paved Speedway
Hampton, Ga.
500-mi. NASCAR Stock Car Race
A. J. Foyt "Mercury" 3:42:16.0
131.375 mph

Apr. 25 "Trentonian 200"
Trenton 1½-mi. Paved Speedway
Trenton, N.J.
200-mi. USAC Championship Race
Mike Mosley "G. C. Murphy Spl."
1:30:58.57 132.562 mph

May 2 "Rebel 400"
Darlington 1⅜-mi. Paved Speedway
Darlington, S.C.
400-mi. NASCAR Stock Car Race
Buddy Baker "Dodge" 3:03:46.0
130.678 mph

May 2 "L & M Grand Prix"
Laguna Seca 1.9-mi. Road Course
Monterey, Calif.
2—76-mi. SCCA Formula A/5000 Races
1st Race:
David Hobbs "Hogan-McLaren-Chevrolet"
:43:47.59 104.125 mph
2nd Race:
David Hobbs "Hogan-McLaren-Chevrolet"
:43:02.44 105.946 mph

May 8 Lime Rock 1.53-mi. Road Course
Lime Rock, Conn.
200.43-mi. SCCA Trans-Am Race
Mark Donohue "Javelin" 2:39:00.0
75.63 mph

May 16 "Winston 500"
Alabama 2.66-mi. Paved Speedway
Talladega, Ala.
500-mi. NASCAR Stock Car Race
Donnie Allison "Mercury" 3:23:32.0
147.419 mph

May 29 Indianapolis 2½-mi. Motor
Speedway
Speedway, Ind.
500-mi. USAC Championship Race
Al Unser "Johnny Lightning 500 Spl."
3:10:11.56 157.735 mph

May 31 "World 600"
Charlotte 1½-mi. Paved Speedway
Charlotte, N.C.
600-mi. NASCAR Stock Car Race
Bobby Allison "Mercury" 4:16:20.0
140.442 mph

May 31 Bryar 1.61-mi. Road Course
Loudon, N.H.
152-mi. SCCA Trans-Am Race
George Follmer "Mustang" 2:01:10.41
75.32 mph

June 6 Milwaukee 1-mi. Paved Speedway
West Allis, Wis.
150-mi. USAC Championship Race
Al Unser "Johnny Lightning 500 Spl."
1:18:19.246 114.858 mph

June 6 "Mason-Dixon 500"
Dover Downs 1-mi. Paved Speedway
Dover, Del.
500-mi. NASCAR Stock Car Race
Bobby Allison "Ford Torino" 4:03:40.0
123.119 mph

June 6 Mid-Ohio 2.4-mi. Road Course
Lexington, Ohio
180-mi. SCCA Trans-Am Race
George Follmer "Mustang" 2:19:59.4
77.15 mph

June 13 "Motor State 400"
Michigan 2-mi. Paved Speedway
Cambridge Junction, Mich.
400-mi. NASCAR Stock Car Race
Bobby Allison "Mercury" 2:41:13.0
149.567 mph

June 20 "Golden State 400"
Riverside 2.6-mi. Road Course
Riverside, Calif.
400-mi. NASCAR Stock Car Race
Bobby Allison "Dodge" 4:17:05.0
93.622 mph

July 3 "Shaefer 500"
Pocono Raceway 2½-mi. Paved Tri-oval
Speedway (Inaugural)
Long Pond, Pa.
500-mi. USAC Championship Race
Mark Donohue "Sunoco McLaren-Offy Spl."
3:36:22.312 138.649 mph

July 4 "Firecracker 400"
Daytona 2½-mi. Paved Tri-oval Speedway
Daytona Beach, Fla.
400-mi. NASCAR Stock Car Race
Bobby Isaac "Dodge" 2:28:12.0
161.493 mph

July 11 Road Atlanta 2.52-mi. Road Course
Flowery Branch, Ga.
195-mi. SCCA Can-Am Sports Car Race
Peter Revson "McLaren-Chevrolet"
1:00:42.09 111.17 mph

July 17 Road America 4-mi. Road Course
Elkhart Lake, Wis.
200-mi. SCCA Trans-Am Race
Mark Donohue "Sunoco Javelin"
2:10:15.0 92.119 mph

July 18 "Northern 300"
Trenton 1½-mi. Paved Speedway
Trenton, N.J.
300-mi. NASCAR Stock Car Race
Richard Petty "Plymouth" 2:29:34.0
120.347 mph

July 18 Michigan 2-mi. Paved Speedway
Cambridge Junction, Mich.
200-mi. USAC Championship Race
Mark Donohue "Sunoco McLaren Spl."
1:22:09.0 144.898 mph

July 25 Watkins Glen 2.3-mi. Road Course
Watkins Glen, N.Y.
199.096-mi. SCCA Can-Am Sports Car Race
Peter Revson "McLaren-Chevrolet"
1:32:54.0 129.087 mph

Aug. 1 "Dixie 500"
Atlanta 1½-mi. Paved Speedway
Hampton, Ga.
500-mi. NASCAR Stock Car Race
Richard Petty "Plymouth" 3:52:05.0
129.061 mph

Aug. 7 Seattle Raceway 2.25-mi. Road
Course
Kent, Wash.
2—100-mi. USAC Championship Races
1st Race:
Jim Dittemore "Lola-Chevrolet" 101 mph
2nd Race:
Sam Posey "Surtees-Chevrolet" 104 mph

Aug. 15 "Tony Bettenhausen Memorial"
Milwaukee 1-mi. Paved Speedway
West Allis, Wis.
200-mi. USAC Championship Race
Bobby Unser "Olsonite Spl." 1:49:42.33
109.386 mph

Aug. 15 "Yankee 400"
Michigan 2-mi. Paved Speedway
Cambridge Junction, Mich.
400-mi. NASCAR Stock Car Race
Bobby Allison "Mercury" 2:40:58.0
149.799 mph

Aug. 22 "Talladega 500"
Alabama 2.66-mi. Paved Speedway
Talladega, Ala.
500-mi. NASCAR Stock Car Race
Bobby Allison "Mercury" 3:25:28.0
145.915 mph

Aug. 22 Mid-Ohio 2.4-mi. Road Course
Lexington, Ohio
192-mi. SCCA Can-Am Sports Car Race
Jackie Stewart "Lola-Chevrolet"
95.777 mph

Aug. 29 Road America 4-mi. Road Course
Elkhart Lake, Wis.
200-mi. SCCA Can-Am Sports Car Race
Peter Revson "McLaren-Chevrolet"
109.102 mph

Sept. 5 "California 500"
Ontario 2½-mi. Paved Speedway
Ontario, Calif.
500-mi. USAC Championship Race
Joe Leonard "Samsonite Spl."
3:16:54.515 152.354 mph

Sept. 6 DuQuoin 1-mi. Dirt Track
DuQuoin, Ill.
100-mi. USAC Championship Race
George Snider "G. C. Murphy Spl."
1:03:24.82 94.617 mph

Sept. 6 "Southern 500"
Darlington 1⅜-mi. Paved Speedway
Darlington, S.C.
500-mi. NASCAR Stock Car Race
Bobby Allison "Mercury" 3:48:55.0
131.398 mph

Sept. 11 Indiana Fairgrounds 1-mi. Dirt
Track
Indianapolis, Ind.
100-mi. USAC Championship Race
Al Unser "Johnny Lightning 500 Spl."
1:01:52.80 96.962 mph

Sept. 12 Donnybrooke 3-mi. Road Course
Brainerd, Minn.
210-mi. SCCA Can-Am Sports Car Race
Peter Revson "McLaren-Chevrolet"
1:45:45.643 119.137 mph

Sept. 13 Bonneville Salt Flats
Wendover, Utah
1-mi. Straightaway Stock Car Record
Bobby Isaac "Dodge" :16.639
216.945 mph

Sept. 26 Edmonton 2.527-mi. Road Course
Edmonton, Alberta, Can.
202-mi. SCCA Can-Am Sports Car Race
Denis Hulme "McLaren-Chevrolet"
2:07:47.1 94.922 mph

Oct. 3   Trenton 1½-mi. Paved Speedway
Trenton, N.J.
300-mi. USAC Championship Race
Bobby Unser   "Olsonite Spl."   2:07:51.65
140.771 mph

Oct. 3   Watkins Glen 3.377-mi. Road Course
Watkins Glen, N.Y.
199.243-mi. Formula I U.S. Grand Prix
Francois Cevert   "Tyrell-Ford"   1:43:51.991
115.092 mph

Oct. 3   "Mission Bell 200"
Riverside 2.5-mi. Road Course
Riverside, Calif.
201.4-mi. SCCA Trans-Am Race
George Follmer   "Javelin"   2:02:00.4
98.679 mph

Oct. 10   "National 500"
Charlotte 1½-mi. Paved Speedway
Charlotte, N.C.
500-mi. NASCAR Stock Car Race—
Halted at 357 miles due to rain.
Bobby Allison   "Mercury"   2:49:38.0
126.140 mph

Oct. 17   "Delaware 500"
Dover Downs 1-mi. Paved Speedway
Dover, Del.
500-mi. NASCAR Stock Car Race
Richard Petty   "Plymouth"   4:03:40.0
123.254 mph

Oct. 17   Laguna Seca 1.9-mi. Road Course
Monterey, Calif.
171-mi. SCCA Can-Am Sports Car Race
Peter Revson   "Gulf-McLaren"   1:33:00.0
109.210 mph

Oct. 23   Phoenix 1-mi. Paved Speedway
Phoenix, Ariz.
150-mi. USAC Championship Race
A. J. Foyt   "ITT-Sheraton Spl."   1:21:18.0
110.333 mph

Oct. 23   "American 500"
Rockingham 1.017-mi. Paved Speedway
Rockingham, N.C.
500-mi. NASCAR Stock Car Race
Richard Petty   "Plymouth"   4:24:43.0
113.405 mph

Oct. 31   "Los Angeles Times Grand Prix"
Riverside 3.25-mi. Road Course
Riverside, Calif.
201.3-mi. SCCA Can-Am Sports Car Race
Denis Hulme   "Gulf-McLaren"   1:37:36.0
123.727 mph

Dec. 12   "Texas 500"
Texas 2-mi. Paved Speedway
College Point, Texas
500-mi. NASCAR Stock Car Race
Richard Petty   "Plymouth"   3:28:20.0
144.00 mph

1972

Jan. 23   "Western 500"
Riverside 2.62-mi. Road Course
Riverside, Calif.
500-mi. NASCAR Stock Car Race
Halted at 390 miles due to darkness.
Richard Petty   "Plymouth"   3:45:11.0
104.016 mph

Feb. 6   Daytona Speedway 3.81-mi. Road
Course
Daytona Beach, Fla.

6-hr. SCCA Sports Car Race
Mario Andretti/Jacky Ickx   "Ferrari"
124.716 mph

Feb. 20   "Daytona 500"
Daytona 2½-mi. Paved Speedway
Daytona Beach, Fla.
500-mi. NASCAR Stock Car Race
A. J. Foyt   "Mercury"   3:05:42.0
161.550 mph

Mar. 5   "Miller High Life 500"
Ontario 2½-mi. Paved Speedway
Ontario, Calif.
500-mi. NASCAR Stock Car Race
A. J. Foyt   "Mercury"   3:56:06.486
127.060 mph

Mar. 12   "Carolina 500"
Rockingham 1.017-mi. Paved Speedway
Rockingham, N.C.
500-mi. NASCAR Stock Car Race
Bobby Isaac   "Dodge"   4:23:50.0
113.785 mph

Mar. 18   Phoenix 1-mi. Paved Speedway
Phoenix, Ariz.
150-mi. USAC Championship Race
Bobby Unser   "Olsonite Eagle"   1:27:31.63
102.805 mph

Mar. 25   Sebring 5.2-mi. Airport Course
Sebring, Fla.
12-hr. Sports Car Race
Mario Andretti/Jacky Ickx   "Ferrari"
1346.8 miles   12:04:40.0   111.508 mph

Mar. 26   "Atlanta 500"
Atlanta 1½-mi. Paved Speedway
Hampton, Ga.
500-mi. NASCAR Stock Car Race
Bobby Allison   "Chevrolet"   3:53:37.0
128.214 mph

Apr. 16   "Rebel 400"
Darlington 1⅜-mi. Paved Speedway
Darlington, S.C.
400-mi. NASCAR Stock Car Race
David Pearson   "Mercury"   3:13:00.0
124.426 mph

Apr. 23   "Trentonian 200"
Trenton 1½-mi. Paved Speedway
Trenton, N.J.
200-mi. USAC Championship Race
Gary Bettenhausen   "Sunoco-McLaren Spl."
1:22:29.0   146.211 mph

May 7   Alabama 2.66-mi. Paved Speedway
Talladega, Ala.
500-mi. NASCAR Stock Car Race
David Pearson   "Mercury"   3:43:15.0
134.400 mph

May 7   Lime Rock 1:53-mi. Road Course
Lime Rock, Conn.
200.43-mi. SCCA Trans-Am Race
George Follmer   "Javelin"   2:15:45.2
88.658 mph

May 27   Indianapolis 2½-mi. Motor
Speedway
Speedway, Ind.
500-mi. USAC Championship Race
Mark Donohue   "Sunoco-McLaren Spl."
3:04:05.54   162.962 mph

May 28   "World 600"
Charlotte 1½-mi. Paved Speedway
Charlotte, N.C.

600-mi. NASCAR Stock Car Race
Buddy Baker   "Dodge"   4:13:04.0
142.255 mph

June 4   "Rex Mays Classic"
Milwaukee 1-mi. Paved Speedway
West Allis, Wis.
150-mi. USAC Championship Race
Bobby Unser   "Olsonite Eagle"
1:22:28.179   109.131 mph

June 4   "Dover 500"
Dover Downs 1-mi. Paved Speedway
Dover, Del.
500-mi. NASCAR Stock Car Race
Bobby Allison   "Chevrolet"   4:12:47.0
118.679 mph

June 11   "Motor State 400"
Michigan 2-mi. Paved Speedway
Cambridge Junction, Mich.
400-mi. NASCAR Stock Car Race
David Pearson   "Mercury"   2:43:40.0
146.639 mph

June 11   Mosport Park 2.459-mi. Road
Course
Bowmanville, Ontario, Can.
200-mi. SCCA Can-Am Sports Car Race
Denis Hulme   "Gulf-McLaren"   (No Time
Given)

June 18   "Golden State 400"
Riverside 2.62-mi. Road Course
Riverside, Calif.
400-mi. NASCAR Stock Car Race
Ray Elder   "Dodge"   4:03:32.0
98.761 mph

June 18   Watkins Glen 3.377-mi. Road
Course
Watkins Glen, N.Y.
2—84.425-mi. SCCA Sports Car Races
1st Race:
Brian Redman   "Chevron"   :45:12.767
112.036 mph
2nd Race:
Graham McRae   "Leda"   :44:41.029
113.363 mph

June 18   Watkins Glen 3.377-mi. Road
Course
Watkins Glen, N.Y.
2-hr. SCCA Trans-Am Race
George Follmer   "Javelin"   94.886 mph

June 25   "Lone Star 500"
Texas 2-mi. Paved Tri-oval Speedway
College Station, Texas
500-mi. NASCAR Stock Car Race
Richard Petty   "Plymouth"   3:28:04.0
144.185 mph

July 4   "Firecracker 400"
Daytona 2½-mi. Paved Speedway
Daytona Beach, Fla.
400-mi. NASCAR Stock Car Race
David Pearson   "Mercury"   2:29:14.0
160.821 mph

July 9   Road Atlanta 2.52-mi. Road Course
Gainesville, Ga.
189-mi. SCCA Can-Am Sports Car Race
George Follmer   "Porsche"   113.96 mph

July 15   Road America 4-mi. Road Course
Elkhart Lake, Wis.
200-mi. SCCA Trans-Am Race
Warren Tope   "Mustang"   2:13:25.0
89.834 mph

July 16 "Northern 300"
Trenton 1½-mi. Paved Speedway
Trenton, N.J.
300-mi. NASCAR Stock Car Race
Bobby Allison "Chevrolet" 2:22:38.25
114.030 mph

July 16 "Michigan 200"
Michigan 2-mi. Paved Speedway
Cambridge Junction, Mich.
200-mi. USAC Championship Race
Joe Leonard "Samsonite Spl." 1:26:08.10
140.685 mph

July 22 Watkins Glen 3.377-mi. Road
Course
Watkins Glen, N.Y.
6-hr. Sports Car Endurance Race
Mario Andretti/Jacky Ickx "Ferrari"
658.515 miles 6:01:11.26 109.39 mph

July 23 "Dixie 500"
Atlanta 1.522-mi. Paved Speedway
Hampton, Ga.
500-mi. NASCAR Stock Car Race
Bobby Allison "Chevrolet" 3:47:05.0
131.295 mph

July 23 Watkins Glen 3.377-mi. Road
Course
Watkins Glen, N.Y.
202.62-mi. SCCA Can-Am Sports Car Race
Denis Hulme "Gulf-McLaren" 1:46:14.044
114.44 mph

July 29 Pocono 2½-mi. Paved Speedway
Long Pond, Pa.
500-mi. USAC Championship Race
Joe Leonard "Samsonite Spl." 3:13:49.315
154.781 mph

Aug. 6 "Talladega 500"
Alabama 2.66-mi. Paved Speedway
Talladega, Ala.
500-mi. NASCAR Stock Car Race
James Hylton "Mercury" 3:22:09.0
148.728 mph

Aug. 6 Mid-Ohio 2.4-mi. Road Course
Lexington, Ohio
192-mi. SCCA Can-Am Sports Car Race
George Follmer "Porsche" 2:04:02.185
92.876 mph

Aug. 13 "Tony Bettenhausen Classic"
Milwaukee 1-mi. Paved Speedway
West Allis, Wis.
200-mi. USAC Championship Race
Joe Leonard "Samsonite Spl." 1:47:28.61
111.652 mph

Aug. 20 "Yankee 400"
Michigan 2-mi. Paved Speedway
Cambridge Junction, Mich.
400-mi. NASCAR Stock Car Race
David Pearson "Mercury" 2:58:31.0
134.416 mph

Aug. 20 Road Atlanta 2.52-mi. Road
Course
Flowery Branch, Ga.
160-mi. SCCA Formula 5000 Race in 2 Heats
1st Heat—87 miles
Brett Lunger "Haggar Lola/Chevrolet"
:46:54.8 112.97 mph
2nd Heat—73 miles
Brian Redman "Valvoline Chevron-
Chevrolet" :39:11.2 112.97 mph

Aug. 27 Road America 4-mi. Road Course
Elkhart Lake, Wis.
200-mi. SCCA Can-Am Sports Car Race
George Follmer "Porsche" (No Time)

Sept. 3 Ontario 2½-mi. Paved Speedway
Ontario, Calif.
500-mi. USAC Championship Race
Roger McCluskey "American Marine
Underwriters Spl." 3:21:20.978
151.540 mph

Sept. 4 "Southern 500"
Darlington 1⅜-mi. Paved Speedway
Darlington, S.C.
500-mi. NASCAR Stock Car Race
Bobby Allison "Chevrolet" 3:54:46.0
128.124 mph

Sept. 4 Lime Rock 1:53-mi. Road Course
Lime Rock, Conn.
2—53.55-mi. SCCA Formula 5000 Races
1st Race:
Bert Lunger "Haggar Lola/Chevrolet"
:29:56.0 107.346 mph
2nd Race:
Bert Lunger "Haggar Lola/Chevrolet"
:31:40.0 101.845 mph

Sept. 17 "Delaware 500"
Dover Downs 1-mi. Paved Speedway
Dover, Del.
500-mi. NASCAR Stock Car Race
David Pearson "Mercury" 4:08:57.0
120.560 mph

Sept. 17 Donnybrooke 3.0-mi. Road Course
Brainerd, Minn.
210-mi. SCCA Can-Am Sports Car Race
Francois Cevert "McLaren-Chevrolet"
1:46:43.269 118.065 mph

Sept. 24 Trenton 1½-mi. Paved Speedway
Trenton, N.J.
300-mi. USAC Championship Race
Bobby Unser "Olsonite Spl." 2:05:06.24
143.236 mph

Sept. 24 Riverside 2.6-mi. Road Course
Riverside, Calif.
2—96.9-mi. SCCA Formula 5000 Races
1st Race:
Brian Redman "Bobcor Chevron-Chevy"
:49:40.0 116.59 mph
2nd Race:
Brian Redman "Bobcor Chevron-Chevy"
:49:32.89 116.88 mph

Oct. 8 Charlotte 1½-mi. Paved Speedway
Charlotte, N.C.
500-mi. NASCAR Stock Car Race
Bobby Allison "Chevrolet" (No Time)

Oct. 8 Watkins Glen 3.377-mi. Road Course
Watkins Glen, N.Y.
199.2-mi. Formula I U.S. Grand Prix
Jackie Stewart "Tyrell-Ford" 1:41:45.1
117.483 mph

Oct. 15 Leguna Seca 1.9-mi. Road Course
Monterey, Calif.
171-mi. SCCA Can-Am Sports Car Race
George Follmer "Porsche" 1:34:18.39
108.79 mph

Oct. 22 "American 500"
Rockingham 1.017-mi. Paved Speedway
Rockingham, N.C.
500-mi. NASCAR Stock Car Race
Bobby Allison "Chevrolet" 4:13:49.0
118.275 mph

Oct. 29 Riverside 3.3-mi. Road Course
Riverside, Calif.
201.3-mi. SCCA Can-Am Sports Car Race
George Follmer "Porsche" 1:38:31.65
122.585 mph

Nov. 4 Phoenix 1-mi. Paved Speedway
Phoenix, Ariz.
150-mi. USAC Championship Race
Bobby Unser "Olsonite Spl." 1:10:31.38
127.617 mph

Nov. 12 Texas 2½-mi. Paved Speedway
College Station, Texas
500-mi. NASCAR Stock Car Race
Buddy Baker "Dodge" 3:24:00.0
147.059 mph

Photo Credits

The author and the publishers wish to thank the following for their kind permission to reproduce the photographs which appear on the pages noted: *Charles L. Betts Collection,* pages 89 (bottom left) and 92 (top and center); *The Birthplace of Speed Association, Inc.,* pages 29 (top) and 34 (center); *Bernard Cahier, Briggs Cunningham Collection,* page 193 (left); *Daimler-Benz Ag.,* page 162; *Daytona International Speedway,* pages 142–143 (top), 142 (bottom), and 143 (center); *Automotive History Collection, Detroit Public Library,* pages 14, 15 (top, center, and bottom right), 16–19, 24 (top and bottom), 26, 32 (top), 34 (top), 36–41, 42 (bottom), 46 (top), 47, 56 (bottom), 66 (right), and 95; *Jean and Jack Dolan,* page 196; *E. I. Du Pont de Nemours & Co.,* page 192 (left); *Fiat S.p.A.,* pages 52 (bottom), 59, 73, and 74 (top); *Firestone Tire & Rubber Co.,* page 125; *Ford Motor Co.,* pages 25, 140–141, 185 (bottom), and 203; *Automobile Reference Collection, Free Library of Philadelphia,* pages 15 (bottom left and bottom center), 27 (bottom), 32–33 (bottom), 35, 43 (bottom), 56 (top), 71 (top), 72 (bottom), 75 (top and bottom left), 76 (bottom), 78 (top), 79 (top), 84 (right), 90–91, 93 (bottom), 94 (top), 99–101, 105, 111–115, 124, 151 (top), and 187 (bottom); *Chevrolet Division of General Motors Corp.,* pages 142 (left) and 191 (bottom); *Goodyear Tire & Rubber Co.,* pages 126–127; *Bernard Cahier for Goodyear Tire & Rubber Co.,* pages 174–175 and 176 (bottom); *Peter Helck Collection,* pages 13, 21 (center and bottom), 54, and 58 (left); *Pete Biro for Shelby American, Deke Houlgate Collection,* page 186; *Dave Friedman for Shelby American, Deke Houlgate Collection,* pages 180–181; *Indianapolis Motor Speedway,* pages 24 (center), 29 (bottom), 34 (bottom), 60–61, 70, 71 (bottom), 74 (bottom left and right), 78 (bottom), 79 (bottom), 80 (top), 82–83, 84 (left), 86 (right), 88, 89 (bottom right), 93 (top and center), 94 (bottom), 97–98, 102 (left), 103 (top), 104, 106–107, 110, 118 (bottom), 138 (top), 151 (center and bottom), 152–153, 171, 173, and 198; *Mel Leighton Collection,* pages 65 and 77 (top); *Long Island Automotive Museum,* pages 30–31, 42 (top), 43 (top), 49 (bottom), 52, 55, 56 (center), 57, 58 (right), 63, 66 (left), 67, 68 (top and center), 72 (top), 74 (center), 75 (center and bottom right), 81 (top), and 103 (bottom); *Charles Lytle Collection,* pages 21 (top), 27 (top), 49 (top), 64, 86 (left), 92 (bottom), 156 (bottom), and 157; *National Association for Stock Car Auto Racing,* pages 130 and 132 (top); *National Hot Rod Association,* pages 120–123 and 148; *Radio Times Hulton Picture Library,* pages 12, 154, 161, and endpapers; *George C. Rand Collection,* pages 116–117, 118 (top), and 119; *Renault,* page 62; *Road & Track,* page 135 (top); *Russ Kelly for Road & Track,* page 159 (bottom); *H. C. Smith,* page 163; *Sports Car Club of America,* page 191 (top and center); *STP Corp.,* pages 138 (bottom), 149, and 200–202; *The Sun Oil Co.,* page 194 (bottom); *Theatre Collection, The New York Public Library at Lincoln Center, Astor, Lenox, and Tilden Foundations,* page 46 (bottom); *Bob Tronolone,* pages 133, 134 (bottom), 139 (top), 145, and 147 (top); *United States Auto Club,* page 150; *Viceroy,* page 144 (bottom); *Cam Warren,* page 176 (top); *Watkins Glen Grand Prix Corp.,* pages 156 (top) and 179 (right); *White House Press,* page 206; *Ted Wilson Collection,* pages 68 (bottom), 76 (top), 77 (bottom), 80 (bottom), 81 (bottom), 85, 89 (top), and 102 (right).

Albert R. Bochroch's photographs appear on pages 131, 132 (center and bottom), 134 (top and center), 135 (bottom), 136–137, 139 (bottom), 143 (bottom), 144 (top), 146, 147 (bottom), 155, 158, 159 (top), 160, 164–165, 168–170, 172, 177–178, 179 (left), 184, 185 (top and center), 187 (top), 188–190, 192 (right), 193 (right), 194–195 (top), 195 (bottom), 197, 199, and 204–205.

Selected Bibliography

Andretti, Mario, and Bob Collins. *What's It Like Out There?* Henry Regnery Co., Chicago, 1970.

Bliss, Carey S. *Autos Across America: A Bibliography of Transcontinental Automobile Travel, 1903–1940.* Dawson's Book Shop, Los Angeles, 1972.

Bloemker, Al. *Five Hundred Miles to Go: The Story of the Indianapolis Speedway.* Coward-McCann, Inc., New York, 1961.

Bond, John. *Sports Cars in Action.* Henry Holt & Co., New York, 1957.

Borgeson, Griffith. *The Golden Age of the American Racing Car.* W. W. Norton & Co., Inc., New York, 1967.

Bradley, W. R. *Motor Racing Memories, 1903–21.* Motor Racing Publications, London, 1960.

Catlin, Russ. *The Life of Ted Horn.* Floyd Clymer, Los Angeles, 1949.

Clutton, Cecil, and others. *The Racing Car: Development and Design.* B. T. Batsford, London, and Robert Bentley and Co., Cambridge, Mass., 1962.

Court, William. *Power and Glory.* Macdonald, London, 1966.

DePaolo, Peter. *Wall Smacker.* DePaolo Publishing, Pittsburgh, 1935.

Engel, Lyle K. *Indianapolis 500: The World's Most Exciting Auto Race.* Four Winds Press, New York, 1970.

Eyston, George, and Barre Lyndon. *Motor Racing and Record Breaking.* B. T. Batsford, London, 1935.

Fitch, John, and William F. Nolan. *Adventure on Wheels.* G. P. Putnam's Sons, New York, 1959.

Fox, Jack C., ed. *The Indianapolis Five Hundred: A Pictorial History of the Greatest Spectacle in Automobile Racing.* World Publishing, Cleveland and New York, 1967.

Gauld, Graham, *Jim Clark.* Paul Hamlyn, London, 1968.

Georgano, G. N., ed. *The Complete Encyclopedia of Motorcars: Eighteen Eighty-Five to Nineteen Sixty-Eight.* E. P. Dutton, New York, 1968.

Georgano, G. N., and Albert R. Bochroch, eds. *The Encyclopedia of Motor Sport.* The Viking Press, Inc., New York, 1972.

Granatelli, Anthony. *They Call Me Mister 500.* Henry Regnery, Chicago, 1969.

Helck, Peter. *The Checkered Flag.* Charles Scribner's Sons, New York, 1967.

Hinsdale, Peter. *The Fabulous Porsche Nine Seventeen.* Jonathan Thompson, South Laguna, Calif., 1972.

Hodges, David. *The French Grand Prix.* Temple Press, London, 1967.

Hodges, David. *The Le Mans 24-Hour Race.* Temple Press, London, 1963.

Jackson, Robert B. *The Steam Cars of the Stanley Twins.* Henry Z. Walck, New York, 1969.

King, Charley B. *A Golden Anniversary, 1895–1945.* Larchmont, N.Y., 1945.

Levine, Leo. *Ford: The Dust and the Glory: A Racing History.* Macmillan, New York, 1968.

Libby, Bill. *Parnelli: A Story of Auto-Racing.* E. P. Dutton, New York, 1969.

Montagu, Lord Edward J. *The Gordon Bennett Races.* Cassell, London, 1963.

Motor Highlights of History, 1904–1929.

Nolan, William F. *Barney Oldfield.* G. P. Putnam's Sons, New York, 1961.

Nolan, William F., and Phil Hill. *Yankee Champion.* G. P. Putnam's Sons, New York, 1962.

Partridge, Bellamy. *Fill'er Up! The Story of Fifty Years of Motoring.* McGraw-Hill, New York, 1952.

Pelkin, Dwight. *The First Ten Years of Road America.* Sheboygan Press, Sheboygan, Wisconsin.

Posthumus, Cyril. *The Land Speed Record.* Crown Publishers, New York, 1972.

Quattlebaum, Julian K. *The Great Savannah Race of 1908, 1910, 1911.* Savannah, 1957.

Roberts, Peter. *Shell Book of Epic Motor Races.* Arco Press, 1965.

Rose, Gerald. *A Record of Motor Racing, 1894–1908.* Royal Automobile Club, London, 1909.

Rueter, John C. *American Road Racing.* A. S. Barnes & Co., New York, 1963.

Scarfoglio, Antonio. *Round the World in a Motor-Car.* Grant Richards, London, 1909.

Scott-Moncrieff, David. *Veteran and Edwardian Motor Cars* B. T. Batsford, London, 1955. (*Veteran Motor Cars.* Charles Scribner's Sons, New York, 1956.)

Segrave, Sir Henry. *The Lure of Speed.* Hutchinson & Co., London, 1928.

Shaw, Wilbur. *Gentlemen, Start Your Engines.* Coward-McCann, Inc., New York, 1955.

Shelby, Carroll, and John Bentley. *The Cobra Story.* Trident Press, New York, 1965.

Shuster, George N., and Tom Mahoney. *The Longest Auto Race.* John Day, New York, 1966.

Talbot, F. A. *Motor Cars and Their Story.* Cassell & Co., London, 1912.

Tubbs, D. B., and Ronald Barker. *Automobiles and Automobiling.* The Viking Press, Inc., New York, 1965. Patrick Stephens, Cambridge, England, 1973.

Tuthill, William R. *Speed on Sand.* Daytona Beach, 1969.

Valent, Henry. *Road Racing at Watkins Glen.* Watkins Glen, 1958.

Van Valkenburgh, Paul. *Chevrolet-Racing . . . ?* Walter Haessner, Newfoundland, New Jersey, 1972.

Wagner, Fred. *Saga of the Roaring Road.* Floyd Clymer, Los Angeles, 1949.

Walkerley, Rodney. *Motor Racing Facts and Figures.* Robert Bentley, Inc., Cambridge, Mass., 1962.

Wilkie, David J., and the Editors of *Esquire. Esquire's Pictorial History of the American Automobile.* Harper & Row, New York, 1963.

Not included in the bibliography are magazine and newspaper articles. Particularly helpful in this category were Russ Catlin's series on AAA racing that appeared in *Speed Age* between December 1954 and August 1955. Also most useful were Bob Kovacik's review of the Corona races from the *Riverside Press-Enterprize* in March 1966; chapters two and three of *Automobile Quarterly* publications; Oldsmobile, the first 75 years; and the Keith Marvin–Arthur Lee Homan piece on Walter Christie which first appeared in the *Upper Hudson Valley Automobilist* in December 1960.

Referred to regularly were the American performance publications: *Autoweek, Car and Driver, National Speed Sport News, Road & Track,* and *Sports Car.* Back issues of England's *Motor* and *Autocar* proved indispensable, as were early volumes of America's first automobile magazines: *The Horseless Age* and *The Automobile,* the latter which became *The Automobile and Motor Review Weekly* (which absorbed *The Horseless Age* in 1918) and, later, *Automotive Industries.* Charles Betts prepared a bibliography of racing articles appearing in *The Automobile* between October 1899 and June 1940 that was published in the spring 1954 issue of the *Antique Automobile.*

Official AAA Record Books published by Floyd Clymer, the USAC Yearbook, NASCAR's Annual Record book, the 500 Fact book issued each May by the Indianapolis Speedway, and the Automobile Almanac were all sources of valued information.

Index

80 H.P Peerless Car
Mr L. Mooers

Napier Car
45 H.P Mr S.F. Edge.

ENGLAND

UNITED STATES

Mr Alex Winton

80 H.P Winton Car
Mr Percy Owen.

Mr J.W Stocks

Mr Ch. Jarrott

The Gordon Bennett Trophy

Chv R de Knyff

FRANCE

Mr W Vous

Jenatzy

GERMANY

Baron de Caters

70 H.P Mors Car
M. Gabriel

60 H.P Mercedes Car
Mr Foxhall Keene.

70 H.P Panhard Car
Henri Farman.

A HUGH FISHER